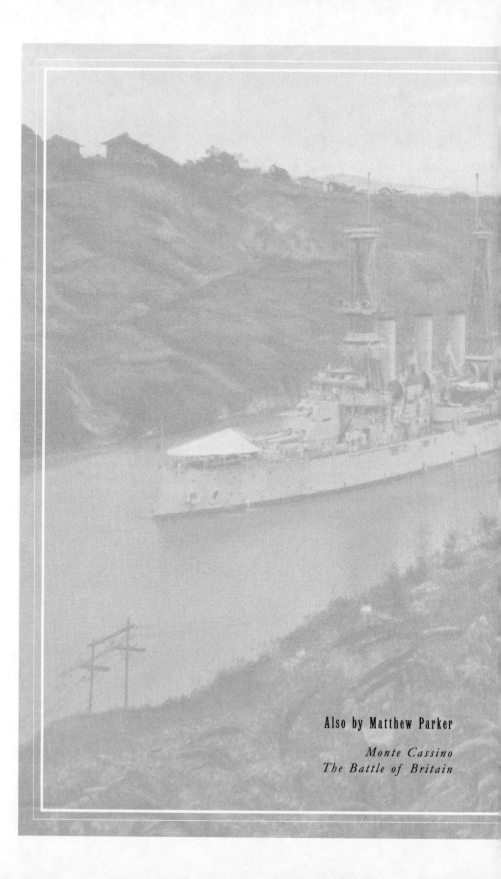

Also by Matthew Parker

Monte Cassino
The Battle of Britain

Panama Fever

The Epic Story of One of the
Greatest Human Achievements of All Time—
the Building of the Panama Canal

Matthew Parker

DOUBLEDAY
New York London Toronto Sydney Auckland

PUBLISHED BY DOUBLEDAY

Originally published in the United Kingdom by Hutchinson, London in 2007.
This edition published by arrangement with Hutchinson.

Published in the United States by Doubleday,
an imprint of The Doubleday Broadway Publishing Group,
a division of Random House, Inc., New York.
www.doubleday.com

DOUBLEDAY and the portrayal of an anchor with a dolphin
are registered trademarks of Random House, Inc.

Illustration credits appear on pp. ix–xii.

Library of Congress Cataloging-in-Publication Data
Parker, Matthew.
Panama fever : the epic story of one of the greatest human achievements of all time—
the building of the Panama Canal / Matthew Parker. —1st ed.
p. cm.
Includes bibliographical references and index.
1. Panama Canal (Panama)—History. I. Title.
F1569.C2P368 2008
972.87'503—dc22
2007017995

ISBN 978-0-385-51534-4

PRINTED IN THE UNITED STATES OF AMERICA

1 3 5 7 9 10 8 6 4 2

First U.S. Edition

In loving memory of Roger Durman

CONTENTS

Part Three
THE AMERICAN TRIUMPH

ILLUSTRATIONS

Insert One

Maps

Text Illustrations

ACKNOWLEDGMENTS

I am very grateful to the K. Blundell Trust, administered by the Society of Authors, for their generous contribution to the research expenses of this book. Many people in a number of countries have helped me. For my research trips to the United States I am indebted to the staff of the New York Public Library, the Library of Congress, and the National Archives, in particular Jackie Cohen, who went far beyond the call of duty in guiding me through the enormous amount of material—particularly the French records—held at NARA. I was also well looked after in the United States by Peter Sollis and his family in Washington and by Ben and Louise Edwards in New York. I have also been lucky enough to receive help and encouragement from Roman Foster in New York and Eunice Mason in California as well as Barbara Adamson, Lesley Hendricks, Dr. Philip C. Breunle, Donald Paine, and Professor Hugh Brogan.

For help in researching the Jantje Milliery story I am indebted to Danielle Susijn and Patrick van Griethuysen in Holland. In the

United Kingdom I was lucky enough to have the enthusiastic and invaluable support of the Panamanian consul and ambassador, Liliana Fernandez, who was able to open many doors for me in Panama. I must also acknowledge my debt to the staff of the British Library (where much of this book was written), the London Library, the Public Records Office, and to Carol Morgan at the Institute of Civil Engineers. Mrs. Primose Mallet-Harris has been kind enough to let me quote from her grandfather's letters and offered hospitality at her home in Somerset. James Spence has provided much assistance on the engineering side of the story, and I am grateful to Dr. Mary Allwood for her checking of the medical material. In France I was greatly helped by Jane Martens, Jean-Yves Mollier, and Gérard Fauconnier.

The time spent in Panama on several visits was a great pleasure of researching this book. If nothing else, I am delighted to have seen the amazing canal up close, an experience I can recommend to anyone. My greatest debts are to Judy Dixon and John Carlson, both of whom provided invaluable help with introductions and research material. I was also lucky enough to be taken under the wing of Gisela Lammerts Van Bueren at the Technical Resource Center at Balboa, Panama City, who provided enthusiastic assistance. In Panama I would also like to thank all those who gave me their time for interviews or assisted in other ways: Marc de Banville, Dr. Angeles Ramos Baquero, Ned Blennerhassett, Foster Burns, Walter Clarke, Georges Colbourne, Graciela Dixon, William Donadío, Victor Echeverria, Terry Ford, Egla Gooden de Lynch, Cecil Haynes, Dr. Stanley Heckadon-Moreno, Eric Jackson, Maria Esperanza Lavergne, Dr. Hedley C. Lennon, Melva Lowe de Goodin, Jim Malcolm, Gerardo Maloney, Mercedes and Charles Morris, Marc Quinn, Lidia Ricardo, Carlos Russell, Enrique Sanchez and all at SAMAAP, Leonardo J. Sidnez, Henry F. Smith Jr., Omar Jeán Suárez, and Juan Tam.

I have been very lucky in having editors of great experience, skill, and patience—Tony Whittome at Hutchinson and Adam Bellow at Doubleday in New York—and I am grateful to all at their companies for their efforts on behalf of this book. I would also like to thank my agents, Julian Alexander in London and George Lucas in the United States, for their encouragement and advice. Richard Collins has performed a very careful and skillful edit of the manuscript, and Reg Pilkington has drawn maps of real distinction and character.

Above all, I am indebted to my family—Anne and Paul Swain, who read early drafts of this book and provided invaluable advice and encouragement as well as a bolt-hole to write in. My parents, Sheila and David Parker, read, translated, and noted numerous works in French and Spanish respectively as well as commented on early drafts. And my immediate family—Oliver, Thomas, Milly, and their mother, Hannah—while endlessly asking how many more pages I had to write, put up with good grace with my frequent absences on research trips and the many years of distraction that writing such a book as this entails.

ATLANTIC OCEAN

Caribbean Sea

Toro Point
Colón Harbour
Colon
Cristóbal
Manzanillo Bay
Limón Bay
Mount Hope
Remnants of the French Canal
R. Chagres
Gatún Locks
Gatún Dam

Canal Zone boundary

CANAL CENTRE LINE

Old Railway

L A K E

Relocat
Panam
Railw

Barro Colorado Island

G A T Ú N

R E P U B L I C   O

PROFILE OF THE CULEBRA CUT

feet 400

Final width 1800 feet

feet 400

Planned width 670 feet

300

300

Obispo diversion

200

200

100

100

0

300 feet

0

Feet 900 800 700 600 500 400 300 200 100 0 100 200 300 400 500 600 700 800 900 feet

////// Initial French excavation: 19,000,000 cubic yards (14,526,545 cubic metres)

▓▓▓ Final American excavation: 96,000,000 cubic yards (73,396,800 cubic metres)

THE PANAMA CANAL
and the boundary of the old Canal Zone

| 0 | | 5 | | 10 | | 15 miles |

| 0 | 5 | 10 | 15 | 20 | 25 km |

N

Madden Lake

Continental Divide
(watershed)

Madden Dam
constructed 1935

Culebra (Gaillard)
cut 9 miles

Pan-American
Highway

East Culebra slide

Cucaracha slide

Canal Zone boundary

Paraiso
Pedro Miguel

P A N A M A

Culebra
slide

Pedro Miguel
locks

Miraflores
locks

Old Panama

Miraflores
Lake

Ancón

Balboa
(previously
La Boca)

Panama City

Naos Island
breakwater
Perico

P A C I F I C

O C E A N

Naos

Flamenco

PREFACE

The Battle to Build the Canal

> You here who are doing your work well in bringing to completion this great enterprise are standing exactly as a soldier of the few great wars of the world's history. This is one of the great works of the world.
>
> —*President Theodore Roosevelt to*
> *the American canal workforce, 1906*

Every year, on the anniversary of the opening of the Panama Canal on August 14, 1914, there is a special celebration. A small motor launch takes a group of about twenty-five on a short boat ride from a dock near the top of the Pedro Miguel Lock. In August 2004 almost everyone is of Antillean descent, mainly from Jamaica or Barbados. The commemorative trip has been organized by Panama's British West Indian community. All ages are represented, and the vast majority are Panama-born. The others are from the islands, and one visitor with her young daughter has come all the way from Boston.

As the boat sets off from the dock, huge container ships loom past. One is a giant German carrier, crewed by Filipinos, on the way to the U.S. East Coast. Another is transporting car parts from China to Brazil. We are floating in one of the world's key commercial arteries. Since the opening of the canal, over a million ships have used it to travel between the great oceans, some fourteen thousand a year, now passing through twenty-four hours a day. In places the sides of the canal consist of sheer rock, in others there are elaborate terraces of crumbly, reddish soil mixed with dark boulders. Where the ground is flat lie neat, clipped lawns, the rich tropical jungle kept at a respectable distance. As it is before noon, the container carriers are heading from the Pacific to the Atlantic (traveling in a northerly direction). They have sailed past Panama City and ascended the double locks at Miraflores, crossed the small lake, and climbed the single lock just behind us at Pedro Miguel. They are now at the top of the "bridge of water," 85 feet above sea level. Beyond the narrow and windy stretch ahead, the canal opens up into the huge man-made Gatún Lake, created by the damming of the Chagres River with a massive earthen structure. At the other end of the lake, the vessels will descend through the spectacular triple lock at Gatún, and thence out into the Caribbean Sea and away.

Within a few minutes we are approaching the infamous Culebra Cut, the site of the maximum excavation for the canal. Here, for up to twenty years, thousands of men, the vast majority British West Indians, labored in torrential rain or in burning heat to break the back of the Continental Divide, the rocky spine that links the great mountain ranges of North and South America.

The occasion is a celebration of the contribution made to the canal by the Antillean workers, but also a solemn memorial of their sufferings and losses. Between the two highest mountains of the Cut, where the sides of the canal rise almost vertically, the boat stops for petals and flowers to be thrown on the water. With all the passengers crowded out on the small deck, prayers are said by several of the rectors present, and hymns are sung as the warm tropical rain starts pouring down.

◄◄◄◄◄- -►►►►►

*B*ahamas-born Albert Peters was twenty years old when, in 1906, he and two friends decided to head for the Isthmus. "We were all eager for some adventure and experience," he wrote. "My parents were against the idea. They told me about the Yellow Fever, Malaria and Small Pox that infested the place but I told them that I and my pals are just going to see for ourselves."

He was in for a shock. Seeing the working conditions, and the "heavy rain and mud," he wanted to be back at home, but having spent all his money on the trip, he had no choice but to stick it out. Within a month he had malaria, and was hospitalized. "The first night in there the man next to me died," he wrote, "and that's when I re-membered my parents' plea and wished I had taken their advice."

"Death was our constant companion," remembered another West Indian worker, Alfred Dottin. "I shall never forget the trainloads of dead men being carted away daily, as if they were just so much lum-ber. Malaria with all its horrible meaning those days was just a house-hold word. I saw mosquitoes, I say this without fear of exaggerating, by the thousands attack one man. There were days that we could only work a few hours because of the high fever racking our bodies—it was a living hell. Finally typhoid fever got me . . ."

Although the hardships of the construction period were shared in part by all the numerous nationalities who built the canal—French, American, Spanish, Italian, Greek, and many others—the West In-dian workers were three times as likely as the others to die from dis-ease or accidents, and their startling accounts are dominated by stories of appalling conditions and dangerous work. The loss of life was astronomical. With safety precautions incredibly primitive by modern standards, accidents "were numberless." Constantine Parkin-son, a Jamaican born in Panama, lost his right leg and left heel when the spoil-carrying train he was working on crashed off its rails. He was taken to the hospital and operated on. "After coming out of the operation in the ward," he wrote, "I noticed all kinds of cripples around my bed without arms foot one eye telling me to cheer up not to fret we all good soldiers."

"Some of the costs of the canal are here," wrote a sympathetic American policeman in his account of visiting the main hospital's black wards, which were always situated on the least favorable side of the building. "Sturdy black men in pyjamas sitting on the verandas or in wheel chairs, some with one leg gone, some with both. One could not help but wonder how it feels to be hopelessly ruined in body early in life for helping to dig a ditch for a foreign power that, however well it may treat you materially, cares not a whistle blast more for you than for its old worn-out locomotives rusting away in the jungle."

Certainly the West Indians were treated as cheap and expendable by both the French and Americans. The working conditions were described by one as "some sort of semi-slavery," and, particularly under the Americans, there was a rigid apartheid system in place throughout the Canal Zone. Nonetheless, in spite of obvious resentments, the West Indian accounts are full of pride in knowing they were part of a great, heroic, and civilizing achievement. "Many times I met death at the door," wrote one worker fifty years after the completion of the canal, "but thank God I am alive to see the great improvement the Canal had made and the wonderful fame it has around the world." Another commented: "We worked in rain, sun, fire, gunpowder, explosions from dynamite . . . but our interest was to see the Canal finished because we came here to build it . . . most of us came here with the same spirit as a soldier going to war, don't dodge from work or we will never finish it."

The men who built the canal did indeed go to Panama as soldiers to a great battle and the fight to build the canal can be compared with an armed conflict. It has been estimated that three out of four of the French engineers who set out to be part of Ferdinand de Lesseps's heroic dream were dead within three months of arriving on Panama's "Fever Coast." Yellow fever and a mysterious and particularly vicious form of malaria known as "Chagres Fever" accounted for thousands.

Many others were carried off by accidents, pneumonia, or sheer exhaustion. The most conservative estimate of the death toll is 25,000, five hundred lives for every mile of the canal. Many, many more were maimed or permanently debilitated by disease. Even in 1914, when the Isthmus was supposedly "sanitized" by the Americans, over half the workforce was hospitalized at some point during the year.

Apart from actual wars, it is the costliest project ever yet attempted in history, as ambitious a construction as the Great Pyramids. Hundreds of millions of francs were invested—and lost—during the ten-year struggle by the French in the 1880s, and the Americans spent nearly $400 million between 1904 and 1914, in the days when a couple of dollars a day was a good working wage. Although much shorter than the canal at Suez, it cost four times as much and required three times the amount of excavation. Mountains, literally, had to be moved. One observer called it the "greatest liberty ever taken with nature."

And "nature" was not going to be conquered easily. In the way of the "path between the seas" were huge, geologically complex mounains, thick jungle teeming with deadly creatures, and seemingly bottomless swamp. For eight months of the year there was almost continual rain. Because of the peculiar geographical configurations of the Isthmus it is one of the wettest places on earth. Two inches of rain have been known to fall in one hour. This made the Chagres River, which lies along the path of the waterway, a powerful and unstable force to have as a bedfellow to the canal. Rising up to 30 yards in an hour, it would regularly burst its banks, sweeping away men and materials. Vast mud slides buried workers, supplies, and machines. And in the swamps and puddles, fever-carrying mosquitoes bred in their millions to launch themselves on the toiling laborers.

⋘⋙

What impresses now about the story of the canal is not just the extraordinary number of "firsts" its achievement entailed—financial, technical, and medical—but the astonishing, almost arrogant ambition of it all. Nothing like it had ever been attempted in the tropics before. The leaders of the project, be they French or American, simply believed they could do anything, that innovation and technology—the forces of progress, of the Industrial Revolution and the great Victorian age—were able to conquer any challenge.

The French effort, in particular, powered as it was by private capital and a sublime belief in emerging technology, sees this age overreach itself, with tragic consequences. The Americans were driven less by idealism than by national, racial, and military ambition, but they too would be humbled by the challenges that the jungles of Panama presented. The U.S. construction project succeeded because of state funding, local political control, and access to scientific and technical expertise beyond the reach of the French. But it also opened the door to a new era where the efforts of individuals would be controlled and channeled by the state for its own purposes, the machine age that was ushered in by the industrial slaughter of the western front.

In both cases, and throughout the history of the canal dream, almost everyone involved with the project, from the humblest pick-and-shovel man to the most venal Wall Street speculator, became gripped by the "great idea" of the canal, by "Panama Fever." For many, the canal would become an obsession. But it is striking, too, how much controversy and how many enemies the project attracted through its history. Vested interests feared the change in the status quo that such a radical altering of the geography of the world would usher in. The Americans, in particular, were fiercely opposed to a foreign power controlling any transcontinental waterway. The French attempt would bring heavy criticism of the "overoptimism" of its promoter, Ferdinand de Lesseps, and its failure would see his ruin and disgrace, as well as financial and political disaster for France. The American project was even more controversial, entailing at its inception the murky maneuvers of political lobbyists and a vivid demonstration of a new kind of United States, casting off its historical aversion to imperialism and aggression on the international stage.

The successful opening of the canal in August 1914, at almost precisely the moment when Old Europe was embarking on a ruinous war, was the climax of the United States' spectacular rise to world power. The Isthmus was the key to the struggle for mastery of the Western Hemisphere as well as to wider international commercial and naval strength. With the successful completion of the Washington-funded and dominated canal, the United States emerged as a truly global power and the "American Century" could begin.

In Panama itself, the canal was the realization of a dream that went back four hundred years. It had been the destiny of the Isthmus ever since 1513, when the Spanish conquistador Vasco Núñez de Balboa ventured inland from Panama's Caribbean coast and, "silent upon a peak in Darién," discovered a previously unknown great ocean separated from the Atlantic by only a narrow bridge of land forty miles wide. Balboa's discovery immediately engendered a belief that a waterway could be built linking the two oceans. Thereafter the Isthmus became of crucial strategic importance and the focus of fierce international rivalry among Spain, France, Great Britain, and, as it emerged, the United States.

Not only was Panama a magnet for empire builders; its transit route—first a paved road, then a railway—had brought the world to the Isthmus even before a canal was started. An international crossroads a hundred years before the *Mayflower* landing, Panama played host at times to traders, bullion carriers, pirates, missionaries, soldiers, and then a California-bound gold rush. The canal dream would bring explorers, doctors, engineers, more soldiers (this time to stay), and, at one time, a workforce of fifty thousand from twenty-seven different countries. Many of the canal builders believed that fever was the result of vice, but that did not prevent Panama's two cities from becoming roaring dens of gambling, drinking, and prostitution. All this descended on an unstable region still struggling to find political solutions to its problems. At times the canal has been an awkward destiny for Panama.

In the wider world, the great dream of the canal attracted idealists, dreamers, and scoundrels from the very outset. The four hundred years after Balboa's discovery saw Panama's unique geography inspire grandiose canal schemes from each age's greatest engineers, promoters, and visionaries. It was the great unfulfilled engineering challenge. But for those four centuries all efforts had ended in failure or disaster.

Panama Fever

PART ONE

The Golden Isthmus

Do but open these doors, and trade will increase trade, and
money will beget money.

—William Paterson, 1698

CHAPTER ONE

"THE KEYS TO THE UNIVERSE"

What had motivated the voyages that led to the discovery of the New World was exactly what the Panama Canal would eventually deliver—a through passage to the East. On his fourth voyage, in 1502, Columbus, by then embittered and sickly, sailed all along Panama's northern coast, obsessively searching every tiny cove for a "hidden strait." At one point he anchored in Limón, or "Navy," Bay, now the Atlantic terminus of the canal. Even after Columbus's failure to find an open passage to the East, the idea died hard. In 1507, the first map ever printed of the New World optimistically showed an open strait about where the Isthmus of Panama is located.

But Columbus did report back that the *Tierra Firme* he had discovered was rich in gold and pearls. West of Limón Bay he had encountered Indians wearing solid gold breastplates, which they were happy to exchange for a couple of hawk's bells. Having set out to discover a route to the wealth of the East, the Spaniards had effectively found far greater riches on the way. At the end of 1509 a settlement

4

was established, Santa María de la Antigua del Darién, some sixty miles southeast of what would later be named Caledonia Bay. Then in 1513 the colony's leader, Vasco Núñez de Balboa, his curiosity aroused by Indian stories of a Great Ocean across the mountains, put together an expedition of 190 Spaniards, accompanied by a number of bloodhounds, which the natives found particularly terrifying. On September 6, having sailed up the coast, they set off across the mountains on a route about a hundred miles east of the modern canal, their heavy loads of supplies carried by a mixture of press-ganged local Cuna Indians and black slaves. The expedition's rate of advance through the Darién jungle was at times only a mile a day. The rivers were in spate and numerous bridges had to be improvised from tree trunks. Even in the sweltering jungle, the Spaniards wore helmets and breastplates of polished steel, thick leather breeches, woolen stockings, and thigh boots. Heatstroke, hostile Indians, and disease began to thin their numbers. On September 25, with only a third of his men left, Balboa reached a small hill. From its summit, promised the guides, you could see the Great Ocean. Balboa set off alone at midday. At the top, he turned one way and then the other; he could see both oceans quite clearly. He fell to his knees in prayer and then called up his men, "shewing them the great maine sea heretofore vnknowne to the inhabitants of Europe, Aphrike, and Asia."

They struggled down to the shore, on the way defeating and then befriending Indians who had barred their route to the ocean. On the afternoon of September 29 they reached the sea. That evening Balboa, in full armor, waded into the muddy water and laid claim in the name of Ferdinand of Castile to what he called the "South Sea."

The party remained on the Pacific coast for over three months, exploring the bay and trading trinkets with the local Indians. Balboa heard stories of a rich land away to the south, but wrongly deduced that he must be close to Asia. He at last returned, heavily laden with pearls and gold, to Santa María and a hero's welcome. Along with a fifth of his treasure, Balboa sent the King of Spain a report, which included, rather as an afterthought, the musing of a Castilian engineer, Alvaro de Saavedra—a suggestion that although the search for a strait between the two oceans should continue, if it was not found, "yet it might not be impossible to make one."

Five years after Balboa's discovery, a land route had been established linking Nombre de Dios, a port on the Caribbean, with a new Spanish settlement at Panama, a prosperous Indian village on the Pacific coast. The transit route opened up the Pacific. Although Magellan found a way around the southern tip of the continent in 1519–21, the voyage was so remote and hazardous that it did nothing to discourage the quest for a way through the Isthmus to the newly found ocean. In 1522 explorers sailing north from Panama discovered Lake Nicaragua. The following year Hernando Cortés, the conqueror of Mexico, was ordered by Charles V to continue the search for an open strait. By 1530 it was clear that no such waterway existed in the tropics, and in 1534 Charles ordered that the Chagres River be mapped and cleared as far as possible in the direction of Panama City, and that the intervening land be studied with a view to excavation. This was the first survey for a proposed ship canal through Panama, and it more or less followed the course of the current Panama Canal. At the same time, the San Juan River, which runs from Lake Nicaragua to the Caribbean coast, was also to be surveyed as part of a possible canal. The great rivalry between the two routes was thus started.

Detailed, reliable information on these very early surveys has not survived, although Charles seems to have received mixed messages. Some reported that the project was totally unfeasible; others, like the Spanish priest Francisco López de Gómara, writing to the king in 1551, thought anything was possible. In an early example of the hubris that the canal dream attracted throughout its history, the priest wrote: "If there are mountains there are also hands . . . To a King of Spain with the wealth of the Indies at his command, when the object to be attained is the spice trade, what is possible is easy."

Then Spanish priorities in Panama changed. Philip II, Charles V's successor and a religious fanatic, shared little of his enthusiasm for a canal, seeing it, among other evils, as "unnatural," as meddling with God's creation. More important, the conquest of Peru led to concerns that an Isthmian canal could be a strategic liability. As early as 1534, the governor of Panama had warned against the construction of a canal as it "would open the door to the Portuguese and even the French." By the 1560s most believed that it was safer to have an unbroken wall of land between the gold and silver of Peru and Spain's maritime enemies in the Atlantic. Similar strategic concerns would arise three hundred years later when the United States debated building a canal.

With the conquest of the Incas, the Panama Isthmus became the overland route for the treasure pouring back to Europe, whose value dwarfed anything that could have come from the Indies. Once a year a grand fleet would arrive at the Pacific terminus of the trail and unload the bullion, which would be transferred across the Isthmus to waiting ships at Nombre de Dios. One witness recounted that he saw twelve hundred muleloads of precious metal leave Panama City in 1550. The "Royal Road" was now the most important thoroughfare in the Spanish empire, and the Isthmus the key to the Spanish commercial and defense system in the New World. Panama City quickly became one of the three richest centers in the Americas, outshone only by Lima and Mexico City. At the other end of the trail, Nombre de Dios grew into an important port, and the site of an annual trade fair of dazzling opulence, where European goods were bought for transshipment throughout Spanish America. The experience of visiting the fair was described by a traveling Englishman, Thomas Gage, as highly risky: it was "an unhealthy place . . . subject to breed fevers . . . an open grave." But, he wrote, "I dare boldly say and avouch, that in the world there is no greater fare."

The great wealth and strategic importance of Panama led to numerous attacks from Spain's enemies. In 1572, Francis Drake carried back to Plymouth an enormous pile of looted silver; he returned twenty years later to attempt to capture the Isthmus for England, only to die of dysentery off Nombre de Dios. The infamous

buccaneer Sir Henry Morgan, under orders from the British governor
of Jamaica, sacked Panama City in 1671, causing a new city to be built
in a more secure location nearby. He reportedly returned to Jamaica
with over £70,000 in loot.

Other arrivals came intending to stay. The famous "Darién Disaster," the calamitous effort at the beginning of the eighteenth century
to establish a Scottish colony in Panama, has many parallels with de
Lesseps's French adventure nearly two hundred years later. Each was
financed by a host of small investors in their own countries and motivated by idealism, patriotism, and naïveté, as well as by the chance
to make a fast buck. Both had leaders with more front than particular expertise. William Paterson was born in Dumfriesshire, Scotland,
in 1658, and as a young man had traveled, as part missionary, part
buccaneer, to the West Indies. Returning to England, he had made his
fortune in business and had become a "projector," a promoter of
speculative moneymaking schemes. But ever since his sojourn in the
Caribbean, Paterson had been in the grip of a "Great Idea," the venture to cap everything. He was not the first, nor would he be the last,
to fall for the "lure of the Isthmus." It was so obvious. If ports could
be established on both coasts, cargoes could be transferred over the
narrow strip of land, saving ships the long and dangerous voyage
around Cape Horn. News from British coastal raiders had identified
a spot where there was "no mountain range at all" and where "broad,
low valleys" extended from coast to coast. It was perfect enough to
envisage not just a road, but, in time, a waterway. Paterson, with more
than a few ideas before his time, intended to welcome traders from
all over the world to the new settlements, regardless of race or creed.
It would be a truly global entrepôt, to rival any in the world, and whoever controlled it, proclaimed the Scot, would possess "the Gates to
the Pacific and the keys to the Universe." "Do but open these doors,"
said Paterson, "and trade will increase trade, and money will beget
money."

The Scottish Parliament backed the scheme in spite of warnings
that Paterson "talks too much and raises people's expectations," but

then money raised in England was withdrawn after pressure from vested interests such as the East India Company. However, a wave of patriotic indignation in Scotland saw money pouring in from all quarters and all levels of society. As for the French public in the 1880s, for Scottish investors the scheme was a means of reestablishing national pride. From 1,400 individuals, including craftsmen and servants, £400,000 was quickly raised, about half the country's available capital. It was a colossal risk for so much of the national silver.

Like so many of the subsequent Panama schemes, it was doomed from the start. As soon as the 1,200 Scotsmen landed in the New World, naming their anchorage Caledonia Bay, fierce protests from English merchants and the Spanish led to an embargo on the colony. For a settlement established as a trading station, it was a fatal blow.

Everything started to unravel. The death rate from fever rose steadily. It soon emerged that far too many of the settlers were "gentlemen," with neither the inclination nor the strength for the hard labor required for starting the settlement. The "valleys" "extending coast to coast" turned out to be a fiction, and no realistic attempt was made to open up an overland route to the Pacific as planned. The only trading partners were the local Indians, who had no use for the heavy cloth and 1,500 English-language Bibles the settlers had brought with them as their start-up stock. Scarcity of food brought increasing weakness, disease, and demoralization; among the first to die was Paterson's wife. Within six months, nearly four hundred settlers had perished of fever or starvation. The onset of the rainy season in May, and the concurrent further worsening of living conditions, was the final straw.

On June 20, 1699, "Being starved and abandoned by the world," as one contemporary letter from Panama described it, the Scots abandoned Panama and sailed for New York, en route to Europe. Only half of the weakened settlers were still alive at the end of the journey. The survivors, described by an eyewitness in New York as looking "rather like Skelets than men, being starved," barely numbered enough to fill one ship on the cross-Atlantic voyage back home. Two

further expeditions, dispatched from Edinburgh before news had arrived of what had happened, met the same fate, the last being driven
away by local Spanish forces.

In all, Paterson's "Great Idea" cost over two thousand lives and
the precious savings of an entire nation. As de Lesseps and many
others would discover, the Isthmus could be a graveyard of men,
dreams, and reputations.

The "Darién Disaster" hastened the coming of the Act of Union
that dissolved the Scottish Parliament. Seeing the futility of trying to
compete with England, and stripped of capital from the disaster,
Scotland was merged into Great Britain in 1707, an early but spectacular casualty of Panama Fever.

⧺⧺⧺⧺ ⧻⧻⧻⧻

*R*egardless of their abandonment of the Scots, the English Navy
continued to flex its muscles in the region, and frequent plans were
laid to seize the Isthmus. To take Panama, it was believed, would end
Spanish rule in the Americas, and open up the Pacific to English
trade. In 1739, during a period of official war with Spain, the English
admiral Edward Vernon, leading six ships of the line and nearly three
thousand men, took the Caribbean port of Portobelo and destroyed
its defenses, although he was unable to cross the Isthmus to seize
Panama City itself.

Confronted by growing threats on the Caribbean side of the Isthmus, in 1748 the bullion ships abandoned the Panama route and
started sailing around Cape Horn. Thus Panama City lost her place as
the treasure-house of the New World. Soon afterward, the famous
fair declined and ceased. Panama was attached to the viceroyalty of
New Granada based in Bogotá, beginning a century and a half of
struggle on the part of the Panamanians to regain their autonomy.

During the rest of the eighteenth century Panama, tied to a fast-
fading empire, shared her colonial masters' steep decline. Weakened
by incessant European warfare, falling birth rates, and intermittent

bankruptcy, Spain gave way to the new aggressive mercantile and maritime powers of northern Europe. However, economic decline on the Isthmus was not matched by a falling off of geopolitical or military importance. Spain's new rivals in the Caribbean, now a key arena of international conflict, were more interested than ever in the strategic value of the Isthmus.

In 1735 the French government had sent an astronomer through Central America on a scientific expedition to investigate the possibility of a trans-Isthmian canal. He had reported back in 1740 to the French Academy of Science advocating a canal at Nicaragua, making use of the San Juan River that flowed from Lake Nicaragua to the Caribbean coast. In the same year, however, the British were establishing control over a section of the Nicaraguan coast through an alliance with the Mosquito Indians, who refused to recognize Spanish sovereignty. It was not a coincidence that this gave the British control over the mouth of the San Juan River, and therefore the Atlantic terminus of any future Nicaraguan canal. But France still made the running—over the next twenty years no fewer than four French trans-Isthmian canal proposals were made.

With the independence of Gran Colombia,* officially declared on November 28, 1821, the dead hand of Spanish rule was at last removed, and a major barrier to the construction of a canal disappeared at the same time. Furthermore, there was now a new emerging power to the north beginning to take a keen interest in Central American affairs.

---

*Gran Colombia consisted of modern-day Panama, Colombia, Venezuela, and Ecuador. This federation dissolved in 1830, with the latter two becoming independent and the remainder renamed the Republic of New Granada, which became Colombia in 1863.

CHAPTER TWO

RIVALRY AND STALEMATE

Even in the midst of the American Revolution, Benjamin Franklin, then the United Colonies' representative in Paris, became gripped by the idea of a trans-Isthmian canal. In 1781 he printed on his own press a pamphlet written by a French peasant called Pierre-André Gargaz, which advocated the cutting of canals at Panama and Suez. This, Gargaz proposed, would bring about world peace through enhanced commerce and communication. When Thomas Jefferson became the U.S. ambassador to France, he, too, became interested in a canal at Panama. Jefferson saw expansion southward as the natural destiny of the United States and was intrigued by rumors, in fact untrue, that there had been recent Spanish surveys of a canal route at Panama. "I am assured . . . a canal appeared very practicable," he wrote in 1788 to a fellow U.S. diplomat in Madrid, "and that the idea was suppressed for political reasons."

Before independence from Spain, revolutionaries in Latin America had looked to the United States and Britain as their natural allies.

When freedom from Spanish rule, having been achieved, was subsequently threatened by the French-led Holy Alliance, British foreign secretary George Canning contacted the leadership of the United States to ask them to make a joint declaration warning of their shared opposition to the reconquest plans. But President Monroe was persuaded to make a statement purely on behalf of the United States. His famous doctrine, delivered in a message to Congress on December 2, 1823, is of huge importance to the Panama Canal story: "The American continents," he announced, "are henceforth not to be considered as subjects for future colonization by any European Powers."

In the meantime, impetus for a trans-Isthmian canal had received a major boost with the publication of "A Political Essay on the Kingdom of New Spain" in 1811. Its author, the German Alexander von Humboldt, had recently explored the regions of South and Central America on an epic journey that thrilled readers all over the world. Although he never actually visited any of the sites, he identified five possible Central American routes for a trans-Isthmian canal. Going from north to south, they were the narrowing of Mexico at Tehuantepec; in Nicaragua, using the giant inland lake; at Panama; and two using the Atrato River in modern-day northern Colombia. Humboldt's book was widely read and admired, and can be seen as the inspiration for all the many subsequent surveys of the Isthmus looking for the best route for a canal. The account was full of errors—he calculated the height of the Continental Divide in Panama at three times its correct elevation—but it was a hugely exciting work nonetheless. Humboldt reckoned a canal was possible and, furthermore, "would immortalise a government occupied with the interests of humanity."

One of those inspired by the book was the poet Goethe, who in 1827 predicted the "incalculable results" of a "crosscut" through the South American Isthmus. With remarkable prescience he also foretold how intimately interwoven would be the destinies of Panama, the United States, and the canal. "I, however, would be surprised if the United States would miss the chance to get such a work into her hands," he wrote. "It is entirely indispensable for the United States to

THE PRINCIPAL RIVAL ROUTES
(Present-day international boundaries are shown)

make a passage from the Gulf of Mexico to the Pacific Ocean, and I am certain that she will accomplish it."

It was also the climax of the "canal age" in Europe and the United States. The 1820s saw the opening of the Erie Canal, joining the Hudson River and the Great Lakes, as well as Telford's monumental achievement in linking the Atlantic and the North Sea across Scotland, which included twenty-eight locks of a size big enough for most of the oceangoing vessels of the time. All across Europe and North America, canals transformed communication, slashing journey times and transport costs for raw materials and finished goods. Crucially, steam power had arrived, and with it the possibility of vessels transiting canals without the need for towpaths. A steam tug was first used on the Forth and Clyde Canal in Scotland as early as 1802, and by the time of the independence of Gran Colombia in 1821, the prospect of a trans-Isthmian canal seemed much closer.

Simón Bolívar chose Panama City as the site for his Latin American Congress, which finally met on June 22, 1826. For Bolívar, Panama was the "veritable capital of the world, the centre of the globe, with one face turned toward Asia and the other toward Africa and Europe." Britain and the United States were both invited to send delegates. Bolívar was passionately in favor of a canal, and soon after independence a stream of proposals were put to him, first by an American army officer (a relative of Benjamin Franklin), then by a British naval captain, then by a Jamaican merchant. All were focused on the narrow Isthmus at Panama. Each was rejected by his Congress, quite rightly, as unrealistic, and the Bogotá government tried unsuccessfully to get funding from London to build the canal itself. Then, in 1827, Bolívar granted permission for a survey to be carried out by a British army captain, John Augustus Lloyd, and Captain Maurice Falmarc, a Swedish officer in the Colombian military. Hampered by bad weather, they nonetheless produced the most reliable survey yet of the Isthmus, even though construction never started. Their plan was to use the Chagres River up to its junction with the Trinidad, then build a railway to the coast. In due course, this would be replaced by a ship canal. Labor would be supplied by British convicts, who would be accompanied by colonizing settlers. This body combined would, Lloyd suggested, "present a human barrier of such formidable power, as to limit . . . any attempts of the United States towards aggrandizement and increase of territory . . ." Lloyd had little time for the Panamanians, whom he described as "superstitious . . . Billiards, cockpits, gambling and smoking in low company, are their exclusive amusements . . . Their best quality is great liberality to the poor, and especially to the aged and infirm."

In fact the Panamanians were almost all desperately poor. The long economic decline that started in the mid-eighteenth century had continued unabated since independence. A visitor from Bogotá in the 1830s was shocked by what he found at Panama City: buildings in ruins, vagrants everywhere, and prices fallen to unbelievable levels. The population of the Isthmus had shrunk, with many who had the will or the means leaving to find prosperity elsewhere. Those remaining knew they had to reestablish the transit route that had always been the reason for Panama's existence. In 1829 Bolívar was petitioned by the Panamanians to do what he could to facilitate the construction of a "clear route or canal."

There was also a real fear that Panama would lose out to Nicaragua or some other site on the Isthmus as the beneficiary of a future canal. Like Panama, Nicaragua played host to a multitude of optimistic surveyors and explorers from the United States, Britain, France, Italy, Denmark, and Holland. Their backers were sometimes private companies, sometimes kings or emperors. The king of the Netherlands and Louis-Philippe of France were at various times interested in trans-Isthmian canals. Telford himself proposed a "grand scheme" for a canal at Darién, starting at the ill-fated Caledonia Bay. The Great Idea of the canal now attracted not only proven engineers such as Telford, but almost all the millionaires, dreamers, amateur engineers, and crackpots of the nineteenth century.

In Panama itself, concessions to build a canal or railroad were handed out freely after 1834. An eccentric, and probably insane

Frenchman was the first concession holder, but his scheme came to nothing. In 1835, U.S. president Andrew Jackson, alarmed by Dutch efforts to secure a monopoly in Nicaragua, ordered Charles Biddle to visit Nicaragua and Panama and to document the possibilities of building a canal or railroad. Biddle's effort, too, ended in failure when he ignored Nicaragua and negotiated a concession for Panama on his own behalf, but from then on American policy toward an interoceanic canal was established: if such a waterway could be built, it would not be allowed to be under the sole control of any foreign power.

At the same time, New Granada still hoped to have any future canal under its sway, and petitioned the governments of the United States, France, and Britain to act as funders and international guarantors of its sovereignty over the Isthmus. In response to this, in 1843 the French government sent a senior civil engineer, Napoléon Garella, to map the Panama route. His survey was the most complete yet, although he failed to find the lowest pass over the Continental Divide, and his plan for a canal included nearly forty locks as well as a huge tunnel over three miles long. Humboldt himself was among those denouncing the scheme as "an absurdity." The next concession was more modest—for a French syndicate to build a railroad over the Isthmus.

All this activity by the French had not gone unnoticed in London. In fact, British steamers had started operating out of Panama in the 1830s, and several reports were sent back to London detailing the possibilities of a canal or railway there. In 1836, however, an incident occurred that was to sour relations between New Granada and Great Britain. After getting involved in a fight with a local resident, Joseph Russell, Her Majesty's vice-consul in Panama City, was given a stiff prison sentence. This led, in true gunboat diplomacy style, to British warships blockading the mouth of the Chagres River and the harbor of Cartagena. War was averted only when the local authorities agreed to release Russell and pay an indemnity. It was all part and parcel, however, of an increasingly high-handed and interventionist approach on behalf of the British. Everyone in Panama and Washington feared that the British, using another excuse, might one day seize the Isthmus. There was also American concern about the railway concession given to the French syndicate, which might be operated as a monopoly. Thus, at the end of 1845, the United States sent a new chargé, Benjamin A. Bidlack, to Bogotá to ensure that "no other nation should obtain either an exclusive privilege or an advantage." He did not have high hopes, such was Britain's regional dominance, but found that the new president, Tomás Cipriano de Mosquera, who had been minister to London, had also come to fear British aggression and presented a sympathetic ear.

Much of the subsequent treaty negotiated by Bidlack with the New Grenadan foreign minister, Manuel María Mallarino, was humdrum, concerning the removal of discriminatory tariffs on American products. The key article, which would shape relations between the two countries and decisively affect the story of the Panama Canal, was number thirty-five: this guaranteed "that the right of way or transit across the isthmus of Panama upon any modes of communication that now exist, or that may be hereafter constructed, shall be open and free to the Government and citizens of the United States . . ." In return, the United States guaranteed "the perfect neutrality of the before-mentioned Isthmus, with the view that the free transit from the one to the other sea may not be interrupted." Mallarino declared that "to surround the isthmus with the vigorous will of a powerful and benign democracy . . . was to save the isthmus."

It was clear that the treaty, by which the United States would protect the Isthmus from British seizure in return for transit rights and favorable customs rates, would come perilously close to an "entangling alliance," something the United States Senate had set its face against. So the New Grenadans emphasized British aggression, warning that British ambitions would soon stretch from the Cape to California. The treaty was ratified by the U.S. Senate in 1848, and, at a stroke, Mosquera had reversed Bolívar's traditional policy of using Britain as a balance against the potentially more powerful United

States. More than that, he had, in fact, effectively handed control of the Isthmus to a foreign power, as French diplomats and others in Bogotá warned at the time. From now on, the United States had the right to land troops on the Isthmus if "free transit" was threatened. For the United States it was a unique treaty, the only foreign alliance ratified throughout the nineteenth century, and for almost the first time, the country had a strategic interest outside its continental borders.

The treaty also further escalated tensions in the region between Britain and the United States. Seeing the Panama route now under U.S. control, the British moved to strengthen their hold over the Caribbean terminus of any potential Nicaraguan canal. They were also alarmed (as was the whole of South America) by the acquisition by the United States at the end of the war with Mexico of vast territories including California. The southward march of American power seemed unstoppable, even to the extent of taking over all of Central America and threatening British colonies and investments in the entire hemisphere. Nicaragua protested British incursions on their territory and asked for—and received—the backing of the United States, which then negotiated a treaty with Nicaragua that gave it exclusive control over a canal there.

On both sides the saber rattling increased ominously, and there was talk of war. In December 1849 British foreign secretary Lord Palmerston sent Sir Henry Lytton Bulwer to Washington to try to find a solution to the standoff. The result was the Clayton-Bulwer Treaty, at the heart of which lay the desire by both sides to avoid having a canal exclusively controlled by the other. In effect, the fear of a foreign-controlled canal—which would hand to its owner total dominance of the region—was greater than the benefits that such a waterway might provide. The treaty stipulated that neither the United States nor Great Britain would take exclusive control over any waterway in Central America or try to fortify any that might be built. The canal was now on hold, with the hands of the United States firmly tied.

But there were still other ways of improving the Isthmus transit route. Because of the upheavals in Europe in 1848, the French syndicate that had been granted a railway concession failed to raise the initial surety, and the contract was taken over by a syndicate headed by William Aspinwall, a New York businessman, who had been lobbying for permission to build a railway for some years, and who was running a new steamship service between Panama and San Francisco. His concession gave him exclusive transit rights across the Isthmus at Panama to a point ten miles south of Caledonia Bay, including the first option to build a canal within this zone.

The timing was, to put it mildly, fortunate. On January 24, gold was discovered near Colonel Sutter's sawmill in the vicinity of Sacramento, California. "The Eldorado of the Spaniards is discovered at last," announced the *New York Herald* after President Polk himself confirmed that the rumors of huge deposits were true. With the transcontinental railroad still twenty years away, the quickest and safest way to get from the East Coast to California was by traveling to the Chagres River, taking a boat upriver to Gorgona, crossing overland to Panama City, then sailing up to San Francisco. Once more, in a different way, Panama was to become "the Golden Isthmus."

CHAPTER THREE

GOLD RUSH

The small steamer the *Falcon* left New York on the first of December 1848 with sacks of mail and twenty-nine passengers bound for California via Panama. The majority were government officials and missionaries. On the way the boat docked at New Orleans. But in the meantime the news of the discovery of gold in California had swept the nation, and by the time it left New Orleans on December 18, the *Falcon* carried 193 passengers. The new arrivals were Southern backwoodsmen bearing pans, picks, and axes and all the paraphernalia of the gold hunter. The small ship was swamped; efforts by the captain to reduce the number boarding had been met with brandished revolvers.

The impatient party arrived off the mouth of Chagres River on December 27, 1848. From that moment on, the Isthmus was transformed forever. After a decade of hard times on the East Coast of the United States, there was a flood of young men eager to try their luck in the California goldfields. The Panama route was the most expensive, but the quickest, and speed was vital if the best claims in Sacramento were to be staked out. Following the *Falcon*, one ship after another arrived, and within a few weeks more than five hundred prospectors had crossed the Isthmus to Panama City, which had not known such commotion and wealth since the early days of the Spaniards.

Because of a sandbar, arriving vessels had to anchor about a mile from the landing place, the small village of Chagres, on the south side of the river, a "low, miserable town, of thirty thatched huts," as an early traveler reported. Native canoes carried them ashore across the swirling muddy water. Chagres did not make a good impression, and reaffirmed the Americans' sense of superiority. One wrote to his mother back in Alabama, "The houses are only hovels that in the States, would not even do for Negro quarters or even for a respectable cow house." The people, too, were seen by the Americans as little better than savages: "Half are full-blooded negroes ... The dress for the men is little short of indecent."

The locals were not slow, however, to realize that they, too, had struck gold. The prices charged to the new arrivals were exorbitant— to get ashore cost $2; a place in a boat upriver to Gorgona up to $10. For many, however, it was worth the money just to get away from Chagres near the river mouth, "one of the filthiest places we ever saw." The town also quickly acquired a reputation as "the birthplace of a malignant fever," as an English traveler, Frank Marryat, noted. Within the town and in a new shanty across the river, known as "American Chagres," bars and brothels soon sprang up. At the Silver Dollar Saloon drinks were seven times as expensive as in New York, but there were plenty of takers. The working girls, who soon flocked to the area from as far away as New Orleans or Paris, in the total absence of law enforcement took to carrying guns, a practice one British traveler called "as disconcerting as hell. All the time she kept one hand on her blasted six-shooter." Soon there were more than two hundred prostitutes working in Chagres alone.

The journey to Gorgona was along fifty miles of winding river, which took about three days. Most went in "bungos," hollowed-out logs used for transporting bananas. Many of the travelers marveled at their first sight of the lush, tropical jungle. "The bright green at all times charms the beholder," wrote Frank Marryat. "The eye does not become wearied with the thick masses of luxuriant foliage, for they are ever blended in grace and harmony." Alligators lazed in the shallows, and birds of every type and hue flitted through the treetops.

At Gorgona, originally a small town of a few hundred people, there was pandemonium. It quickly became a bottleneck in the flood across the Isthmus, as the eager gold hunters waited impatiently for scarce transport on the next leg of the journey. Such was the shortage and demand that to hire a riding mule could cost up to $20. Numerous tents and shanties sprang up on the hills above the town.

For the journey onward to Panama City, the "road" was diabolical. Over much of the twenty-one miles it was a trough rather than a track and if it was the wet season it would be swampy gunge, with mud up to five feet deep. Mules and horses, jolting over the rough, uneven cobbles, carried the travelers and their loads, but often it was local porters. Some of the men carried as much as three hundred pounds over the journey of a day and a half. Many of the smarter travelers were even carried in chairs strapped to the bearers' shoulders.

The whole experience of crossing the Isthmus was for one American "so like a nightmare that one took it as a bad dream—in helpless silence." But at last the weary travelers could descend to the Pacific and Panama City, which they found had quickly realized the money to be made from the prospectors. "The old ruined houses have been patched up with whitewash," wrote Frank Marryat, adding that "the main street is composed almost entirely of hotels, eating houses and 'hells' [bars]." Most were American-owned and run. In the city much of the rushing stampede hit a brick wall, as there were at first insufficient ships to take the men on the next leg of their journey. Arriving steamers would be mobbed as a mass of people fought to get on board. The situation was made worse by the fact that most of the ships entering San Francisco lost their crews, who chose instead to join the gold rush. Soon abandoned ships lay seven deep in San Francisco harbor. The result was a huge throng stranded in Panama City, at one point more than four thousand. Those who could not find or afford a bunk set up filthy camps on the outskirts, where what they inevitably called "Panama Fever"—malaria, yellow fever, and dysentery—began to strike them down. Some were so desperate to leave that they even set off for California in canoes. The frustration was increased when men started appearing on their way back to the East Coast, a lucky few carrying a fortune in gold dust and nuggets.

There are many accounts of returning prospectors having their precious gold dust stolen from them. With the prospectors had arrived on the Isthmus not only cholera, gambling, and prostitution but also an epidemic of armed robbery. One homeward-bound gold hunter reported of his disastrous trip in the spring of 1851: "I knew nothing of the great risk in travelling alone, as the natives two years before appeared to me an exceptionally honest people. But . . . contact with American roughs had changed them to thieves and murderers, and the whole route . . . was infested with American, English and Spanish highwaymen."

Some contemporary accounts blame the lawlessness, violence, and chaos of the gold trail on the "weak sway of the New Granada Republic . . . powerless to control the refuse of every nation which meet together upon its soil." Occasionally, when squabbles at the gaming tables or in the bars got out of hand, the local "soldier-police" were called in. But they were few in number, bore rusty old muskets, and very often marched unshod. The force of law was not helped by the chronic political instability on the Isthmus at the time. Between 1850 and 1855, there were no fewer than fourteen different governors of the province, and political violence added to the problems for the authorities.

It was not only gold prospectors but also the great and the good who used the Panama route. Nevertheless, on the whole the Americans traveling through the Isthmus were not good ambassadors for their country. "Terribly bullied by the Americans were the boatmen and muleteers," reads one account by a hotel proprietess from Jamaica. "[They] were reviled, shot, and stabbed by these free and independent filibusters, who would fain whop all creation abroad as they do their slaves at home."

━━◄◄◄◄◄━━►►►►►━━

It was the acquisition by the United States of vast Pacific territories at the end of the Mexican War that had inspired William Aspinwall and his partners to establish steamer services from Panama City to San Francisco and from New York to Chagres. In this, they were supported by the U.S. Navy, and by promised payments from the federal government for carrying mail and officials to and from the West Coast. Crucially, they were also protected by the Bidlack Treaty.

With the interior of the United States largely unsettled and unpacified, the Isthmus was seen in Washington as a key strategic artery linking the two coasts of the country. Aspinwall also had a plan for a railway across the Isthmus, and with the gold rush in full swing there was new impetus to start the construction straightaway. Gold seekers were paying up to $100 to cross to Panama City, so the potential profits were there for all to see.

In spite of this, the initial stock offer was a disappointment with only about half of the $1 million worth being taken up by the public. Undeterred, the directors purchased the remainder themselves, and work started on surveying a route for what would be the first railway ever built in the tropics.

The first and best choice for the Atlantic terminus of the railway was the old harbor of Portobelo, but a New York speculator had bought all the surrounding lands and held out for a huge sum. So the railway engineers were forced to choose Limón Bay, otherwise known as Navy Bay, where Columbus had anchored during his search for the mythical strait. It was an unfortunate beginning, which would have long-lasting repercussions, for the harbor provided little shelter from the occasionally fierce north winds—"northers"—and the land bordering the bay was little more than a swamp. In fact, it was just about the wettest and unhealthiest place on the Isthmus. In the bay was an island, known as Manzanillo, and here it was elected to start work in May 1850. As a contemporary account has it, "No imposing ceremony inaugurated the 'breaking ground.' Two American citizens, leaping, axe in hand, from a native canoe upon a wild and desolate island, their retinue consisting of half a dozen Indians, who clear the path with rude knives, strike their glittering axes into the nearest tree; the rapid blows reverberate from shore to shore, and the stately cocoa crashes upon the beach."

Contracted as engineers were two men with experience of the tropics—they had recently completed a short canal in New Grenada—but even for them this was a forbidding prospect. "It was a virgin swamp," a contemporary wrote, "covered with a dense growth of the tortuous, water-loving mangrove, and interlaced with huge vines and thorny shrubs. In the black, slimy mud of its surface, alligators and other reptiles abounded, while the air was laden with pestilential vapors, and swarming with sand-flies and mosquitoes." As the island was cleared, a storehouse was erected, but it was found impossible to occupy on account of the insects, so the workers and American engineers were forced to live on an old wooden hulk anchored in the harbor. There, the myriad cockroaches and the constant movement of the ship in the unsheltered bay further weakened their spirits and constitutions. The huge demand for porters, muleteers, and boatmen made it impossible to recruit sufficient local laborers (who were thought "indolent and lazy" by the Americans anyway), so in June some fifty workers were brought from Cartagena in New Grenada, almost all descendants of the black slaves imported by the Spanish. The next month the same number of Irishmen arrived from New Orleans. There was surplus American labor in the United States at this time, due to the large number of men demobbed after the end of the Mexican War, but it was felt that they would demand too high a wage, and might be too prone to organizing themselves.

Meanwhile the surveyors pushed on, locating the track, often wading up to their armpits in the deep marshes that lay beyond the island. One, it was reported, "carried his noonday luncheon in his hat . . . and ate it standing, amid the envious alligators and water snakes."

The surveyors did have one spectacular success, finding at a place called Culebra (Spanish for "snake") a pass across the mountainous spine of the Isthmus at only 275 feet above sea level, when they had been expecting to have to site the line at 600 feet. But by now fever was carrying off the workers at an alarming rate, and in time the white members of the party "wore the pale hue of ghosts."

Nevertheless, in August the construction work was commenced. A decrepit steamer replaced the hulk, and Manzanillo Island was filled in enough to build a few more huts. As the jungle was cleared, the clouds of insects lessened. But by the end of the first year, even though the workforce had increased to a thousand, only four or five miles of temporary track had been laid across the swamp on wooden trestles. Wooden docks were built on Manzanillo Island in April 1851, but by then the rainy season had restarted, the original capital was all expended, and the directors were compelled to keep the work going on their personal credit.

By October 1851, eight miles had been constructed and the railway reached to Gatún. But in New York the promoters began to doubt that the line would ever be completed. The value of the stock went into free fall, and the work came to a standstill.

CHAPTER FOUR

"A NATURAL CULMINATING POINT"

It was a fierce southwesterly storm off the Caribbean coast of the Isthmus that saved the railroad project. In December 1851, two ships from Georgia and Philadelphia, filled with over a thousand hopeful gold hunters bound for the Chagres River, found themselves in serious trouble and were driven to take shelter in Limón Bay. The impatient passengers swarmed onshore and demanded to be taken inland by rail. The railroad engineers protested that there were no passenger cars, but the prospectors eagerly piled into wooden cattle trucks and were transported the eight miles to Gatún. It cut a precious day off the transit and after that everyone demanded the same. The railway never looked back; and from then on, as fast as the beleaguered workers pushed on across the Isthmus, the California-bound passengers were right behind them. What's more, they were prepared to pay huge sums, sometimes more than $25, for their tickets. The initial rates set by the railway managers were, one admitted, "intended to be, to a certain extent prohibitory, until we could get things in shape," but there were plenty of takers and the planned reduction in fares was never necessary. So from that day on, the "goose began to lay golden eggs with astonishing extravagance."

Early the following year, the Panama Railroad Company formally inaugurated the growing town on Manzanillo Island, the Atlantic terminus of the route. They named it Aspinwall, after the company's American boss, but the locals were having none of this, passing a law calling the town Colón, after Christopher Columbus. For a while confusion reigned, as the local post service refused to deliver mail addressed to Aspinwall, and eventually the American name was dropped. Up the coast, the town of Chagres at the river mouth quickly lost its previous importance, declined, and then disappeared altogether. Colón was now the key port and town on Panama's Atlantic coast. For the hundreds of thousands of men and women who would come to Panama over the next sixty years for the railway or to build the canal, it would be their first sight of the Isthmus.

For almost all, it was a hugely dispiriting experience. Although streets and squares were laid out, there were neither paved roads nor sewers. The town was separated from the mainland by a small channel, known as Folks River, slightly above the tide level, where vultures hovered, attracted by the offensive and rotten stench that circulated with the breeze coming from the swamps. When travelers arrived from Panama or New York, the population of eight hundred would be doubled, and the town would come to life of a sort. An account published in 1855 describes how "the hotels—great, straggling, wooden houses—gape here with their wide open doors, and catch California travelers, who are sent away with fever as a memento of the place, and shops, groggeries, billiard rooms, and drinking saloons thrust out their flaring signs to entice the passer-by." All the buildings, with the exception of the Railroad office and the "British consul's precarious corrugated iron dwelling," were of wood, and many were on rickety stilts over the stinking morass that almost surrounded the island.

"I thought I had never seen a more luckless, dreary spot," wrote one visitor in the 1850s. "It seemed as capital a nursery for ague and fever as Death could hit upon anywhere." Colón, the wettest and filthiest place on the Isthmus, was indeed a death trap for the workers the company imported to push the railway project along. A huge recruitment drive saw arrivals from all over the world. Among the Europeans were Englishmen, Irishmen, French, Germans, and Austrians. In 1852, one thousand Africans were brought in, and the following year some eight hundred Chinese workers were contracted. A number died on the way from Canton, on transport, according to a historian of the railway, "as filthy and odorous as any slavers." The terms of the contract were not far removed from slavery, either. The contractor was paid $25 per man per month, of which the workers saw about $4, with food and clothing thrown in. The men were expected to labor up to eighty hours a week, even in the drenching rain. Right from the start the Chinese proved particularly susceptible to the local strains of malaria. After less than a year, only some two hundred of the original intake had survived and these shattered remnants were shipped off to Jamaica.

It was to this island that the Railroad Company now looked to solve its labor crisis. Jamaica, along with the other sugar islands, was in a chronically depressed state. Malnutrition was rife, worsening the effects of the devastating cholera epidemic of 1850. Thus there was a great response when the Railroad Company's recruiting agent, Hutchins and Company of Kingston, starting advertising for workers, promising food and doctors, and wages of 3s 2d per day minimum.

By July 1854 two to three thousand adult males had left Kingston for Panama, and by the end of the following year almost five thousand had made the journey. One newspaper editor claimed: "We could name many persons who were walking the streets of the City for a long period of time,—literally starving because they could not get employment,—who are now doing well in Chagres." The West Indians quickly acquired a reputation for being the best pick-and-shovel men and the hardiest of the imported workers.

A large proportion of the Jamaicans were more or less resistant to yellow fever, the disease most dreaded by Europeans on the Isthmus. Like Panamanians, many would have had a mild dose during childhood, thus becoming immune. But they readily succumbed to malaria and especially to environmental diseases such as pulmonary infections, tuberculosis, and pneumonia, and many contracted these complaints on arrival, partly because they turned up in a malnourished state and thus had no resistance.

Typhoid, dysentery, smallpox, hookworm, and cutaneous infections were also endemic on the Isthmus. No record was kept of the number of workers who died during the railroad construction, but estimates are from six to twelve thousand. The worst year was 1852, when a cholera epidemic killed unnumbered workers and all but two of the fifty American technicians then on-site. One railroad historian reckoned that on average over the five years of construction one in five of the workers died every month. An account written in 1912 describes how "workers who toppled over in the jungle [and] managed to drag themselves to the tracks . . . were picked up and taken to the hospital in Aspinwall . . . Others swallowed by the sinkholes or eaten alive by ants and land crabs, disappeared without a trace."

Food was scarce and expensive. Although strips of dried jerked beef were a staple, workers and whites alike ate monkey, iguana, or snake stew to survive. Often it was best not to ask what was put in front of you in the so-called hotels. Water was also hard to come by. In Panama it came from a spring about a mile outside the city, and was carried in earthen crocks holding three gallons, and sold for ten cents a crock, which was almost a fifth of the daily wage for a worker. Alcohol, in contrast, was cheap and plentiful. American technicians drank champagne cocktails for breakfast, with quinine instead of bitters. According to a local newspaper, it was this intemperance that led to many falling ill. "In most cases," the paper wrote, "sickness and death have occurred from imprudence in drinking spirituous liquors, gluttony and a careless exposure to wet weather."

The lawlessness of the gold trail was also a real problem for the railway construction. Finding the local police inadequate, the Railroad Company bosses made a secret deal with the provincial governor to set up their own force. In 1852 they imported a notorious Indian fighter and former Texas Ranger called Ran Runnels to lead a small but heavily armed company of about forty men, described by a contemporary as "a bare-footed, coatless, harum-scarum looking set." Brushing aside the local police force, they had the power of life and death on the Isthmus, liberally engaging in whipping, imprisonment, and shooting. On several occasions dozens of men were hanged along the seawall in Panama City. In 1853 the vigilante force broke up a strike by railway workers, in the process publicly flogging the Panamanian official who had been instrumental in organizing the action. The force was also useful for providing surveillance of their contracted workers, to prevent them from taking up agricultural plots or going to work in the better-paid transit business. As well as withholding wages, the Railroad Company authorized lashings by overseers and the use of stocks to keep men on the job.

All the time the railway, tiny in length, but a massive undertaking considering the conditions, was steadily lengthening. By July 1852, the track had reached Barbacoas, about halfway across the Isthmus, where it was to cross the Chagres River. At this point the work was returned to a contractor, whose first job was the construction of a bridge there, where the Chagres flowed through a rocky channel, some three hundred feet wide.

It was the first taste of the power and unpredictability of the Chagres. A bridge was built, then promptly destroyed when a freshet swept away one of its spans. The Railroad Company was once again compelled to take the enterprise into its own hands.

The bridge was rebuilt and in May 1854 the track reached Gorgona, and work started in Panama City heading up the Río Grande Valley. Although incomplete, the railway was by now making serious money. In 1854, with thirty-one miles in operation, 32,000 were transported, and the outfit's gross income exceeded a million dollars. This was in spite of a falling off of the stream of gold prospectors; by now the Isthmus was one of the major passenger routes of the world, and still the best way to get from the East to the West Coast of the United States, whoever you were. The Bishop of California crossed in December 1853 and left a vivid account of the "pale and miserable" Irish workers, and the "oaths and imprecations" of the "ruffians" and "women of the baser sort" he encountered at Las Cruces.

Setbacks continued even as the line neared completion. A forty-foot-deep cut was dug near Paraíso high in the mountains. When the first rain came, the surface became saturated and the greasy soil moved into the cut, burying the railroad to a depth of some twenty feet. In December 1854 a hurricane from the northeast exposed the weakness of Limón Bay, destroying every ship anchored in the port. Nevertheless, at midnight on January 27, 1855, under a torrential tropical rain, two work crews met, bringing into existence the first railroad that crossed a continent. In many ways it was a heroic achievement, and that is certainly how it was viewed in the international press. The project was officially inaugurated on February 15, 1855, with elaborate celebrations. The *Aspinwall Daily Courier* described the whistles blowing from the heights to the Pacific lowlands, while for another English-language paper, the *Star and Herald*, originally established in 1849, it was first and foremost a triumph of Yankee entrepreneurship ability.

Indeed, a precedent had been set of American engineering ingenuity and success in the tropics. More than that, Panama was now the site of an internationally important transport breakthrough. In an age where commerce and progress were the drumbeats of the world, the excitement was irresistible. The official history of the railroad construction, published in 1862, eulogized that "no one work . . . has accomplished so much, and . . . promises for the future so great benefit to the commercial interests of the world as the present railroad thoroughfare between the Atlantic and Pacific Oceans at the Isthmus of Panama . . . it forms a natural culminating point for the great commercial travel of the globe."

Because of the railroad, the prospect of a canal had improved almost immeasurably. It was a giant step forward. Not only had the lowest pass in the entire Continental Divide outside Nicaragua been discovered at Culebra, but also the railway, with its "slender feeler of progress," had opened up the interior. The railroad would serve as the right hand of the canal builders, and it would offer a great advantage to Panama when the "battle of the routes" would be fought with Nicaragua.

But the greatest lure that the railroad presented to those who dreamt of a trans-Isthmian canal was financial. It had cost a fortune to build—estimates are as high as $7 to $9 million, or $170,000 per mile—but for those who had put up the money, the payback was huge. Even before it was finished, a third of the cost had been recouped. In a single month, March 1855, receipts topped $120,000. Fares remained incredibly high and steamship companies happily paid huge sums—one-half of their entire freight costs—to unload onto the railway and then reload at the other end.

Panama was not the only trans-Isthmian transit route. In Nicaragua, the American entrepreneur Cornelius Vanderbilt had established a transit for passengers, which involved flat-bottomed craft sailing up the San Juan River and across the lake where they were transferred to carriages for the trip to the Pacific. He also commissioned a detailed canal survey in Nicaragua, but was unable to raise the capital to start work. Although many thousands chose Vanderbilt's route, it didn't hurt the business at Panama. In the first six years after it was finished, the Railroad Company made profits in excess of $7 million. Dividends were 15 percent on average and went as high as 44 percent. At one time, Panama Railroad stock was the highest-priced on the New York Exchange. Panama seemed indeed the golden Isthmus once again.

But amidst the euphoria there were plenty of lessons that later canal builders could have learned—had they not been blinded by the financial and heroic success of the railroad. The appalling death rates, the political instability and labor troubles, the dangers of the Chagres

River and landslides would be the bitter enemies of the next generations of West Indians, Americans, and Europeans who went to "the
golden Isthmus" to build a canal. The experience of nonwhites at
the hands of the prospectors and U.S. bosses also looks forward to
the confused and unfortunate racial attitudes of the American construction period. Indeed, the railroad, which had put Panama on the
map as never before, was to turn out, for the people of the country,
to be something of a mixed blessing.

In effect, the transit route had become a company town. Panama
was the railway. The Company kept for itself the arrangement of accommodation and food for its employees, and everything was imported, just as all the expertise, labor, capital, materials, and tools for
the railway construction had been. In effect, the local businessmen
lost their control of cross-Isthmian freightage and storage—Panama's
primary resource—and the entire transit zone came under the control and ownership of British or American interests. In the same way
the New Grenadan authorities found themselves outmanned and outgunned by the railway's men, and deferred to the foreigners. The dollar replaced the peso as the common currency and English became
almost as common as Spanish. Attempts to impose a toll for the local
economy on tonnage on the railroad were defeated. The railroad and
foreign interests, backed by the almost continual presence of the U.S.
Navy, under the terms of the 1846 Bidlack Treaty to keep the transit
open, were just too strong.

In the early 1850s Panamanian landowners had made small fortunes renting or selling properties for hugely inflated sums. But with
the opening of the railway and the falling away of the gold rush,
demand for accommodation and other services collapsed and the
Panamanian economy went into a deep slump, even as the railway
prospered.

It was boom and bust for the poor of the country as well. The demands of the gold rush had led to a bonanza for the country's muleteers, oarsmen, and porters, but the opening of the railway had ended
those trades forever. In the meantime, thousands of men had flooded

to the two terminal cities looking for work, causing chronic over-crowding and attendant filth and disease. Between 1842 and 1864, the population of Panama City had swollen from five thousand to thir-teen thousand and a massive slum had grown up outside the city walls. With the completion of the railway, there was widespread un-employment. In fact, the lot of the majority of Panamanian citizens had actually worsened.

The huge influx of black workers also caused a great challenge to the region's delicate social structure and narrow, class-based political system, and hopeful laborers were still arriving from Jamaica even af-ter the main construction work was finished, leading to calls for mi-grants without work to be turned away at Colón. The previously loose social stratification based on color had been magnified and so-lidified by the advent of the Americans. One observer described the situation in Colón in the mid-1850s: all the railroad officials, hotel and barkeepers were white, mainly American; the "better class of shop-keepers are Mulattoes from Jamaica," while "dispensers of cheap grog, and hucksters of fruit and small wares are chiefly negroes."

Influenced by the spread of European liberalism, and inflamed by the exclusion of local people from the prosperity of the railway, there was growing popular opposition to the foreign presence in Panama. In many ways Washington replaced Bogotá not just as the real power in Panama, but also as the focus of growing nationalist efforts to rid the Isthmus of empire-building foreigners.

Panama was now essentially an American protectorate. This did not go unnoticed around the world, and in 1857 Britain suggested that this new state of affairs was in violation of the Clayton-Bulwer Treaty, offering instead to be one of a triumvirate of "protecting powers" alongside the United States and France. Showing early signs of the abandonment of the idea of a "neutral canal," the Americans rejected the solution, citing the Bidlack Treaty as taking precedence.

New Grenada's rule on the Isthmus weakened further during its six-year civil war beginning in 1857, essentially a struggle between federalist, secular liberals and centrist, clerical conservatives, complicated by the regional rivalries of the scattered population. Together with economic depression, the 1860s in Panama saw constant turmoil or revolts, coups d'etat, and revolutionary conspiracies that so depleted the treasury that at one point mid-decade many public schools were forced to close through lack of funds. In response to separatist convulsions, as well as the "mob" threatening the railroad (or, more precisely, foreign or white elite Panamanian interests), U.S. troops were landed five times during the decade, sometimes at the request of Bogotá, sometimes not.

Between 1861 and 1865, the United States was, of course, fighting its own civil war, and the Panama route was used several times for moving troops, materials, and bullion from coast to coast. In the buildup to the war, and during the armed conflict itself, America's European rivals were quick to take advantage. The French emperor, Napoléon III, had long been obsessed with Central America, dreaming of control of a canal, and of a buffer against the alarming expansion of the United States. In 1861 and the following year, there were expeditions to Mexico from Spain, Britain, and France to demand payment of debt. But for France it was more than that. Troops were landed, and control established over much of the country. An Austrian Habsburg, Maximilian, was established as emperor. Never recognized by the United States, he was overthrown in 1867 after the withdrawal of French troops decimated by disease. But a legacy of deep distrust of French activities in the region had been firmly established in the United States. This would have profound effects on later canal efforts.

The United States leadership emerged from the Civil War determined to reverse creeping European intervention in their backyard and to point the United States in an outward-looking and expansionist direction. The vague aspirations of the Monroe Doctrine now became national dogma, and from being a defensive strategy it became a license for U.S. intervention throughout the hemisphere.

The directions of the expansion of American influence and interest—southward to Peru and Chile, producers of valuable raw materials such as nitrate of soda, copper and tin; and westward to the newly opened up markets of China and Japan—focused attention on the need for a trans-Isthmian canal. It was now becoming a corner-stone of American strategic ambitions, and part and parcel of the country's Manifest Destiny.

In 1866, the Senate requested that the Navy report on possible canal sites. Rear Admiral Charles H. Davis, having consulted the mishmash of Spanish, French, and other sources, came back with nineteen possibilities, including six in Panama and three in Darién, in modern-day Colombia, based on the Atrato River.

Late the same year, the U.S. minister in Bogotá negotiated a con-cession with Colombia for the exclusive right to build a canal, but the treaty, and further efforts over the next three years, never satisfied both sides. The Americans demanded a large measure of control and freedom of action in the transit zone, while Bogotá was fearful of further loss of sovereignty on the Isthmus, and tried to limit the number of U.S. employees or troops in Panama at any one time. On the Isthmus itself, the failure of these efforts was dismaying and fur-ther fueled secessionist temperament.

As the civil war raged in Colombia, sometimes sweeping into its northernmost province, then sweeping out again, Panama faced the prospect that even its key business (albeit foreign owned and con-trolled), the railroad, had seen its best days. The opening of the transcontinental railroad in the United States on May 10, 1869, ended the Panama Railroad (PRR)'s monopoly almost overnight. The previ-ous year had seen record revenue for the business, but after that the line on the graph heads ever southward. Arrogant mismanagement of the railroad did not help, either. Panama sank further into poverty and sporadic anarchy, with U.S. troops landing twice more in the 1870s and Colombian soldiers in 1875.

However, the opening of the transcontinental railway did nothing to quiet calls in the United States for a trans-Isthmian canal. Never before had it been so plain that the United States was now truly a continental power, with two oceans separated by an enormous but, on paper, highly avoidable distance. The inauguration in 1869 of Ulysses S. Grant as the eighteenth American president brought further new momentum to U.S. canal policy. For one thing, Grant had actually been on the Isthmus. In his first address to Congress, the new president laid out his canal ambitions and soon established a new Inter-Oceanic Canal Commission—headed by Admiral Daniel Ammen—to investigate possibilities, and conduct and weigh new surveys of all the possible routes.

So for the first time, every possibility, however remote, was to be meticulously and systematically explored. What's more, the methodology would be the same everywhere so real comparisons would now be possible. At last myth would be separated from reality about the true prospects of an interoceanic canal.

CHAPTER FIVE

THE COMPETING ROUTES

The field was still open. Aside from Nicaragua and Panama, there had been surveying expeditions in Mexico, where, as elsewhere, concessions were granted, then resold, but no work was ever started. The San Blas route, where the Isthmus spans only thirty miles, had been visited by British and American explorers, who had expressed optimism about a "very remarkable depression" in the area's 1,000- to 1,500-foot mountainous spine, not that they had actually reached it. The region that had attracted the most excitement, however, was Darién, the section of the Isthmus spanning the present-day Panama-Colombia border, still inhospitable jungle today.

In 1850, an Irish doctor, Edward Cullen, had announced in England that he had found a short and convenient canal route from Caledonia Bay to the Gulf of San Miguel, with a break in the Continental Divide at only 150 feet above sea level. He also claimed that the previous year he had painlessly walked the route from coast to coast in a few hours. It seemed a sensational discovery. But subsequent investigations by an internationally manned surveying team had found no pass across the Continental Divide at this point at less than 1,300 feet above sea level. During the course of the exploration, several teams got lost and were either ambushed by hostile Cuna Indians or died of starvation or disease.

"It is proved beyond all doubt," the leader of the surveyors had reported, "that Dr. Cullen never was in the interior, and that his statements are a plausible net-work of fabrications." The Irish doctor wisely disappeared, though he emerged later as an army medic in the Crimea. It seems that his entire story was a gigantic lie, a dream built on wishful thinking, which had cost the lives of more than a dozen men.

But many were undeterred and optimistic stories still circulated. South of Caledonia Bay, a broad river, the Atrato, penetrates deep inland, offering a canal excavation of as little as twenty-eight miles. For this reason several French and British expeditions had been organized and sent to the area. Soon after Cullen's sensational claim, Wall Street millionaire Frederick M. Kelley heard a rumor of a "Lost Canal of Raspadura" linking deep inland, tributaries of the Atrato and the Tuyra rivers flowing to opposite oceans. In 1852 Kelley funded an expedition to investigate, led by John C. Trautwine, one of the experienced Panama Railroad engineers. His report was emphatic—there was no "Lost Canal"—but Kelley, described in his later years as "mystical and imaginative," was clearly a man in the grip of an idea. As well as corresponding with and meeting the by now ancient Humboldt, he toured the capitals of Europe looking for support for a canal, and over the next twenty years spent an estimated $150,000 of his own money on further optimistic surveys in Darién, few of which even managed to venture far inland.

Rear Admiral Charles H. Davis, in his 1866 report for the U.S. Senate, had also favored Darién, in particular the more westerly route between Paterson's Caledonia Bay to the Gulf of San Miguel. On the map it looked simple: the narrow barrier between the oceans, the probable route taken by Balboa, is only forty miles, and large rivers promised to reduce further the necessary length of a canal there.

So the destination was Caledonia Bay when the first Grant expedition to leave the United States for the Isthmus headed out from Brooklyn Navy Yard on January 22, 1870, commanded by thirty-three-year-old Lieutenant Thomas O. Selfridge. "The Department has entrusted to you a duty connected with the greatest enterprise of the present age," read his orders from Admiral Ammen. The weather was clear and bright.

For two months his hundred-man team, heavily armed to deter Indian attacks, searched the high mountain range near the Atlantic coast, but found no sign of Cullen's pass, and their thoroughness, something of a new departure for Darién surveys, left no room for doubt. From there Selfridge moved on to San Blas. There, like previous expeditions, they were turned away by Cuna Indians before completing an overland crossing of the Isthmus, but they saw enough to bury the hope of a "remarkable depression" and quickly to discard a sea-level or lock canal. Even if the long string of locks needed to lift ships to over a thousand feet could be built, every lock canal needs a supply of water at its summit elevation. Each time a lock is used, thousands of gallons of water pass "downstream." At the top of the mountains of San Blas there were only trickling brooks. The only option was a tunnel, as others had concluded, and this time the estimate was at ten miles long. Nevertheless, because it was still the shortest route, Selfridge refused to rule it out as he led his exhausted team back to New York.

He was back in Darién at the end of the year, still chasing shadows. On December 29, 1870, he sailed to the deep, beautiful Gulf of Urabá into which flows the Atrato River. This was where Balboa had founded the now abandoned town of Santa María more than three hundred years before and where Kelley's explorers had hoped to find the "Lost Canal."

Selfridge himself was now succumbing to the wishful thinking, or "excessive optimism," that is a recurring part of the canal story. He was much taken by the Atrato basin and allowed himself to imagine that "it [would] one day be covered with sails from every clime." Selfridge had been joined by fellow naval officer Edward P. Lull, who carried out a hydrographic survey of the river's gulf, while Selfridge himself headed upstream. He eventually came up with a plan that involved more than twenty locks and a tunnel five miles long. Tunnels were particularly problematic, even without geological considerations. They had to be high enough for the tallest sail-bearing masts, but there was also the problem presented by the accumulation of steam from engine-powered vessels. Nevertheless, Selfridge was keen, and further expeditions were sent to take another look.

Meanwhile, separate expeditions had set off to investigate the other possibilities suggested by Humboldt, Davis, or both. On November 11, 1870, a party of surveyors landed at Tehuantepec, the narrowest point in Mexico, where the Isthmus is 130 miles wide, with a low range of mountains. Although it was the possible canal site nearest to the United States, the surveyors found little else to recommend it. The lowest pass was over 750 feet above sea level, and the only possible canal would be 144 miles long and need an impossible 140 locks.

There were two Grant expeditions to Nicaragua. The first got off to a calamitous start, when the commander of the expedition was drowned while attempting to land. But a second expedition headed by Selfridge's previous companion Edward Lull and Cuban-born Ancieto Menocal (who had worked on the Vanderbilt survey back in 1849) conducted a thorough survey, running a line of levels from coast to coast, measuring river flows and depths, and preparing tables, maps, and charts. They confirmed the earlier survey's findings that there existed a pass only 153 feet above sea level in the narrow neck of land between Lake Nicaragua and the Pacific. This was more than 100 feet lower than anything found at Panama. Lull and Menocal suggested a canal with ten locks on either side, estimated to cost nearly $65 million.

It was not until the beginning of January 1875, after a further expedition had explored other routes around the Atrato River, that the Panama survey team left New York for Colón. From the surveys conducted for the railway, the Panama route had been the best known at the outset, so it was left to last. The expedition was led by Lull and Menocal, and for two and a half months some one hundred men explored and measured the land between Colón and Panama and up into the Chagres watershed. Nevertheless, both Lull and Menocal had pretty much decided on their preference for the Nicaragua route, and they were unable to imagine a realistic design for a canal at Panama. The line of their proposed waterway largely followed that of the present-day canal. It was to be a lock canal, with a summit level of 124 feet, reached by twelve locks at either side. The problem with Panama, they correctly judged, was the volatility of the Chagres River. They suggested that what was needed was a huge, 2,000-foot-long viaduct sufficiently high to allow the floodwaters to pass under it. But the river was required as well, to supply water to the summit level, so the engineers decided that ten miles of aqueducts would have to be built. In all, it was just too impractical and expensive.

When the Inter-Oceanic Canal Commission reported in February 1876, there was a firm majority in favor of a route through Nicaragua. Tehuantepec was dismissed out of hand. Darién was too remote and wet; and the various Atrato schemes were too ambitious. All myths about "lost canals" and low passes in those areas had been exposed. Panama was too expensive, and what's more, "the deep cut would probably be subject to land-slides, from which the Panama Railroad has suffered seriously, and the canal would be exposed to serious injury from flood."

From then on, for the next twenty-five years, U.S. canal policy was firmly focused on Nicaragua, which became lodged in the minds of the public as well, who were beginning to demand an American canal under American control rather than the neutral and open-to-all arrangement favored by the Grant Commission. In 1877, treaty negotiations were started with the Nicaraguan government. In contrast, the United States did not even have a diplomatic representative in Bogotá. Slowly, draft treaties were drawn up, while private companies jostled for the concession, and Ancieto Menocal prepared another, even more thorough, Nicaragua-bound surveying party.

Then, in May 1879, the United States public read in their papers news from Paris that upset all previous plans. Le Congrès International d'Etudes du Canal Interocéanique had approved the digging of a canal at Panama and events were moving fast. It seemed that there would be a canal, but it was going to be built by the French.

PART TWO

The French Tragedy

We are, gentlemen, soldiers under fire; let us salute the comrade who falls in the battle, but let us think only of the fight of tomorrow and of victory.

—*French engineer and lobbyist*
Philippe Bunau-Varilla

CHAPTER SIX

"LE GRAND FRANÇAIS"

Paris in the spring of 1879 was awash with frenetic financial speculation. Money was more plentiful and mobile than ever before. The expansion of the railway and telegraph networks had brought new branch banks to provincial France, and the reach of those seeking to raise capital had widened considerably. Penalties for debt and bankruptcy had been eased, and restrictions on issuing shares had been lifted. In the Paris bourse, young stockbrokers noisily wheeled and dealed, betting on pretty much anything and often making huge sums for themselves. One such was the artist Paul Gauguin, who would later work on the Panama Canal. In 1879, he made 30,000 francs, a fortune at the time.

In spite of endemic political instability, everywhere there was optimism and energy, a spirit of *revanche*. Humiliated by the Prussians in the war of 1870, France was determined that it would be great again, and would recover its prestige not through fighting, but through, as Victor Hugo put it "astonish[ing] the world by the great deeds that can be won without a war." In the spring of 1878 Paris held a great exposition, which covered sixty-six acres of the city and attracted thirteen million visitors. It cost a fortune, but it demonstrated to the world France's recovery and new ambition.

The embodiment of this spirit of *revanche* was the builder of the Suez Canal, Ferdinand de Lesseps, called by Gambetta *"Le Grand Français."* Untainted by the events of 1870, he represented a new patriotism based not on war but on achievement for all mankind.

De Lesseps had followed his father into the diplomatic service, and in 1832, aged twenty-seven, had been appointed vice-consul at Alexandria and served in various roles in Egypt for the next five years. During this time he befriended the son of Egypt's viceroy and also became interested in the idea of a canal linking the Mediterranean to the Red Sea.

After several positions in Europe, de Lesseps left the diplomatic service in 1849, but returned to Egypt six years later as the guest of the new viceroy, his friend Said Pasha, who had just succeeded his father. Although de Lesseps had neither expertise nor money, after just over two weeks' stay he had persuaded Said Pasha to sign the concession that gave the Frenchman the right to build the Suez Canal.

A plan was drawn up by two French engineers and approved by an international commission of civil engineers, but there were plenty of critics of the scheme. In Britain, Robert Stephenson said he believed it to be a folly on a huge scale, and Lord Palmerston, now prime minister, called it "an undertaking which, I believe, in point of commercial character, may be deemed to rank among the many bubble schemes that from time to time have been palmed upon gullible capitalists." In fact, the British feared the alterations in the status quo that the canal would bring. Other doubters at home and abroad predicted that the trench would fill with sand from the desert as quickly as it was dug.

But nothing could dishearten Ferdinand de Lesseps. Supported by Emperor Napoléon III and Empress Eugénie, who was a cousin of his, de Lesseps succeeded in rousing the patriotism of the French and obtaining by their subscriptions more than half of the required capital of 200 million francs. The other half of the shares were taken up by the Egyptian government, who also forced thousands of local laborers to work on the project in conditions of semi-slavery. The excavation operations through the desert took nearly eleven years, during the course of which numerous technical, political, and financial problems had to be overcome. The final cost was more than double the original estimate, but the canal opened to traffic on November 17, 1869. De Lesseps, then sixty-four, was world famous.

Celebrated as the greatest living Frenchman, he was honored around the world. In 1870 he visited England, and *The Times* eulogized him as a "man eminent for originality enterprise courage and persistence . . . moral qualities of the highest order." At a banquet in his honor at Stafford House he was toasted by both Gladstone and Disraeli, and six days later more than twenty thousand people filled London's Crystal Palace for a reception in his honor.

He was praised for having the unshakable confidence to believe in his project even when virtually no one else had done, but in France in particular he was also seen as a man of the people for having built the canal with the capital of twenty-five thousand small investors, rather than the big banks. Following Suez he was never out of the Paris papers, and the fact that he had a pretty, young wife and a brood of adorable children made him perfect fodder for the new illustrated magazines. When in the early 1880s he ascended to the pantheon of the French Academy, he was praised thus: "You exercise a charm. You have that supreme gift which works miracles . . . the true reason for your ascendancy is that people detect in you a heart full of sympathy for all that is human . . . people love you and like to see you and before you have opened your mouth you are cheered. Your adversaries call this your cleverness; we call it your magic."

There was a special magic, too, about the nature of his achievement in Egypt. In a stroke, India had been brought nearly six thou-

sand miles closer to Europe. Furthermore, in a Victorian age determined to take on and conquer the world with innovation, engineering, and entrepreneurship, the Suez Canal was the perfect
marriage of commerce, transport, and industry, the forces that were
changing the world. It was also seen as a great civilizing achievement,
which "will help to wed the whole universe into one great unit, polit-
ically, industrially, and religiously," as was written at the time."The two
sides of the world approach to greet one another . . ." wrote a British
commentator in a similar vein.

But it was not just about high ideals. By the late 1870s, the benefits of the canal to European manufacturers were more than apparent, as the raw materials of the East, as well as its markets, had been
brought so much nearer. More than anything, the canal gave Europe
a critical advantage over the frighteningly fast-growing economy of
the United States' East Coast. For the canal's original backers, too, it
was a bonanza. Initially the share price of de Lesseps's company had
slumped. It soon turned out that his promises made during the construction for the traffic through the canal had been wild overesti-
mates. But by 1879 a 500-franc ($100) share was trading for over
2,000 francs, and the company was paying dividends of 14 percent.
Suez had made a lot of people rich.

Bathed in public adulation, de Lesseps, although by any reckoning
now an old man, was not going to content himself with just the Suez
Canal. "Is it not a glorious thing for us to be able to carry out . . . vast
projects," he wrote, "thus affirming the progress made by our race
and age, in which all obstacles seem to have disappeared." In 1873 he
became interested in a project for uniting Europe and Asia by a railway to Bombay, with a branch to Peking. He subsequently got involved in a harebrained scheme to break through a low-lying ridge in
Tunisia to create a huge inland sea in the Sahara.

It was an international geographical conference at the Louvre in
Paris in 1875 that saw the launch of de Lesseps's Panama ambition.
Four years before, a similar meeting in Antwerp had commended the
work of a succession of French explorers, who had claimed that

there was a low pass between the headwaters of the Tuyra and Atrato rivers in Darién. None of them, however, had actually reached it.

Ferdinand de Lesseps had become a leading light in the Paris Geographical Society, under whose auspices the conference was held. Undoubtedly the star of the show, he spoke about his experience with the Suez Canal, but then went on to lay out for the first time his ambitions for an American waterway. Even at this early stage, he said he hoped that it would be possible to construct in Central America a canal *à niveau*, at sea level, without locks. Swayed by the optimistic claims of the French explorers, he announced that his personal preference was for a route in southern Darién. An American delegation was present reporting on the results of the Grant surveys, but their careful measurements in Darién seem to have been discounted. Instead, de Lesseps suggested, there should be new surveys undertaken in Darién. There was another crucial advantage to this area for de Lesseps that had nothing to do with surveys or geography: it was outside—just—the limit of the Panama Railroad's transit monopoly as granted by their concession from Bogotá.

Following the conference, the Paris Geographical Society established a special committee, with de Lesseps as president, to study the canal question. There were two Colombian delegates included, and it was hoped that scientists from all over the world would be involved, with the idea of further exploration being jointly undertaken and financed. It was an idealistic beginning.

But at this point a private syndicate emerged and offered to fund the work itself. Led by General Istvan Türr, a Hungarian who had fought with Garibaldi during the unification of Italy, the group, which called itself the Société Civile Internationale du Canal Interocéanique de Darién, included eminent figures from the worlds of letters, industry, and finance. There were some less salubrious characters, too, as would emerge later. In total their capital was 300,000 francs, represented by sixty shares of 5,000 francs each. De Lesseps was not a shareholder, but he was a friend of Türr and a number of the others.

By November 1866 a seventeen-man survey team had been assembled. In charge of the party was Lieutenant Lucien Napoléon
Bonaparte Wyse, a twenty-nine-year-old naval officer, brother-in-law
to Türr and fellow syndicate member. Wyse had experience of exploration on the Isthmus and was distantly related to his famous name-
sake. Second in charge was thirty-three-year-old Armand Reclus, a
naval officer and friend of Wyse.

Surveying work started on the Pacific side of the proposed
Atrato–Tuyra route. At first Reclus enjoyed himself, imagining, as
Selfridge had done fifteen years earlier, what their work might bring
about: "Our hope," he wrote in his diary, "is to fill these waters with
all the ships which will bring world commerce to the canal: clippers
with their huge hulls, three-masters letting their white sails fill to the
breeze, busy steamships ploughing through the water with all the
force of their steel lungs, brigs, all sails set, vessels of every nation."

But the jungle, exciting at first, soon became monotonous and
frightening. Everyone seemed to be ill with something or other; mosquitoes made their nights a misery. It soon became clear that the
claims of the earlier French explorers were "swarming with errors."
By the time the rains brought exploration to an end in March, two of
the team had died of disease; a third succumbed during the voyage
home.

Wyse and Reclus arrived back in Paris thoroughly disheartened.
When they met de Lesseps and the rest of the Société's Committee
of Initiative, they made it clear that a sea-level canal in Darién was out
of the question without a huge tunnel, and even a lock canal would
require a tunnel as well. This was not to de Lesseps's liking. He had
made up his mind that only a canal à niveau would do, and he urged
Wyse to return to the Isthmus and widen his investigations. De
Lesseps later told American reporters that he ordered Wyse specifically to investigate a sea-level canal along the line of the Panama Railroad, suggesting that he had given up on Darién and decided to bite
the bullet about the PRR's local transit monopoly.

The party, with many of the survivors from the first trip on board again, left for Panama at the end of 1877. This survey would be the first that would result in actual canal construction. Again, it was a small and inexpert group dispatched by the private syndicate, in contrast to the huge U.S. Navy teams that had been sent out from the United States. More striking still is that in spite of the supposed instructions from de Lesseps, the second Wyse expedition spent its first two months looking at the San Blas and southern Darién routes. Then, leaving Reclus in charge, Wyse headed for Panama. There, he traveled along the route of the railroad, before ordering Reclus to cut short his explorations in Darién and return to Panama. From what he had seen, Wyse had decided a preference for linking the Chagres and Río Grande valleys, effectively following the route of the railroad. The valleys were the lowest and longest in the region, had been comprehensively surveyed, and were served by the railway. "You should start preparations immediately to study the route of an inter-ocean canal at sea level, but with a tunnel," Wyse wrote to Reclus. Waiting for Reclus in Panama would be a "succinct version" of the American engineer Lull's report (though not the unpublished accompanying maps and charts), the maps made by the Frenchman Napoléon Garella in the 1840s, and the American railroad survey from the 1850s. Wyse himself left for Bogotá on February 25, to negotiate a new concession that would allow a canal to be built right on top of the American-controlled railway route.

Reclus's work in the river valleys of the Chagres and the Río Grande, which largely determined the route of the French canal, remains highly controversial, and would be viciously attacked by the enemies of the canal, in particular the Americans. It was indeed unfortunate that the surveying of the route later adopted was granted such a small proportion of the two expeditions' time—less than six weeks. In addition, the small party was hampered by disease, a fire in Panama City that destroyed much of their papers and tools, and an early start to the rainy season, which rendered further surveying impossible.

Meanwhile, Wyse had more clear-cut success. Meeting the

Colombian president on March 14, he was given all encouragement and presented a draft contract the very next day. Five days later, after only minor amendments, the deal was signed. Under the terms of the "Wyse concession" the Türr syndicate was granted exclusive right to build an interoceanic canal through Panama. As a provision of the deal, the waterway would revert to the Colombian government after ninety-nine years without compensation. It was also stipulated that the exact route of the canal should be determined by an international commission of competent engineers, just as had been the case with Suez. The syndicate could sell the concession to a private company but not to a government. Colombia was to receive a percentage of the gross revenue rising from 5 percent over time, with a minimum amount of $250,000 per annum. It was left to the concession holders to negotiate "some amicable agreement" with the Panama Railroad concerning its rights and privileges.

Back in France, Wyse and Reclus worked on collating their information. The date of the "International Commission," as demanded by the terms of the Wyse concession, was set for May the following year, and in the meantime Wyse, Türr, and Reclus, in concert with Ferdinand de Lesseps, prepared a series of plans to present.

Just before the conference Wyse put together a table of seven options, to be decided by the delegates. Four were in Darién or San Blas, all of which required extensive locks, tunnels, or both. The fifth and sixth options were the Panama Railroad Colón–Panama route. One was Lull's twenty-five-lock canal from the Grant surveys, the other was at sea level with ("or even without") a 5- to 8-kilometer tunnel. Wyse estimated that this could be built in six years at a cost of 500 million francs. The last option was in Nicaragua, with twenty-one locks. The disadvantages of this route were stressed: the complete absence of suitable ports, political instability, and the fact that the land over which the canal would pass was disputed between Nicaragua and her southerly neighbor, Costa Rica. In his conclusion, Wyse was unambiguous about his preferred option: the sea-level Panama route, and in his part of the published report Reclus expanded this to include five variations, one of which, seen as uneconomical by its author, dispensed with the tunnel altogether. Although Wyse acknowledged the difficulties presented by the Chagres River, he stressed that they were outweighed by the advantages this route offered, which included, somewhat surprisingly, the political stability of the province of Panama.

In all, some one hundred pages of maps, notes, and data were collected together. To the great disappointment of Reclus and Wyse, the detailed tables and maps from the United States' Grant surveys had, in the end, not been forthcoming from the Americans. All versions of the canal were designed to accommodate what was then the largest ship in the French Navy, which had a draught of 7.9 meters. The tunnel would be 24 meters wide and rise 34 meters above the water level to allow ships through without lowering their masts. For Wyse and Reclus, the construction of such a massive tunnel was not the impossibility it might seem now. Seven years earlier had seen the completion of the Mont Cenis Tunnel through the Alps. Thirteen kilometers long, it was built with the help of key new technologies— dynamite (electrically ignited) and pneumatic drills. An even longer Alpine tunnel, the Saint Gotthard, was currently under construction, and in England, work had started on a seven-kilometer tunnel under the River Severn. In 1875, bills had been passed in the French and British governments for the construction of a tunnel under the Channel, an astonishing distance of about thirty miles. Geological surveys for the project had started in France the following year.

As the Le Congrès International d'Etudes du Canal Interocéanique assembled in Paris on May 15, 1879, many of the leaders of these projects were present. From Britain came Sir John Hawkshaw, in charge of the Severn tunnel; Ribourt, one of the engineers of the St. Gotthard Tunnel, was there, although as an observer rather than a delegate. In all there were 136 delegates from twenty-two nations, including financiers and businessmen as well as civil and military engineers. The American contingent included Ammen, Menocal, and Selfridge. All had been personally invited by de Lesseps. The delegates included a large proportion of Frenchmen—over seventy—and among this group were a number of *Le Grand Français*'s Suez cronies. One was Abel Couvreux of Couvreux, Hersent, the giant contracting firm that had helped build the Egyptian canal.

By this stage de Lesseps seems to have insinuated himself into every aspect of the canal planning process. It was Wyse who did the deal with the Colombian government and had led the surveying expeditions, but all the talk was of the involvement of Ferdinand de Lesseps. Nevertheless, Wyse knew he needed the support of a man of de Lesseps's stature if his plan was not to join the host of schemes that had come to nothing.

De Lesseps had a proven track record from Suez. He never professed to be a trained engineer. But he was someone who could make things happen. More than anything, he was a communicator, one who could conjure up both the necessary capital and the dedication among the workforce that a project like the Panama Canal would demand. He had the reputation, energy, and charisma to turn fantastical schemes into reality. In many ways, after so many disappointments and false starts, he was just what was needed to deliver to Panama its destiny as a crossroads of the world. Inevitably, though, his strengths were also his weaknesses. His confidence was not only in himself, but also in his age. His lack of concern about the extraordinary challenges of the task ahead had its foundations in his faith in the serendipitous nature of emerging technology. He was sure that the right people with the right ideas and the right machines would somehow miraculously appear and take care of all the seemingly impossible challenges, just as had happened at Suez.

De Lesseps was not alone in riding a wave of confidence in engineering and technological progress. As well as those amazing Alpine tunnels, the previous decade had seen the creation of London's sewer system and the first electric streetlights; 1869 had witnessed the opening of the Union Pacific Railroad across the United States, as well as the Suez Canal. The Brooklyn Bridge was under construction in New York. Increased world trade had driven the development of new iron-screw ocean steamers. Alongside spectacular recent advances in chemical and electrical science, cheap steel, made by the Bessemer or Siemens-Martin hearth methods, together with new techniques in precision manufacturing, had made possible a huge range of new goods at affordable prices. Improvements gave birth to further progress and commerce, in a seemingly endless virtuous circle. All this was celebrated in international "expositions," such as the American Centennial in Philadelphia in 1876, which in its machinery hall showcased cutting-edge new technologies. Most impressive was the gigantic 1,500-horsepower Corliss Steam Engine, taller than a house, which alone powered thirteen acres of machinery.

Dreams of ever more powerful machines, of cheaper and quicker transport and communication, of opening up the world to increased trade and "civilization," gripped the public imagination as an endless stream of amazing new inventions and mind-bogglingly ambitious engineering projects were introduced to the world. De Lesseps's Panama Canal, which embodied so much of this forward-looking confidence, would surely, it was believed, take its rightful place amongst these great achievements.

CHAPTER SEVEN

THE FATAL DECISION

The news from Paris, carried on the newly laid submarine cable from Jamaica, was keenly followed in Panama. At home, however, they had their own concerns. At the end of the previous year there had been an armed uprising against the state president; a district judge and two others were killed during violence in Panama City's sprawling and volatile suburbs. On April 17, a month before the conference opened in Paris, there was another attempted revolution led by soldiers of the Colombian garrison. "Tragic scenes," wrote the *New York Tribune*'s local correspondent, "fighting in the streets and many persons killed." Although the conspirators surrendered, martial law came into force. "Business has been paralysed," reported the British consul Hugh Mallet, "and trade diverted from the Isthmus by constant apprehensions of danger to life and property." Disorder continued even as the delegates in Paris were debating the future of Panama. On May 24 there were violent scenes, including gunfire, in the provincial assembly building. Two weeks later, General Rafael

Aizpuru, who had been state president on Wyse and Reclus's first visit to the Isthmus, led a revolt of his supporters among the racially mixed lower classes in Colón, while Benjamin Ruiz, another radical, tried unsuccessfully to seize power in Panama City.

None of this political turmoil seems to have registered with the delegates at the Paris conference who met in the afternoon of May 15 in the sumptuous surroundings of the headquarters of the Société de Géographie on Rue Saint Germain, in Paris's Latin Quarter. It was the best time of year to be in Paris: the sun was shining and the young chestnut trees that lined the street were in new leaf. Crowds had gathered to see the multinational delegates, clad in top hats and morning coats, alight from their carriages and make their entrance into the beautiful, lofty auditorium. Here, there was seating for nearly four hundred: de Lesseps, his officers, and the titular head of the Congress, a grand French admiral, de La Roncière-Le Noury, were on the small stage. The front rows were reserved for delegates, while all other seats were taken by spectators.

The opening session was purely ceremonial: the admiral made some remarks, then de Lesseps stood to great applause, welcoming the delegates "with all his heart." Particular fuss was made of Rear Admiral Daniel Ammen, the head of the American delegation, who was made a vice president, and seated on the right of de Lesseps.

The real work of the Congress would be performed by five committees, investigating different aspects of the challenge ahead, from potential tolls to issues of navigation. As work got under way, an early conclusion of the financial or operational aspect of the undertaking was the overwhelming desirability of the canal being at sea level, a feeling shared by the majority of the delegates. A sea-level canal could be open twenty-four hours a day, without any restriction on the number of ships passing. Only one ship can pass through a lock at one time, with serious implications on operational revenue.

The most important of the five groups was the Technical Committee, which would decide the location, cost, and the type of canal that should be built. The day after the opening ceremony, Ammen

was asked to start the debate for this committee, but as the trunk
containing the American maps and charts had been delayed, Selfridge was the first to take the floor, extolling the virtues of a sea-
level route in Darién that he himself had visited. Immediately, the
American delegation began to squabble among themselves. To Ammen, Selfridge was off message: there was no good route in Darién,
as the Grant Commission had decided. So why did Selfridge push
for this? It is a recurring theme of the canal story that time and
again those in the grip of the "great idea" were also passionately
committed to a certain type and location for the canal. For de
Lesseps it had to be a sea-level canal, whatever the cost. For Menocal, Lull, and Ammen, it had to be in Nicaragua using the lake, which
presupposed a lock canal. Selfridge had been the leader of the
American surveying effort in Darién; if it was built there it would be,
in a way, his canal, and he was just as blind to the huge disadvantages
of the area as de Lesseps would prove to the monumental folly of
attempting a sea-level canal in Panama.

The next day Ammen and Menocal laid out their arguments for a
lock canal in Nicaragua. This was followed by Wyse, outlining his various plans for a sea-level canal from Panama City to Colón. By now,
all other options, from Mexico through San Blas to Darién, had been
pretty much discounted; the battle was between Panama and
Nicaragua, which corresponded, to a large extent, to a battle between
the French and the American points of view. On May 20 Menocal described the American plan for a Panama Canal involving the huge
aqueduct over the Chagres and some twenty-four locks, but made it
clear he thought this too expensive and impractical. He then went
through his arguments against Wyse's scheme for Panama: a sea-level
canal was impossible, he said, because of the volatile Chagres River,
which would have to drop over forty feet into the canal, causing a
dangerous cataract. Another objection was then raised by Ribourt,
actually a Frenchman. He reckoned that the tunnel envisaged by
Wyse and Reclus, if possible at all, would alone cost over 900 million
francs and take nine years to build. Even if it was shorter than what

he was attempting through the Alps at St. Gotthard, the diameter of the ship tunnel was many times what was required for a railway tunnel.

Following this, two subcommittees of the Technical group were formed: one to deal with the tunnel versus open cut question at Panama; the other to investigate the cost and engineering issues behind the Nicaragua lock plan. Very quickly the former, staffed by some of the most eminent engineers of the Congress, ruled out the construction of a sea-level tunnel and also concluded that a canal *à niveau* "involved so much uncertainty . . . that it would be impossible for any engineer to arrive at an approximate estimate of its probable cost." The much-respected British Severn tunnel engineer, Sir John Hawkshaw, also added his opinion that a sea-level canal at Panama would have to "provide for the whole drainage of the district it traversed [which] . . . would require the canal to be 160 meters wide."

According to Menocal, the report and the comments of Hawkshaw were "met by the friends of Lieutenant Wyse with the affirmation that M. de Lesseps would positively refuse to accept the presidency of any other canal company except that of Panama—a statement which had the desired effect of bringing back to their party some who had deserted to the sides of the best engineers, who seemed to be in favor of the Nicaragua Canal."

For the de Lesseps party, things were clearly beginning to get out of hand. So on Friday, May 23, *Le Grand Français* "threw off the mantle of indifference," as one delegate wrote, and convened a general session. Striding confidently in front of a large map, he addressed the Congress. He spoke spontaneously, without notes, in simple, direct language, and with great conviction, if not abundant knowledge, making everything sound right and reasonable. The map, which he referred to with easy familiarity, clearly showed that the one best route was through Panama, as it had been, he argued, for centuries. It was the route that had already been selected to develop the cross-Isthmus railroad. There was no question that a sea-level canal was the correct type of canal to build and no question at all that Panama was

the best and only place to build it. Any problems would resolve themselves, as they had at Suez. His audience was enthralled.

Wyse and Reclus, however, had been stung by the criticisms of
their Panama project, and, to their credit, refused to participate in the
wishing away of the problems of the Chagres River and the massive
excavation required by an open-cut, sea-level waterway. Later the
same day, they presented a new plan that had been devised by Baron
Godin de Lépinay, a senior French civil engineer and a delegate at the
Congress. Although de Lépinay had never been to Panama, he had
worked in South America on a railway project, where most of his
workforce had been killed by yellow fever. De Lépinay's idea was to
create an "artificial Lake Nicaragua" in Panama by damming the Chagres as near to the Atlantic as possible as well as the Río Grande near
the Pacific. In between would be created a vast artificial lake some 80
feet above sea level, accessed by a small number of locks. In a stroke
the amount of excavation would be limited to a short and relatively
shallow cut through the Continental Divide, and the Chagres River
would be tamed. Amazingly, the de Lépinay design contained all of
the basic elements that ultimately, after years of mistakes and heart-
break, were designed into the current Panama Canal.

De Lépinay himself, although favoring Panama over Nicaragua,
predicted that an attempt at a sea-level canal would be a catastrophe.
For a start, he argued, the cost would be in billions of francs, a level
of debt that could never be serviced by a private company. Secondly,
working in a tropical climate such as Panama's was totally different
from anything experienced by the vast majority of the delegates: iron
rusted in no time, labor was scarce and unreliable, coal and provisions
were expensive. And then there was disease. De Lépinay shared the
current, though mistaken, belief that tropical fevers were caused by a
poisonous emanation— "mal air" (hence "malaria")—from rotted
vegetation in the ground. The huge excavations, he warned, would release this to devastating effect. To persuade European or American
technicians to work there would require tripling their normal salaries,
and the death toll, which he estimated at fifty thousand, would re-

quire constant replenishment of the workforce. In perhaps the most telling attack on de Lesseps and the confidence that underwrote the whole Congress, he turned the comparison with Suez on its head: "They want this canal to be made after the model of the Suez Canal, that is to say, without locks—and yet its natural conditions are so very different. In Suez there is no water, the soil is soft, the country is almost on the level of the sea; in spite of the heat, the climate is perfectly healthy. In tropical America there is too much water, the rocks are exceedingly hard, the soil is very hilly, and the climate is deadly. The country is literally poisoned. Now to act thus after the same fashion under such different circumstances is to try to do violence to nature instead of aiding it, which is the principal purpose of the art of engineering."

Wyse later admitted that this plan was put forward in large part to spike the guns of the official American Panama plan as earlier outlined unenthusiastically by Menocal, as it required far fewer locks. If there were to be a lock plan for Panama, at least it would be a French one. But by the time he came to write his account of the conference in late 1885, the plan had far higher visibility and he claimed that he had investigated its potential on all his visits to the Isthmus in the early 1880s, and was convinced of its merits.

Many of the delegates at the time were impressed by de Lépinay's vision, although this included neither de Lesseps, for whom locks were totally unacceptable, nor the American contingent. With some justification, Ammen complained that the plan seemed to have been conjured out of thin air—it hadn't even been mentioned ten days earlier—and Menocal pointed out that none of the necessary surveys, particularly in the placing of the all-important dams, had been carried out. He also argued that the new lake would be large enough neither to provide water for the locks in the dry season, nor to deal with the Chagres when the rains arrived. Although estimated by the Technical Committee as being cheaper than both the Menocal Nicaragua plan and the Panama sea-level scheme, de Lépinay's idea disappeared from the reckoning.

Meanwhile, de Lesseps worked feverishly behind the scenes, twisting arms and calling in favors to secure the votes he needed for his dream of an "Ocean Bosporus" at Panama, as the arguments between the two routes, and the two types of canal continued in the Technical Committee, becoming more heated and personal by the hour. "A great deal of interest and feeling [was] manifested," Ammen wrote, "amounting, at times, to disorder." On May 27 Selfridge spoke for the last time, again infuriating Ammen and Menocal by attacking the Nicaragua option. It would be impossibly expensive to improve Greytown harbor, he argued, and, what was more, Nicaragua was prone to earthquakes and volcanic activity, the first mention of what would later be a crucial factor in deciding the American Panama Canal. On Wednesday, May 28, the committee finally made its recommendation after a stormy session during which twenty of the delegates, nearly half the committee, staged a walkout. The next day, as heavy rain fell, the full Congress met to hear the committee's report and to vote on its recommendation. The hall was packed as it was announced that a decision had been made: "the committee, standing on a technical point of view, is of the opinion that the canal, such as would satisfy the requirements of commerce, is possible across the Isthmus of Panama, and recommend especially a canal at the level of the sea." The cost of the work, including interest on the capital, was estimated at 1.2 billion francs, or about $240 million, with completion in twelve years.

Soon after, it was put to the vote. It was highly public and highly charged. In alphabetical order each delegate stood up and voted on what was essentially the de Lesseps plan. Henri Bionne, the secretary of the Congress, read out the names. Daniel Ammen abstained, saying that only professional engineers should be entitled to vote. By the time it was de Lépinay's turn, 76 of the delegates had voted, 43 for, with most of the others abstaining. De Lépinay, the French canal's own Cassandra, rose to his feet, declaring, "In order not to burden my conscience with unnecessary deaths and useless expenditure I say 'no!' " He sat down to widespread boos and jeering. Next up was de

Lesseps himself. "I vote 'Yes!,' " he declared in a loud voice. "And I have accepted command of the enterprise!" The room erupted in cheering and applause.

In the end, the resolution passed with 74 in favor and 8 opposed. Afterward, de Lesseps told the conference, "It has been suggested by my friends that after Suez I ought to take a rest. But I ask you: when a general has just won one battle and is invited to win another, why should he refuse?"

His adoring public in the onlookers' seats were ecstatic. At the end of the Congress, the chairman, the elderly Admiral de La Roncière, underlined that it was *Le Grand Français* himself who had carried the day: "May that illustrious man, who has been the heart and soul of our deliberations," he declared, "who has captivated us by charm, and who is the personification of these great enterprises, may he live long enough to see the end of this work, which will bear his name forever. He has not been able to refuse to assume its command, and in so doing he continues to carry out the mission which has made him a citizen of the whole world."

With the benefit of hindsight there were warning signs everywhere. Thirty-eight delegates had conveniently absented themselves from the vote and 16 had abstained. The predominantly French pro votes did not include any of the 5 delegates from the French Society of Engineers. Of the 74 voting in favor, only 19 were engineers, and of those, only one, a Colombian who had a vested interest in the Wyse concession, had ever been in Central America.

❮❮❮❮❮ ❯❯❯❯❯

To the Americans the whole affair had been an appalling travesty. At the heart of their displeasure was outrage that anyone else, particularly the French, should dare to presume to build a canal in their backyard, in what was effectively a United States protectorate. On his return to the United States, Menocal wrote an article for the *North American Review* entitled "Intrigues at the Paris Canal Conference." It was introduced by a short piece by the journal's editor, which gives some indication of the vitriol of the Americans. As far as the editor was concerned, it was all a conspiracy among hard up prominent Bonapartists, who had lost their means of subsistence with the fall of Napoléon III. "A careful examination of the names of the French delegates to the Canal Congress shows how entirely it was packed with subservient friends of the fallen dynasty; nor is it well to overlook the fact that the shares of the Türr company were largely held by them." "These people once went to Mexico to seek their fortunes in a Franco-Mexican empire," he went on. "It seems passing strange that the conspicuous defeat of those plans, which embraced the destruction of the American Union, should have failed to teach them some degree of caution before affecting to . . . tamper with American interests in America."

This suspicion predated the conference. In February 1879 Wyse had traveled to Washington to ensure American attendance at the Congress. He had met President Hayes and Secretary of State William Evarts. The latter was openly hostile to any further French "adventures" in Central America—it can't have helped that Wyse had "Napoleon" in his name—and might well have been instrumental in blocking Wyse and Reclus's access prior to the Congress to the detailed American maps and surveys.

When Menocal and Ammen reported back to Evarts at the end of the conference, they confirmed his misgivings, saying the decision for Panama had been determined not by "relative consideration of natural advantages," but from "personal interests arising from the concession." If Nicaragua had been chosen, then the Wyse concession would have been worthless. It had been a foregone conclusion, a shoo-in, what another American delegate, William E. Johnston, called "a comedy of the most deplorable kind."

Menocal, for his part, was sure that the whole Panama project was doomed to early failure. But this was just as much a worry as the scheme's completion. Johnston, among others, feared that if de Lesseps could get the stock into the hands of a mass of ordinary

Frenchmen, as he had done with Suez, the canal's inevitable failure would lead to the intervention of the French government. In terms of the sacred Monroe Doctrine, this was worse even than a French-controlled private company meddling in American affairs.

Ammen and Menocal's reports were widely covered in the U.S. press, the *New York Tribune* being particularly concerned by the "shenanigans" in Paris. In government too, there was disquiet about the outcome of the conference, a New England senator moving a resolution to the effect that the United States "viewed with serious disquietude any attempt by the powers of Europe to establish under their protection and domination a ship-canal across the Isthmus." The *New York World*, which would be another implacable opponent of the French canal, went further, declaring that the project "prefigures for us an era of complications and difficulties in regard to the foreign policy and the commercial relations of this country more serious than any we have had to deal with in the last twenty years of our history."

In Panama itself, where civil and political disturbances continued through June, the news from Paris was warmly welcomed, though not without a certain amused detachment. On May 29, the *Star and Herald* reported: "The Wyse Panama route is the one likely to be adopted. Indeed, many said before the Congress met that the acceptance of this route was a foregone conclusion." The following day, reporting the final vote of the Congress as soldiers enforced martial law in the streets outside their offices, the same paper added, "It may amuse some of our readers in Nicaragua to know that a recent publication cites another objection to their route, and that is the 'political instability' of the country. We presume the author was satirizing Colombia at the time." Nonetheless, to those in Panama it seemed that at last prosperity was around the corner.

-⋘⋙-

*J*n France, de Lesseps swung into action. Raising 2 million francs from selling "founders shares" to a syndicate of 270 rich and influential friends, he started negotiations to buy out the Türr syndicate, including their concession and all their maps and surveys. The deal, for 10 million francs, was concluded on July 5, 1879, and for the Türr syndicate it was almost all profit. Next, de Lesseps embarked on a whirlwind tour of France. As with Suez, he aimed to raise the starting capital, set at 400 million francs, directly from the public.

However, times had changed in France, and the power of the financial institutions and the press had risen considerably since the 1860s. This time, the banks showed their displeasure at being cut out of the lucrative issue by organizing a campaign against the canal venture. Costs had been underestimated, the venture would never pay, suggested Marc Lévy-Crémieux, vice president of the powerful Franco-Egyptian Bank. Emile de Girardin, proprietor of the mass-circulation *Petit Journal*, was another opponent. Panama's climate was a death trap, it was argued; plus, the Americans would never allow work even to start. It was rumored, too, that the vibrant de Lesseps was now in his dotage and had lost his winning ways. "The financial organs were hostile," de Lesseps later told American reporters, "because they had not been paid."

Consequently, the issue, on August 6 and 7, was a severe disappointment. Only 30 million francs of the desired 400 million was raised. Almost anyone other than de Lesseps would have given up right then.

CHAPTER EIGHT

THE RICHES OF FRANCE

Public subscriptions live or die on confidence. It did not take a promoter of the experience and skill of de Lesseps to realize that some urgent public relations were now needed to allay fears about the Panama project. To calm concerns about the technical and practical issues of the canal, de Lesseps announced that he would himself go to Panama together with a Technical Commission of international experts. He would even take his young wife and three of his children with him, showing that fears about disease were unfounded. To counter claims that the United States opposed the project, de Lesseps would tour that country reassuring officials and drumming up support.

The first move, however, was to set up a bimonthly journal, the *Bulletin du Canal Interocéanique*, which aimed to counter the "lies" of the press with stories alleging, among other things, that Panama was "an exceedingly healthy country." The magazine, which included

The French Sea-level Plan

—┼— Original railway Colón–Panama.   —↦ River barrages
--- Planned river diversions

(Compare with the modern canal route shown on pp. xvi–xvii)

extracts from favorable press coverage in France and abroad, was first published on September 1, 1879.

The following month a young engineer, Gaston Blanchet, from Couvreux, Hersent, went to Panama to investigate the route for his bosses. Already the Franco-Belgian company was being lined up to be the contractor for Panama. Blanchet himself had made his name building for the firm a metal bridge over the Danube near Vienna. When he returned from Panama with a favorable report, additional engineers were sent out in November to take test borings. In December, de Lesseps himself boarded the *Lafayette* at Saint-Nazaire bound for the Isthmus. The expedition was funded by Couvreux, Hersent, and on board was Abel Couvreux's son as well as Blanchet, who was particularly keen to return to Panama as he had met and fallen in love with a local girl, Maria Georgette Loew, the daughter of the proprietor of the Grand Hotel. Also on the trip was Jacob Dirks, a Dutch engineer who had built the Amsterdam Canal; Henri Bionne, who had been secretary of the Paris Congress; and a number of other technicians.

Lieutenant Wyse had been promised by de Lesseps that he would head up the operation in Panama. But no such appointment had actually materialized, and he had not been invited along. In the end he paid for his own passage, and engaged during the voyage in several heated rows with de Lesseps. The latter was not one to share leadership responsibilities or glory; Wyse was effectively dropped.

The arrival of de Lesseps in Panama was one of the biggest news stories the local press had ever covered. "Mr. Lesseps' enterprise," the *Star and Herald* proclaimed, "will ... take rank with Columbus' discovery of America."

The *Lafayette* entered the harbor of Colón a little after 3:00 p.m. on December 30. The party could not have arrived at a more clement, or misleading, moment: the dismal rainy season had just ended, the skies were cloudless, and the northwest trades blew in pleasantly from the Caribbean. Coming alongside the wharf, the boat was met, the *Star and Herald* reported, by "the committee of reception appointed by the government, the delegation from the State Assembly, and a large number of invited citizens." At a little after 4:00 p.m. the landing stage was put on board, and all repaired to the spacious saloon of the *Lafayette* for formal addresses of welcome. One of the reception committee was an American diplomat, businessman and journalist Tracy Robinson. He remembered de Lesseps, in perfect Spanish, responding "very pleasantly" to the welcome, "wearing the diplomatic smile for which he was noted. He was then over seventy years of age, but was still active and vigorous: a small man, French in detail, with winning manners, and what is called a magnetic presence. When he spoke the hearer would not fail to be convinced that whatever he said was true." All the time, the "enthusiasm from every class knew no bounds," the *Star and Herald* wrote. "The flags of all nations were displayed, with the notable exception of that of the United States, and the reception can be said to have been a decided success."

The next morning, together with his entourage of "distinguished engineers," de Lesseps "made an examination of the harbour," all the time holding forth about his enthusiasm for the project. Tracy Robinson remembered him invariably concluding every phrase with the assertion, "The Canal will be made." " 'There are only two great difficulties to be overcome,' " the *Star and Herald* reported de Lesseps as saying, " 'the Chagres River, and the deep cutting at the summit. The first can be surmounted by turning the headwaters of the river into another channel, and the second will disappear before the wells which will be sunk and charged with explosives of sufficient force to remove vast quantities at every discharge.' "

At ten o'clock that same morning, a party arrived from the United States. This included Trenor Park, the diminutive boss of the Panama Railroad. On his visit to the United States prior to the Paris Congress, Wyse had met Park to discuss the "amicable agreement" stipulated by the Wyse concession from Colombia. Park, a successful Wall Street speculator, knew he had Wyse over a barrel—if an arrangement was not forthcoming, the Wyse concession was worthless. Wyse had offered to buy the railroad, and Park, who personally owned fifteen hundred shares, was happy to sell—at $200 a share, twice the market value. Several other Railroad board members were on the trip, along with a journalist from the *New York World*, José Rodrigues, and two American engineers who had agreed to be part of the Technical Commission: an army engineer named W. W. Wright, and Colonel George Totten, who had been in charge of the construction of the railroad back in the 1850s.

An hour and a half later, the entire party left Colón for Panama on the railroad. Halfway across, the train was met by the president-elect of the state, and "a fine lunch was provided on the train, with wines &c., &c., and everything gave great satisfaction." Yet another reception committee of local dignitaries and generals was waiting at Panama station in a specially erected tent. Also in attendance, it seemed according to Rodrigues, was "every one of the [city's] 14,000 inhabitants . . . shouting, struggling to get a glimpse of the distinguished guest." Following more speeches, the party was conveyed in carriages to the Grand Hotel. Houses along the route were decked in French and Colombian flags, and no expense had been spared in cleaning up the city in honor of the "Great Engineer." According to an occasional correspondent for the *New York Tribune*, "Such an air of neatness and real cleanliness has not pervaded this city of pigs and smells within the memory of its oldest inhabitants."

That night the hotel hosted a state banquet. The only woman present was Madame Louise-Hélène de Lesseps. She had been only twenty-one when she had married de Lesseps, then sixty-four, in 1869. She was as beautiful as the first Madame de Lesseps had been witty and brilliant. According to Tracy Robinson, she "gave éclat to the occasion . . . Her form was voluptuous, and her raven hair, without luster, contrasted well with the rich pallor of her Eastern features." After the dinner, dancing and singing, spilling out into the plaza, went on for most of the night.

The next morning, the first of the New Year, de Lesseps was up early, in full regalia, for the inauguration of the new president, Damaso Cervara. After that, making good on his promise to dig the first spade of earth for the Panama Canal, de Lesseps organized a special ceremony at which his seven-year-old daughter, Ferdinande, would do the honors of turning the first sod. The symbolic act was to take place at the mouth of the Río Grande, scheduled to become the Pacific entrance to the future canal.

The steam tender *Taboguilla* took de Lesseps and a party of distinguished guests—which included the British consul Hugh Mallet and his twenty-year-old son, Claude—three miles to the site on the Río Grande where the ceremony would take place, following appropriate feasting and festivities on board. However, since late arrivals had delayed the *Taboguilla*, the Pacific tide had receded such that the vessel could not land at the designated site. Undaunted, de Lesseps was ready with a solution. He had brought a special shovel and pickax with him from France especially for the occasion. Now, declaring that the act was only symbolic anyway, he arranged for his daughter to strike the ceremonial pickax blow in an earth-filled champagne box. Each member of the Technical Commission then in turn took a swing at the box, and the whole work was blessed by the bishop of Panama. The passengers landed back at Panama City at 8:00 p.m., according to a local newspaper, "unanimous in their expressions of gratification with their delightful trip."

The following day, it was down to business. The Technical Commission was run by Dirks and Totten, while the detailed work was parceled out among the more junior members. All the surveyors reported in to Dirks and Totten every three days. De Lesseps took a hands-off role, except for impressing on the men one vital factor. As the *Tribune*'s correspondent reported, "His mind is unalterably made up on one point—he will have nothing to do with a canal with locks."

As the surveys continued, de Lesseps threw himself into the coincident celebrations of the new president, the New Year, and the new canal venture. On January 3 there was horse racing: "Mr. Lesseps is an accomplished horseman, and joined in the pleasures of the day with all the zest and activity of youth," reported the *Star and Herald*.

On other days there were excursions with his children, two boys aged nine and ten, who, with their sister, seven, had also caught the eye of the locals. Robinson called them "as dark as Arabs and as wild." On January 10, there was another ceremonial commencement of the canal work when a huge dynamite charge was exploded near the summit of the Continental Divide. Champagne flowed once more.

A great highlight of the trip was the wedding of Gaston Blanchet and Miss Maria Georgette Loew, the beautiful daughter of the owner of the Grand Hotel. For observers, it was the perfect embodiment of the new friendship and shared future between Panama and France. Held in the cathedral, "bright with myriad lights, and gay with the presence of a multitude of ladies and gentlemen of the best of our Panama society," it was blessed with a performance at the piano by the French vice-consul and singing by Madame de Lesseps herself, "with great sweetness and expression." The party afterward, inevitably held at the Grand Hotel, continued well beyond midnight.

There were balls and dinners most nights. All were resplendent with toasts and speeches. "You have seen the soldiers of Count de Lesseps," one of the French party announced to a reception given by Colombian officials. "We have the faith to move mountains, or at least, in the present age, rend them asunder." No one could believe the energy and enthusiasm of Ferdinand de Lesseps, now in his seventy-fifth year. He would dance "all night like a boy," noted Tracy Robinson, and still be on the train at seven on some expedition "fresh as a daisy."

In this atmosphere, optimism about the work of the Technical Commission abounded. De Lesseps proclaimed that the job at Panama would be easier than Suez, writing to his thirty-nine-year-old son Charles, in charge of affairs at home, that he couldn't believe that it hadn't been done already. The local press, too, reported that the new geological survey had shown the estimates of the Paris Congress to be pessimistic: "The engineering difficulties . . . are being solved one by one," wrote one paper, "and when the present surveys are concluded the project will assume so positive and practical a shape that financial men in Paris and elsewhere will not hesitate to give it the attention and support it deserves."

"Elsewhere" to all intents and purposes meant the United States, which remained the ghost at the banquet. Everyone knew that the United States was de Lesseps's next destination, and the *Star and Herald* anticipated a great welcome there for the builder of the Suez Canal. The publication of the Commission's report on Panama and de Lesseps's charm would, the paper concluded, gain "the moral, if not the material support of the people and Government of the United States."

The same issue of the newspaper reported the provisional findings of the Technical Commission, which, it emphasized, were based on maximum costs. Further details were to be worked out during the trip to New York. With only a few minor modifications and improvements, the open-cut plan and route of Wyse and Reclus were approved. There would be a 40-meter-high dam at Gamboa to retain the Chagres, along with a channel running alongside the canal for the regulated flow of the river to the sea. Another smaller channel would keep river water from the canal on the opposite side. At Colón, a 2-kilometer breakwater would be constructed to protect the port, while at the other end of the canal a tidal lock would be required.

A study of the stability of rocks had led to the adoption of slope for the canal of 1:1, or 45 degrees, except on the summit division at Culebra, where a slope of a quarter to one was considered sufficient because of the hard rock. In the Culebra Cut, the canal would be 24 meters wide at the bottom, 28 meters at the waterline, with a water depth of 9 meters. Elsewhere, the canal would have a waterline width of 50 meters, but otherwise similar dimensions.

The cost of diverting the Chagres was increased substantially from the Congress estimate, as was the amount of spoil to be removed, now judged to be some 75 million cubic meters. Nonetheless, the overall increase in cost was slight, helped by the reduction of the contingency fund from 25 to 10 percent. Not including the expense

of purchasing the railroad, interest on the capital, administrative out-
lay, and the sums due to the Türr syndicate and the Colombian
government, the cost was now estimated at 843 million francs
(US$168,600,000). The comparable figure from the Congress had
been 765,375,000 francs (US$153,075,000). The time of construction
was reduced from twelve years to eight. In Paris, the *Bulletin du Canal
Interocéanique* crowed that in all, the work would be easier and quicker
than had been previously believed.

This overall sum seemed eminently affordable. The Congress had
estimated tonnage through the canal at six million a year. At 15 francs
per ton, this would bring in 90 million francs annually, producing 10
percent a year on a capital of 900 million francs. If 15 francs a ton
seemed high compared to Suez's 8 francs, the current cost of moving
freight on the railway, including loading and unloading, was nearly 80
francs per ton.

However, there is no doubt that, overall, this was an optimistic estimate. With hindsight, the slopes deemed sufficient were wildly
wrong; the plan for the Chagres would prove a minefield; furthermore, the reduction of the contingency fund to hold down the cost
seems to be taking "putting a favorable gloss" to the point of dishonesty. In contrast, U.S. estimates under the Grant surveys had always
included a contingency fund of 100 percent, a sensible move considering that the Suez Canal, for example, had gone over its original
budget by some 128 percent.

The de Lesseps party left Panama on February 15. They depart,
wrote the *Star and Herald*, "vastly to the regret of the people of the
Isthmus of all nationalities . . . during their stay on the Isthmus they
have taken possession of the public heart to an extent never before
witnessed among us. The importance of Mr. de Lesseps' mission, a
preparatory step to one of the greatest undertakings the world has
ever witnessed, did not prevent that courteous and affable gentleman
from taking a vivid interest in our rather dull isthmus life, into which
he and his amiable lady have infused new vigor and animation." He
headed for New York, "with heartiest best wishes."

There were dissenting voices. Wyse, cast out from the project, wrote from Panama to Reclus on January 24: "Blanchet does nothing . . . the tachometers are broken. There is total disorder, waste, and disorganisation." De Lesseps, Wyse alleged, was making a nuisance of himself by trying to grope *"les tétons des femmes."* Tracy Robinson, who was so impressed with de Lesseps, and believed that "from first to last he was perfectly conscientious and honest," pronounced him "too old, too eager, too vain of the glory it would add to his already great reputation."

◀◀◀◀—▶▶▶▶

*D*e Lesseps's expedition to Panama and his imminent arrival in the United States had created a great deal of comment in the newspapers of that country. In general, they were cynical about the realistic prospects for the sea-level canal, concerned about the repercussions for the favored Nicaragua option, and hostile to the perceived international weakness of the United States that the European-led project revealed. It was the United States, said the *New York World*, who had "proper predominance over the seas to be united by any Isthmian or Central American ship-canal." What was needed was massive and accelerated naval expansion, along with naval stations near the future canal. The *New York Times* thought that the sea-level canal was practicable and desirable, but that its cost would make it uneconomic. Nevertheless, it praised the energy and determination of de Lesseps compared to his rivals in the States: "While they protest and discuss and reflect and hesitate, he goes ahead." The *New York Tribune* agreed: "All this looks like business." The paper interviewed the Panama Railroad boss, Trenor Park, on his return from Panama in late January. Park, who must have been rubbing his hands together at the killing he knew he could make by selling the railroad to the French, announced that he had gone to the Isthmus with "grave doubts of the success of the project," but returned reassured by de Lesseps: "He is certainly a great man, and his enthusiasm is contagious."

As the day of de Lesseps's arrival neared, the *New York Tribune* urged decisive action: "Now is the time for the Government to make up its mind what to do . . . If it merely continues to make no sign, foreign capital will get committed, and then foreign Governments will be drawn in to protect the capital of their citizens, and the Monroe Doctrine will have disappeared like a morning fog . . . We are unwilling that the successors of Napoleon III, should attempt another foothold on the soil of the continent, even in the seductive guise of a peaceful triumph of engineering skill." The answer, according to the *Tribune*, was to get the Nicaragua project up and running as soon as possible, and thereby see off the interlopers' Panama scheme.

⤙⤙⤙⤙ ⟫⟫⟫⟫

*D*e Lesseps arrived in New York on February 24. On the journey from Colón he had completed the report of the Technical Commission, cutting the estimate to 658,600,000 francs ($131,720,000). Half this amount, he announced, was reserved for American subscribers.

De Lesseps never expected to raise this money in the United States. Before his trip he wrote to an American friend, who was busy setting up meetings, that he expected the Americans, and, to a lesser extent, the British, to fall for "inaccurate objections." The capital for the project, de Lesseps believed, would come from France, "where one is used to working for the civilization of the world."

He had never visited the United States before, and, as in Panama, de Lesseps enjoyed himself enormously. He set up court in the Windsor Hotel, which flew a tricolor from its mast in his honor. There, he was waited on by a committee from the American Society of Civil Engineers, who took him to see Hell's Gate and the East River Bridge. Later he visited the uncompleted Brooklyn Bridge, the Erie Railroad Station, and the docks and grain elevator in Jersey City. In the evening, there were receptions given by the Geographical Society, the French expatriate community, and on March 2 there was a great dinner in his honor at Delmonico's, which had been decorated with elaborate confectionary symbolizing the achievement of the Suez Canal—sphinxes, dredges, elephants, and bales of goods. One of the welcoming speakers was John Bigelow, the publisher and diplomat. Everywhere De Lesseps was honored as the builder of Suez, and the press were fascinated by his energy and charm.

But as de Lesseps had predicted, there was little interest in investing in the Panama project, and even at dinners with handpicked guests there were dark mutterings about the Monroe Doctrine, and predictions that a foreign government might take over the canal. In fact, while de Lesseps had been in Panama, the French government had sent a clear message to Secretary of State Evarts, formally notifying him that "the enterprise of M. Lesseps is of an entirely private nature and has no political color or protection at all," as the Panama *Star and Herald* reported of the news. "This dumfounds the speculators, adventurers, contractors and others," said the paper, "who have spread . . . rumors of war within six months, and of a tremendous European alliance against the United States."

At Delmonico's, de Lesseps tried to answer the fears of his audiences: "He spoke rapidly in a distinct but quiet tone," reported a journalist onlooker. "Occasionally when criticizing or indirectly ridiculing theories opposed to his own, he dropped into a sort of chuckle." It had to be at Panama, rather than Nicaragua, because it had to be a sea-level canal; his project had nothing to do with any government, so the Monroe Doctrine did not apply, de Lesseps argued. The outfit would be based in Paris only because it was there that company laws gave the best protection to shareholders. "I have offered America 300,000 of the shares. If she takes that much she will have a controlling voice in the enterprise," he told a *Tribune* reporter the following day. "But even though no shares are sold here, I shall still build my canal . . ."

From New York, de Lesseps traveled to Washington. There he met President Rutherford Hayes and Secretary Evarts and appeared before the House Interoceanic Canal Committee. He was received politely enough, but it was plain that his scheme infuriated everyone from the president down. On March 8, Hayes declared in a special message to Congress: "The policy of this country is a canal under American control. The United States cannot consent to the surrender of this control to any European power or to any combination of European powers." So what if the Clayton-Bulwer Treaty committed the United States to share control with Great Britain? This should "by just and liberal negotiations" be altered. "The capital invested by corporations or citizens of other countries in such an enterprise must, in a great degree, look for protection to one or more of the great powers of the world," Hayes continued. "No European power can intervene for such protection without adopting measures on this continent which the United States would deem wholly inadmissible. If the protection of the United States is relied upon, the United States must exercise such control as will enable this country to protect its national interests." The canal, he proclaimed, will be "virtually a part of the coast line of the United States."

"When M. de Lesseps gets ready to leave Washington tomorrow," said the *New York Tribune* the following day, "he will have no reason to complain that he has been left in the dark as to the attitude of the Government of the United States toward the interoceanic canal project."

But, as ever, de Lesseps was undaunted. Ignoring the threat of takeover implicit in Hayes's statement, he welcomed the interest shown by the American leadership in his project. Of course, as he had said time and again, no European governments would be invited to become involved in the canal. But if the United States, clearly the major power in the region, wanted to offer protection to the capital he was planning to raise, then that was to be celebrated. The next day he expressed "his delight with the President's message," "because it would certainly be advantageous to have the protection of the United States during the work, and after the opening of the canal." He had just sent a message to his son, which would be printed in the *Bulletin*, saying that the "President's message assured the political stability of the canal." It was just what his home audience wanted to hear.

From Washington, de Lesseps traveled to Boston, Chicago, and nearly twenty other U.S. cities. However, everywhere he went, although there were flattering attentions, there was still a marked paucity of financial backing.

Back in Europe, de Lesseps threw himself into a new round of speeches and lectures in France, Britain, Holland, and Belgium. Everywhere there were reassurances that the United States was on board. "In these provincial tours," reported one infuriated American critic, "he everywhere gave the impression that the governments of France and the United States were equally favourable to the enterprise; the flags of the two nations were everywhere united over his head when he spoke."

De Lesseps was in Liverpool on May 29, specially invited to be present at a banquet in honor of the Queen's birthday. The 150 guests included foreign consuls and numerous naval officers in full uniform, as well as all the principal merchants of the city. At the town hall, "loyal toasts [were] enthusiastically drunk [and] a glee choir was in attendance." American opposition to the scheme, de Lesseps announced, was "a phantom and a bugbear." As he had for the United States, de Lesseps offered to keep back some shares especially for British investors.

In Britain, however, he found a cautious response. There was certainly support for the idea of a canal. In a leading article written in response to Hayes's statement to Congress, *The Times* drew a picture of the "few miles of oozy quagmire and jungle" separating the Atlantic and Pacific at Panama as "a heavier tax on the industry of mankind than a war or a famine." The paper also strongly criticized the U.S. president's statement: "an inter-oceanic canal," it wrote, "would form as much or as little a part of the European coastline as of that of the US ... All that Europe wants is that a block of earth which it is growing to regard as it might a sunken ship in the Medway ... should be cleared away, whether in the manner proposed by M. de Lesseps or in some other manner." Interestingly, the president's claim of local hegemony was both resented and acknowledged. "That the US, by furnishing the money, should obtain a special right to watch over the safety and peaceable use of the new channel is what Europe, and particularly Great Britain, would most of all desire."

For British investors, if de Lesseps's claims that the United States was now on side were widely believed, he was less successful in persuading them that the climate of Panama was "salubrious." "It is a region," wrote the *London Standard*, "endemic with tropical diseases and notoriously more pestilential than any part of the desert of Suez." Also "In Panama [de Lesseps] has no gangs of Fellaheen forced to work for scant wages, no enthusiastic Khedive willing to command the resources of the state for the benefit of the undertaking."

In France, though, it was a different story. It was incorrectly rumored that Couvreux, Hersent had signed a contract to build the canal for even less than de Lesseps's most optimistic estimate. No one rushed to deny this. In August, a new subscription was announced, to be held at the beginning of December. On offer would be 600,000 shares of 500 francs each, a total of 300 million francs, which was all the French legislature would authorize. The shares were expensive when 500 francs was nearly a year's wages for about half the working population of France. But the terms were attractive—25 percent down with six years to pay off the difference. During the time of construction, shareholders were to receive 5 percent on their paid installments. Once the canal was completed, they were to get 80 percent of the net profits. A huge publicity campaign was launched: much was made of the fact that 500-franc shares in Suez were now worth more than 2,000 francs and paying a dividend of 17 percent; there were special picnics; de Lesseps was everywhere, staging conferences and banquets, urging the purchase of shares as a patriotic duty; there were advertisements trailed from hot-air balloons; handbills of various eye-catching colors were pasted on every highway; purchases from shops were sent home with advertisements attached; a silver medal was offered to every individual to whom five shares of stock were assigned.

Even more important, de Lesseps had now decided to play on the terms of those who had wrecked his first share offer in August the previous year. This time, the banks would handle the subscription. A syndicate of commerical and investment houses was formed by Marc Lévy-Crémieux, a vicious opponent of the first issue. For the price of a 4 percent commission, or 20 francs a share, the opposition of the financial community melted away. The press, too, was brought on board. One of the chief opponents the first time round, Emile de Girardin of *Le Petit Journal*, was offered and accepted a place on the Company's board of administrators. Elsewhere simple payments were made to editors and journalists, to a total, it emerged much later, of some one and a half million francs. Papers previously scathing about the project were now falling over themselves to find rhetoric sufficient to describe its attractions. "Capital and science have never had such an opportunity to make a happy marriage," the *Journal de Débats* announced. "Success . . . is certain," said *Le Gaulois*. "One can see it, one can feel it." *La Liberté* proclaimed: "The Panama canal has no more opponents . . . Oh, ye of little faith! Hear the words of Monsieur de Lesseps, and believe!"

The opening of the sale of the stock on December 7 marks one of the most extraordinary moments in the history of finance capitalism. Within three days more than 100,000 people had subscribed for 1,206,609 shares, more than twice the number available. Eighty thousand were small investors, buying one to five shares each. Sixteen thousand were women ordering shares in their own names. Mothers sent de Lesseps their children's savings wrapped in handkerchiefs. Whether or not they had actually met de Lesseps and been a victim of his overwhelming charisma, the fever of the Great Idea had clearly taken grip of the entire country as no great financial enterprise had ever done before. Together with the influence of the press, de Lesseps's trips to Panama and the United States, or more exactly, his version of them, had won over all doubters. The riches of the ordinary French family were now committed to the great project.

A French commentator later wrote: "At that time they realized the poetry of capitalism . . . This is private enterprise, this is the shareholders' democracy which is gradually changing the face of the world and setting humanity free." As it would turn out, as the share issue stoked the fires of speculation on the bourse and kept the whirlwind of dealing spinning along nicely, a massive time bomb had been laid under the financial structure of the Third Republic.

◄◄◄◄◄ ─►►►►►

𝒯wo weeks later, Armand Reclus was offered the job of *Agent Supérieur* of the canal company to head up the operation in Panama. He left for the Isthmus on January 6, 1881, together with his deputy, a Franco-Colombian lawyer named Louis Verbrugghe, who had accompanied Wyse on his trip to Bogotá to secure the concession. In Paris, a sumptuous headquarters was purchased for a million francs. The first shareholders' meeting was held on January 31 with more than five thousand people in attendance, and on March 3 the new company, the Compagnie Universelle du Canal Interocéanique, was officially incorporated. De Lesseps was president, Henri Bionne was secretary general. Charles de Lesseps, who had urged his father not to take on such a mammoth task but who had promised his support when he saw the old man was unmovable, was appointed a director. On the same day the second general meeting of the Company was held. Wasting no time, de Lesseps outlined the program for the year ahead: to clear the line of the canal of vegetation; to study the hydrography of Colón and Panama bays, their tides, currents, and winds; to build houses for the accommodation of the employees and hospitals for the sick; and to build work yards. All preliminary work was to be completed by October, when Culebra would be attacked, and in November and December dredges would start work on the soft soil on the lower parts of the line. De Lesseps announced that the canal would be open to traffic by 1888, predicting that the job would be far easier than what he had achieved at Suez. His comments were greeted with cheers and applause.

News of the incorporation of the Compagnie Universelle

reached Panama about a week later. "The company now has a legal existence and a name," wrote the *Star and Herald*. "It is no longer in the realm of inchoate projects like its rival institution the Nicaragua Canal project, but is a solid and substantial entity, commanding un-equaled resources and unrivaled influence. The news is welcome, and we hasten to offer it to the public."

In the United States, however, the success of the subscription fanned rising fears about an open ship lane through the Isthmus. "The worry is that it will weaken the United States strategically," wrote the *New York Tribune*. The only option, the paper continued, would be "to exercise such control over it as will prevent the passage of the fleets of any Nation with which we may be at war." What this would mean would be an abandonment of the long-held policy to avoid "such vast and costly naval armaments as are kept afloat by En-gland, France, Germany and Spain . . . Otherwise we would find our Western coasts, from San Diego up to Sitka, exposed to attack within a few weeks after the breaking out of hostilities with any country that can keep a formidable squadron in the West Indies . . . Suppose the canal was open and a sudden quarrel were to arise between the United States and Spain," the paper wondered prophetically. "What is to prevent Spain from sending a dozen ironclads through the Isthmus to bombard our California towns?"

Such was the success of de Lesseps's money raising that the specter of the canal had changed from being distant and uncertain to an almost done deed, and the dire strategic repercussions of an open waterway under the control of a hostile power were also debated in the House of Representatives, where it was suggested that the United States "insist on acquiring from Colombia the territory through which it runs, in order to be able to fortify its mouths and control its operations in time of war." But, as the *New York Tribune* reported in mid-February, such was the new wealth of the Compagnie Uni-verselle that it was surely only a matter of time before they controlled the bankrupt Colombian government. To its fury and frustration, the United States seemed powerless.

CHAPTER NINE

"TRAVAIL COMMENCÉ"

On February 1, 1881, de Lesseps read to an enthusiastic French press a telegram from Reclus on the Isthmus, which the journal *La France* described as "eloquence in a few words": *"Travail Commencé."* It was thrilling news.

Reclus and Verbrugghe had arrived in Panama at the end of January, together with thirty-five engineers, five of whom brought their wives with them. As always, there was a warm welcome from the people of Panama. Also of the party was Gaston Blanchet, the representative of Couvreux, Hersent, who were to be contracted to do the actual work, although under the overall control of Reclus. The giant engineering firm had an excellent reputation based on their business on three continents. But none of their directors had ever worked in Central America. Alarmingly, Abel Couvreux had made a speech in Ghent at the end of 1880 saying that the so-called deadly climate of Panama "was nothing but an invention of the canal's adversaries." In March 1881 a contract was signed between Couvreux and the

Company that allowed for two years of preparation, assembly of machinery, and preliminary studies, which would determine the costs for the actual excavation. The directors of Couvreux were old friends of de Lesseps from Suez days, and the preliminary contract was loosely drawn and generous.

Following the arrival of the first party from France, almost every boat from Europe brought its share of engineers, office workers, or adventurers hoping to profit from the vast new project. At the beginning of 1881, Henri Cermoise was twenty-two years old and recently qualified as an engineer. French technical schools, run by and for the state, were the finest in the world, with rigorous entrance examinations, strict rules, and a rigid, theoretical approach. After his grueling training as a civil engineer, Cermoise was keen to see something of the world outside "lecture theatres and blackboards." Having had his application to work in Panama accepted, he sailed from Saint-Nazaire on the hardworking *Lafayette* on March 6, 1881, on the third shipment of personnel to the Isthmus. To gain employment with the company had been difficult, he writes, and he was aware that the journey was long and hard, that he ran the risk of meeting yellow fever "nose to nose," and that the tropical sun could kill you "like a cannon ball." *"Mais, bah!"* he writes, he was going all the same.

Those words—*"Mais, bah!"*—typify the bravery and foolhardiness of the French years. Whatever de Lesseps, Abel Couvreux, or the *Bulletin* said, it was common knowledge that Panama was an extremely dangerous posting. But like a young man volunteering for service in a war, there existed for Cermoise and many of his contemporaries a belief, first, that the worst would always happen to someone else; that their country and the general progress of humanity demanded that they take the risk; and that at the end of the day, amazingly, they were prepared to die for the Great Idea of the canal.

Cermoise's account of his journey to Panama is full of excitement and exuberance. After a storm in the Atlantic, on the sixteenth day of the journey they entered calm seas. It became hot and sunny, and the air was now "charged with the perfumes of tropical earth." There were more stops, at Martinique and on the South American mainland, before at last the *Lafayette* neared Colón. All that morning the passengers remained on deck, excitedly scanning the horizon with their binoculars. Soon a long blue blurred line appeared in the distance. Then, little by little, the wooded summits of the Isthmus came into view. Everyone fell silent. "A great thoughtfulness took hold of us all," writes Cermoise, "even those least given to contemplation. Silently, we thought of these lands where we were going to engage in the great scientific battle, and where, like in all battles, there would be the wounded and the dead."

The party went ashore, and at the railway station were met by Gaston Blanchet. "He was tall," writes Cermoise, "with an energetic look about him." He seemed straightforward and kind. Blanchet had a list of his new arrivals, but when he went through it he found that most of the men were not what he had been expecting. Either through bureaucratic mix-ups, or because those applying to work in Panama had lied about their qualifications, Cermoise and a friend he had made on the voyage called Montcenaux turned out to be the only two qualified engineers in the entire group. Blanchet was furious.

Nonetheless, squeezed in amidst sacks of rice and other provisions, the group traveled on the train to Panama City. Cermoise describes the low-lying marshy land behind Colón, continuing through Gatún, Bohío Soldado, and Buena-Vista, native villages along the line made up of huts "built of bamboos thatched with palms or oleanders." After Gorgona there was a gradual rise up to Matachín, where the short, limp vegetation gave way to a taller and more solid mass of green. The railroad was single track, and at Matachín they had to wait on a siding for the train coming in the opposite direction to pass. They had time to disembark, and were offered an array of provisions including water that was "twenty-five degrees [centigrade] in the shade," and hard-boiled lizard and iguana eggs. Even more daunting was their first look at the jungle close up. The forest here reached right to the edge of the line. It seemed utterly impenetrable, a "horrifying tangle of trees, a wall of creepers." At last on the move again, they climbed further, to the top of the Continental Divide. At Emperador they saw a gang drilling for rock samples, the first signs of canal work in progress. Then they descended, the railtrack taking alarmingly tight curves down the slope to the Río Grande Valley and Panama City. That evening Cermoise was introduced to Armand Reclus. To Cermoise he was already a legend, having been involved in the canal project from the earliest surveying days. The *Agent Supérieur* welcomed him warmly.

Reclus's first priority in these early months was to secure sufficient roofs to protect workers and machinery from the rains, due at the beginning of May. Time was of the essence. Within a week of the arrival of the first French engineers, Colón had been transformed into a busy port. A new wharf was speedily constructed, and ships started docking every day carrying prefabricated wooden buildings from New Orleans and countless railway sleepers and rails. At the same time, all sorts of machinery started arriving from the United States and Europe: drills, locomotives, wagons of all types, dredges, barges, steam shovels, and cranes. All were transported in bits and had to be reassembled.

Louis Verbrugghe was now in charge of recruitment, a job in which he had local experience running his family's plantations in Colombia. The initial workers were from nearby—from Darién, Cartagena, or from the Jamaican community left over from the construction of the railroad. They were set to work expanding Colón's port facilities and assembling buildings—machine shops, a sawmill, wooden cottages for the white technicians and larger barracks for the workers. The Grand Hotel in Panama City was purchased by the Company and refurbished as its headquarters. Along the line of the railway the scattering of native villages were to be transformed. At Emperador a huge clearing was made for a work camp. Outside Gatún on the Chagres a new settlement, grandly called Lesseps City, was to be established.

After a week or so to acclimatize, Henri Cermoise reported to Blanchet to start work. Blanchet outlined the progress so far. The initial party of engineers, he said, had found much of the proposed canal line covered by impenetrable virgin forest. While the general route was known—which valleys the canal would follow—details such as where the axis of the canal passed from one valley to another were still to be determined. In addition there was much drilling to be done to discover the type of rock or soil that would have to be removed. Therefore all of the engineers were to be employed either in surveying and taking soundings along the axis of the canal, or in the central office collating the reports as they came in from the field. Blanchet offered Cermoise the choice of work: "I hadn't come to Panama to be stuck in a study again," he wrote. "The idea of the virgin forest, with tigers, crocodiles swirled round in my head; the life of a pioneer, penetrating into the unexplored depths of this isthmus was an irresistible temptation." The next day, still with his friend from the boat over, Montcenaux, he set off for Gamboa.

This is where the Chagres River, what Cermoise called the "implacable enemy of our great enterprise," met the line of the canal at right angles. From Gamboa through to Barbacoas, the river followed the same route as the planned waterway. While other work parties set about clearing a 50-meter-wide strip along the line of the canal and began to take detailed measurements, it fell to Cermoise and Montcenaux to survey the site of the huge dam planned to regulate the flow of the river at Gamboa. Leaving the train at Matachín, the two men were punted upriver in a hollowed-out canoe. Twenty minutes later they arrived at Gamboa and took possession of the two huts, one for "chiefs" and one for the thirty or so workers, which constituted the camp already established. There they met a Belgian, Blasert, a veteran of the North American West, who was acting as quartermaster and administrator of the work camp. Cermoise found him an impressive figure. "He laughed at the climate, the snakes and at Yellow Fever ... he considered himself invulnerable." Blasert had even brought his wife and ten-year-old daughter with him to the camp. The latter "passed her days à *vagabonder* barefoot and bare-headed" around the camp.

It was immediately apparent to Cermoise that this work would have "nothing in common with what one does in Europe . . . When we saw the thick forest which covered the mountains we were thoroughly daunted." The first task was to begin clearing pathways through the jungle toward those summits that seemed the highest. The plan was for the crucial dam to be constructed between two hills, each about 250 meters high, and some 500 meters apart. In Europe, comments Cermoise, both could have been surveyed in a morning. But here in the tropical jungle it was another matter altogether. The jungle was so thickly matted that one could see only a few yards in any direction, hopeless for taking measurements. The heat and humidity, like "a steam bath," sapped the strength, making legs and arms as heavy as stone. The narrow pathways gradually cleared in the jungle were "suffocating [as] the high branches met each other overhead, forming a vault which kept out the light and the air."

Most of the workers were local mulattoes, who were instinctively hostile toward Europeans, and to taking commands, often replying, Cermoise notes, with the declaration, "I am a free man." They had to be handled with great tact, and at one point the Europeans, fearing a mutiny, took to carrying arms and guarding their hut by night. On the whole, however, Cermoise is generous in his praise for his workers. "In spite of the faults, the Colombians . . . did us great service with the clearing." They knew the forest, and were experts with their machetes. "Bamboos, creepers, even trees fell before them like hail." Sometimes, however, the party would meet a colossal tree that, because of the hardness of its wood, would take a whole day to cut down by ax. Progress was slow.

Few animals, apart from the odd parrot, were encountered in the jungle. However, there were plenty of snakes. More than a hundred had been killed during the clearing of the space for the camp alone. The locals seemed to be adept at dispatching them with a single machete blow, but the clearing still required constant alertness as huge specimens could fall on the men from branches above their heads. Most feared were the coral snake and the *mapana*, otherwise known as a bushmaster. The coral snake is quite small, some twenty-four inches long, and brightly colored with black, yellow, and red bands. It was most usually encountered in the early morning or at dusk. Its bite contains a neurotoxic venom that attacks the nervous system and is frequently fatal. The bushmaster is much larger, up to ten feet long, with enormous fangs that cling to the victim the better to inject its venom, which is hemotoxic, killing by destroying red blood cells, causing internal bleeding and rapid tissue and organ degeneration.

These snakes soon became attracted to the camp, or more exactly to the vermin that attacked the party's stores and feasted on their waste. Great care had to be taken by the quartermaster, Blasert, when fetching provisions from their storehouse. The Blasert family shared the single officers' hut with Cermoise, Montcenaux, and a Colombian translator, Jeronimo. All slept in hammocks suspended in the corners. Madame Blasert was heavily pregnant, and the Frenchmen urged her to return to Panama City, but she and her husband insisted there was plenty of time. Soon after Cermoise's arrival, however, she went into labor. With the assistance of an "ancient black crone," she successfully gave birth in the tiny hut to a second daughter. All the while the two young French engineers tried to sleep in their hammocks, "smoking cigarettes when the din became too loud."

The team of Europeans became very close, and Cermoise enjoyed the challenges of the work, despite the privations. Everyone got stomach illnesses from drinking the river water, and fevers came and went regularly. For the Europeans, this could prostrate them for days, although, Cermoise notes, the locals, while just as susceptible, seemed to be able to recover after only a few hours. Vampire bats and tarantulas, which took to climbing down the ropes of their hammocks, tormented them at night. The jungle also teemed with ticks and *niguas*, small insects that would burrow under the skin to lay their eggs, threatening to cause gangrene. Evenings would be spent digging them out of each other.

At night, the jungle came to life. "Above all, there was an invasion of insects," Cermoise wrote. "With each step, one's foot crushed hundreds of them; with each movement of the hand, one picked up a fistful, and with each nod, one's face brushed swirls of them flying in the darkness. One breathed them in, as one went along! Moreover, the flame of a lamp was extinguished within minutes under the heaps of their small corpses . . . a monstrous buzzing filled the forest and rose all the way to the sky, while in this clear tropical night the huge trees . . . flamed with millions of fireflies."

⤙⤙⤙⤙⤙ ⤜⤜⤜⤜⤜

At the end of April, just before the rains were due, Reclus carried out a tour of inspection. At Colón, he was pleased to see a great deal of activity. Jamaican workers were busy creating new port space by filling in the marshes to the southwest of town. Nevertheless, such was the volume of material being unloaded daily that there was considerable confusion. Just outside Colón at Monkey Hill could be seen the first actual excavation in progress, where rocks and earth were being dug out to provide the filler for the marshes below. This had generated great excitement, and was the destination for American visitors curious to see the French actually at work on their great project. At Gatún, Lesseps City was well established, with wharves for unloading from the river, and adequate shelters for the workers. Reclus inspected other work camps at Emperador and Culebra, and at La Boca, the Pacific terminus of the canal, new wharves had been constructed and a railway line laid to nearby Panama City.

But, as he explained in his report to the Company in Paris, there were great difficulties as well, many of which, indeed, would also be encountered in the early years of the American project. The first criticism that Reclus made was leveled at the choice of men. The executives and technicians chosen and sent from Europe by Couvreux were, he said, both insufficient in number and, above all, mediocre in quality. On April 30, Reclus wrote from the Grand Hotel to Charles de Lesseps in Paris that the contractors seemed to be sending over men who "would be accepted nowhere—people who have dabbled all over and have never done anything well—nutters, drunks, incompetents etc. They send us traveling salesmen for mechanics, for blacksmiths men who've never been behind a forge." Cermoise's group, it seems, had been pretty typical. In the terminal cities and the camps, Reclus wrote in the same report, he had seen far too much liquor, both purchased and homemade, as well as endemic gambling with dice and cards. All combined to produce frequent violent disputes.

Addressing the question of the railroad, Reclus reported that his "personal relations with [the manager] M. Woods continue to be most cordial but that doesn't prevent frequent unpleasant incidents from happening." It was essential, Reclus wrote, that the Company purchase the railroad as soon as possible. He even suggested that the railroad bosses were being deliberately obstructive in order to hold the Company for ransom and secure the best price for their business.

In fact, negotiations had been going on for some months. Trenor Park, the boss and majority shareholder in the Panama Railroad, was now holding out for $250 a share in cash. The value of the railroad had been falling steadily since the opening of the transcontinental U.S. railroad in 1869, and the real share price was nearer $50. It was a "hold-up," and there was nothing the French company could do about it. In the end, to cover all expenses and the railway's own sinking fund, de Lesseps parted with just short of $20 million, nearly half his start-up capital. It was a severe early blow to the finances of the new Company. One-fifth of the balance was to be paid every year with 6 percent interest due on the rest. The Panama Railroad retained possession and management of the property until the whole amount was paid, and a majority of the seats on the board of directors, who still sat in New York. In spite of the buyout, then, the railroad would remain American for now.

Park, who retired from the board but put his son-in-law in charge instead, cleared $7 million on the deal. However, interestingly, he retained a strong interest in the project, and according to his daughter never doubted that the de Lesseps venture would succeed. He visited the Isthmus several times before his untimely death in December the following year, on board a steamer from New York to Colón.

As well as tourists and grateful railroad shareholders, the United States government also maintained a keen interest in the canal, and kept up serious efforts to take further control of the Isthmus. In turn, the various European diplomats in Washington, Paris, Panama, and Bogotá kept an eye on what the Americans—and one another—were up to in the region. The previous year, President Hayes, to give body to his aim of "a canal under American control," had sent U.S. naval vessels to investigate sites for coaling and naval stations on either side of the Isthmus, near the future canal termini. The move angered the British, who saw it as incompatible with the Clayton-Bulwer Treaty, and was blocked by Bogotá after a furious popular anti-American reaction in Colombia. Nevertheless, the controversy carried into the next year, with Congress, in March 1881, voting $200,000 specifically for the establishment of permanent military bases near the canal.

In the meantime, the U.S. envoy to Colombia, Ernst Dichman, did everything in his power to persuade the Bogotá government that their country was "menaced by a grave danger." "Turning away from the United States which had been her firm friend, ally, and protector," he said, "Colombia recklessly and ungratefully concludes with an adventurous Frenchman, a contract for the opening of a Canal." Dichman pressed for an updating of the 1846 Bidlack Treaty that would allow the United States to establish a permanent garrison in Panama, while Secretary of State Evarts demanded that the United States be given the right to veto any Canal concessions, future, present, or past.

Seeing "all alliances with the United States as an exemplification of the fable of the wolf and the lamb," Colombia started sounding out European capitals over a multilateral guarantee of the waterway and considered denouncing the 1846 treaty. For the aggressive and anti-British new U.S. secretary of state James Blaine (later to be nicknamed "Jingo Jim" by the press), this was totally unacceptable. In June 1881 he wrote to the British foreign minister, Earl Granville, citing the Monroe Doctrine and condemning the plans, which he said came close to "an alliance against the United States."

Blaine's domestic audience was delighted, and in Congress there was a growing determination to act unilaterally on the canal question. The Clayton-Bulwer agreement that forbade such a move was debated in the House and referred to as "a singular and ill-omened treaty," which should be abrogated.

None of this went unremarked upon in London when it came to reply to Blaine's June letter. For a long time, there was a haughty silence. Blaine was an upstart troublemaker, it was felt—he had already waded into disputes with Britain over other matters. In the meantime, Granville confidentially sounded out the European capitals about this possible international guarantee that had so annoyed Blaine.

One by one, the replies came in from Britain's European ambassadors. Every power was in favor, in principle, but no one wanted to make the first move. France was keen to provide support for beleaguered Colombia, but could not be at the forefront as it was a French company at work on the Isthmus. In September, Britain's Madrid representative reported that Spain "would be glad to see England and France take joint measures to check the pretensions of the United States' Government with regard to the interoceanic canal, but that Spain hesitated to place herself *'en premiere ligne'* in opposition to the United States, in view of the consequences which might ensue in the island of Cuba, where a fresh insurrection could easily be fomented by American influence." In Germany, Bismarck, who still held German ambitions in check, declared himself neutral in the matter, and said that it was a question for the Clayton-Bulwer Treaty between the United States and Britain.

In November a reply eventually made its way to Washington from the British Foreign Office, taking issue with details of Blaine's pronouncements and slapping down the pretension of the Monroe Doctrine. By now, Blaine, encouraged by favorable press support at home, had written to the British again on the subject, this time asking that the clause in the Clayton-Bulwer Treaty that forbade the fortification of the Canal be revoked. Because the United States had no navy to speak of, he argued, the only way that their vital strategic interests could be protected was through the establishment of permanent military power on the Isthmus itself. Otherwise, the primacy of the Royal Navy would make British control of the waterway a done deed. Privately, Blaine made a contingency plan to build a railway through Central America to Panama to "enable the United States to keep military possession of the canal in the event of a war with Great Britain."

But for now, Britain was not prepared to be bullied by a power with huge potential, granted, but no real international strength. Granville replied that it would be "manifestly unjust" for the Americans to request abrogation. Soon after, as the new president, Chester Arthur, took control, Blaine was out of office and out of favor. This coincided with a popular feeling that unilaterally breaking a treaty with Britain would have been unwise. "Did Blaine want war?" asked the newspapers, mirroring the sudden popular recoil from pushing the mighty European powers too far. "Mr. Blaine had overshot the mark and misjudged public sentiment," decided the *New York Herald*, only days after backing his aggressive approach.

If the Americans remained stalemated by the Clayton-Bulwer Treaty, they were still responsible under the original 1846 Bidlack Treaty to keep the transit passage on the railroad open, and more often than not, there would be United States Navy gunboats standing off Panama City and Colón. By now, Colón was unrecognizable from six months earlier. There had been an explosion of wooden huts and shanties out into the swamp around Manzanillo as the town's population doubled. In the harbor there was a constant coming and going of steamers, and on the reclaimed land to the south of the island was a grid of warehouses, offices, and residences, many in a grand style.

Inland, Blanchet and his men pressed on. By the middle of 1881, there were some two hundred technicians and about eight hundred laborers, and the number was increasing. The engineers were from not only France but also Germany, Britain, Switzerland, Russia, Poland, and Italy. Many of the mechanics were American, who came along with equipment purchased in the United States. The workers were not only Colombians, but also Cubans, Venezuelans, and West Indians.

In Gamboa, Cermoise's camp was transformed by the influx of a considerable number of new personnel and a batch of prefabricated buildings from the United States. "Everyone had his own room!" he exclaims. Now in charge was a distinguished French engineer called Carré, who brought with him an expert Belgian cook and much improved provisions. There were even regular deliveries of ice. Because of the importance of dealing with the problem of the Chagres, the Gamboa camp was now a key site on the Isthmus.

By the middle of September, Cermoise's surveying work was completed. While Carré remained behind to start mapping the giant area to be flooded by the dam, Cermoise was given a new job in Panama City. His friend Montcenaux was sent to Gatún, the most notoriously sickly area of the Isthmus. After nearly seven months in the bush, Cermoise writes, "We said goodbye with a certain sadness to this corner of the world where we had more than once shivered with fever, but also where we had passed many good days, busy with cheerful work in the company of devoted friends." His new task was to work on the detailed maps and charts being prepared from the reports now flooding in from all along the line. As well as measuring levels, the engineers were sinking five great wells to test the ground along the summit of the Continental Divide. The greatest was some 150 feet, three times deeper than any well drilled during de Lesseps's visit early in the year, but still less than half the planned depth of excavation. The findings encouraged the canal planners—there seemed to be a lot less hard granitelike rock than had been factored into their costs. Before, drills had hit solid rock in several places, sometimes at 20 feet or less, and stopped. Now, with improved drill bits, the rock was passed through and in some cases found to be only 2 feet thick, an "angular boulder of dolerite." Below, there was "brown clay and pulverized rocks, seamed with diverse colors."

In fact, the ground was nothing like anything the majority of the geologists had ever seen before, bearing no resemblance whatever to the terrain in Europe mined and dug by many of those present. The unique geological history of the Isthmus, with the land bridge sinking below sea level and then rising again in a series of cycles and a long record of ancient volcanic activity, had created bewilderingly complex strata, including layers, at various angles, of breccia, limestone, coral, carb, sand, gravel, volcanic lava, and clay. In the forty-odd miles from Colón to Panama City there are six major faults, five substantial volcanic cores, and seventeen fundamentally different types of rock. Every well told a different story. But the engineers focused on the positive: at least it was not all solid rock. In fact, the surveys had said it all: dig here, and you do not know what you are going to find. As it turned out, it would have been easier had it been solid rock.

Blanchet himself turned his attention to the rivers, establishing observation posts on the Chagres, Trinidad, Obispo, and the Río Grande; these were equipped with fluviographs, which confirmed the challenge that the rainy season would bring to the successful construction and running of the canal, with rivers rising 20 feet in as many hours and their rate of discharge increasing overnight from 3,000 to over 60,000 cubic feet per second.

By October 1881, much of what de Lesseps had outlined back in March had been achieved. That month the *Bulletin* published details of the "second campaign" for the next twelve months, which included settling the question of the dam for the Chagres, the digging of a waterway between Colón and Gatún, and the removal of five million cubic meters of spoil from Culebra, the point of maximum elevation. In addition, all the necessary machinery was to have been ordered.

But not all was going according to plan. Engineers had been experimenting with different excavating machinery and had found that the plant that had built the Suez Canal was proving too light for the heavy clay of the Chagres valley. Even more worrying was the question of labor. Only one in ten newly arrived laborers had remained on the job for more than six months. There were two thousand men at work at the end of the year, but de Lesseps had promised there would be ten thousand. Worst and most ominous of all, though, it was becoming obvious that the Isthmus was nothing like the healthy place that de Lesseps and Abel Couvreux had promised.

◄◄◄◄ ►►►►

As early as March 1881, only two months after the arrival of the first French engineers on the Isthmus, the *Panama Star and Herald* reported that "Mr. de Lesseps contemplates making up what is short in the labor supply on the Isthmus and the neighbouring coast states of Colombia, with laborers from the West Indies. Barbados and Jamaica are spoken of as the principal source of supply."

The British islands had not prospered in the years after the construction of the railroad. Since the then all-time-low sugar price of 1850, the value of the colonies' principal export had fallen a further 30 percent. After emancipation in 1834, many former slaves, keen to establish their independence and a different life from that of plantation labor, had opted to set up small plots, producing food for themselves and for market. But most of the freeholds were under five acres—large enough for one family perhaps, but not enough to afford a livelihood for their sons and daughters, much less their grandchildren.

Furthermore, blacks remained condemned by the West Indian social structure to a permanent lower-class status, denied real recognition of their freedom, autonomy, or even humaneness. In response to this, a tradition of emigration grew up throughout the islands. Only by going abroad could a Jamaican or Barbadian find levels of reward for labor sufficient for their needs as well as lower levels of abuse.

Nevertheless, it is wrong to see the emigrants solely as passive objects, or victims of these conditions. In spite of everything, black West Indians had developed a strong sense of independence and personal dignity. The trend toward emigration also points to the ambition of the ex-slaves' descendants to "better themselves"—to see the world outside their small island, and to earn enough to improve their conditions at home, to be masters of their own destiny. The Caribbean basin offered many good opportunities for work, not only on the Panama Railroad in the 1850s, but on other railway projects as well, in goldfields and metal and rubber industries, in logging or in plantations being set up throughout the area. The islands also exported teachers, missionaries, and ministers as well as colonists to previously unsettled areas.

In many ways the emigration to Panama during the French period is part of this pattern. There were particular "push" factors, such as the severe drought in Jamaica in 1879, but the project, in the eyes of the emigrants, also offered great opportunities. They made the journey to Panama not just to escape poverty at home, but just as much to "see the world," "learn a foreign language," or "seek adventure." The chance of work on the canal was seen as a means of truly freeing themselves through their own efforts.

Nevertheless, the 1880s represent a quantum leap in West Indian emigration. Although records are incomplete, there seem to have been some five hundred British West Indians working on the canal by October 1881, 40 percent of the total workforce. The following year and for the rest of the project this percentage rose to 60 percent, as the overall workforce ballooned to over twenty thousand by 1884.

Early in 1881, the Company took on the services of Charles Gadpaille, a Jamaica-based Frenchman, to handle recruitment in the islands. Straightaway, he started posting advertisements in the local press. One such read:

A trip to Colón?
Wanted immediately!
10 000 labourers
for the
Panama Canal Company.
No indenture. Passengers returning when they like.
Both passage and food given.
$1.50 to $3.00 a day.*
Medical care given when sick.
Apply to Charles Gadpaille
Hincks Street,
Agent, Panama Canal Company.

Daily wage rates in Jamaica for a field laborer in the 1880s were between sixpence and two shillings, less for women and children, so this was a great offer. If it seemed too good to be true, that is because it was. Gadpaille had no right to make many of these promises, as shall be seen. As well as newspaper advertisements, the agent posted flyers and sent runners into rural areas to drum up recruits.

Gadpaille concentrated his efforts in Jamaica, Barbados, Saint Lucia, and Martinique. Although the Company might have favored the French-speaking Martinicans, in fact they were less than impressed with workers from the Gallic Caribbean islands, considering them "pretentious, and always complaining, for they had been ruined by the political customs in vogue in the old French colonies." So the vast majority of the workers on the French canal came from Jamaica, with Saint Lucians the next largest group. The first arrivals, in 1881 and 1882, tended to be skilled laborers and artisans who were not involved in cultivation on small freeholdings, but had drifted into the towns and cities as they were displaced from estate labor. After this

---

*Wages here, as throughout the French period, are in Colombian silver dollars, equivalent to about US$0.65–0.70.

first period, the typical migrant was male, an agricultural worker, twenty-five to thirty-five years old.

Henri Cermoise was highly impressed with the new arrivals from Jamaica. "They were excellent workers," he wrote, "much more active and energetic than the Isthmians and easier to manage." Back at home, some of the planters were less than pleased at seeing their pliant labor force leave the country, but for now the governments of the islands saw the money that would be sent home outweighing the disadvantages to the planters. The governor of Jamaica's annual report of 1882 commended the returning emigrants, "bringing with them money with which they arrange their affairs and aid their families."

But for every laborer returning with his pockets rattling with coins, there was another who came back in a different state, or didn't make it back at all. Some Jamaican workers, Governor Musgrave reported in 1882, "are left when ill to die in the streets of Colón." His main complaint was that his government was "put to large expenses for the relief, burial, or return to the colony of any natives whose case comes before the British consular authorities. And, moreover, many of those who return are so broken down by Chagres Fever, and other disorders, that they become a burden upon the community, and the poor rates." It was clear that, already, disease was taking a toll on all sections of the workforce.

CHAPTER TEN

FEVER

The beginning of the project's first wet season had seen the initial serious outbreaks of disease. The first high-profile death among the thousand-odd employees occurred in the second week of June 1881, soon after the beginning of the rains. A distinguished and experienced engineer named Etienne died on July 25, supposedly of *"ataxie cérébrale"*—"a fit of the brain." On the Isthmus at the time, on a two-week tour of inspection, was thirty-nine-year-old Henri Bionne, the Company's secretary. On July 9 he had dined in Henri Cermoise's mess hut at Gamboa for which the excellent Belgian cook had pulled out all the stops. "He drank to our success on the Isthmus," remembered Cermoise. "We drank to his good luck." Bionne boarded a boat home for France on the evening of Sunday, July 24, and at the captain's table that night he reported himself feeling poorly and without appetite. The following afternoon he was visited in his cabin by Georges Hopkins, the ship's doctor, who found him in the throes of a violent shaking fit, which was followed by a high fever.

According to the doctor's report, reprinted in the *Bulletin*, Bionne was given quinine, and, the next day, a mustard bath. After this he felt better, and even had a little to eat. The doctor was much encouraged that his patient seemed to show no signs of the symptoms of yellow fever. But on the Thursday morning, he was "evidently in a state of delirium." He was given more quinine and mustard treatment, but "his state worsened quickly; after a fit, he fell into a coma during which he died . . . the last symptoms indicate kidney failure." His body was hastily disposed of, shunted overboard in the Gulf of Mexico.

The doctor's diagnosis was that Bionne had died of a breakdown of his nervous system. For the benefit of readers of the *Bulletin*, he was keen to stress that it had not been yellow fever. This illness held a particular fascination and horror for Europeans and North Americans. Emerging in the Caribbean in the 1640s, supposedly from the Mayans on the mainland, or, as recent theories suggest, from mosquito stowaways on the slave ships from Africa, the disease spread to Barbados and Cuba, where it killed one-third of the island's inhabitants. Outsiders in the region seemed particularly vulnerable. In 1665, it claimed the lives of all but 89 of an English squadron of 1,500 stationed in Saint Lucia. Spaniards on imperial duty carried it back to their home cities, where it wreaked havoc. For the next two hundred years, the disease also came and went along the southern and eastern coasts of the United States over a hundred times, on one occasion killing more than 5,000 in the Mississippi Valley. In 1793, the city of Philadelphia was decimated by yellow fever, or "yellow jack" as it became known. Famously, Napoléon's Polish legion of 25,000 men, sent to recapture Haiti from Toussaint L'Ouverture and to reestablish control of France's North American empire of Louisiana and New Orleans, was wiped out by yellow fever and retreated, vanquished, home.

Yellow fever is an almost uniquely distressing, disgusting, and terrifying disease. There is still no cure, apart from treating the results of the disease, such as kidney failure, and in the 1880s a strong adult would have only about an even chance of surviving an attack. At that time it was treated with whiskey, mustard seed, brandy, and cigars. If you do survive, you are then subsequently immune. Thus the disease, to flourish into an epidemic, needs an influx of nonimmune subjects. Caused by an arbovirus, a small virus transmitted by the bites of certain mosquitoes, the early symptoms include headaches, loss of appetite, and muscle pain. A high temperature follows, accompanied by severe back pain, which many described as like being on the rack. After that comes a burning, agonizing thirst, the telltale jaundice as the face and eyes yellow, and the dreaded *"vomito negro"*—vomiting up choking mouthfuls of dark blood, as the virus causes liver and kidney failure and multiorgan dysfunction and hemorrhage. The brain is often affected as well, producing delirium, seizures, and coma. The medical shock, caused by extreme fluid loss, can in itself be fatal.

Part of the terror of the disease was in its mystery, how it arrived from nowhere, created havoc, and then just as inexplicably disappeared. As well as there being no effective treatment, there was little idea of how the disease was transmitted. Some doctors suggested that it was due to a certain wind off the sea; others were sure it was some sort of fungus. One insisted that it came from eating apples. Most agreed, though, that it was airborne, and as it was so often found around ports, that it had to have something to do with mud, filth, or dead animals. Worst of all for causing infection, it was believed, was the patient himself, or anything that he had touched. Victims were shunned, given a hasty burial, and their clothes destroyed.

Fevers came under many names on the Isthmus. As well as yellow fever there is mention of *calentura*, miasma, the shakes, blackwater fever, the chills, *paludisme*, ague, pernicious fever, putrid fever, and, particularly nasty, "Chagres" or "Panama Fever." Yellow fever was the most feared by whites, but these versions of malaria were actually the biggest killers.

Caused by a parasite that is transmitted to humans through the bites of an infected *Anopheles* mosquito, malaria remains a huge scourge at the beginning of the twenty-first century, killing around a million people a year in Africa alone. The parasites migrate to the liver and then infect red blood cells, where they multiply, rupturing the cells, then spread further. The weakening and disruption of the body's blood results in many symptoms that are similar to those of yellow fever: uncontrolled shivering, chattering teeth, high fever, sweating and a burning thirst, headaches, nausea and vomiting, muscle pain, and anemia. This can lead to jaundice, convulsions, coma, rupture of the spleen, and subsequent massive hemorrhage. If you live, you will be severely weakened mentally, as well as physically. Unlike yellow fever, malaria attacks confer no instant immunity and can recur to those who survive, often killing on the third or fourth attack. The only effective treatment at the time was the administration of quinine, a palliative made from the bark of the cinchona tree, a trick learned from the Incas of Peru. Quinine stops the disease's progress by interfering with the growth and reproduction of the parasites in red blood cells. But when malaria patients stop taking quinine they relapse. This was more common than might be thought: quinine not only tasted disgustingly bitter, it also had side effects including nausea, painful earache, deafness, and, most dangerous of all, hypoglycemia.

For centuries, people had believed that malaria was caused by "miasma"—toxic emanations from the rich corruption of tropical soil. That is why de Lépinay had argued during the Paris Congress that to dig up so much earth in Panama would be particularly dangerous. In the early 1880s, recent studies near Rome had led to the theory that it was a bacterium in the soil, made airborne when released, that caused the malaria symptoms. Although isolated individuals had suggested that neither yellow fever nor malaria were airborne but were transmitted by mosquitoes, and numerous experiments with this idea were being carried out in Cuba as early as 1881, the development and acceptance of the theory were some years away. Until that time, the "miasma" theory held sway, and the Isthmus was consequently a death trap.

Two days after Bionne had boarded his steamer to France, Blasert, Cermoise's "indestructible" Belgian friend from the Gamboa camp, put his wife and children on the boat back to France. The very next day he took sick, with yellow fever according to Cermoise, and died soon after. He, too, had been at the Bionne dinner.

As others of his companions starting sickening and dying, including the much-praised Belgian cook, even Cermoise's optimism and humor faltered. "There was a dismal period for the administration," he wrote. "It seemed as if a wind of death was blowing on its employees." Even at Emperador, high in the mountains and seemingly the healthiest spot on the line, there was a bad outbreak of yellow fever. "The situation looked bad," said Cermoise. "These successive deaths . . . had shaken our courage, striking the imaginations of even the bravest men; everyone anxiously began thinking of steamers home; in a word, we were struck by one of those moral weaknesses from which a panic is born."

Armand Reclus was away in Paris, having left Louis Verbrugghe in charge. On October 5, 1881, the lawyer wrote to France: "At the moment, the state of health conditions in Panama is distressing: an upsurge of disease is occurring . . . the morale of our personnel is a bit shaken by the sudden deaths . . . Natanson and Marinovitch are leaving Panama. All the pretty promises they made to Abel Couvreux have been broken." This panic, the fear of disease, was almost as bad for the project as the actual fatalities.

Inevitably, rumors reached Europe, but de Lesseps, addressing a Geographical Congress at Vienna that month, insisted: "No epidemic of maladie had manifested itself at Panama. Only a few cases of yellow fever had appeared, and these had been imported from abroad." But even worse was to come. In November, Gaston Blanchet, whose marriage the previous year had made him a popular figure in Panama, became shivery and feverish while on an expedition mapping the headwaters of the Chagres. He made it back to Panama City, but died two days later. "Mr. Blanchet's death is an irreparable loss to the Company," the British consul reported back to London. "Operations will be almost entirely at a standstill until his successor arrives."

The "casualty figures" from the French construction period were argued over at the time, and have been ever since. Contemporary American newspapers hostile to the project doubtlessly exaggerated their reports, claiming that among the couple of hundred white technicians alone nearly seventy had perished in the first twelve months. The Company retaliated by ridiculing the figures. The best estimate is that about fifty men died in the first year, from an average workforce of about a thousand for this period. Many more, though, were incapacitated by illness.

As part of his pitch to investors in the canal, de Lesseps had promised up-to-date hospitals would be built to serve the workers on the project. And he was as good as his word. A hundred-bed hospital was constructed in Colón, and work started on a huge five-hundred-bed establishment on Ancón Hill, a salubrious and breezy spot high above Panama City. Huge sums were spent—a million dollars on the Colón hospital and more than five and a half million dollars at Ancón, on a seventeen-building complex that included its own fresh water supply, a vast laundry, an abattoir, and a farm that provided the patients with an abundance of milk, eggs, and fresh vegetables. Outside the ward windows, patients could enjoy a well-laid-out garden, irrigated on a terrace system, bright with herbs and flowers. Inside, as a contemporary noted, "the hospital rooms are so vast and well-ventilated that, even in the ones occupied by Negroes stricken with marsh fever, visitors with the most acute sense of smell could not detect the slightest odour." It was by some distance the best hospital anywhere in the tropics.

A further half a million dollars was spent on building an extensive sanatorium on the island of Taboga, about an hour and a half by steamer out into the Bay of Panama. In its lavish and beautiful surroundings, employees could convalesce after a time in one of the hospitals, or just take a break from the feverish climate of the mainland.

In charge of the medical operation was the former head of the sanitary division at Suez. He ran a team of six doctors and thirty nurses from the order of St. Vincent de Paul, led by Sister Marie Roulon. Their care, though medically primitive by later standards, was much praised. "She is one of those rare women whose personal zeal is contagious," wrote the *New York Herald*'s occasional Panama correspondent of Sister Roulon in October 1881. "Every one of her Sisters has caught the trick of her cheery kindness . . . When all healing is unavailing, they make even the scorched death of yellow fever easy if such a thing can be."

But in November the rains ended, and as the pools of stagnant water on which the mosquitoes depended to hatch their young dried up, so rates of infection fell away. In addition, according to Henri Cermoise, the skillful and courageous leadership of Louis Verbrugghe did much to calm exaggerated fears. But now that the small window of dry weather had returned, it was imperative that work be pushed ahead with as much urgency as possible.

◀◀◀◀ ▶▶▶▶

By November 1881, Henri Cermoise's task of mapping the precise axis of the canal was completed and it was time to set it out on the ground, with a line of stakes either side of the area to be excavated. Together with Montcenaux, he was given a ten-kilometer section to mark out in the area of Gorgona. Cermoise was happy to be back out in the field, and to be reunited with his friend, who, as Cermoise had predicted, had caught a fever while working near Gatún, and had very nearly died. At first, writes Cermoise, Montcenaux had presented the symptoms of the dreaded *vomito negro*—yellow fever—but as he had survived, Cermoise deduces, it must have been something else. "There's only one certain way to diagnose fever," he wrote. "Did he die? Then it's Yellow Fever. Did he recover? Then it is only an attack of bilious fever."

At Gorgona they camped out in an open shack in the middle of the village until, fifteen days later, a prefabricated house was sent up to them by the Company. In the meantime, they started the job of clearing vegetation from their ten kilometers. They were all too familiar with this arduous task from their surveying work at Gamboa, but this was now on a different level. Previously, their *"tranches"* had been fairly haphazard—they had been able to bypass obstacles or particularly enormous trees—but now they had to stick exactly to the route on their maps as well as create a much wider and more complete clearance.

Missing the Belgian cook, Cermoise now found the available provisions scarce and expensive. As elsewhere on the Isthmus, the local retailing (the single shop) was run by a Chinese gentleman, in this case married to a local. As more and more foreign workers arrived on the Isthmus, so prices climbed with demand.

Many of the people turning up, Cermoise complains, were still of dubious qualifications or even competence. At one point a carpenter working on the accommodation requested thirty nails from the workshop in Panama, carefully carving a piece of wood in the exact dimensions and size of what he required. A fortnight later the order duly arrived, to exactly the right dimensions, but each one made of wood and so utterly useless. In all, there was a feeling of muddling through.

Among the imported workers, reported the *Star and Herald*, there was also dissatisfaction. At the beginning of January 1882 a general strike broke out in Colón, based on demands for $1.50 rather than $1.20 a day. The following day, January 6, the strike was "in full blast," and had drawn in workers on the railway, the steamers, and the canal itself. Fearing wider trouble, the American consul summoned the U.S. Navy. The standoff continued for a week, with the works of the Isthmus at a standstill, while the Company tried in vain to import enough new men to cover the gaps. On January 13, the bosses offered $1.35, but the workers stuck to their guns, citing the huge rise in the prices of provisions over the previous twelve months. The *Star and Herald* sympathized with this, but urged the strikers to do the right thing and take the offer, as soon the Isthmus would be flooded with labor and their negotiating power would be gone. Finally, on January 14, the paper could report the end of the strike: "The railway wharf is again a scene of life and animation . . . The price paid for labor by the Railway Company is $1.50 per day." When the U.S. warships arrived two weeks later, all was peaceful.

On January 20, 1882, the first spade load came out of the actual line of the canal at Emperador. This was fitting, as here was the highest position on the canal route, the point at which the depth of the trench to be dug to reach sea level was over 350 feet. The French called the area *"la section de la grande tranchée."* A spectacular explosion in the presence of a number of invited guests launched the work, after which the great and the good retreated to Panama for a banquet followed by a gala dance.

It was a great boost for the project that actual excavation was under way, but for the next four months of the dry season the Company was unable to get mechanical diggers into place and operational. The work fell to some seven hundred men, mostly Jamaicans, toiling away with pick and shovel, so progress was slow. Much of the overall workforce was still employed with erecting buildings, laying track, and improving access to the site.

From Matachín to Gatún work was still needed pegging out the line, which was not entirely cleared of vegetation until May. In February, Henri Cermoise and Montcenaux had been sent to San Pablo, an isolated spot offering few diversions apart from watching the trains go past and hunting for iguanas and local wild turkeys. Two months later, just as their time there was coming to an end, Cermoise suddenly felt "invaded by a persistent tiredness." He had a headache, could hardly eat, and was left indifferent by even the most succulent iguana eggs. For him, the attack seemed inevitable. Montcenaux had done his time while at Gatún, now it was his turn. Soon, he felt dizzy, then overcome with aches and was unable to stand up. After that he suffered a high fever for two days, during which, "unfortunately, my reason left me on several occasions." He was convinced that he had been taken with yellow fever. Montcenaux, however, did not panic, dosing his friend with quinine and calling for help from a passing train, which took Cermoise to Panama City.

To his relief, at the hospital Cermoise was diagnosed with *calentura*, rather than yellow fever. But for fifteen days he suffered a high fever and delirium, never sure if he was awake or asleep. When he regained his senses, he felt lucky compared to the man he saw in the bed next to him who, weakened by fever and blood loss from vampire bat attacks, also had some type of larvae in the top of his nose, which in a few days burrowed into his head and killed him.

But the new hospitals were far from full, in spite of the fact that the labor force was increasing quickly on the Isthmus, mainly as a result of Charles Gadpaille's efforts in Jamaica. In May 1882, the British consul reported three thousand men at work along the line, and that "The sanitary condition is very favourable. There are about forty-two cases of various types of fever, none of which are of an alarming nature. The average is fourteen cases in 1,000, which I consider a very feeble percentage, owing to the nature of the work the men are engaged in. I am happy to say that the natives of the West Indies stand the climate very well, and supply the Company with a good nucleus." By this time the entire line had at last been cleared to a width of 300 meters, a task that had taken much more time and effort than had been anticipated.

The following month, June 1882, de Lesseps told the third annual shareholders' meeting of the details of the purchase of the PRR and asked for a bond issue to pay for this expenditure. He also announced that excavation work had now started at Gatún, Gamboa, Bas Obispo, Culebra, Gorgona, and Paraíso. In twelve months' time, he breezily predicted, 5 million cubic meters would have been removed from Culebra. There was more good news. In February a contract had been signed with an American company, Huerne, Slaven & Company, to dig a channel to a depth of 2.5 meters between Colón and Gatún. The excavation was reckoned at 6 million cubic meters, which would take eighteen months from a start date of August 1882. This, de Lesseps explained, would bring American mechanical skill and might to the project, and bury forever the fear that the United States was opposed to the canal. Shareholders were delighted and readily approved a bond issue to be held that September.

There were increasing numbers of Americans on the Isthmus. The process of parceling out the work to contractors had continued through the year, with another American company taking on the dredging at the Pacific end. Machinery was purchased by the Company and then rented out to the contractors, who were to be paid per cubic meter excavated. But the arrangement was not to the liking of the *Agent Supérieur*, Armand Reclus, who complained about the over-favorable terms given by the Company and the bureaucratic chaos the approach was engendering. In fact, Reclus was losing heart. Since the return of the rains in May, frequent flooding of the works at Culebra had brought digging there to a standstill, and the hospitals were again filling up with fever patients and accident victims. Complaining of overwork, exhaustion, and confused leadership from Paris, Reclus resigned in June 1882. He was given a job in the Paris office, but his time of influence over the canal, going back to the first Wyse expedition five years before, was now at an end.

In September, there was a further setback, when the Isthmus suffered an earthquake. Although there was only one fatality, the railway bridge over the Chagres was thrown out of line and the tracks damaged in many places. A Canadian doctor, Wolfred Nelson, who had been living on the Isthmus for six months and who would become a fierce critic of the French effort in Panama, cabled a report to the *New York Herald*. The piece when printed "all but produced an earthquake among M. De Lesseps' shareholders," Nelson writes. "He at once informed the world that there would be no more earthquakes on the Isthmus. Strange to say, despite the utterances of this celebrated man, the earthquakes kept on, to the unstringing of our nerves . . ." Cermoise described the quake in less doom-ridden terms, despite tearing muscles in his legs jumping off a first-floor balcony to make his escape from a collapsing building. Cermoise would leave Panama a few months later, he says "for family reasons," but in contrast to naysayers like Nelson he shrugged off the difficulties and frustrations of his time there. In fact, he was sad to be leaving the Isthmus, "where," he said, "I have spent two of the best years of my youth." Looking back while writing his account the following year, he missed the strangeness, novelty, and the unexpectedness, "and the friendship of good and loyal companions, with whom we have, together, played our part, however modest, in the most gigantic of all modern enterprises."

The earthquake also failed to dampen the enthusiasm and optimism of de Lesseps and his *Bulletin*. In November, *Le Grand Français* announced that "After two years' work . . . we are much farther advanced than we were at Suez after six years." Of the 75 million cubic meters to be excavated, crowed the *Bulletin*, a quarter had been allocated to contractors. It was almost as if the work was already done.

In the U.S. press, the French Company was dismissed as "incompetent," and in Panama the *Star and Herald* warned that "exaggerated statements" were causing "doubt and distrust." In France, however, confidence remained rock solid. The bond issue in September was a great success and massively oversubscribed. Although there were warning signs—the interest on the money had crept up from the share issue and yet more sweeteners were handed over to the financial institutions—it was a distinct setback for those predicting the imminent demise of de Lesseps's project. With "applications for shares showering him from all quarters of France," wrote the anti-canal *New York Tribune* soon after, "he can now reckon with confidence upon the resources required for so vast a scheme. He can get the money . . . Englishmen and Americans may as well reconcile themselves to the situation."

Then, at the end of the year, there occurred another setback on the Isthmus: the contractor Couvreux unexpectedly used a loophole in their contract to pull out of the project. It turned out that the veterans of Suez had found all their expertise worthless. As de Lépinay had predicted, Panama had nothing in common with Egypt. If anything the experience of Suez had actually hampered the efforts of Couvreux. The loss of Blanchet had hurt, too, with no one of similar stature from the company willing to go out to Panama. The break was amicable, Couvreux arguing that since smaller contractors were now in place, having a middleman between them and the Compagnie Universelle was a waste of money. The real reason for their defection emerged later, when the ashes of the Panama project were raked over in Paris ten years later: "The truth is that during the trial period," a government report reads, "Couvreux and Hersent had been able to form a shrewd idea of the difficulties of the enterprise but were unwilling to undermine the [canal] company's credit by frank admission of the motive behind their retirement."

With the works now stuttering after just two years, perhaps Ferdinand de Lesseps should have taken personal charge on site, as he had at Suez. But that, he calculated, would have sent a disastrously alarmist signal to the markets. Appearance and confidence were all to a project living or dying on credit with the public investor. De Lesseps was needed in Paris. He was also distracted by the events at Suez, where the British had seized control, and by his ongoing eccentric scheme to flood the Sahara. Another explanation, put forward by de Lesseps's American detractors, was that age had finally caught up with the "Great Engineer." The Paris correspondent of the *New York Tribune* reported that de Lesseps on his return from his latest trip to Africa had "aged a good deal . . . His handwriting, which was so clear and vigorous when he returned from Panama, is now a shaky scrawl."

So instead of Ferdinand, his son, Charles de Lesseps, was sent to the Isthmus for a monthlong visit. Charles, who possessed none of his father's verve or showmanship, would increasingly shoulder the burden of leadership of the project. With him was the first *Directeur Général* of the works, Jules Dingler (pronounced *Danglay*), one of the most senior civil engineers in France. He had been appointed with a salary of the equivalent of $20,000, far more than anyone else in the French organization was being paid. He looked unprepossessing—short, bald, and round-shouldered—but his arrival at Panama, at the beginning of March 1883, would usher in the great heroic period of the French effort.

CHAPTER ELEVEN

JULES DINGLER

By the end of the following year, Dingler's leadership had transformed the canal project. Even Wolfred Nelson described 1884 as a time when Panama was "busy . . . and bright with hope." "The work moves steadily on," reported the *Star and Herald* in November of that year. "The progress which is being made is apparent to everyone who crosses the Isthmus."

Dingler was passionately in love with the Great Idea of the canal, but he was experienced enough on large-scale engineering projects to see on his arrival that the effort on the Isthmus was drifting. His first move was to reorganize the company's chaotic office in Panama City. From the Company's paperwork, a clean break is apparent dating from the arrival of the new *Directeur Général*. Armed with total authority on the Isthmus, unlike Reclus or Blanchet, Dingler set about trying to tighten up payment procedures, demanding exact descriptions of articles requisitioned "especially so where machine parts are required," and generally attacking the bugbears of waste and fraud.

There was also a purge of the workforce, with many of the unsuitable adventurers and strays—whom Dingler referred to as "idlers and traitors"—being sacked or moved from their comfortable offices out into the jungle. In the process the new leader made plenty of enemies, but also earned the respect of the majority of the workforce.

Next, he toured the line and put together the first truly detailed plan for the canal. This included a policy of creating much more gradual slopes for the trench, which, together with the idea of riveting the sides of the canal with vegetation, was designed to deal with the growing problem of landslides. The result was a large jump in the estimate of spoil to be excavated—120 million cubic meters, 45 million more than judged necessary by the 1880 Technical Commission. In early autumn 1883, he returned to Paris to present his plan to de Lesseps and his board of advisers. Dingler got the go-ahead, although de Lesseps did not feel it necessary to revise either his costs or his scheduled completion date for the canal, which remained 1888.

When Dingler returned to the Isthmus, he brought with him his wife, son, daughter, and her fiancé, as well as his collection of thoroughbred horses. The message of long-term commitment to the project was unmistakable, as was his belief that there was nothing to fear from Panama's climate. Dingler went further, announcing, "I intend to show the world that only the drunk and the dissipated will die of Yellow Fever." The family were an instant hit in Panama society. The *Star and Herald* reports a reception given by the *Directeur Général* in December 1883: "Their rooms were crowded with many ladies, and a number of our most distinguished native and foreign residents. The handsome rooms were still further beautified with floral decorations and other adornments; the music was good, and gave a zest to dancing, whilst the cultivated hosts spread a charm through the scene of enjoyment." The young Dinglers set about exploring the Isthmus, enjoying picnic and riding excursions.

Back in France, investors were also impressed with the new leadership. In October 1883 there was a second bond issue, which was again massively oversubscribed. "This result has surprised all," reported the Panama press, "except those who know the popularity which Count de Lesseps enjoys, and the confidence investors feel in his projects." Eleven months later there was a further bond issue. This time it didn't quite sell out, in spite of even more favorable terms. Nonetheless, French support remained solid.

By now, nearly 700 million francs had been raised. Dingler was spending it fast, giving out huge orders aiming to double or even triple the number of steam shovels, locomotives, and other machinery in operation on the Isthmus. Along with the new machinery came a host of new contractors. In May 1883 alone, Dingler signed seventeen contracts for excavation. Once back from France with his family, the *Directeur Général* divided the line of the canal into three divisions, each under the control of a single French engineer. The first covered Limón Bay and lower reaches of the Chagres; the second, the Upper Chagres and the hills between Matachín and Culebra; the third from Culebra to the approaches to the Bay of Panama.

The key contractor in the First Division was the American outfit Huerne, Slaven & Company, which had been taken on back in February 1882. The driving force of the company was H. B. Slaven, a Canadian-born drugstore owner from San Francisco. He had known nothing about excavation but, "determined to have a finger in the canal pie," had, as Tracy Robinson put it, "with an audacity akin to inspiration" put in, and had accepted, a bid to take on some of the work. Raising capital from a New York banker, he ordered the building of a series of huge, custom-made dredges 36 meters long and 9 meters wide. Although work on his section was supposed to have started in August 1882, it was not until April the following year that the first of these monsters had been completed in Philadelphia and, with great difficulty, towed to the Isthmus. The first to arrive was destroyed by fire in Colón Harbor, but the next—the *Comte de Lesseps*—arrived during the summer and was laboriously fitted out. A 20-meter wooden tower was assembled in the center with a huge wheel on the top. Attached to this was a chain with a series of large steel buckets on a boom that was lowered over the side. Each of the buckets scooped up a cubic meter of soil from the bottom of the channel and hoisted it to the top of the tower, where it was emptied by jets of water into large pipes that extended 55 meters on either side, dumping the spoil clear of the work site. The whole contraption moved on huge legs, or "spuds," "by means of which," says Robinson, "she walked step by step into the material to be excavated." The *Comte de Lesseps* started inland from the mudflats of Limón Bay in October 1883. Able to extract 5,000 cubic meters a day, it made a huge impression. It seemed just the sort of fantastic machine that de Lesseps had promised would miraculously turn up.

In January 1884, an American naval officer, sent to estimate progress on the canal, reported back to Washington that "this powerful and excellent machine" had already "dug a passage 1075 meters long, 34 meters wide, and 4 meters deep; so that vessels of 13 feet draught may now, at this point, pass up the line of the canal for a distance of half a mile." Another monster dredge arrived during the year, and in October, the *Star and Herald* reported that Colón and Gatún were soon to be in connection by water. "So the visitor to Gatún . . . can easily satisfy himself that there is something serious and practical in this canal enterprise."

Further up the line, work was undertaken on diversionary channels for the Chagres and digging up the alluvial silt of the river valley. This was managed by a Franco-Dutch firm, Artigue et Sonderegger, which had twenty smaller Belgian-made ladder dredges at work.

On the Pacific side of the Isthmus, much deepening work was needed in the Bay of Panama. This was started out by self-propelled dredges built by Lobnitz and Company of Renfrew, Scotland, which were sailed to Panama under their own steam. The first arrived in May 1883, having covered the five-thousand-mile journey from the Clyde in only a month. Such was the quality of their design and manufacture that they were kept on by the canal builders right up to 1914. Meanwhile, lighter dredges pushed up the valley of the Río Grande. It was steady progress, if less spectacular than that at Colón.

Inland, in *la grande tranchée*, it was a different story, with much more labor-intensive work being required. By the end of 1883 pilot trenches had been run the ten-mile length of the Continental Divide and a contract had been signed with Cutbill, de Longo, Watson and Van Hattum—usually referred to as the Anglo-Dutch Company. The excavation work commenced with hand pick and shovel, and the soil was removed in small iron cars, running on portable tramways. Once the trench was a few feet deep, a track was laid connecting with the main line of the Panama Railroad, and upon this steam excavators were brought up mounted on trucks. Most were U.S.-built by Osgood or Otis. These machines commenced digging down in a series of stepped terraces, each about 5 meters wide and 5 meters deep, which was how far the excavators could reach. The spoil was loaded onto flatcars, then taken away. "From morning till night," reported an American visitor, "trains are moving about removing the excavations of the laborers and of the excavating machines, which latter do their work very well and very cheaply."

Nonetheless, there remained a lot of hand excavation, and it was here that the majority of the canal laborers were concentrated. In mid-1883, the British consul reported some twelve hundred workers in this small space, mainly Jamaicans, Martinicans, and Italians. "The Anglo-Saxon element prevails a great deal here in the way of officials

French ladder dredge

and clerks," he went on. The steam shovel operators and mechanics were also British or American.

So as well as ordering masses of new machinery, Dingler also determined to increase the number of laborers available to the contractors. There were ten thousand by September 1883, fifteen thousand by January the following year, and by the end of 1884, there were over twenty thousand on the payroll, making a total wage bill of some $40,000 a day. The majority of the workers were from Jamaica.

⊰⊰⊰⊰⊷ ⊶⊱⊱⊱⊱

There was good money to be made on the Isthmus. Most workers earned about $1.50 a day, and as the pay was calculated on a piecework basis, extra labor would bring even more. This was a big deal for the impoverished inhabitants of the West Indian islands, particularly Jamaica. Soon large steamships were making the run from Kingston to Colón as frequently as every four days. Nonetheless, there were near riots at the docks as people fought each other to get a place on a ship. "A stampede took place which is hardly possible to describe," reported the Jamaican paper *Gall's News Letter* in early 1884 of the scene at Kingston docks. "Men with trunks on their backs, women with little children tugging through the crowd, all trying to gain admission to the ship. In a few minutes the deck was crowded."

Money being sent home to relations and the return of men from the Isthmus with their fortunes visibly transformed and further fueled Panama Fever on the island. "Now and again," complained a planter, "you see a great swell with a watch and gold chain, a revolver pistol, red sash, big boots up to his knees, who swaggers about." Such returnees soon became known as "Colón Man," an almost mythical figure on the island, the subject of many skits and verses, both admiring and gently ridiculing. "One two three four/Colón Man a come," goes one. "With him watch chain a knock him belly bam bam bam/Ask him for the time/and he look upon the sun/With him watch chain a knock him belly bam bam bam."

As the "Panama Craze" spread, even those few with stable and secure jobs joined the rush to Colón. "The infatuation to go seems to have taken hold on the whole of them who are able to go," reported the *Gleaner*. During the French construction period, some eighty-four thousand made the journey to Colón from Kingston, at a time when the entire population of the island was under six hundred thousand. Whole areas of the island became depopulated, and the demographics of those left behind were radically altered, leading to a decline in marriage and other unions, and women and children taking up the work previously done by men. The birthrate fell, and women became heads of families as never before. Children were frequently left to fend for themselves, as families were split up, often forever.

At the same time, the money coming back from Panama was invested in land, livestock, and housing, leading to rising peasant proprietorship and ownership of goods, appliances, and tools, in all contributing to an economic revival on the island at the end of the century. "Colón Man" also brought home a new, less subservient attitude, his flash dress and accessories "a flag of liberation."

Official reaction to these huge changes was mixed. "We are not of those who think it a calamity that so many of our people are going to the great Canal Work," wrote one of the mouthpieces of the ruling plantocracy, the *Jamaica Witness*, in early 1884. "It is a great enterprise this, the joining of two great oceans . . . We wish it God speed; and we feel rather proud that we can supply so large a portion of those who are to perform that necessary toil . . . Let them go by all means. It will give many a lesson in labour which they never had before—a hard day's work for good wages. Many will gain money, and return to acquire property; and they will be more men than they ever were, men who have felt their manhood, and who will more than ever prize their position and privileges as citizens of a great Empire." But as early as mid-1883, Jamaican plantation interests in London were lobbying the secretary of state for the colonies to restrict "the great outflow from the Colony of labourers, artisans, and respectable young men, who are properly described as the bone, sinew and hope of the country."

The planters spread stories about the terrible risks of disease in Panama, and that the Company ran a brutal regime, but were unable to stem the tide. The *Witness* explains: "the dangers and drawbacks of life on the Isthmus are counterbalanced by material advantages of an appreciable character." As one of the West Indian work songs has it:

Kill my partner
Kill my partner
Kill my partner
Somebody's dying every day.
I love you yes I do, you know it's true,
And when you come to Panama how happy you will be,
'Cause money down in Panama like apples on a tree.

On the Isthmus, the West Indians found themselves doubly vulnerable as foreigners working for a foreign company. There was no labor law in Colombia except for the "freedom to work," and the workers' backgrounds mitigated against concerted labor action. Churches, community burial clubs, and mutual support organizations were established, but there was little organization in the workplace. Eight or nine strikes broke out on the Isthmus during the 1880s, yet these tended to be confined to the port or railway workers, whose stoppage could cause serious delays and backlogs for the steamer companies. The employers, however, found the Colombian authorities sympathetic to their side, and several strikes were broken up by soldiers. More than anything, though, the flood of new arrivals meant that there were always men to replace those who tried to improve their wages or conditions. Instead, to the frustration of the Company, the men would simply move to another area in order to get better pay, or to be with their friends. "They have a way of shifting for themselves," the *Star and Herald* reported in early 1884, "and selecting their own masters and places of work ... go[ing] about from section to section wherever they can best suit their own particular ideas as to wages and other circumstances."

Panama had a sensitive racial and social mix ill-suited to such a huge influx of "aliens." The arrivals from Jamaica, who came from a cultural background radically different from that of Panama or greater Colombia, were seen as a threat and deeply resented. Antagonism was exacerbated by the hardships of the construction camp setting. As the number of Jamaicans grew, so too did instances of disturbances and bloodshed along the line of the canal. In March 1883, five Jamaicans and three Colombians were killed in fighting at Culebra, Obispo, and Matachín, and the British consul requested armed protection for British subjects. But the attitude of the soldiery was just as antagonistic as that of the Colombian workers: "I perceive that these men are partial in their protection and disorderly and brutal in their conduct," the consul wrote.

Tension now simmered all along the line. "Both sides are armed," said the *Star and Herald* on April 3, 1883, "both prepared, and alike expectant . . . the works between Matachín and Gorgona . . . are practically deserted." More by accident than design—Colombians started refusing to work with Jamaicans—the two warring parties now lived and worked in separate areas, but friction was still building through the following year, threatening to spill out into open armed conflict.

⟪⟪⟪⟪‒⟫⟫⟫⟫

For the moment, however, these labor troubles were not the greatest of Dingler's worries. In spite of the progress since he had taken over, the project was now beset with very serious difficulties. For one thing, the harbor and warehouses at Colón could not cope with the huge volume of machinery and supplies being imported. Often, steamers would have to be unloaded by lighters, "a ruinously expensive method," wrote a visiting reporter from the *New York World*. "The cost of coal is increased two thirds. It is worth £3 per ton in the harbour and £5 when landed." Furthermore, the railway, in spite of a great expansion of rolling stock, did not have the capacity to move machinery inland as fast as it was arriving. So valuable equipment was left out on the waterfront at the mercy of the climate. "Damage amounting to thousands of dollars daily is known to be going on," reported a visiting journalist. The machinery itself came from many quarters—France, the United States, Belgium, and elsewhere. It was constantly being modified and used in experimental, often ingenious, combinations, but much of it was found to be unequal to the task. A growing accumulation of discarded, inoperative equipment along the canal line testified to earlier mistakes. A later American engineer, piecing through the abandoned French plant, would describe it as "of a character and complexity to defy description ... some parts could only be classed as freaks. Apparently every crank who possessed influence was allowed to exploit his notions in the furnishing of machines to the company." The experimentation and increasing number of small contractors combined to produce a host of contradictory specifications for spare parts, railroad track, and truck gauge. At one time there were eleven different types of flatcar running on six different gauges. It was as far from a "joined-up system" as can be imagined.

For all Dingler's efforts at improving efficiency, the Company was hemorrhaging money through a combination of mismanagement, extravagance, and corruption. More than a hundred racehorses were imported from Europe and lavishly stabled at the Company's expense. There was also widespread pilfering. Inspectors sent to check on the contractors' excavation quantities were often bribed. One estimate was that the Company lost some 10 percent of the work it paid for. The worst offenders were the Huerne, Slaven men, who were even accused of dredging soil from one side of their barges, for which they were paid, and then simply dumping it back into the water on the other side. The workers, also, became adept at exploiting the Company. "There was no system or organisation," reported a Nicaragua-born canal workman. "A man can work on five different jobs a day, and when the week ended you collect for all five jobs. Their timekeeping system was poor." The local Panamanians were also making a lot of money out of the Company, charging exorbitant rates for land the French needed, or bringing endless expensive legal cases against them. Like Reclus, Jules Dingler and his wife had to entertain a constant stream of visitors from Europe, Colombia, and the United States during the dry season, and, in urgent need of an adequate house in which to entertain them, found no one willing to build something for less than $100,000. There was similar mass collusion over food supplies. Traders would board incoming ships carrying provisions, buy the entire cargo, and then fix the price of the goods on the Panama market.

As well as administrative difficulties, engineering problems were now beginning to pile up. In *la grande tranchée*, the rainy season brought continual landslides, which buried rails and machinery under thousands of cubic meters of sticky mud. The contractors in this section had to keep cutting the slopes back to flatten them, creating seemingly endless amounts of extra work. By the end of 1884 it had been decided that the gradient would have to be as gentle as one in four. This would have made the trench, had it been dug to sea level as planned, as much as three-quarters of a mile across in several places.

The spoil was removed in small dump cars to a convenient nearby valley, where a track would be laid on the brow of the hill. The cars were then tipped or laboriously emptied by hand, with the dirt thrown over the side. When a terrace had been formed, new track was laid on it and the process repeated. But the dump areas also became unstable, with terraces slipping away, destroying track and trains and leading to the whole system breaking down and the excavators lying idle.

"The rainy season, at last set in, is making up for lost time by pouring down oceans of water all over the Isthmus," the *Star and Herald* reported at the end of May 1883. "The effect on new embankments, fills &c., made by the Canal Company during the dry season, is not pleasant to contemplate. The work of months disappears in a day." Almost exactly a year later, it was the same story: "The heavy downpours of late are making short work of earth cuttings . . . A few hours of tropical rain caused the mighty Chagres to rise three feet. When it subsided the cut was found to be filled to within three feet of the top. The work of many days costing a great deal of money has disappeared as if by magic ... This Chagres question is a mighty one."

As had been anticipated back at the 1879 Congress in Paris, the problem of the Chagres was indeed among the most formidable faced by the French engineers. Dingler, in his grand plan, had stuck with the suggestion that to stop the river flooding the canal, a huge earthen dam should be constructed at Gamboa, with another smaller dam twenty-five kilometers upriver. But this filled no one with confidence. There was no adequate rock formation at this site upon which to found such an enormous structure, and few believed that it would hold the pressure of the river at its most swollen. In addition, the basin behind the dam, in which it was hoped up to 6,000 cubic meters of water would be held, had still not been adequately surveyed.

It was planned that the remaining flow of the river would be drained by a series of diversions running parallel to the line of the canal. But as the canal ran along the lowest points of the river valleys, the surface water of these diversions would be about 70 feet above that of the canal proper, requiring very strong guard banks. In effect, as a critic of the French plan pointed out, "the water will have to be hung up on the sides of the mountains." And just one of these channels would have to be thirteen miles long, with similar dimensions to the main canal. It was as if the canal had to be constructed two or three times. In all, every time the French engineers turned around, the task ahead seemed to have grown exponentially.

In all great construction projects the greatest cause of delay and financial loss—and the reason that considerable slack is worked into budgets—is generally termed "unforeseen ground conditions." Panama had these in spades. "Fresh engineering difficulties present themselves," wrote a British visitor in late 1883, "and the magnitude of the work to be accomplished seems to increase." It became clearer and clearer that, right from the start, de Lesseps had totally underestimated the task he was setting for his engineers. And as the problems mounted, in order to maintain the confidence of investors and sell new bond issues, de Lesseps kept up a stream of promises and impossibly high targets. In June 1882 he had told the Company's annual general meeting that 5 million cubic meters would be excavated from Culebra in the next twelve months; the figure achieved in that period was only 660,000. The following year he reaffirmed his promise that the canal would open in 1888, and predicted a monthly excavation figure overall of 2 million cubic meters. But the workforce on the Isthmus was not exceeding a quarter of that. The more expectations were raised, the further de Lesseps had to fall. "A day of reckoning is coming," wrote the *Montreal Gazette* in August 1884.

Although the press in France remained onside, elsewhere criticism of the project, and of the exaggerated reports of the *Bulletin*, was mounting. In August 1884, the American *Engineer* magazine printed the report of a correspondent who had spent two months on the Isthmus, who estimated that the Company would need another twenty-four years and hundreds of millions of dollars more to finish the canal at the current rate of excavation, an analysis with which several U.S. naval officers, sent to investigate progress, concurred. It was also now openly stated in Britain and the United States that the French press had been bribed to hide the truth from domestic investors.

In August 1884, the *Montreal Gazette*'s correspondent, back in Panama after having visited the works six months earlier, reported that "little substantial progress has been made . . . valuable plant remains unhoused, including locomotives, boilers &c." The fault, as far as he was concerned, was with misplaced priorities: "Time that might be used in building proper sheds is frittered away embellishing banks near houses, setting out tropical trees and plants to make the landscape attractive. *C'est magnifique*," he concluded, "*mais ce n'est pas le canal*." In November the *New York Herald*, usually a fair judge of the project, accurately predicted, "It is probable the present company will go into bankruptcy or liquidation within three years and the enterprise be taken up and completed by a new company or a government."

On the Isthmus itself it was felt that real progress was being made, but the huge expenditure of capital had not gone unnoticed. Among many of the canal employees an air of heroic unreality had descended, as if infected by de Lesseps's fantastical pronouncements from Paris. One of the American "inspectors" remarked on the "tendency on the part of the canal officers to exaggerate everything that had been done by the company." Others, though, testified that several of the Company's managers were privately saying that the project was catastrophically behind schedule. In July 1884, twenty-four-year-old acting consul Claude Mallet reported back to London, "It is generally believed here that the present Company can never finish the work, as the cost so far has greatly exceeded expectations." For him, such a project could never be completed by private capital. Only a government could carry through such a task. The *Star and Herald* agreed, in the same month goading the U.S. government to take on the job: "It would be a pity," it wrote, "that a work such as this should be left partially completed as a monument of the folly and gullibility of Capital." A government had to step in, and "it would be well for Americans to remember that the government of France would have the most powerful motives to undertake it. There would be the natural desire to prevent the loss of French Capital, and the price of control and influence abroad is not a forgotten sentiment in France."

A British observer, Admiral Bedford Pim, blamed the weaknesses of the original Wyse-Reclus surveys for the problems, and dismissed the sea-level plan as impossible. His only praise, after an extensive tour of the work, was for "the gallant employees who have struggled manfully to carry out the wishes of their chief." The *New York Herald*, reporting the pessimistic analysis of the latest U.S. naval investigation, commented, "Under such circumstances, there is something amounting to heroism in the persistence of the French Company at Panama."

◄◄◄◄◄-►►►►►

*S*he French engineers and their workers were now facing more than just financial or engineering difficulties. Their very lives were at stake. In 1882, 126 people had died in the hospitals, mainly from yellow fever or malaria. The following year, as the workforce tripled, so did the number of deaths, to over 400.

But the official tally did not tell the whole story. Many died before they reached the hospital. According to a lurid account by a *New York Tribune* correspondent, a number of workers ended up in unmarked graves. "Death becomes a grim joke, burial a travesty," he reported. "An unconsidered laborer is buried under a hundred feet of earth— and very simply; rolled down an embankment, and twenty carloads of earth rolled after him." Although the Company itself covered hospital expenses for its employees, the vast majority were on the payroll of contractors, who were charged a dollar a day for the care of their workers in the hospital. It was alleged that some simply dismissed their men at the first sign of sickness rather than foot the bill. In addition, the hospitals themselves were feared and shunned, and with good reason. If you did not have malaria or yellow fever when you went in, you were likely to have it soon afterward. In the absence of knowledge of the transmission of these diseases by mosquito there were no efforts to isolate known fever victims or to keep the insects from the wards. Furthermore, to protect the hospitals' much-admired gardens from leaf-eating ants, waterways had been constructed around the flowerbeds. Inside the hospital itself, water pans were placed under bedposts to keep off ants and other crawling pests. Both insect-fighting methods provided excellent and convenient breeding sites for mosquitoes carrying yellow fever or malaria. Doctor William Gorgas, who led the medical effort on the Isthmus during the American construction period, later wrote, "Probably if the French had been trying to propagate Yellow Fever, they could not have provided conditions better adapted to the purpose."

Gorgas reckoned that for every death in one of the hospitals, two occurred outside, which would put the 1883 toll at nearer 1,300 than 419. This is conjecture, of course, and should be treated with caution. Nevertheless, there is fairly overwhelming anecdotal evidence to back up this claim. Charles Wilson, a half-Scottish, half-French sailor, was twenty-one when he arrived on the Isthmus in 1882 and started work for the Panama Railroad. Wilson was what was known as a "tropical tramp." He was born on board a ship and never belonged in any place except where there was money to be made. He found that working on the Isthmus earned him far more than the $20 a month he had been getting as a sailor. But there were, he said, "thousands dying with yellow fever, malaria, and all kinds of diseases . . . everywhere, in the streets and under houses." "As for the men," reported the *Montreal Gazette*, "they die on the line and are buried, and no attention is paid to the matter. Two American carpenters are in an unnamed grave near Emperador . . ." Wolfred Nelson, the Canadian doctor, remembered an endless procession of funeral trains, reckoning that during the wet seasons of 1882 and 1883 "burials averaged from thirty to forty per day, and that for weeks together."

The correspondence of the British consulate also draws a picture of illness growing into unmanageable proportions. The staff themselves were forever sickening and pleading to be allowed to leave the Isthmus to recover in Jamaica or back in England. Consul Edward March was invalided home in April 1882 after just a month in Panama, and six weeks later his replacement, Courtenay Bennett, reported that he had malaria, or "miasmic affections" as his doctor described it. By June the following year his replacement was also ill and had to leave the Isthmus. The melancholy pattern, which was shared by all the other European consulships, was repeated for the rest of the 1880s, which meant that the young Claude Mallet was acting consul for much of the decade.

Mallet reports a huge increase in the consul's workload as a result of having to sort out and return the effects of dead Jamaican laborers. He was also called on to help those abandoned by their employers, sometimes collecting sick men from the streets and conveying them to the hospital. Often Mallet would have to pay for the care out of his own pocket and take his chances that a tightfisted Foreign Office would refund the expense.

At the beginning of 1884 it was hoped that the advent of the dry season would again reduce the cases of fever, but it was clear that Panama was now in the grip of a major epidemic. Carelessly discarded spoil from the works had blocked watercourses and created permanent stagnant pools—ideal mosquito breeding grounds—all over the Isthmus. On January 21 the *Directeur Général* Jules Dingler's daughter Louise, a pretty, dark-haired girl of about eighteen, died, in miserable agony, of yellow fever. The family was beyond grief. "My poor husband is in a despair that is painful to see." Madame Dingler wrote to Charles de Lesseps in Paris. "My first desire was to flee as fast as possible and carry far from this murderous country those who are left to me. But my husband is a man of duty and tries to make me understand that his honour is to the trust you have placed in him and that he cannot fail in his task without failing himself. Our dear daughter was our pride and joy." The day after her death Dingler was back at work at the usual time.

It did not stop there. A month later Dingler's young son, Jules, sickened with the same disease and died three days later. The *Star and Herald* reflected the horror and grief of the whole community: "Mr. Dingler was but 20 years of age, the picture of physical health and strength . . . Sympathy is weak, and words are powerless in such a cruel blow, to convey to the grief stricken parents the sense of loss and sorrow which these sad events have occasioned in the minds and hearts of all." Soon after, Louise Dingler's young fiancé, who had come with the family from France, contracted the disease and also died.

The high-profile deaths in early 1884 caused a panic akin to that following the deaths of Etienne and Bionne back in 1881. Some three hundred French engineers applied to return home, and were refused. Nonetheless, men deserted from all parts of the line. For others, however, the specter of death served to raise their work to higher, sublime levels of heroism. They were sacrificing themselves, one young engineer wrote, "as surely as those who fought at Lodi or Marengo laid down their lives for France." Although the teachers in the engineering schools in France were now quietly trying to deter their pupils from serving in Panama, idealistic young Frenchmen continued to journey to the Isthmus. One such was twenty-five-year-old Philippe Bunau-Varilla, who arrived that year and would become a key figure in the history of the canal. He had met Ferdinand de Lesseps in 1880 and ever since had been in the grip of the Great Idea of the canal. He was the apogee of graduates from the elite Ecole Polytechnique, France's top engineering college, where military uniforms were worn and the motto was *La Patrie, les sciences, et la gloire.* For Bunau-Varilla, the canal was "the greatest conception the world has ever seen of the French genius." "The constant dangers" of yellow fever, he wrote in his autobiography, "exalted the energy of those who were filled with a sincere love for the great task undertaken. To its irradiating influence was joined the heroic joy of self-sacrifice for the greatness of France."

-◄◄◄◄◄- -►►►►►-

As Dingler pushed ahead with the work during the rest of 1884, achieving, in the circumstances, great progress, the death toll kept rising. In July, an outbreak of dysentery struck in Panama and Colón, filling the hospitals, while in the flood plains of the valleys, ideal breeding ground for mosquitoes, six out of seven Europeans working there during mid-1884 had contracted malaria or yellow fever. By the late summer of that year work was almost impossible in these sectors. One engineer told an American doctor that he had come over with a party of seventeen young French engineers. In a month all but one had died of yellow fever. At any one time, more than a third of the laborers were sick, making a mockery of Dingler's strenuous efforts to increase the workforce.

In October 1884 a floating hospital was set up in Colón Harbor to deal with the overflow from the hospital, where the nurses, the sisters under Marie Roulon, were also dropping like flies. By the end of the year all but three of the original twenty-four nurses were dead, and the annual figure for mortalities in the hospitals alone had tripled from the year before to nearly twelve hundred. If Gorgas's estimate of the true level of fatalities is to be believed, this meant that more than ten people were dying every single day.

Many on the Isthmus put these deaths from yellow fever down to the "abominable neglect of all sanitary measures" in the terminal cities. Where the French had jurisdiction, such as in Cristóbal, the new town built on reclaimed land to the side of Manzanillo Island, or in the settlements along the line, it was another story, but in Panama City and Colón the French were powerless. According to Charles Wilson, in Colón, "There was green water, and all kinds of rubbish and rotting things in the center of the streets." Certainly the lack of sewers and clean water would have contributed to the problems with dysentery, but, of course, they had nothing to do with yellow fever.

Others still subscribed to Dingler's original theory that "only the drunk and the dissipated die of Yellow Fever." The *Star and Herald* put the yellow fever deaths in Colón down to the "host of idle loafers, who infect the town and load the air with their obscene and vulgar epithets at every hour of the day." In April 1883 Wolfred Nelson was taken ill, but recovered, he said, "thanks to abstemious habits." "Woe to the feeble person who doesn't know how to quench his thirst!" wrote a senior French engineer. "He falls into drunkenness, and soon, aged, faded, with haggard eyes, shrunken, face drawn, yellow-skinned, he drags his broken spirit along in a body lacking in all vigour. And certainly he deserves it. It is fair that this shameful vice should be severely punished by nature."

There was certainly no shortage of "vice" in the terminal cities and along the canal line. In Panama, there were numerous bars, "designed for nothing but hasty drinking," according to a French engineer, ". . . horrible dens that look and smell like the filthiest grog shops." Colón, which retained its frontier town atmosphere, and where the bars would always stay open later than in Panama City, was the worst, "a veritable sink of iniquity," according to an American visitor. The single main street, running along the waterfront, he reported, "was composed almost entirely of places for gambling, drinking and accompanying vices . . . and these diversions were in full progress day and night with such abandon as to make the town uninhabitable for decent persons." Claude Mallet described the town as "the hardest drinking and the most immoral place I have ever known."

According to Tracy Robinson it was the fault of the "spirit of venality and corruption [that] pervaded almost the entire French Company," which "spread beyond the service itself, to debauch (there is no other word for it) the whole Isthmian community." Wolfred Nelson blamed the myth that any human being in hot climates requires alcohol. "Another point in this connection," he continued. "There is a general belief held by many intelligent people that a residence within hot countries has a marked tendency to increase the sexual instincts. Such is not the case. The real explanation is this. The majority are away from the refining influences of early culture and home life—generally they are single men,—in a warm climate where all the conditions are supposed to produce general relaxation. There is a little society open to such men. If they become 'one of the boys,'—and the vast majority do, that is the end of it, and generally of them too, for this means late hours, gambling and other distractions, largely *pour passer le temps*. Such men readily become victims to disease."

Doubtless, huge quantities of wine, champagne, and *anisado* were consumed during the French years. On one road in Colón where bars and prostitutes vied for trade, so many bottles were thrown out into the street that in time they formed a solid surface beneath the mud and when pavement-laying crews arrived years later there was no need for them to put down a gravel base. Supplies were imported from France and sold at wholesale prices to Company employees, who would then sell them on to their friends. Claude Mallet reported that he "could get claret for 6d a bottle . . . wines were so cheap that there was a habit of starting the day with a pint of champagne frappé 'to kill the microbes.' " There was, of course, a sensible reason for this, as Mallet explains: "No one dared drink the water that was sold in small measures from barrels." In addition, as Nelson says, there were few other ways *pour passer le temps.*

In mid-1883 de Lesseps announced that he had ordered the opening of "assembly rooms, provided with books, periodicals, and various indoor games" where employees could gather, but there is no evidence that this actually happened. Instead, in Panama City, employees had a choice between the "horrible" local establishments or the Grand Hotel. A young French engineer described the scene there: "A great enormous hall with a stone floor was the bar-room." In the center were two huge billiard tables and beyond them a vast bar. "In front of these rows of bottles with many coloured labels, most of the commercial business of Panama is transacted;—standing and imbibing cocktails,—always the eternal cocktail!" Across the hall was a little room crowded with people, "where roulette was going on." After each throw the croupier "announced the number in three languages: 'Treinta y seis, colorado! Thirty-six red! Trente-six, rouge!' Oh, this roulette, how much it has cost all grades of canal employees!"

"It was useless," he went on, "to look for other pleasures. They were nowhere to be found. In this town there was neither theatre, concert nor cafe, nothing but the hall of the Grand Hotel, to which one must always return."

Furthermore, as one French visitor explained, "passions run high owing to the constant proximity of death." Another wrote that "the Sword of Damocles hangs over everyone." The threat of fever, he said, explained the fever of gambling that gripped the Isthmus. "In this country," wrote Henri Cermoise, "death and *la fête* are perpetually hand in hand. Yellow fever threatens always and one is so unsure of tomorrow that one throws oneself into pleasures."

The fast, frontier-town lifestyle contributed to a general lawlessness on the Isthmus. In addition, the money being poured into the

great ditch had attracted to Panama numerous "foreign men of dubious reputation," in effect desperate and vicious characters from all
over Central America. The *Star and Herald* from this time is full of accounts of robberies and murders. In May 1883, for example, a man
was stabbed to death during an argument, "which as usual was occasioned by the vile rum which is sold so freely at all points on the
line . . . Human life," the paper concluded, "is held at too cheap a rate
on the Isthmus." The situation worsened as the West Indians started
arming themselves with revolvers to defend against machete attacks
from their Colombian enemies. As always, Colón fared the worst,
where the people were "an agglomeration of all nations, and tribes
and tongues, drawn from all lands and swayed by a thousand senti-
ments and impulses." During the rainy season, when the work on the
canal fell off, there were hundreds of unemployed in the town as the
steamers continued to arrive from Kingston, and "Fighting, drunkenness and the like are of everyday occurrences." Charles Wilson was
living in Colón's Washington Hotel. "There were all kinds of people
living in the town, and some of the worst kinds," he wrote. "When
you took a trip into it at night it was a question whether you would
come out alive or dead."

During 1884 there was widespread political instability in the
province, exacerbated by high inflation, food shortages, and the general social unrest the canal project was causing. At one point, in October, there were two rival state presidents, each with men under
arms in Panama City. The following year, this would lead to full-
blown civil war on the Isthmus, with serious consequences. Under
such circumstances, the authorities were utterly incapable of policing
the volatile streets of either of the main cities. Europeans and Americans increasingly looked to the foreign warships, frequently anchored in the bays of the terminal cities, for their protection. The
small police force was ineffective and partisan, preferring to extort
money from West Indians on the pretext of fines for vagrancy than
solve any crimes. Dingler offered to contribute money to the estab-

lishment of a new three-hundred-strong police force, but this foundered on local objections.

There was to be one more personal tragedy for the *Directeur Général.* Around Christmas 1884 Madame Dingler started showing the unmistakable symptoms of the dreaded yellow fever. She died on January 1, 1885, completing the total destruction of his family. At last, Dingler's heroic steadfastness was beaten. His wife had frequently gone riding on one of two magnificent horses worth 25,000 francs, which had been a gift from Gadpaille in Jamaica. After her death, the director did not wish to encounter anyone else on the streets of Panama riding these horses, so he ordered the beasts to be killed. The staff refused to carry out the command. Finally they found a poor fellow who was given the role of executioner, but at the last moment his hand trembled and he could not finish the job. For hours the horses were heard, partially disemboweled, screaming in agony. In the end they were shot dead. This execution figures in the accounts of the Company, and is billed as a hole of 33 meters paid at fifty piastres per cubic meter. Dingler was a broken man, deeply pitied by the canal workforce. He stayed on the job for another six months, but his wife's death ended his dynamic leadership of the canal project. He returned to France in June 1885 and, exhausted and heartbroken, was himself dead before the end of the year.

CHAPTER TWELVE

ANNUS HORRIBILIS

At least once a year U.S. naval officers would tour the canal works and then write lengthy and detailed reports back to Congress on the progress, or lack of it, of the French project. Sometimes these reports can read as if the authors had somehow become infected by the enthusiasm of their always generous hosts, or just by the sheer ambition of it all. But for the most part, with a crescendo as the years go past, the reports concluded that the current sea-level plan was running disastrously behind time and over budget. In the United States, de Lesseps's "friends"—many, officially or not, on the payroll of the Company—continued to defend the canal against its attackers. U.S. factories and workshops were kept busy supplying Panama's endless thirst for new and bigger equipment. But many shared the *New York Times'* view that the chance of the project ending in failure was "not unlikely." In the circumstances, commented the paper with not a little schadenfreude, "we can congratulate ourselves that it is chiefly foreign capital that will be swallowed up by it."

Occasionally, a different voice was heard. "Americans would much prefer that the American canal should be the work of Americans," wrote a Commander Gorringe in the *New York Sun.* "Evidently Americans had neither the courage nor the means to undertake it. The Frenchmen had; they have gone quietly to work; they ask us for nothing," What's more, he continued, all their efforts would assist no country more than the United States, "quite as much as British commerce and the British commercial marine were benefited by their work at Suez." Not that respect for the French travails should hamper strategic good sense. It did not matter who did the work, he argued, because, "When it is completed, if it becomes necessary or even important to our national welfare and safety that we should control it, there is no doubt that we shall take possession of the canal and the country through which it passes, with as little hesitation and trouble as the British recently took possession of Egypt and the Suez canal."

The U.S. Navy, deterred from establishing naval bases on the Isthmus, was now sniffing around a bay on the north coast of the Dominican Republic, strategically placed to guard the passageways into the Caribbean basin and a canal wherever it was situated, "which might," the British foreign secretary was warned by one of his diplomats in December 1884, "be so fortified as to become a second Gibraltar."

The same month, not coincidentally, saw the climax of the early American efforts to build a canal, for and by themselves, in Nicaragua, which remained their favored location for a waterway. Soon after the decision of the Paris Congress to plump for Panama, Ancieto Menocal, along with Admiral Daniel Ammen, ex-president Ulysses Grant, and others had formed the Maritime Canal Company, to fulfill their vision of the breakthrough happening in Nicaragua, regardless of what the French were doing in Panama. In 1880 Menocal had negotiated a concession from the Nicaraguan government to build his canal. Late the following year, they succeeded in getting a bill introduced in the Senate for political and financial guarantees to be given to the company by the government. The bill was passed around interminable committees, until at last, in mid-1882, it was voted on, narrowly failing to win the necessary two-thirds margin, helped by lobbying from de Lesseps's men in Washington and a feeling, as the *New York Times* put it, that "the time for guarantees and subsidies of bonds has gone by." The great railway boom had been underwritten by the federal government, but now the power of the railroad barons was a national bugbear. "Let them have protection and charters," the paper went on, "but let them persuade the capitalists of this country or of the world that they have a good thing and obtain their funds in a legitimate and business-like way. Therein at least they may take a lesson from de Lesseps."

Ammen was furious that support had been denied, telling the British ambassador that he was going to "abandon it as an enterprise backed by the United States' Government, and to seek the necessary capital in English and German markets for carrying out the work." Rather than being an American canal for Americans, it would be neutral and free to all, multilaterally guaranteed.

Blaine's successor as secretary of state, Frederick Frelinghuysen, was disappointed by the failure of the bill, for precisely this reason, muttering darkly to the British ambassador, "there is reason to believe that direct overtures were made to the German Government by parties interested in the Menocal Concession." But these efforts failed and the concession lapsed.

Frelinghuysen kept up negotiations with the British Foreign Office over altering the Clayton-Bulwer Treaty, albeit at a less shrill pitch than that of Blaine. But the Americans had little to offer in return for a move that would clearly benefit the United States at the expense of Britain, and got nowhere. Nevertheless, at the end of 1884 Frelinghuysen started fresh negotiations with Nicaragua for a canal treaty. A deal was signed on December 1. Anticipating ratification, Ancieto Menocal prepared to depart once more for another survey in Nicaragua, this time not as an employee of a private company, but of the secretary of the navy.

On December 10, the president, Chester Arthur, sent the treaty to the Senate with a strong message of recommendation. The work was too important to be left to private capital, he said. The Nicaragua canal would unite the country without recourse to the railway corporations, he went on, and deliver great benefits to U.S. trade and shipping. European grain markets would be brought in reach of the Pacific Coast states, and China would be opened up to East Coast manufacturers, who would now find themselves "midway between Europe and Asia." By building the canal, he argued, the United States would make itself the center of the world.

As the prospect loomed of two rival canals, the Mexican ambassador in Washington took the opportunity to pitch his homeland to the British ambassador there, Lionel Sackville-West. If the French and Americans were going to have their own canals, he told the ambassador, Britain should also have one, built at Tehuantepec. Sackville-West brushed this suggestion aside, but was keeping a close eye on the Frelinghuysen deal, which was in clear breach of the Clayton-Bulwer Treaty.

When it came to the vote, the "much divided" Senate found itself in a quandary, as Sackville-West reported back to London. If it was rejected, it would "be understood by European governments as a practical abandonment of the Isthmian policy, and entail humiliation. On the other hand its ratification would test the position of the British Ministry that the Clayton-Bulwer Treaty is still in force . . . but is the United States prepared for a controversy which might result in something more serious than diplomatic correspondence?" To overturn an international treaty was a very serious step, as was reflected by concerns in the country and press.

The treaty, which would have seen a U.S. government–funded Nicaragua canal, was rejected, with 32 in favor and 23 against, narrowly missing by five votes the two-thirds majority needed for ratification. Party jealousies contributed to the defeat, but the Senate was also swayed by another argument in favor of delay: the canal would be a liability, fortified or not, until the United States had a competent navy to police the strategically vital waterway. A motion to reconsider the vote was introduced, but the inauguration of Grover Cleveland in March 1885 saw a change in policy and outlook. In his inaugural address Cleveland signaled a return to the traditional aversion to "entangling alliances." He was also opposed to government involvement in "big business." Shortly afterward, he withdrew the treaty.

Thus America's canal effort passed back from government to be once again the responsibility of the "folly and gullibility of Capital." As hopes faded for Nicaragua, attention returned to Panama, where, whatever the setbacks, there were more men and machines at work than ever before. Suspicions of the French were mounting, with many believing that they were on the road to declaring a protectorate over a Panama state grateful to be detached from Colombian rule. In March 1885, the British minister in Bogotá had a conversation with his United States opposite number, who had recently been in Panama, in which the American "described every Canal functionary as, in his opinion, a French Government Agent in disguise." De Lesseps, he went on, was set on introducing French colonists to Panama, before annexing the whole of the Isthmus.

All the time, the political situation on the Isthmus was worsening. The scene was set for a show of military force by the United States.

◄◄◄◄— ►►►►►

The civil war in New Granada in the late 1850s had ended with the triumph of the Liberal faction, and the drawing up, in 1863, of a new constitution that enfranchised the lower classes, reined in the influence of the Church on national affairs, and gave considerable autonomy to provinces within the country, now to be called the United States of Colombia. This decentralization suited Panama, which had always been more racially and ecclesiastically mixed, liberal, and outward looking than distant Bogotá. But after a depression in the 1870s, caused in part by collapsing prices for Colombia's cash crops, there was a conservative backlash in 1884 led by the new President Doctor Rafael Núñez.

Núñez's efforts to reverse the Liberal reforms prompted civil war in mainland Colombia, which quickly spread to Panama, at a time when the French canal effort did not need new problems. In July 1884 an attempted Liberal coup in the province was suppressed with difficulty, and after further disturbances, martial law was declared and a military governor appointed.

Amid the growing anarchy, foreign consuls on the Isthmus hurriedly telegraphed for gunboats to be sent for their nationals' protection and on January 18, 1885, the U.S. Navy's *Alliance* was brought up alongside Colón dock, trained her three-inch guns on the town, and stationed men on the wharf and around the Panama Railroad offices, with particular attention to safes and vaults. The demonstration of American power provoked the resignation of the mayor of the town in protest, but calmed the situation for a while.

Allegedly the landing of U.S. troops had been at the request of the military governor, General Vila, but in Washington the Colombian minister shared his grave concerns with the British ambassador. Apparently, he had received a telegram from the government in Panama reporting that "the sovereignty of the State was in jeopardy." According to the Colombian, the danger "arose from the intrigues carried out by the United States' Government to obtain control over the Isthmus." The United States, he said, was "fearful of the establishment of a French colony . . . and would use the excuse of anarchy on the Isthmus to establish a filibustering colony."

In Colombia, the revolutionary party was in the ascendant, with Cartagena on the Caribbean coast threatened by a powerful Liberal army. The Colombian president responded by requesting that Vila send a loyalist force from Panama for the defense of the city. The general raised taxes further in the province and introduced conscription, but this merely led to another series of demonstrations against his regime. So Vila instead proceeded to the mainland with five hundred soldiers from the regular garrison. As it turned out, his action saved the city, and may have turned the course of the civil war, but it left only 250 loyalist troops in the province, most of whom were stationed in Colón. So it was in Panama City that Núñez's opponents first seized their chance.

On March 23, acting British consul Mallet brought the Foreign Office up to date on events in Panama. "My Lord, I have the honour to inform you," the letter begins, in the customary way, "that a Revolution broke out in this city on the morning of the 16th inst., . . ." "At 2 a.m. on the 16th," the *Star and Herald* reported a few days later, "General Aizpuru gathered his men, 247 in number, at the garden of Paraíso, where after receiving some drinks to fortify them for the dangerous enterprise on which they were about to embark, they proceeded to enter the city." The barracks and police station were speedily captured, but fierce fighting, in which some twenty people were killed, continued around the town hall, where the depleted Colombian garrison had taken refuge.

As soon as the diminished garrison departed from Colón on the railway to deal with this emergency, another Liberal leader, Pedro Prestan, seized his opportunity. With 80 men, he overpowered the small police force left guarding the Atlantic port and took control of Colón. Prestan, a mulatto and fervently anti-American, had a strong following among the poor and nonwhite in the town.

The Americans responded by landing troops from a warship, the *Galena*, to guard the railway and the wharf. Meanwhile, Prestan did his utmost to secure arms for his growing band of followers for the inevitable confrontation with government troops. After an uneasy truce of a few days, while in Panama City the government forces ousted Aizpuru, the hastily purchased weapons arrived in Limón Bay on a steamer from the United States.

The steamship line's agent in Colón was John Dow, an American with little love for Prestan or his followers. Dow refused to land the arms. Prestan was furious, and immediately arrested him, another Pacific Mail employee, the American consul, and two officers from the *Galena*, who had been with their men at the railroad.

Prestan also threatened to fire on any of the crew of the U.S. warships who disembarked and warned the U.S. commander in the bay, "Any aggression against us on the part of the U.S. ships will imperil the lives not only of the hostages but also those of your fellow-countrymen living in Colón." Prestan is quoted as saying to his staff, "I wanted to prove to these people that their nationality and race does not protect them from my revolutionary authority. For the first time in the history of America a mulatto has dared put his hands on white U.S. citizens, and this fills me with pride because I have vindicated by my act the dignity of the negro, outraged by the white man across the centuries." The quote has the whiff of subsequent invention or embellishment, but the sentiment is accurate. The U.S. consul, in fear for his life, urged Dow to deliver the arms. Dow consented, and the hostages were released. However, at this moment the captain of the *Galena* took possession of the shipment of weapons in the name of the government of the United States, and the hostages were quickly rearrested and taken to the rebel's position on Monkey Hill.

Here, Prestan's men were awaiting the rumored return of government forces from Panama City. One hundred and sixty men were indeed on their way by train. They disembarked at Mindi and proceeded to attack the rebel positions at dawn on March 31. Hopelessly outgunned, Prestan's men were driven back to Colón, where fierce combat continued for the next eight hours. At one point the fighting reached the walls of the British vice-consulate, where "rebel bullets and cannon balls . . . completely riddled the building." At four in the afternoon, with Prestan's forces on the brink of defeat, a fire broke out in the north of the city. Colón, almost entirely built of wood and lacking piped water or any sort of fire brigade, was soon an inferno, and in no time a rumor was circulating that it was Prestan himself who had ordered the fire to be started. Helped by a strong northeasterly wind, the fire burned for another twenty-four hours. Almost every building in the town was destroyed. Men were landed from the European warships in the bay to help save the foreign enclave of Cristóbal, happily separated from the main city by a shallow inlet, and soon the Americans and government troops were restoring order by shooting suspected looters. Within two days, the rebels had been destroyed or captured, although it seemed that Prestan himself had escaped.

In Panama City, Aizpuru had taken advantage of events at the other end of the railroad to launch a fresh attack. Fighting continued for eleven hours. "The firing was hot and reckless in the extreme," Mallet later reported. "Thousands of cartridges were burned as the scarred and wrecked appearance of walls and interiors sufficiently prove." By the end of the day, Aizpuru was victorious, and on April 1 declared himself the military and civil chief of the city.

The bloody fighting and the tragic events in Colón had, however, given everyone a moment of reflection. Neither the government forces, now in control of what remained of Colón, nor Aizpuru in Panama City had sufficient force to overwhelm the other, and they signed an agreement to suspend hostilities for a month, "to preserve the capital from criminal elements, and to give security to interoceanic traffic." It seems it was an effort to prevent foreigners from having an excuse to intervene.

But U.S. naval forces, including marines, were arriving in strength. The USS *Shenandoah* anchored off Panama City on April 6. The *Alliance* returned on April 8. Two days later the USS *Tennessee*, with an admiral aboard, appeared off Colón, together with a steamer of the Pacific Mail line packed with marines. More vessels arrived and by April 15 an entire marine brigade, along with two or three support battalions of bluejackets, was in place. Together with four field pieces, 170 men were ordered ashore on April 8, and armored railway cars to protect the transit were improvised with weapons and boiler plate from the ships. By April 18, according to Mallet, there were some five hundred U.S. troops based around the railway station in Colón, armed with a battery of Hotchkiss and Gatling guns and

Dahlgron howitzers. In Panama City were a further three hundred men, with another two hundred scattered along the railway line. Offshore at either end of the line were half a dozen U.S. warships with a further 1,800 men and thirty more field guns. It was the largest overseas military expedition to be mounted by the United States between the Mexican War of 1846 and the war with Spain in 1898.

In mainland Colombia, Núñez's party was gaining ground against the revolutionists, and a loyalist force was being assembled at Buenaventura to depose Aizpuru in Panama. The general started erecting barricades in the city and preparing for a siege.

To the Americans, this was unacceptable. To protect foreign property and interests, troops were ordered out of their barracks and off their ships to take control of the city. Barricades were removed, and key positions in the city secured. All the bars and saloons in the town were closed down, and Aizpuru, together with his senior officers, was arrested. "The entry of the American marines into the city was a complete surprise for everyone and occasioned great excitement," Mallet reported. "The belief among natives was that the city was to be taken away from them; patriotic feelings were raised to a fever pitch, and threats were openly made that unless General Aizpuru was released and the American force withdrawn every foreigner would be assassinated, and the town reduced to ashes." The U.S. commander reassured the Panamanians that "the presence [of the U.S. force] is only temporary and simply to restore law and order. The idea of occupation or annexation of the Isthmus is one that has never occurred to the American mind." On the evening of April 25, Aizpuru was released, having promised to respect foreign nationals and not to fight within the city limits. The U.S. force, now 1,200 men with twelve howitzers, retreated back to the railway station and everyone waited for the arrival of the Colombian loyalist soldiers.

Two days later, their ships were seen anchoring off Taboga Island in the Bay of Panama. By now, Aizpuru had lost too many of his men to desertion to risk fighting, and he surrendered to Colonel Rafael Reyes, the loyalist leader, on April 29. The next day, the Colombians landed and over the following week the American troops retired to their ships.

Aizpuru was later fined and exiled, and a witch hunt was launched against his and Prestan's erstwhile supporters, with Jamaicans and Haitians singled out for special treatment. Many were shot out of hand, and others languished in jail without a trial for up to four months. Two were hanged on May 6 for starting the Colón fire, even though, while incarcerated on a U.S. warship, they had helpfully signed testimonies which pointed the finger of blame at Prestan.

Prestan himself had escaped to the state of Bolívar but after the fire found himself friendless and soon fell into the hands of government troops, who returned him to Colón to face trial for arson. Held on August 17, it was a military tribunal on which sat a motley collection of soldiers and locals, all enemies of the accused. Four witnesses were called for the prosecution, foreigners, none of whom actually saw the fire being started, although they testified that Prestan had threatened to burn the city at some point or other. In fact, it is unlikely that Prestan was responsible. He owned property in the town, had his wife and daughter living there, and had nothing to gain militarily from the act. But the verdict was never in doubt. None of the witnesses requested by Prestan in his own defense appeared, and the tribunal ordered that Prestan be hanged. The sentence was carried out the next day at noon, on a scaffold made out of railroad ties erected in one of Colón's main streets, a stone's throw from the entrance to the new canal. "I saw no sign of fear," wrote Claude Mallet, who was a close witness to the execution. "As he was dying he made no struggle and kept moving his arms as a sign of farewell to the crowd."

-◀◀◀◀◀-▶▶▶▶▶-

The whole dramatic episode had many important repercussions. It had now been firmly established that the real power on the Isthmus was the U.S. military, and with the defeat of the Liberals, control of

nasty coda to the whole affair. On May 3, the tensions simmering between the Jamaican and Colombian workers came to a grisly head.
That night there was to be a circus performance near the work camp
at Culebra. The men had just been paid. The local *alcalde* (mayor) requested a picket of Colombian troops to keep order. Five men were
sent, but these were, according to Mallet, part of Reyes's newly arrived force, who "were ignorant of Isthmian affairs, and knew nothing of Jamaicans . . . and were animated only by a blind prejudice
against all people who did not speak their language." The soldiers
tried to go through the camp to reach the site of the entertainment,
but there was a rule that no armed men were allowed in the camps.
The Jamaican watchmen, not knowing for sure if the Colombian
troops were government soldiers or rebels, who were still roaming
the countryside in small parties, disarmed them, on the orders of the
camp chief, who said he didn't want a guard for the entertainment.
The men returned to their base at Emperador and reported what had
happened. Their commanding officer was incensed and ordered out
his whole force. On the way they were joined by a mob of Cartage-
nians armed with machetes and revolvers. The whole crowd seems to
have been well oiled, and there were raucous cries of *"Viva Colombia."*

It was about two in the morning when the troops reached the labor camp. The offending watchmen were tracked down first. Arthur
Webb, a Jamaican who had been on the Isthmus since 1882 and was
in No. 4 barracks, saw what happened: "I heard the watchman outside challenge some one who answered 'Colombian.' I opened the
door, and saw four men around one of the watchmen chopping at
him with machetes." Webb took to his heels, was spotted, and fired
at. The soldiers, some twenty-five in number, then attacked Webb's
barracks, where it was believed another watchman had taken refuge.

At three in the morning, when volley after volley had crashed into
the building or cut down the Jamaican workers as they tried to flee,
the door was smashed down with machetes. Jamaican Samuel Anderson had taken shelter under his bunk. From there he saw "a number
of Jamaicans killed and hacked to pieces, their boxes and trunks were

then broken open and robbed of their contents. Some Colombians then came into the barracks with kerosene oil and tried to set light to it. When I saw they intended to burn the barracks I left my hiding place. Several Colombians then seized hold of me, tied my hands, and struck me all over the head and body with the flat side of their machetes. I didn't resist and I was then made to accompany them to Emperador." Another Jamaican was also taken prisoner, but they turned out to be the lucky ones. Arthur Webb returned to his barracks early the next morning "and counted 23 Jamaicans lying killed, and hacked to pieces on the ground, and in their bunks. Some of them had their legs and arms chopped off, and many had their skulls split in pieces. Many of the dead appear to have been killed whilst attempting to dress." He found that his possessions had been stolen, including $200 he had saved in the last three years. The floor of the barracks was awash with blood and the whole place scattered with the ransacked contents of the workers' trunks and boxes. Isaiah Kerr, a Jamaican who lived at nearby Las Cascadas, came to Culebra that morning as usual and "on entering No. 4 Camp I saw my brother Augustus Kerr, who worked there, lying dead on the ground, his throat had been cut and one of his legs were gone. Many other Jamaicans were lying about dead and wounded." He found that his brother's clothes and money had "been taken away, and I could find nothing belonging to him."

The Colombian authorities suggested that the Jamaicans had started the aggression by firing on the Colombians, but the witness statements, carefully gathered by the British diplomats, contradict this story. "I have never before witnessed anything so horribly sickening as the scene of the butchery at the camp," C. H. Burns, an American canal contractor, told Claude Mallet. "Some of these unfortunate labourers lay upon their beds with only a night shirt on." He saw no weapons among the mutilated bodies. "It is not the first outrage upon Jamaicans, and all growing out of the prevailing hatred which the natives bear the 'Chombo,'" he said.

Samuel Anderson, taken prisoner that night, was confined in jail at Emperador. "I remained in prison for nine days," he said, "four days of which I was kept with my feet in the stocks, and I was without food or water for 48 hours. On Monday 12th of May the judge at Emperador told me if I gave him fifteen dollars he would let me go. I had a watch in my possession, which I pledged for seven dollars which I gave to the judge, and he released me. On my return to the camp at Culebra I found all my clothes, and money had been stolen, and I am left without anything."

A shocked and furious Claude Mallet demanded an investigation, but met only delay and prevarication. Important papers had, it seemed, gone missing. Rafael Reyes, now promoted to general, wrote to the *Star and Herald*, trying to excuse his men, but the paper did not believe him: "In all these fights between Jamaicans and Colombians," it said, "the former are invariably represented as the aggressors, and as invariably are they beaten, demoralized and cut to pieces . . . it was a massacre, pure and simple." The Panamanian government assured the governor of Jamaica that his countrymen were safe, but Mallet told him that such promises were "worthless," and are only made "with a view of inducing Jamaica negroes to leave their homes and come to the Isthmus." In fact, the massacre was symptomatic of a wider disregard for the rights of the imported workers: "It must also be borne in mind," Mallet wrote to the authorities in Kingston, "that British subjects have suffered as much from constitutional as from the Revolutionary authorities. Alcaldes, prefects, judges and all in authority have paid little attention to the rights of the negro from Jamaica. The poor negro has been the legitimate prey of Executive and Judicial outrage of the gravest and most serious character. The records of this Consulate are made up largely with the story of their wrongs. The powerful Companies that bring them have taken little interest in their welfare and make no active efforts in their favour when they fall into the hands of the authorities."

The fallout was both immediate and long-lasting. The Jamaicans fled the camp at Culebra, and within days no one who had worked there was on the Isthmus any longer. All along the line, Jamaicans abandoned the works to return to the safety of Kingston. Nor did the shocking events of that night lead to any change in the attitude of the locals to the Jamaicans. Those who remained were increasingly forced to arm themselves, and tensions rose further. Although new laborers did continue to arrive from Jamaica, the appeal on the island of "Colón Man" was tarnished forever. Never again was the Company able to marshal such numbers of workers on the project as had been there at the beginning of 1885.

⧸⧸⧸⧸⧸⧸⧸⧸

*E*ven before the civil war, fire, and subsequent events, confidence in the success of the canal was seeming more and more far-fetched. In early March, Mallet had reported to London the visit of de Lesseps's second-oldest son, Victor, along with others high up in the Paris Canal Company. They had professed themselves pleased with what they had seen, "with the conviction," Mallet wrote, "that the enterprise will be ready for the world's commerce at the end of 1888. I may remark in passing," he added, "that there are few intelligent people outside of Canal circles, who share the sanguine expectations of these gentlemen . . . dissatisfaction and anxiety prevail." Apart from anything else, the shock at the death of the last of Dingler's family was still being felt.

With the fire came a worsening of the bottleneck at Colón for the import of machinery and supplies, and the massacre at Culebra had led to labor shortages all along the line. April saw exceptionally heavy rains, which held up the work and exacerbated the problem of landslides. "The Panama canal is in such a state that its ultimate completion is beyond question," wrote the *New York Tribune* in May, "but it appears equally certain that the present company can never complete it . . . In going over the canal route, one gets the impression that the work is practically stopped."

But in some areas the sort of technical breakthroughs predicted by Ferdinand de Lesseps were occurring. Philippe Bunau-Varilla had been appointed chief engineer of the Pacific Division of the canal, even though he was only twenty-six. Through a study of the Bay of Panama he had accurately predicted that submarine trenches dredged there would stay free of mud and sand, thus dismissing a major worry in that sector. In recognition of this progress, in April 1885 he had been appointed head of the Atlantic Division as well. Here there was another breakthrough. The dredges of Huerne, Slaven & Company had been held up by hard rock at Mindi. When such material had been encountered at Suez, for instance between Bitter Lakes and the Red Sea, dams had been laboriously built, the area drained, and excavation had continued "in the dry." But at Mindi, Bunau-Varilla, recalling an earlier experience in France, ordered a series of underwater holes to be drilled in the rock, a yard apart. In each was placed dynamite, which, when exploded, reduced the rock to paving-size slabs, which could then be dealt with by the dredges. Thus the cost of underwater excavation was reduced to that of cutting "in the dry," and with even better methods and machines, Bunau-Varilla surmised, could be made yet cheaper. The realization would lead to a clever suggestion to save the French canal.

It is difficult to get a handle on the extraordinary figure of Bunau-Varilla. There is little doubt that he was an engineer of genius, as well as having other talents, as would emerge later. In his own writings, however, he has an egomania verging on madness. It is reported he spoke—and he certainly wrote—not in sentences but in proclamations. Nevertheless, he was adept at making friends. Short, only five feet four, he had perfect posture and a luxuriant dark red moustache. Many of those who met him found him an eccentric and slightly overwhelming figure. "Mr. Varilla's tremendous mental capacity becomes apparent when one looks at him," wrote an American whom Bunau-Varilla would later befriend. "His brain rises from an active, rather square face, but, as if to contain it, the sides of his head are much larger than the face." "His versatility was fantastic," wrote another admirer. "He had the energy of ten horses." No one who met him ever doubted his fanatical devotion to the achievement of the canal, at whatever cost and by whatever means.

But time was already running out for de Lesseps's sea-level plan. By summer 1885 the excavation was falling seriously behind schedule. Menocal visited in August and reckoned that only 8 million out of the 120 million cubic meters needed had been excavated since the very start of the project. Furthermore, much of the money raised had been spent. In spite of de Lesseps's assurances that all the problems were surmountable, the Panama shares began to fall a little on the bourse. The days of boom in the French financial markets had passed with the collapse of the Catholic Union Générale bank in late 1882. In place of the frantic speculation of the time of the launch of the Canal Company, traders on the bourse were just as likely to be bear raiders, seeking through a variety of schemes to lower the price of the shares in such an enormous company in order to profit on the change in market price. Criticism continued in the newspapers. In London and New York the financial press was loud in its condemnation. In response to the undeniable reports of deaths from illness, a cartoon appeared in *Harper's Weekly* asking: "Is Monsieur de Lesseps a Canal Digger, or a Grave Digger?" Even in France, doubts began to be aired.

At the opening of the Company's July 1885 annual general meeting, the reality of the situation was beginning to undermine the faith of even the strongest believers in de Lesseps's Great Idea. Worries were expressed about the financial state of the company, the falling rate of excavation, the sporadic labor troubles, and the terrible rate of attrition from disease. De Lesseps countered with an inspired bout of oratory, speaking, without notes, for an hour, announcing that he would launch a lottery to raise the extra 600 million francs more he now said were needed. Furthermore, he would personally visit the Isthmus to inaugurate the "final stage of construction." It says much for his magnetism that he was still able to charm an overwhelming vote of confidence from his audience.

It was a lottery bond issue that had saved the Suez Canal. In 1867, after the failure of a bond issue, de Lesseps had issued 5 percent lottery bonds, with four prize draws a year, each offering a 250,000-franc top prize. It had been a huge success and ensured the opening of the canal two years later. But under French law such an issue was restricted to undertakings of national importance and required a specific act of Parliament. Straightaway, de Lesseps found the government of the republic less helpful than had been the Imperial Senate. Although the Company organized, at great expense, a flood of petitions in favor of the legislation, the minister of works took no action until December, when he ordered a senior and scrupulously honest government engineer, Armand Rousseau, to go to Panama to give judgment on the project. In Rousseau's hands, it seemed, was the future of the canal.

In the meantime, after a gap of two months after the departure of Dingler, a new *Directeur Général*, Maurice Hutin, had taken over in September. There had already been drift in the leadership of the project, but Hutin himself left Panama only a month later, struck down with yellow fever. He would survive and return to the canal story later, but again there was a vacuum at the top of the organization on the Isthmus. Into the breach stepped twenty-seven-year-old Philippe Bunau-Varilla, as acting chief engineer.

His duties at either end of the canal had already stretched the young engineer, leaving him time, he says, for only two or three hours' sleep a night, but he took on the new role with enthusiasm. His first initiatives were to improve recruitment and labor relations and to set a monthly excavation target of 1 million cubic meters for the first few months of 1886. With patriotic rhetoric, he urged on his French engineers and technicians.

Before the end of the year, however, disaster struck again on the Isthmus. On December 2 a violent storm lashed the Atlantic seaboard, with winds of up to a hundred miles an hour. Vessels crowded into the exposed harbor of Colón tried to escape out to sea, but at least ten were driven onto the shore. Bunau-Varilla rushed to the port, concerned above all about the safety of the newly built embankment of Cristóbal. At the harbor he was met by a terrible scene. Boats were smashed on the rocks or overturned, with their crews clinging to them like "a human bunch of grapes." The seawall at Cristóbal survived, but more than fifty sailors were drowned. Meanwhile "Rain poured in torrents," the *Star and Herald* reported. "The Chagres River has risen over twenty feet above its level." The river was soon in huge flood, discharging twenty-five times its normal volume of water. In a stroke, much of the work and equipment were submerged.

The next day, with the sky again clear, Bunau-Varilla inspected his sector. "The points where my locomotive passed on the previous day were now covered by fourteen feet of water," he wrote, "so I requisitioned three Indian canoes . . . as we paddled along through a channel apparently cut out of virgin forest all the workings were submerged and the tops of the telegraph poles were scarcely visible above the water." After one canoe was damaged, the party had to crowd into two boats. "The load was almost too much," Bunau-Varilla continues, "and the freeboard was not more than an inch above water. One of the engineers, a M. Philippe, said that he couldn't swim. I told him jokingly, 'There is no danger. I could easily swim with you to the nearest trees.' It was only then that I noticed the strangest phenomenon: the tops of the trees were not their usual green, but a distinct and ever-shifting black; as we drew nearer I saw they were covered with the most enormous and deadly spiders: tarantulas."

The damage from the floods was straightaway noticed by Lieutenant William Kimball, who toured the works soon after to write the latest U.S. Navy report on the construction. At Bohío Soldado he found 3 million cubic meters of sand deposited in the trench by the subsiding waters, with railtrack and spoil cars buried to the depth of 2 meters. Kimball's report provides a fascinating and evenhanded snapshot of both progress on the works, and also, more generally, of life on the project at the turn of 1885–86. In some places he noticed progress from the findings of a report twelve months earlier. Work on the repair of the wharves had proceeded quickly. In *la grande tranchée* between Bas Obispo and Culebra "some very good work has been done," even if a lot of it was by "hand-drills, small blasts, and hand work." At Matachín, the central machinery depot, almost entirely staffed by Americans from New Orleans, seemed efficient and well equipped, although it had cranes too light for the task. In general, the accommodation and infrastructure seemed to have improved, with the exception of the hospitals, which had proved inadequate for the number of sick.

Kimball noted with interest the construction of a dam on the Río Grande to enable dredges to be floated further upriver—testament to Bunau-Varilla's idea to excavate as much as possible "in the wet." It was also hoped that the flooding of the marshes would "improve the sanitary conditions near La Boca, which are at present very bad." The water, it was believed, would prevent the "miasma" disturbed by the excavation from affecting the workmen.

Elsewhere, the lack of overall progress from the year before was more evident. At the site of the crucial dam at Gamboa, work had hardly started, and in the Paraíso section at the Panama City end of *la grande tranchée*, he noticed severe problems with slides. "The slips are not earth slides from the top of the bank," he wrote, "but rather movements of the whole hillside, which in some places carries one bank almost intact across the cut with the top surface unbroken, and with the vegetation undisturbed." Looking up, Kimball could see both the railway line and a channel built to keep the Río Grande from the canal suspended on the hillside 30 and 50 meters respectively above the new ditch. "There is a substratum of greasy clay all along the line," he reported. "It would seem as if both the deflection of the Río Grande and the deflection of the railroad must slide into the canal."

All along the line there was the impression of spoil carelessly dumped, damaging the railroad embankment in one place, narrowing the Chagres in another, contributing to the flooding. The machinery he saw in action was "considerable," but impressed him "as neither large enough nor of the right kind." The American Osgood and Mc-Naughton steam shovels were doing a good job, as were the U.S. and Scottish dredges, but they were too few in number. There was a lack of power drills and the French and Belgian ladder excavators were "ineffective." The miracle machines that had dug the sand out of the Suez Canal had come to grief. "When working in soft earth, free from stones and roots," wrote Kimball, "there is no doubt that the chains-of-buckets machines have a greater capacity than those of the steam-shovel, American type; but these perfect conditions are not to be had."

There was also a lot of idle machinery, testament to failed experiments and other factors. In one place five excavators were seen delayed for lack of spoil trains. This was due to an absence of proper switching arrangements to transport the earth to a dump only half a kilometer away. At Matachín a contractor had stopped work as he hoped to get a higher price for removing rock that had not shown up on borings. In general, the hundred or so small contractors seemed to be getting in each others' way, particularly over spoil removal. Furthermore, some of the companies, Kimball said, were "irresponsible parties," who gave up when the going got hard or less profitable. Others did not have the necessary financial resources for what they had taken on and, forced to borrow from Isthmian bankers at 2 percent per month, soon went under. Either way, the results were delays, machinery standing idle again, and the inevitable demands of new contractors for more favorable terms.

Stoppages were also caused by labor shortages, arising not just from fear of further political violence, but also from the "forethought of others, who decide to leave the Isthmus before they are killed by the climate . . . by the poor quality and high prices of provisions; by the exorbitant rates charged for small drafts by the small bankers, who control such business; [and] by the lack of sufficient guarantees for hospital attendance." Furthermore, the "men are in the habit of returning to their homes to spend what they accumulate, often leaving the works at the very time when from conditions of weather or arrangement of plant they can least conveniently be spared." All this contributed to a turnover of workers of some 80 percent a year.

Kimball also reported the tensions between the French and their U.S. colleagues on the project. Apparently, the Americans were being accused of sabotaging excavators in order to stop the work, so their government could take control of the canal, "and other wild statements." Perhaps Bunau-Varilla's patriotic rhetoric had sharpened divisions. Certainly, Kimball noticed great dedication on the part of some of the French engineers. The acting chief engineer, who showed Kimball "unremitting and repeated courtesies," explained it thus: "The contagion of my confidence in our success had taken hold of all my men," said Bunau-Varilla. "One man who fell was immediately replaced by another, and the battle went on." "It is an impressive fact that there is money value in the prestige of M. de Lesseps, the courage of the French and the determination to finish the canal," noted Kimball, "for otherwise the company would already have become bankrupt under the showing of 500m francs practically spent and not more than one tenth of the work accomplished."

In spite of this gloomy, and, as it turned out, accurate, assessment of progress, Kimball still believed the canal would be built. "That with sufficient expenditure of money, time, brains, energy, and human life, the canal can be finished is self-evident," he concluded, although refusing to estimate "the necessary quantity of all or any of them." If the money from the lottery was forthcoming "the canal will be so far advanced by the time the money for the new loan is expended that the necessity for finishing it will be apparent." Put another way, the temptation to throw good money after bad would be irresistible. This new financing was the key factor. "The Company has doubtless made some grave mistakes, but I am confident it has at its disposition all the necessary brains and energy," wrote Kimball. "As for human life, that is always cheap."

It has been suggested that 1885 was the blackest year of all for deaths from fever. We only have the figures for mortalities in the hospitals. For 1885, there was a similar official death toll as the year before, running at nearly a hundred a month, in spite of a slight lessening of the workforce. Records of burials in, for example, the foreign cemetery (of which Claude Mallet was the treasurer) suggest that these figures do not tell the whole story. On several occasions during the year Mallet was again called out to collect from the streets of Colón or Panama City the bodies of dead British subjects whom no one had been found to bury. There was a pattern of men employed on the canal or the railroad falling sick, being hospitalized at the contractor's expense, but then being discharged before fully fit. While looking unemployably ill, the patient would fall sick again shortly afterward—basically have another malaria attack—and find himself unable to afford to go to the hospital. Claude Mallet fought an ongoing battle with the Foreign Hospital to lower its costs of $2 a day, which he was obliged to pay for such "distressed" Britons. Many of these were railway engineers and laborers displaced from Peru by the war there at the beginning of the decade. But the hospital now had more patients trying to get in than they had space. And, Mallet was told, "under no circumstances would negroes be admitted."

The Company still had its fair share of shocks. In October 1885, Bunau-Varilla was sent two new engineers to be chiefs of division. Both, he reports, were dead from yellow fever within two weeks. "Many a man of them had been happy to enlist," he wrote of the still steady stream of new arrivals at Colón, "but felt his heart sink at the sight of the warm, low and misty shores of the deadly Isthmus. Some bore on their faces the obvious mark of terror . . ." To Bunau-Varilla, and others, it was this very fear that made someone susceptible to fever.

The French consulate had a terrible year, losing three diplomats and two of their wives in the twelve months. Within five months of each other, two Italian consuls had died. Both the Spanish consul and his wife came down with yellow fever. The wife recovered from her delirium to find that her husband was already buried.

The British consulate saw their Colón vice-consul, the young Fred Leay, who had so meticulously taken the witness statements from the Culebra massacre, come down with "Bilious Remittent Fever" and be invalided off the Isthmus. In January 1886, even Claude Mallet's hardy constitution was worn down, and he, too, contracted fever. He remembered lying in bed and hearing one of the three doctors called for consultation say that he would not live to see daylight again. "I had reached a state of semi-coma and did not care what happened," he later wrote.

Fortunately a new consul, Colonel James Sadler, had at last arrived to relieve him. Mallet was allowed to retire for a short while to the healthier climes of Jamaica where he would recover, but he would therefore miss the two vital visits—of the government inspectors and of Ferdinand de Lesseps—the following month. It did not take his replacement James Sadler long to look around and assess the importance to Panama of the forthcoming inspections. Writing to the foreign secretary the Marquis of Salisbury on January 27, he warned of the unpopularity of Núñez and the risk of further revolution on the Isthmus. Taxes and resentment were high. "Crime is frequent," he wrote, "and remains unpunished from want of means to support the cost of imprisonment, though political offenders are treated severely." Everything, he said, was riding on Rousseau's report. If it should be favorable and the lottery issue approved, "the condition of the country may improve." Otherwise, "should the works cease, fresh misery and disturbance would certainly occur on the Isthmus."

CHAPTER THIRTEEN

COLLAPSE AND SCANDAL

*R*ousseau arrived on January 30, 1886. With him, to relieve Bunau-Varilla, was a new *Directeur Général*, thirty-five-year-old Léon Boyer, along with his own handpicked cadre of sixty engineers. Boyer was well known in France, having dabbled in politics, and also had a reputation as a brilliant civil engineer. He was a very good catch for the Company. Also on the boat was Charles de Lesseps, in theory writing a report of his own, but in reality keeping an eye on Rousseau and preparing for the arrival of his father.

Rousseau was accompanied by two other government-appointed experts. For two and a half weeks they toured the works. In the meantime, flags and bunting were dusted off, streets cleaned, speeches and pageants rehearsed, and machinery, whether operative or not, whitewashed. *Le Grand Français*, the "Presiding Genius of the Nineteenth Century," was about to descend once more on Panama.

On January 31, 1886, John Bigelow learned that he had been invited, as a representative of the New York Chamber of Commerce, to accompany Ferdinand de Lesseps on his forthcoming visit to the works at Panama. Bigelow, lawyer, intellectual, former newspaper proprietor, and U.S. ambassador to France, had been at the lavish dinner for de Lesseps at Delmonico's back in March 1881. He was unsure whether or not to accept the invitation, and consulted friends and family. The first advice he heard was to have nothing to do with it, "that it was probably a scheme to use my name as an ex-Minister to France to bolster the stock of a chimerical enterprise." But then another friend urged him to "embrace any opportunity of associating my name with such a magnificent enterprise." Bigelow asked whether he could take his daughter Grace, for "her company and assistance." The reply came back in the positive—and all would be at the Company's expense, including "a satisfactory remuneration" for himself. "This point, I confess, weakened my scruples about going," he wrote in his private diary.

He accepted, but then spent a week worrying if he had made the right decision. Some big names, he learned, had said no. He was also worried about the illness on the Isthmus, and checked with a friend on the political situation to be reassured that the U.S. Navy was there in force.

On February 10 he left with Grace on the steamer *Colón*, together with a journalist and other representatives from U.S. chambers of commerce. A party had already left from France. Throughout their voyage, de Lesseps kept the fifty or so businessmen, engineers, and diplomats entertained with "witty lectures" and stories of his time in Egypt. "He is indefatigable and inexhaustible!" exclaimed Gustave de Molinari, an accompanying journalist from the *Paris Economiste*. For the benefit of his readers in France, de Molinari spelled out the huge responsibility resting on the shoulders of *Le Grand Français*: "The success of the Panama business does not only interest the investors in the Company, it interests all of France. We live in a time where the power and the vitality of people is measured not only by the deployment of their military might and the success of their weapons, but also by their spirit of enterprise, the grandeur and utility of their works. If the French construction of the Panama Canal were to fail, the Americans (who are well disposed towards the idea) would take it upon themselves to buy out the project that we have given up on. As a result, with a lack of confidence in ourselves, the prestige of France would suffer for a long time in both countries. It would be like losing a battle. Let's hope that the battle is won!"

The party from France reached Colón on February 17, 1886, just as Armand Rousseau was preparing to leave, his inspection completed. As before, de Lesseps, now eighty-one, had come at the best time of year and the weather was bright and dry. But Colón was still a wreck. A few houses had been rebuilt, and there were huge improvised market stalls. But in between, writes de Molinari, were "vast open spaces left by the fire where stagnant rainwater, blackened beams, corrugated tin twisted by the heat, broken bottles and plates accumulate." Mud and rubbish were everywhere, infested with toads, rats, and snakes, and "a myriad of mosquitoes breed in these low lying areas and spread through the mostly windowless houses and seek out their prey."

John Bigelow's party arrived the next day, after twenty uncomfortable days at sea, and in the evening met de Lesseps for dinner on the USS *Tennessee* anchored in the bay. Grace Bigelow was seated on de Lesseps's left. "I was pleased to find that Grace and the old Baron got on admirably together," wrote John Bigelow in his diary. "Went to bed about eleven but was too heated and excited by the events of the day and evening to sleep well."

For the next three days there was an exhausting schedule of visits to the nearby works and workshops, and trips on boats along the river and the completed section of the canal. Bigelow was suffering in the heat, changing his clothes twice a day, was horrified by the price of clean water and the filthy latrines, but was impressed with much of what he saw. At one chantier, he noted how the black laborers gave de Lesseps a warm reception: "When we left they gave us repeated cheers which the old Baron returned with bows." On board one British-built dredge, he noted approvingly its "immense power."

New, even bigger machines were just around the corner, the visitors were constantly told.

Bigelow struck up a close and lasting friendship with Bunau-Varilla and also got on well with Charles de Lesseps, whom he called a "very clear headed and capable man." One evening, however, he was shocked to hear Charles confidentially and sadly prophesy that "two or three years hence the United States would follow the example of England in the case of the Suez Canal, purchase an interest in [the Panama Canal] and take a share in its management." In his diary Bigelow also noted private conversations he had with fellow Americans based on the Isthmus. Several who worked for the steamship companies told him that the Company would never finish the canal. Another told him that for the past nine years the corruption on the canal and on the PRR had been "shameless and that the Americans out there on the PRR rather excelled the French on the Canal."

After three days, the party headed across the Isthmus. For the arrival of de Lesseps in Panama City a huge pageant had been arranged. Everywhere de Lesseps was acclaimed on his passage round the town by "Vivas," shouts of "Long life the Genius of the Nineteenth Century; long live the Man of Progress, the Grand old Frenchman." Celebrations continued into the night with a torch-lit procession and, reported an exhausted de Molinari, "banquets, dancing, lights, fireworks and who knows what else . . ."

The party stayed for a further week, exploring the Pacific side of the works by day and dancing and banqueting by night. As before de Lesseps was "indefatigable," restoring confidence everywhere he went. "His stay is one continued fête . . ." wrote the new British consul James Sadler back to London. Had it been up to the people of Panama, he said, the lottery loan would be assured. De Lesseps confidently predicted that the year ahead would see 12 million cubic meters excavated; the next, 1887, would achieve twice that; and by 1888 there would be a monthly rate that would produce 36 million cubic meters for the year. With the same rate carried into the following year, he said, the sea-level canal would be completed by July 1889.

As the visitors prepared to return home, with no illness suffered, almost everyone declared themselves highly impressed. "I am delighted to say that our expectations were exceeded," de Molinari concluded. "Even if the piercing of the Isthmus presents enormous difficulties, the effort made to conquer them is in proportion. Never has such a colossal work been undertaken, never have capital and science so united to deploy such a powerful machine to bring to an end the resistance of nature."

John Bigelow was also overwhelmed by the grandeur of the project's ambition and size, writing that it had "no parallel among private enterprises in all history." He would remain a "convert" to the cause of Panama, infected with its fever, for the rest of his life. But in his widely read report he also repeated many of the criticisms of Kimball—that machinery was idle or discarded due to lack of leadership or system; that contractors were unreliable and corrupt; the challenges of the Chagres and the deep excavation in the Cut were not being met; that information from the company was "often conflicting and rarely more than approximative."

The fact that it was the dry season had not prevented him from noticing the "insalubrity" of the Isthmus, particularly in the swamp area at the Atlantic end. "You have a climate," he wrote, "where it may, without exaggeration, be said that—'Life dies and death lives.'" Although, he said, "human life is about the cheapest article to be purchased on the Isthmus," wages had steadily risen to keep attracting workers and mechanics to Panama, to a minimum of $1.75 silver a day, rising for skilled work to five times that.

Like Kimball, Bigelow believed that the fate of the canal would be decided by its finances. But he also agreed that "too large a proportion of its cost has already been incurred to make a retreat as good polity as an advance." In the meantime, the "people of small means" who held the Panama stock would stick by de Lesseps, Bigelow believed, because success "would rank among the half dozen largest contributions ever made to the permanent glory of France."

Remarkably, he also anticipated what would be the American

agenda in the next decade, a time that would see a radical change in the international balance of power and a transformation in U.S. foreign policy. An open waterway would, Bigelow suggested, "secure to the United States, forever, the incontestable advantage of position in the impending contest of the nations for the supremacy of the seas." But there was a serious caveat: until the money was secured, and, crucially, the cost of the debt ascertained, it was impossible to say when and on what financial or political terms the work would be finished. "And, for aught I see, this uncertainty must last until near the completion of the work," he concluded, "for nowhere in the world is the unexpected more certain to happen than on such a work at Panama. It is destined to be, from first to last, experimental . . ."

⫷⫷⫷‑⫸⫸⫸

While the Company, indeed, the whole of France, awaited the verdict of Armand Rousseau, de Lesseps tried a new tactic to raise money— selling bonds on the bourse rather than by private subscription. The experiment was not a success, with less than 40 percent of the issue sold, even at an interest rate approaching 7 percent. The decision on the lottery was now more important than ever.

Rousseau's report was submitted at the end of April 1886 to the new minister of public works, Charles Baïhaut. "I consider a cut through the isthmus . . . is a feasible undertaking," Armand Rousseau wrote, "and that it has now progressed so far that its abandonment would be unthinkable," a disaster not just for the shareholders, who were almost all French, but also "for French influence throughout America." If the Company failed, it would, he predicted, certainly be taken up by a foreign company, wanting to exploit the enormous sacrifices and the progress so far made. "I believe that the government should . . . assist it," he decreed. But before sending the lottery bill to the Chamber of Deputies, he warned, the government would have to content themselves that the Company was addressing the project's

"certain grave technical defects." "Important reductions and simpli-
fications" were needed if the project was to be completed in anything
like the time envisaged.

What he meant, though felt it was outside his remit to say, was
that the sea-level plan was unworkable and had to be altered before it
was too late. But, in combination with Rousseau's lofty ambiguity,
others were now spelling it out. Jacquet, another government engineer who had accompanied de Lesseps to Panama, reported to the
Cabinet that the sea-level plan was categorically impossible. It seemed
likely that the bill would never make it to the Chamber unless this issue was resolved. On the Isthmus, too, in spite of continuing strong
excavation figures for the early months of the year, Bunau-Varilla and
others were exploring alternative visions to de Lesseps's "Ocean
Bosporus." Léon Boyer, the new *Directeur Général*, took only a month
to make up his mind that a canal *à niveau* was simply unachievable
with the money and time at his disposal. Now, he urged de Lesseps,
only the rapid adoption of a lock-canal plan could save the project.

◄◄◄◄──►►►►

But de Lesseps was not to be moved. He reluctantly agreed to certain time- or money-saving modifications but on the key issue—the
conversion to a lock canal—he refused to comply with the wishes of
the government inspectors and the urgent appeals of his own senior
engineers on the spot. The promise of an open, sea-level waterway,
and its superior operating profits, had been the whole reason for
choosing Panama in the first place. De Lesseps had from the very
start nailed his colors to the mast by so energetically selling to the
French public the simplicity and beauty of the idea of a canal *à niveau*.
It would have been an embarrassing reversal if he gave in to the pressure.

By an unhappy coincidence, fever at a crucial moment robbed de
Lesseps of two experts who might have changed his mind. In May,

Boyer was suddenly prostrate, then dead. It was, the British consul reported, a particularly severe case of yellow fever. Bunau-Varilla, too, had "been awakened suddenly" one morning soon after the end of de Lesseps's visit, by "a violent vibration of my bed which I thought was a seismic movement." It was "the shakes," followed by a dose of fever, and before the end of April he had been invalided back to France. But even if the pair had been fit, it is uncertain whether de Lesseps would have listened to them. He didn't work by committee. At Suez, everyone had told him he was heading for ruin, but he had confounded his critics by never giving up. Panama, he now at last admitted, had proved many times more difficult than Suez. Yet to show weakness, he calculated, would surely be fatal to confidence.

The first reaction of the French Cabinet to the Rousseau report was to seek to delay making a decision. Then, to everyone's surprise, Minister of Works Charles Baïhaut drafted a bill in favor of the application and presented it to the Chamber. The Chamber appointed a committee, which heard from Rousseau, de Lesseps, and others. But still, as time ticked away for the effort on the Isthmus, nobody wanted to make a decision. On July 8, the committee adjourned for the summer undecided. In the meantime, they asked, could they have a look at the Company's books and contracts?

De Lesseps was incensed. He simply could not wait that long for new money, nor risk the final verdict going against him. And to open up the books would be a clear admission of guilt. It was unthinkable. The following day he withdrew the application, telling shareholders, "They are trying to shelve me—I refuse to be shelved . . . I work on, but not alone, assuredly, but with 350,000 Frenchmen sharing my patriotic confidence."

The last chance to save the French canal had slipped away, through a combination of the dithering of the politicians and de Lesseps's stubborn refusal to give up the sacred sea-level plan. Meanwhile on the Isthmus, of the sixty handpicked engineers Boyer had brought with him, nearly all were sick, demoralized, or dead. Since the advent of the rainy season, more than 80 percent of the chief officials of the Company were out through sickness. Of thirty Italians who had arrived together twelve months earlier, only five now survived.

S. W. Plume was an American railway man, a veteran of South American projects. In 1886, after two years on the Isthmus, he was in charge of a gang of about a hundred workers, replacing rotten ties on the railroad. "Every month or two I would lose a man, perhaps two men," he told a U.S. Senate committee some years later. "I will explain it to you. If a man gets wet there with the rain he is sure to be sick the next morning . . . I never saw such a climate in all my life, and I have worked in the rice fields of South Carolina, and gracious only knows that is bad enough."

The streets now saw a constant stream of funeral processions, and trains ran all the time to the cemetery at Monkey Hill. "When I first went there," said Plume, "we used to run one train—perhaps it would be a car or two boxcars—in the morning out of Colón, to Monkey Hill." But by 1886, it was "bury, bury, bury, running two, three, and four trains a day with dead Jamaican niggers all the time. I never saw anything like it. It did not make any difference whether they were black or white. They died like animals." In response, wrote the "occasional correspondent" of the *New York Tribune*, the Company's senior employees showed "insane recklessness" and took up a "habit of life . . . such as would result in wide-spread disease in any hot climate, even the most salubrious." The drinking of alcohol would start at breakfast and would continue all day. In the evening, when it was too hot to read or play cards, it would be more of the same.

⟪⟪⟪‹-›⟫⟫⟫

*I*n spite of all this, the Company kept up a monthly excavation rate of a million cubic meters through mid-1886, according to Bunau-

Varilla, who returned, after convalescence and now immune to yellow fever, late in the year. In the circumstances this was impressive, but anyone who wanted to could see that this was still not nearly enough to complete a sea-level canal within reasonable time. In the Culebra Cut, which had to be dug in places to a depth of over 300 feet, only an average of 12 feet had been removed, a paltry rate of just three feet a year. The Anglo-Dutch Company had been taken on in December 1884 and contracted to remove from Culebra 12 million cubic meters in four years, but after eighteen months had managed less than 1 million. As Bunau-Varilla wrote, they had proved to be "a dismal failure." "During the dry season," he explained, "the works seemed to justify the best hopes. As soon as the first rains began, the dumps began to slide, the tracks were cut, and general subsiding of the ground inside the cut paralysed any movement of trains, and often overthrew the excavating machines."

They were dismissed and a new contract was awarded to Artigue et Sonderegger. The new contractor's guiding light was Bunau-Varilla, whose brother was also high up in the same company. The new contract was part of a wider reorganization. One outcome of de Lesseps's visit was that in mid-1886 the job of digging the canal was given to six large firms rather than the host of small contractors. This certainly helped reduce the suffocating bureaucracy of the Company and avoid the confusion and waste symptomatic of the "small contractors" period. But it was expensive. Numerous firms had to be paid off, and the new work was inevitably contracted at a higher rate. Huerne, Slaven was kept on, with an even better deal. Artigue et Sonderegger's remuneration was so lavish that it led to the resignation of the Company's secretary in Paris.

There, the Company directors still hoped that the French government would rescue the project. After all, wasn't Charles Baïhaut, the minister for works, telling anyone who would listen that he believed in the canal, whatever the Rousseau report had said? In the meantime, the Company directors issued more bonds with some success, but at a ruinously high interest rate.

At last de Lesseps began to give way. In January 1887, he ordered his technical advisory committee in Paris to meet to consider the possibility of a lock canal. But he remained insistent on the original vision of an open waterway, demanding that all projects that construed permanent locks be excluded. Again, there was a delay. A subcommission was appointed which did not report until the autumn. The result was indecision on the Isthmus, as the latest U.S. Navy inspector, Lieutenant Charles Rogers, reported after his visit in March 1887. The progress of the previous year had, he said, been "creditable," virtually meeting Ferdinand de Lesseps's target of 12 million cubic meters. But he was doubtful whether the rate of excavation could be doubled in 1887, as planned. Moreover, he calculated that the Company had only enough money to continue for another three and a half months.

Nonetheless, Rogers, as many before him, was overwhelmingly impressed with the ambition of the scheme and the dedication of the project's leaders on the Isthmus. "The most bitter opponents were our own countrymen and a few Englishmen or former employees of the canal who had been discharged or had some other grievance against the company," he remarked at the end of his report. Such types "were prone to exaggerated statements . . . or else malice." "The contractors are young, zealous, and energetic men," said Rogers, "the engineers are . . . both clever and capable, and no one can appreciate more than these men the difficulties that lie in their path. Instead of censure and detraction, they deserve the highest praise and respect . . . they wish well to an enterprise fraught with so much good for the human race, and they are doing their utmost under the circumstances to promote its success."

Not all the Frenchmen on the Isthmus, of course, were quite so high-minded. At thirty-seven, Paul Gauguin had gone from riches to rags. His job as a broker had not survived the downturn of 1882, and he had since ruined his finances and his health through his taste for absinthe. In 1886, his long-suffering Dutch wife gave birth to their fifth child, and, with the situation desperate, he called on his wealthy sister, Marie, for help. She agreed to appeal to her husband, Juan N. Uribe, a rich Peruvian businessman who had offices and outlets all over and in particular, of late, in Panama. In the country where France was digging the canal, money was being made by the fistful and Uribe's fortune, it seemed, was benefiting from the project. Gauguin learned that Uribe was setting up a brokerage office and bank and needed someone who knew finance and could be trusted to replace him when he took his holidays in Europe.

In March 1887, Gauguin resolved to try his luck on the Isthmus, writing to his wife, "I will set off for America. I cannot continue to live here swamped by debts, a stultifying and lacklustre existence." The plan was to settle in Panama, in the benign glow of the inspiring great work, and send for his family once he was established.

He arrived at Colón at the end of April, together with his friend, fellow artist Charles Laval. They were unimpressed with the town where, it seems, new hovels had sprung up since the fire, but nothing had been cleared away. In Panama City there was further disappointment. His brother-in-law was not running a bank but a general store, and not a very grand one either. There was certainly no work to be had for Gauguin. Finding that the price of land in Panama had so risen that it was unfeasible for him to settle there, Gauguin headed for the island of Taboga, which he hoped to find "practically uninhabited, free and fertile . . . the fish and fruit can be had for nothing." "I'm taking my paints and brushes," he wrote to his wife, "and will, living like a native, immerse myself far from mankind."

But he was in for another disappointment. Taboga had become something of a tourist trap. It was the favored location for picnickers and day-trippers, and was dominated by the large sanatorium, to which well-favored Company employees would retreat to be free, for a while, of the stultifying heat of the mainland. Well-organized guided tours crisscrossed the island. The "native villages" had long ago wised up, and were now more than a little sham.

Gauguin returned to Panama, but the hotels were expensive, and his money was now running out. His friend Laval got work painting portraits of some of the better-off Company officials. Gauguin declined to do this, instead getting himself taken on as a laborer on the canal works. There he found that rumors were rife of the impending bankruptcy of the Company, and the reality of the job was far from the noble project he had envisaged. Gauguin was set to work with a pickax, chipping out holes for the dynamiters who would follow him. "I have to dig from five-thirty in the morning to six in the evening under tropical sun and rain," he wrote to his wife. "At night I am devoured by mosquitoes." The death toll wasn't that bad, he added sardonically, "only 9 out of 12 of the negroes die while for the rest it is a mere half."

Gauguin resolved to work only as long as it took to earn the fare off the Isthmus. But after a couple of weeks he fell foul of the new law-and-order regime of General Vila, who was back in Panama as Núñez's strongman, determined to stamp out dissent and resistance to firm rule from Bogotá. Gauguin was arrested for urinating in a street, which, he protested, was an open sewer anyway. He was imprisoned and then fined. Eventually back at work, he had just saved enough from his pay of 600 francs a month for the fare to Martinique, when he was laid off, along with a raft of other workers, on orders from France.

Together with Laval, Gauguin left for Martinique on June 8. On their arrival Laval came down with a fever, probably malaria. During one cycle of the disease, he became so depressed that Gauguin had to prevent him from committing suicide. Soon after, Gauguin, too, was ill. "During my stay in Colón," he wrote to his wife, "I was poisoned by the malarious swamps of the canal and I had just enough strength to hold out on the journey, but soon as I reached Martinique I collapsed. In short, for the last month I have been with dysentery and marsh fever. At this moment my body is a skeleton and I can hardly whisper; after being so low I expected to die every night..." His stomach cramps and continued weight loss were probably due to amoebic dysentery, which had by then developed into what would to-day be diagnosed as hepatitis or an abscess of the liver.

The sacking of Gauguin was part of a general freezing of the Company's activities. It was more than indecision about the issue of locks. Money had pretty much run out, as Rogers had predicted back in March. Nothing more could be done until the outcome was known of de Lesseps's latest attempt to float a stock issue.

This time only just over half of the stocks were taken up. It was hardly enough to paper over the cracks. And again the money was ru-inously expensive. By late autumn the Company's finances were once more in a perilous state, and speculators had forced the value of the original canal shares to a new low on the bourse.

But at last, in October, a full two and a half years after the Rousseau report and Léon Boyer's advice had been received, Ferdi-nand de Lesseps gave in to pressure to redirect the works toward the completion of a lock canal. What de Lesseps's commission recom-mended was based on experience on the Isthmus. Following the suc-cess of the excavation "in the wet" at Mindi, after underwater blasting, several contractors had been experimenting with creating ar-tificial lagoons along the line of the canal, and then assembling and launching waterborne dredges. These machines filled barges, which were then towed underneath a fixed-ladder excavator. This emptied them and lifted the spoil onto waiting trains or piped it out of the way. Thus water, rather than rail—vulnerable to rain and slides—would be used to carry out most of the moving of spoil. This led on to the new scheme. If pools could be created all along the route, separated by locks, then underwater excavation could continue with the canal open to traffic. As the various levels were lowered by dredging, the locks—five on either side of the Divide—could be gradually removed until the entire canal was at sea level. In the meantime, a working, and pay-ing, lock canal would have been created, it was estimated, by 1891, but, crucially, only as a means to the completion of what Bunau-Varilla called, "the perfect, the final, project" of a canal *à niveau*.

Characteristically, Bunau-Varilla claims the entire credit for this plan. In fact, he had, in early 1887, built dams at either end of the Cut and experimented with excavating "in the wet." Whoever's idea it was, its strength did not lie in its engineering aspect alone. Indeed, the cost of the gradual transformation would still have been prohibitive. In addition, the constant supply of water to the summit level of the canal, essential to operate the locks, was dependent on vague, unsurveyed schemes to build tunnels or viaducts from higher up the Chagres River. But the beauty of the plan was the distance it went toward reconciling the reality in the Culebra Cut with selling the change of plan to de Lesseps and his army of supporters, who had for years been persuaded of the overwhelming superiority of a sea-level trans-Isthmian route.

There was still the question of finding the new 600 million francs that this work had been estimated to cost. The following month de Lesseps reapplied to the government to run a lottery, outlining the temporary locks plan. At the same time, he announced that France's most brilliant engineer, Gustav Eiffel, had accepted the task of constructing the locks. Eiffel was newly famous as the creator of the giant iron structure just being started in Paris for the 1889 exposition. He was a good catch for the Company, although his name and expertise, it later emerged, came at an outrageous cost.

Eiffel swung into action and by January 1888 his men were on the Isthmus starting the excavation of the lock basins as the giant iron parts began to be shipped from France. In the meantime, de Lesseps set out to sell the new plan to the stockholders, reassuring them that the original vision was postponed, rather than lost, and that by 1890 the canal would be sufficiently advanced for the passage of twenty ships a day.

From the government, however, there was an ominous silence. Then, after two months of deliberation, the Cabinet announced that they would not be submitting the necessary lottery bill to the Chamber of Deputies. Once more the Company launched itself into lobbying, organizing petitions, and, it later came out, outright bribery of politicians. So, in early March, nine deputies of various political complexions introduced the bill the government had refused to back. Yet another commission was appointed to investigate.

De Lesseps could not afford to wait, and had to go with another bond issue. He promised that if the lottery was approved these new bonds could be converted to lottery bonds. But the issue in March 1888, the eighth in as many years, was the worst yet, with only a quarter being taken up. Clearly no more money was going to be forthcoming from this route. Soon after, de Lesseps was forced to borrow 30 million francs at a ruinous rate from his "friends" at the Crédit Lyonnais and Société Générale banks to keep the Company afloat. The lottery was now the only hope.

It looked at first as if the commission would reject the bill, but after the surprising last-minute change of mind of Charles François Sans-Leroy, a hero of the Franco-Prussian War, it was approved by a margin of 6 to 5. The debate in the Chamber, which was packed with canal supporters, on several occasions degenerated into a brawl. Nonetheless, the bill was approved by a wide margin on April 28, and was rubber-stamped by the Senate on June 8, though the Company was compelled to state in its loan prospectus that the granting of permission implied no government guarantee or responsibility.

Shares in the Company, which had fallen to a low of 250 francs in December, now soared. On the Isthmus, Bunau-Varilla believed that nothing could now stand in the way of the successful completion of "his" plan. In the Culebra Cut, he now only had to lower the floor to 140 feet above sea level, rather than 30 below. He was confident he could do this in three years, and now had nearly three thousand men on the site, working around the clock with the assistance of recently installed floodlights. The actual results of his company, Artigue et Sonderegger, do not back up Bunau-Varilla's boasts. In addition, in spite of the harsh regimes of Vila and his Conservative successors, tension and violence among the workers was again on the increase, made worse as the Company was forced to look farther afield for recruits, bringing new communities, such as Africans and Puerto Ricans, into the volatile racial mix. Yet whatever the chances of success with the lottery money secured, it was certain that should the issue fail, then all would be lost.

⤜⤜⤜⤜⤜ ⤛⤛⤛⤛⤛

The lottery bill authorized the Company to borrow an additional 720 million francs, 600 million for the completion of the work and the rest for investment in French government securities to guarantee payment on the bonds and to furnish the cash prizes. Bimonthly drawings promised maximum wins of nearly 700,000 francs. Against their better judgment, the Company was persuaded by their bankers to offer the entire sale of two million bonds in one go. It would start on June 20 and run for six days.

The Company threw everything it had at efforts to promote the sale, spending, it came out later, over 7 million francs on "publicity" and over 3 million francs on "patronage." No one in France was unaware of what was at stake.

On the morning of the start of the sale, someone put a hoax notice out by wire that Ferdinand de Lesseps had died. There was an instant denial, but the damage was done. Two days later speculators dumped Panama shares on the bourse, causing a sharp fall in their value. By the end of the six days, although 350,000 people had subscribed, three times the 1880 figure, less than half of the bonds had been sold. Money, it seemed, was exhausted. Once the sum had been put aside for interest and the prize fund, the Company had gathered in only a little more than 100 million francs, a sixth of what it required.

Still, de Lesseps refused to accept defeat. On August 1, addressing the annual general meeting, he urged his troops on to one final, patriotic effort. "All France," he announced, "is joined in the completion of the Panama Canal. Actually more than 600,000 of our compatriots are directly interested in the rapid success of the enterprise. If each of them will take two lottery bonds or get them sold, the canal is made!"

Then de Lesseps and his son Charles set off on a grueling tour of twenty-six French cities, with Charles now doing most of the speaking, while his father's presence still guaranteed huge turnouts. "Spontaneous" local committees were organized by the Company to recruit new investors.

The remaining bonds went on sale on November 29, with a final exhortation from de Lesseps: "I appeal to all Frenchmen," he said. "I appeal to all my colleagues whose fortunes are threatened . . . Your fates are in your own hands. Decide!" By this time, the price had been cut to just 320 francs, with generous terms for paying in installments. It was decided that unless four hundred thousand were sold the subscription would have to be annulled.

Soon after the opening of the sale, bear raiders made another attack. By December 8, lottery bonds on the bourse were selling for 40 francs less than de Lesseps was asking. The final day of the sale had been set for December 12. The day before, the American journalist Emily Crawford visited the Company's headquarters at 46 Rue Caumartin. The hall of the building was packed with investors, "flushed and excited, but willing to stake their last penny on the hope of retrieving their fortunes . . . They were like desperate gamblers," Crawford would report in the *New York Tribune*, "whose hopes rise highest when their losses have been greatest." The crowd grew in number and noise, until suddenly at 4:00 p.m., it was hushed by the appearance of Ferdinand de Lesseps. The old man clambered onto a counter in the corner of the room and cried out: "My friends, the subscription is safe! Our adversaries are confounded! We have no need for the help of financiers! You have saved yourselves by your own exertion! The canal is made!" So overcome that he was weeping, de Lesseps joined the crush in the room, shaking the hands of his exultant, cheering investors.

No details were given, but soon rumors were circulating that 800,000 bonds had been sold. The next day saw the same chaotic scene in the Company headquarters, and then, late in the afternoon, Charles de Lesseps appeared. How had the subscription gone? everyone asked. "The subscriptions reached a total of 180,000 bonds," Charles began in a low voice. "This being below the minimum fixed by M. de Lesseps, we will commence returning the deposits tomorrow. You see, I am telling you exactly how things are."

There was a shocked, dazed silence. How had the picture changed so radically overnight? someone asked. "My father is younger in spirit than I," Charles replied. "His remarks were made on the strength of a hopeful report . . . the result is bankruptcy or the winding up of the Company."

In desperation Ferdinand de Lesseps placed before the Chamber of Deputies a bill authorizing the Compagnie Universelle to suspend payments of all debts and interest for three months, while he attempted to float a new company. On December 15, the Chamber threw out his bill by 256 votes to 181.

Ten minutes after the vote, a reporter called at de Lesseps's house with the news of the bill's rejection and his company's liquidation. The old man turned pale. "*C'est impossible*," he whispered. "*C'est indigne.*"

⫸⫷

*T*he crash of the Compagnie Universelle was the biggest of the nineteenth century, and the greatest since the markets began. The liquidation wiped out the hard-earned savings of eight hundred thousand private investors. A staggering one billion francs ($280 million) had been expended, and the Company had liabilities of nearly three times that sum. *Le Grand Français* made one last, fruitless effort to save his company, with a spectacularly unsuccessful bond issue in January 1889, but the next month an official receiver was appointed. De Lesseps never recovered from the blow, retiring to his country house at La Chesnaye. His great will finally broken, he quickly lost awareness of the world around him, preferring to stare out into the garden, or sit musing by the fire. By the summer of 1889, he was often confined to his bed.

When the news of the liquidation arrived in Panama, it was, according to Tracy Robinson, "like a stroke of paralysis." Foreign consuls had been predicting fierce riots, and gunboats had arrived offshore from France, Britain, and the United States. There were disturbances, but on the whole a sense of dumb shock prevailed, as contractors and workers alike laid down their tools, the giant machines were shut down, and peace returned to the jungle for the first time in seven years.

All along the line thousands of laborers found themselves suddenly thrown out of work. Shops closed as merchants pulled down their shutters and relocated, the prostitutes and professional gamblers set off for more inviting pastures, the railway closed down stations, and the banks suddenly stopped honoring checks from the Company. Rent rates and land values collapsed just as immediately.

Within no time at all, the workforce had fallen from 14,000 to just 800 involved in basic maintenance. A large number of those laid off left the Isthmus, either for home or for other employment in the region. Many of the workers, however, found they had insufficient funds for the rail fare to Colón, let alone the steamer back to Kingston. Slowly, they made their way on foot to Colón, where they congregated in desperate groups.

"There are hundreds [of destitute Jamaicans] absolutely starving," reported the *Star and Herald* in early April, "who have not tasted food for days . . . Despair is taking possession of the people." Many sought the help of Claude Mallet, who telegraphed the Jamaican government to send steamers to pick the men up. Receiving no reply, he was forced to feed 1,500 out of his own pocket. Eventually the government of Jamaica agreed to start bringing their thousands of destitute countrymen home. In all, 7,244 were repatriated. Some six thousand Jamaican men, women, and children were left behind when the fixed period for repatriation ended, and most took up residence in shanties along the line, growing bananas and other crops for subsistence. Many refused to believe that the project could really be abandoned.

-‹‹‹‹- -›››››-

*I*n France, in the immediate aftermath of the great crash, when attention was diverted by the great exposition of the centennial of the French Revolution, there was a similar refusal to accept the end. Surely the French government would come to the aid of the scheme? But stern warnings from the new U.S. president Benjamin Harrison not to interfere ended what little inclination the French Cabinet might have had to do so. As this realization percolated through the country, the fever of recriminations began.

Petitions from bondholders seeking redress from the government poured into the Chamber of Deputies. At the same time, rumors of wrongdoing in the Company and in the government gathered momentum, and best-selling books were published on the "Scandal of Panama." *Le Grand Français* was a fraud, a cheat, and a liar, one alleged. "What have you done with the money?" the author asked de Lesseps.

An examining magistrate was appointed, whose first step was to summon the eighty-six-year-old de Lesseps, his son Charles, and another senior Canal Company director. Ferdinand de Lesseps, against the advice of his doctor, roused himself, donned his uniform of a grand officer of the Legion of Honor, and went to meet the investigator. According to Charles, "He had apparently recovered all his strength; he remained three quarters of an hour . . . and when he left his face radiated charm and energy as it always did under difficulties. But the reaction soon set in; it was frightful." Back home, the old man took to his bed and hardly spoke to anyone for three weeks, except to say to his wife, "What a terrible nightmare I have had. I had imagined I was summoned before the examining magistrate. It was atrocious."

The magistrate's report, delivered in May 1892, accused the Company of "dissipating" funds "in a manner . . . more consistent with the personal views and interests of the administrators and direc-

tors . . . than with the true interests of the company." Second, they
were culpable of repeated "false announcements of progress," which
concealed the "true situation" and misled investors. The files were
handed over to the public prosecutor, who took his time sifting
through the evidence, while police raided the offices of ex-canal officials and engineers, including Gustave Eiffel.

Meanwhile, revelations came thick and fast. More than a hundred
deputies, it was suggested, had taken bribes from the Canal Company.
The cabinet was forced to resign, duels were fought, and a formal
parliamentary investigation ordered, while criminal proceedings were
brought against de Lesseps, Eiffel, and other Company officers.

Soon "the Panama Affair" had outgrown its original focus and
became a general stick with which to beat one's political opponents.
Out in the country, too, the word *Panamiste* now had a wider meaning
as synonymous with corruption anywhere. On January 6 a large anti-
Semitic rally was staged in the center of Paris, where the speakers
proclaimed the Panama disaster the fault of the Jews, who, they said,
were now laughing at France's misfortune. While most of the crowd
cheered, a small number protested. A fight broke out, which degenerated into a riot. Paris was jumpy. A bomb in a police station was
blamed on anarchists, whose numbers were swelling as disillusion
with the government grew. Then, amidst talk of a royalist coup, military units were put on the alert. Foreign consuls described France as
on the brink of a revolution.

Such was the backdrop for the sensational trial of de Lesseps father and son, Eiffel, and two other Company directors, which started
on January 10, 1893. Ferdinand de Lesseps was excused from attending because of his rapidly fading health. The defendants were well
represented. Neither Ferdinand nor Charles de Lesseps had made any
real money from the canal, their lawyer pointed out. Clearly, neither
had benefited from any fraud. As for maladministration or misleading the investors, didn't every great project run vastly over budget?
The Marseilles Canal was supposed to cost 13 million francs, but was
not finished before an expenditure of 45 million francs; the Man-

chester Ship Canal, too, had massively exceeded its budget. If the de Lessepses had sinned, the defense argued, it was only through "excessive optimism."

But the public clamor for a scapegoat had made the advocate general determined to get a conviction, describing the attempt to build the canal as "the greatest fraud of modern times." Ferdinand de Lesseps and his son were both indicted for fraud and maladministration and given five-year prison sentences. Charles de Lesseps, his face in his hands, wept as the judgment was handed down. It was taken for granted that his father, who, reportedly, was not even aware that the trial was taking place, would not be fit to go to prison. Two other directors got two years and a fine. Eiffel, found guilty of making a 7-million-franc profit for work he had barely started, was sentenced to two years' imprisonment and a fine of 25,000 francs.

Four months later the sentences were quashed on a technicality by the Supreme Court, but by then the situation had worsened for Charles de Lesseps. The parliamentary investigation, carried out in a febrile atmosphere of allegation and counter-allegation, had turned up one sensation after another.

The Chamber of Deputies Committee did genuinely try to answer the question posed back in 1890: what happened to the money? Much, it was immediately apparent, had gone to the large contractors taken on in late 1886. Few of them had achieved a fraction of their contracted total excavation, but some had somehow, nonetheless, cleared huge profits. The various banks and syndicates that handled and occasionally underwrote the bond issues had also made eye-wateringly huge profits from their business with the Company. Some 10 percent of the Company's total receipts, over 100 million francs, had disappeared against the cost of the flotations. Part of this cost was money paid to the press, and not all of it for advertising space. Twelve million francs had been distributed between 1880 and 1888, it emerged, with the largest "subsidy" going to *Le Petit Journal*, which had stayed loyal to the Canal Company right till the end. An astonishing 2,575 magazines and periodicals had received cash payments to plug the canal venture, including, bizarrely, *Marriage Journal, The Poetic World,* and *Foresters' Echo.* Some small journals, it appeared, had been established purely to benefit from the "Panama Check."

And when the Company became involved with the government over the lottery request, it had found a whole new raft of even greedier and more dangerous parasites. Check stubs were found that indicated that the former minister of works, Charles Baïhaut, had received 375,000 francs as payment for forwarding the original lottery bill to the Chamber back in 1885. Among others who had received bribes was Charles Sans-Leroy, who at the last minute had changed his deciding vote and thus ensured the success of the second lottery bill application. The evidence caused a sensation, and a new word, *chéquard*—check taker—entered the French language.

The corruption trial opened in March 1893, with Charles de Lesseps and the Company secretary accused of making bribes, and five deputies and one senator of receiving them. Charles de Lesseps, in prison since December, seemed a different figure from that of the first trial. His "face was drawn and his skin yellowed," and his earlier courteous manner had been replaced by a quiet outrage. He was not guilty of bribery, he argued, but a victim of extortion. The minister for works had demanded a million francs to keep the lottery bill alive, he testified. The 375,00 francs was just the first installment. When the bill was subsequently rejected, Charles de Lesseps had refused to pay Baïhaut any more. Since the failure of the very first share issue in August 1879, Charles said, the Company had found it necessary to pay for press and political support, and for the goodwill of the bourse. "They seemed to rise up from the pavement," Charles said of the *chéquards.* "We had to deal with their threats, their libels, and their broken promises."

Charles Baïhaut tearfully confessed to having received money from Charles de Lesseps for his support of the lottery bill. But Sans-Leroy insisted that although he had suddenly paid off debts to the tune of 200,000 francs, the money had come from elsewhere. Likewise, the other politicians denied any wrongdoing. For the verdict on March 21, 1893, the aroma of whitewash was heavy in the air. All of the deputies but Baïhaut, who "had been stupid enough to confess," were acquitted of the charge of receiving bribes. Nonetheless, Charles and an intermediary he had used were still found guilty of bribery and were sentenced to one year's imprisonment each. Baïhaut was given five years' solitary confinement in the notorious Étampes prison, a huge fine, and was ordered to repay the bribe. Should he be unable to manage this, Charles de Lesseps became liable.

A few months after his second trial, Charles de Lesseps was allowed to leave prison to visit his father on a day release. Accompanied by two policemen, Charles made the journey to La Chesnaye. His father greeted him with "Ah, there you are Charles . . . Has anything new happened in Paris?" The old man never asked about the ever-present policemen, and after a long walk with his father in the woods near the house, Charles was returned by his guards to his prison cell.

Soon after, Charles became ill and was in the hospital when released in September 1893. But within a couple of months he was forced to flee to London, having become liable for Charles Baïhaut's fine. By this time, Ferdinand de Lesseps's mental state was mercifully such that he knew little of what was going on, and he remained sequestered at home within the family circle. He died in December 1894, a few days after his eighty-ninth birthday. However many people had lined their pockets at the expense of the shareholders, de Lesseps had not been among them. His family were so poor that the funeral expenses had to be met by the board of directors of the Suez Canal.

⋘⋙

*T*he waves of scandal did nothing to help the receiver in his battle to rescue something from the mess on behalf of the investors. The option of abandoning the project altogether was seriously considered, but the impossibility of dividing up the remaining assets among the legion of creditors, of all descriptions, and the almost negligible return it would have meant, persuaded the liquidator that the best option was to keep the concern alive—either to press on and build the canal, or sell it to the highest bidder.

A new concession was negotiated with Colombia, and in October 1894 the Compagnie Nouvelle du Canal de Panama was formally incorporated, paid for by contributions extracted under threat of criminal prosecution from those who had made the most outrageous profits from the old Company. Eiffel was one such "penalty shareholder," as was Bunau-Varilla. Only the American company, Huerne, Slaven, "one of the enterprises which made some of the most scandalously excessive profits out of Panama," escaped, having their books in the United States, safely out of reach. In all cases, "penalty shareholders" were forbidden involvement in the running of the new company.

The whole effort of the New Company is characterized by caution and parsimony. In the absence of any firm blueprint, the desultory work undertaken was concentrated in the Culebra Cut, which would need to be lowered whatever the final scheme decided on. Efforts were made to attract investors, while keeping the canal a French project. To make it more sellable, a detailed plan—for a lock canal with a dam at Bohío—was put together by yet another international commission of experts. Bunau-Varilla, acting independently and considered something of a liability by the New Company directors, even managed to catch the interest of the tsar of Russia after a fortuitous meeting with a Russian prince on a train to Moscow. But nothing came of it. No private company had the enormous resources needed for such a project, and no foreign government would dare defy the United States by setting up in their backyard. At the end of 1898, with the original capital almost gone, the directors had only one choice. Reluctantly, clutching their latest plans, they headed to Washington where they were received by President William McKinley.

According to Bunau-Varilla, the Americans received the offer with "scepticism." "It would never have come to anything," he said, "had I not at that moment begun my campaign." How the Americans came at last to take over the Panama Canal, in a U.S.-controlled zone of a newly independent country, is as controversial and murky a story as any from the de Lesseps years.

PART THREE

The American Triumph

What is Costaguana? It is a bottomless pit of ten-per-cent loans and other fool investments. European capital has been flung into it with both hands for years. Not ours, though. We in this country know just about enough to stay indoors when it rains. We can sit and watch. Of course, some day we will step in. We are bound to. But there's no hurry. Time itself has got to wait on the greatest country in the whole of God's universe . . . We shall run the world's business whether the world likes it or not.

—U.S. financier Holroyd in
Joseph Conrad, Nostromo, *1904*

CHAPTER FOURTEEN

HEROES AND VILLAINS—
THE "BATTLE OF THE ROUTES"

The skepticism of the American leadership in late 1898 had noth-ing to do with the principle of a U.S. government–owned and con-trolled canal in Central America, nor with the "entangling alliances" that it would inevitably involve. In fact, the 1890s had seen the United States become more outward looking and expansionist than ever be-fore. Important thinkers like Alfred Mahan, whose *The Influence of Sea Power Upon History* was published in Boston in 1890, were arguing that a canal, guarded by an expanded navy, was necessary not only as a means of commercial expansion for the now preeminent U.S. econ-omy, but as a conduit for sea power (what Mahan saw as the truest judge of a nation's greatness). Above all, the canal presented itself as a way of spreading "superior Anglo-Saxon civilisation" across the re-gion.

The war with Spain in 1898, motivated in part by fears of German ambitions in the region (Admiral Tirpitz had declared an interest in German control of a Panama Canal), had seen the acquisition by the

United States of the Philippines, Puerto Rico, Hawaii, and, effectively, Cuba, and the need for a short sea route to link these new possessions, as well as the two coasts of the mainland United States, seemed more urgent than ever. Before the war, McKinley had set up the Isthmian Canal Commission under Rear Admiral John G. Walker to study the canal question, but it was an incident during the fighting that effectively ended the long-standing objection of Congress to taking on the work as a government-funded project. At the beginning of the conflict, the United States' most powerful battleship, the *Oregon*, stationed in San Francisco, found herself marooned far from the action. The vessel was ordered to proceed at once to the Atlantic, a 15,000-mile course around the Horn. Sixty-seven days later, its heroic progress followed daily by the press, the warship arrived to join the decisive Battle of Santiago Bay. The demonstration of the military significance of a shortcut through an isthmian canal could have been made to order.

"The construction of such a maritime highway," proclaimed McKinley at the end of 1898, "is now more than ever indispensable." The president also instructed his secretary of state, John Hay, to restart negotiations with Britain to rid the United States of the restrictions of the Clayton-Bulwer Treaty.

Already, there was legislation for an American canal progressing through Congress. In June 1898, when it became known that the Isthmian Canal Commission under Admiral Walker intended to recommend the construction of a waterway at Nicaragua, Alabama senator John Tyler Morgan introduced a bill allowing for the building of a fortified Nicaragua canal by the U.S. government. Morgan, who chaired the Senate Committee on Interoceanic Canals, had been a colonel in the Confederate Army during the Civil War, and believed that a canal through Nicaragua would return to the South the prominence it had lost since the war and make the ports of Mobile and Galveston thriving hubs of trade. By the late 1880s the construction of a Nicaragua canal had become an obsession, and he had many times argued unsuccessfully for congressional support for the private company that actually started work on a Nicaragua canal for a short time in late 1889 before going bust. Like de Lesseps, Selfridge, Menocal, and Ammen, Morgan was gripped not only by the Great Idea of an Isthmian canal, but by a clear view of a waterway of a particular type, in this case a lock canal at Nicaragua. His obduracy would have serious consequences. Morgan's bill came up for debate in January 1899, when the ink on the Treaty of Paris with Spain was barely dry. It passed through the Senate with ease, and was presented to the House of Representatives.

Although Walker's commission had visited the French works at Panama, such as they were in early 1898, at no point had the Panama route been considered a serious option. The scandals in Paris, the well-publicized attrition from disease, and the seemingly insuperable engineering and political problems had given Panama a distinct odor of failure. There were a scattering of voices raised for Panama, including that of John Bigelow. Despite his largely pessimistic report in 1886, Bigelow had become infected by the project. But supporters were few and far between and had no representation in either house in Washington. Nicaragua, on the other hand, was seen as a clean slate—free of the taint of poisonous European influence. As the *New York Herald* wrote, "The Nicaragua canal is a purely national affair, conceived by Americans, sustained by Americans, and if later on constructed, operated by Americans according to American ideas, and for American needs. In one word, it is a national enterprise." All seemed set fair for the Nicaragua route, which would make the New Company's property worthless. It appeared it would take a mighty battle and a miracle of persuasion to change the nation's preference.

William Nelson Cromwell and Philippe Bunau-Varilla were two of the most skillful lobbyists ever to work the corridors of power in Washington. It was largely as a result of their efforts that American engineers would, in 1904, arrive to restart work on a canal not, as everyone expected, in Nicaragua, but in a newly independent and U.S.-controlled Panama. Their contribution would also see the

Panama Canal at its rebirth mired, as before, in controversy, scandal, and recriminations.

Cromwell was one of history's great fixers. From a modest Brooklyn family, he was, like Bunau-Varilla, short of stature and fatherless, and he shared the Frenchman's aggression and determination. By the age of thirty-three he had risen to become the guiding light of one of Wall Street's preeminent corporate law firms. Sullivan and Cromwell, as it became known, was a new type of company, born out of the railroad boom, offering all sorts of services from finance and accounting to press relations and political lobbying. Above all, the firm was ferociously well connected. Its clients included the huge railroad companies and the nation's most trusted banks, including JP Morgan; and, starting in 1896, to represent their interests in the United States, the Compagnie Nouvelle du Canal de Panama.

It was a good choice by the directors in Paris. Cromwell knew the Isthmus, having been general counsel, a director, and a shareholder in the Panama Railroad for three years. But, above all, he was a superb operator. Affable, with disarming manners, he was known as "The Fox" because of his extraordinary cunning. "He is one of the readiest talkers in town. No life insurance agent could beat him," wrote the *New York World*, which would lead the investigations into the "Scandal of Panama." "[He] has an intellect that works like a flash of lightning, and . . . swings about with the agility of an acrobat . . . He talks fast, and when he wishes to, never to the point." As well as his contacts and his lawyer's talent for obfuscation, Cromwell had the crucial ability to master such a complicated brief as that presented by the French. He did not come cheap: he would bill the New Company some $800,000 for his services. But when the fee came up for arbitration in 1907, Cromwell was able to argue with justification that his services had "involved almost every branch of professional activity—engineering, law, legislation, finance, diplomacy, administration and direction."

As a "penalty" shareholder in the New Company, Philippe Banau-Varilla was barred from direct involvement with the running of the venture, but he had far from given up on his canal dream and the final accomplishment of "the Great Idea of Panama." Apart from anything else, he had over a million francs of his own money forcibly invested in the New Company. After the collapse of the de Lesseps setup, Bunau-Varilla had unsuccessfully stood for office in France, and then with his brother taken over a newspaper, *Le Matin*, as an alternative outlet for his campaigning for the completion of the French canal. In addition, on the prompting of his friend John Bigelow in New York, in 1892 Bunau-Varilla published a book outlining his plans for finishing the canal at Panama. Bigelow saw that it was distributed widely among opinion formers in Washington.

John Bigelow also provided introductions to influential Americans living in or passing through Paris. Even if Bigelow could not provide a link, Bunau-Varilla made himself the master of "chance encounters" and thereby managed to pitch for Panama to many U.S. citizens who, once converted, would be vital to his later efforts. Frank Pavey, an influential New York lawyer who would soon be working for Bunau-Varilla, described (for the benefit of a later congressional investigation into the whole "Panama Scandal") meeting the Frenchman in Paris. Pavey's attitude prior to the encounter was typical of his countrymen—that "There was a hole in Panama into which a lot of French money had been sunk, and that no canal would ever be possible there." But Bunau-Varilla gave him the full evangelical treatment. "He never let go of an American victim when he got one in that library until he thought he had converted him," said Pavey, "and the first time I dined in his house I stayed until 2 o'clock the next morning, listening to his picturesque and fascinating argument in favor of Panama and against Nicaragua . . . [he] made a special effort to convert me to the cause of Panama, which I am frank to confess he did."

A desire to claim credit for the great achievement of the canal was a weakness that Cromwell and Bunau-Varilla cleverly exploited among their enemies. But it also dominates their own accounts of their involvement in the events that led to the start of the American Panama Canal. In the Frenchman's published writings there is one hero of the story, namely himself, a new, hyperpatriotic *Grand Français* who steps into the breach to steer events and protagonists toward the saving of "the noble conception of French Genius through its adoption by America." Cromwell's version emerged when his 65,000-word justification for his enormous fees at the arbitration court in 1907 was handed to the press. The leak caused a sensation, for Cromwell, naturally putting the best shine on services rendered, claimed to have decisively influenced U.S. government decisions in favor of the Panama Canal to a breathtaking extent.

But Bunau-Varilla, like de Lesseps before him, was not one to share the limelight, calling the claims of the man he disparagingly called "the lawyer Cromwell" "a tissue of erroneous and misleading assertions." Cromwell, in turn, would play down the contribution of Bunau-Varilla and sought to discredit his motives for campaigning for a Panama Canal. Both men talked down their mutual cooperation. Each wanted to be, and subsequently saw himself as, uniquely, the hero who made the waterway a reality. They also shared an obsession with the canal. Bunau-Varilla's was well established, but for Cromwell, too, the longer he was involved, the more it became greater than just another lucrative job. As an American journalist would later write: "Once you have touched Panama, you never lose the infection. Some call it canalitis."

But to others, one or both of the men were the villains, rather than the heroes, of the piece. To his enemies, such as the Nicaragua lobby led by Senator Morgan, and those who objected to the United States' shady involvement in the Panama Revolution, Cromwell's undoubted influence and interest, combined with the taint of a new, runaway Wall Street, made him a perfect scapegoat. He was portrayed as a corrupter of American public life. A congressional investigation was told that Cromwell was "the revolutionist who promoted and made possible the revolution on the Isthmus of Panama." He was, the investigation's leader suggested, one of the most dangerous men the United States had spawned for a long time. Almost worst of all, he was "one of the most accomplished lobbyists this country had ever produced." The *New York World* concurred, writing that Cromwell's "masterful mind, whetted on the grindstone of corporation cunning, conceived and carried out the rape of the Isthmus."

However, to Panamanians the "rapist" was the "traitor" Bunau-Varilla, who, as shall be seen, blackmailed the infant Republic into acceding to a deal with the United States that was patently unfair. The Frenchman, the self-anointed heir of Ferdinand de Lesseps, would stop at nothing to see the Panama Canal built.

It is Cromwell, however, who takes center stage in the early parts of the story. When he was contracted by the New Company in 1896, he told his employers that "no one in the United States doubted that the Panama Canal in itself was an impossibility . . . Public opinion demanded the Nicaragua Canal." In turn, the directors in Paris for the moment kept Cromwell on a tight leash, still hoping that the last resort of selling out to the Americans might be avoided. When, by 1898, this looked impossible, they acceded to Cromwell's pleas to allow him to press energetically the case for a sale to the United States government.

Cromwell straightaway set up a special press bureau for the production and dissemination of anti-Nicaragua and pro-Panama propaganda, at the same time lobbying engineering societies, shipping interests, and influential politicians. "We must make our plans with Napoleonic strategy," he told his French clients. For Cromwell this meant being "ubiquitous and ever present" on Capitol Hill, as one of his enemies would later complain. It was Cromwell, naturally, who set up and presided over the meeting of the New Company directors with President McKinley in early December of that year.

But the president was not impressed, in part because of the clause in the Wyse concession that forbade the sale of the canal works to a foreign government. On December 5, 1898, he sent his message to Congress supporting Morgan's Nicaragua bill.

When this measure sailed through the Senate, Cromwell had to concentrate all his resources on the House of Representatives to prevent Morgan's legislation from becoming law. If the bill passed, then

all his client's assets would be worthless. The job of getting the
Nicaragua bill through the House of Representatives fell to Iowa's
William P. Hepburn. Both the Republican Hepburn and the Demo-
crat Morgan considered the Nicaragua option inevitable and were
maneuvering to secure the honor of the legislation for their party and
themselves. Someone—what a later investigator called "mysterious
influences"—played upon Hepburn's vanity by getting him to intro-
duce a bill of his own, rather than just sponsoring Senator Morgan's
in the House of Representatives. This complicated the passage of the
bill, and Hepburn was persuaded to accept an amendment that called
for a new study to look at all the feasible routes for a canal. Effectively, the bill was killed, and a new commission was ordered, again
under the direction of Admiral Walker, to look once more at the best
route for a canal "under the control, management and ownership of
the United States." To the fury of Morgan, who saw the powerful
transcontinental railroad interests behind the "delaying measure," it
was the first crack in the Nicaragua edifice, and a great victory for the
Panama lobby.

Characteristically, Bunau-Varilla claimed the credit, saying that the
field had been reopened through the efforts of his carefully cultivated American friends. But in this instance, the "mysterious influences" were almost certainly Cromwell, who somehow got himself
invited before the committee studying the bill and argued "for hours
on the most profound study of the technical sides of the question."

Cromwell did not rest on his laurels, however, immediately doing
his utmost to influence the selection of the new Walker Commission.
In this he was only partly successful, failing to block the appointment
of several experts who had already pronounced for Nicaragua on the
previous commission. But he did manage to arrange that the commission's first port of call would be Paris, where all the talk would be
of Panama, rather than Nicaragua. Cromwell left ahead of the Walker
party, sailing for France on August 9, 1899, "to prepare and direct the
presentation of the case."

In Paris, the nine eminent engineers and military bigwigs of the

Walker Commission were subjected to a barrage of plans, maps, and figures by the New Company, but also, because of Cromwell's efforts, elaborately wined and dined. One lunch included six courses and four different wines. Bunau-Varilla popped up, too (that Cromwell did not meet and consult with him at this time if not before is impossible to believe). Supposedly thanks to another introduction from John Bigelow, now eighty years old, Bunau-Varilla had dinner with three of the Commission engineers, including the eminent George S. Morison, whom he subjected to the full Panama treatment. All were converted, or, as Bunau-Varilla puts it, "the scales had fallen from their eyes."

While Bunau-Varilla provided the high notes, Cromwell got down to business on his return to Washington. The key man to get on side, Cromwell decided, was Mark Alonzo Hanna, who had been the chairman of the Republican National Committe during the 1896 election. Hanna was very close to McKinley and was considered the most powerful man in Washington. He also had a long interest in canals, had recently been tasked by the president with getting on top of the Isthmian canal question, and had therefore joined Morgan's Senate Committee on Interoceanic Canals. Cromwell got an introduction from Hanna's banker, who was a client of Sullivan and Cromwell. The meeting opened with Cromwell slapping down on Hanna's desk a $60,000 donation to the party, compliments of the Compagnie Nouvelle. It was an outrageous move—not only was it a vast amount of money, but also no one in Paris had authorized such a payment on the New Company's behalf.

Cromwell's efforts seemed to be paying off when the Republican Party Convention in June 1900 changed its call for a "Nicaraguan" canal to an "Isthmian" one, but on other fronts Panama was stalling. In spite of the lavish hospitality, the Walker Commission had returned from their Paris trip disappointed by the New Company's inability to state either a firm price for their venture, or that they had the legal right to sell to the United States government. Maurice Hutin, who had briefly been *Directeur Général* of the de Lesseps Company back in 1885 before being invalided off the Isthmus with yellow fever, was now in charge of the New Company. In April, Walker had again asked him to name a price. Hutin did not reply for ten weeks, but on April 26 he took the precaution of buying for 5 million francs in gold an extension to the Colombian concession up to 1910. But he still stalled on Walker's demands. Hutin's long-standing and traumatic involvement with the French canal project led him to hope that the United States would somehow be taken on as a partner, rather than simply buying the French out. The result was that Walker, in a preliminary report issued in November 1900, indicated that because of "all the difficulties of obtaining the necessary rights . . . on the Panama route" Nicaragua presented "the most practicable and feasible route." The Panama lobby was in crisis.

A few days later, according to his own account, Bunau-Varilla received an invitation to speak to the Cincinnati Chamber of Commerce, from a U.S. businessman he had met and converted to the Great Idea in Paris earlier in the year. "The bugle-note had been heard," Bunau-Varilla wrote, and set sail straightaway for the United States, arriving at the beginning of January 1901. By a coincidence or not, it was exactly the time it would have taken for Cromwell to summon him after the preliminary report by the Walker Commission.

Bunau-Varilla's whirlwind three-month tour of the United States, reminiscent of those undertaken by Ferdinand de Lesseps in the 1880s, began in Cincinnati on the evening of January 16, 1901, in a large hall decked with the flags of France and the United States. It was an unqualified success. The Frenchman seemed a strange, exotic creature, with his theatrically impeccable manners, grandiloquent gestures, large head, and moustache waxed to two fine points, but his passion for Panama was plain. It was the "intensity of conviction which inspired all your utterances," one of the guests wrote to him, that gave what he said so much impact. "I love a man," the American went on, "who loves a great cause."

In his own account of the tour, Bunau-Varilla maintains that it was "Fate" that ensured he met the key U.S. decision makers. "Every time I was in need of a man he appeared," he writes. In truth, Bunau-

Varilla left little to chance. Several of his converted American friends were working for him at his expense, setting up meetings and opening doors. After Cincinnati, he headed to a business club in Cleveland, supposedly thanks to a "chance encounter" with a friend of a businessman there he had met on the boat over. Again he spoke about the advantages of the Panama over the Nicaragua route—the railroad, the superior harbors, the shorter length and lower cost. He also warmed to a new theme that had made a considerable impact during his first speech, the suggestion that, unlike Panama, the Nicaragua route was bestridden by volcanoes. The Cleveland audience was particularly important as it included key friends of McKinley and Hanna.

At every meeting, Bunau-Varilla, or his friends working behind the scenes, came away with a new invitation. After Cleveland, he headed for Boston, then Chicago. In New York, he dined again with the Walker Commission's George Morison, and then addressed the city's chamber of commerce, thanks to the influence of his old friend John Bigelow. Those present included J. P. Morgan, John D. Rockefeller, and Andrew Carnegie. All the time, Bunau-Varilla was liberally spraying around gifts of cigars, flowers, and theater tickets, giving dinners and writing countless letters seeking introductions or just pushing the case for Panama.

Now Bunau-Varilla considered heading for home, but there then occurred another of the "chance encounters" that he had made his specialty. Reading between the lines of his own account, it was a setup. Bunau-Varilla was staying in the Waldorf-Astoria, as were several key Washington politicians. "Towards midnight," Bunau-Varilla wrote, "as I was about to go out for a breath of fresh air before retiring, I met a party of people in evening dress entering the Waldorf-Astoria. My surprise was great when I saw at the head of them Colonel Herrick [a contact from Cleveland] with a lady on his arm, and behind them a short, stout gentleman who limped slightly. His characteristic face, so frequently reproduced in the newspapers, was familiar to me."

It was Mark Hanna, identified by Cromwell as the key man to get on side. Herrick feigned surprise as he made the introductions, and Bunau-Varilla came away with a pressing invitation to call on the senator in Washington. Not content with this priceless coup, Bunau-Varilla continued to loiter in the lobby of the hotel until another friend, this time one of the "converted" Cincinnati businessmen, happened to come past in the company of the U.S. comptroller of currency. Through him, the Frenchman secured an interview with McKinley himself.

In no time, Bunau-Varilla was in Washington, to "attack the political fortress." He had a number of meetings with Hanna, which, apparently, culminated in the senator from Ohio pronouncing, "Mr. Bunau-Varilla, you have convinced me." The interview with the president was briefer. Bunau-Varilla did not wish to "inflict" a lecture on him. Besides, he knew "that the opinion of Senator Hanna would be his [McKinley's] own." On April 11, Bunau-Varilla sailed for Paris, confident that he had made a significant dent in U.S. public and official opinion in favor of Panama.

How Bunau-Varilla came to be summoned to the United States, and who paid for the lavish trip, remains a mystery. But certainly Cromwell had not been idle in the meantime. On the news that the provisional Walker report would favor Nicaragua, he was on to the Colombians, warning them that the future of their canal was in jeopardy. Bogotá responded by sending a senior politician and close friend of the Colombian president to Washington to press the case for Panama. The envoy met U.S. secretary of state John Hay on March 13, 1901, and early exploratory negotiations between the Colombian envoy, Walker, and Cromwell representing the New Company, went well. Apart from anything else, the Colombian's presence in Washington indicated to Cromwell and his clients that Bogotá was happy for the New Company to sell out to the United States, despite the terms of the Wyse concession forbidding its handing over to a foreign government.

But there were potentially fatal problems and distractions. The Colombians were convinced that the Nicaragua option was a red herring designed to get better terms for the United States, and that Panama was the only serious option from a technical point of view. The United States, for its part, was still involved with the complicated negotiations, initiated in 1898, to change or abrogate the Clayton-Bulwer Treaty with Great Britain, which continued to stand in the way of any unilateral action by the United States on the canal issue. Worst of all was that the New Company still refused to set a price for its assets—demanding instead independent arbitration to settle the issue—or to confirm that it had the right to sell. Utterly frustrated, Walker went to Cromwell in July 1901 to demand that the directors in Paris name a price. Cromwell, equally annoyed, pressed Hutin for an answer in the most direct terms.

For the New Company directors, enough was enough. Not only had Cromwell made free and easy with their money, often in questionable ways, but now he was adopting an unacceptably aggressive tone. In July 1901, he was sacked.

So while the other distractions continued through the summer, the New Company now had no representation in the United States. Naturally, Walker's Commission had to consider the political aspects of the choice of canal location as well as the purely engineering issues, and it did not look good for Panama. On the Isthmus itself, hopeful rumors swirled about, but to those in the know it was clear that the preliminary verdict in favor of Nicaragua was not about to be reversed when the Commission submitted its final report in November 1901.

Then, on September 6, there happened a combination of two of the recurring events of the end of the nineteenth century—expositions and anarchist violence. President McKinley was attending the Pan-American Exposition in Buffalo, New York, when a lone anarchist called Leon Czolgosz fired two shots from a .32-caliber revolver into the president's upper body. McKinley died eight nights later.

On the same day, September 14, 1901, a new chief executive was inaugurated, the former vice president, Theodore Roosevelt. And with his arrival, everything would change for the canal.

◄◄◄◄- ►►►►

In his first address to Congress, the new president promised an American-built and controlled trans-Isthmian canal. "No single great material work which remains to be undertaken on this continent," he declared, "is of such consequence to the American people."

Roosevelt, who was actually descended on his mother's side from one of the survivors of the Scottish "Darién Disaster," had already, while New York State governor, intervened in the canal debate, or, more specifically, the negotiations with Britain for the abrogation or alteration of the Clayton-Bulwer Treaty. Hay's discussions with the British had been slow and laborious, but in February 1900 he had at last signed an agreement with British ambassador Sir Julian Paunce-fote that abrogated the restraining treaty that had prevented the United States from building a canal on its own. But its replacement, which forbade fortification, stipulated that the waterway should be "free and open in time of war as in time of peace, to vessels of commerce and of war of all nations," and looked to an international guarantee, found no favor among the Roosevelt circle. While some press commentators applauded the lack of aggression inherent in the neutrality clause, which gave the United States' neighbors less "cause for suspicion," Roosevelt, a great admirer of Mahan's theory of the importance of naval power, wrote directly to Hay complaining that the "international guarantee" would flout the Monroe Doctrine and took direct issue with the ban on fortification. "If that canal is open to the warships of an enemy," he wrote, "it is a menace to us in time of war; it is an added burden, an additional strategic point to be guarded by our fleet. If fortified by us, it becomes one of the most potent sources of our possible sea strength."

Hay was shocked by these criticisms and sniffily told Roosevelt that such matters of Great Power diplomacy were outside the remit of a mere state governor. But opposition in the Senate, led by Morgan and Roosevelt's friend Henry Cabot Lodge, forced Hay back to the negotiating table. Happily, he found Great Britain in an obliging mood. Embroiled in a costly and internationally unpopular struggle with the South African Boers, and worried about Russian expansionism toward India and the German naval program, the British were keen to nurture an informal détente with the United States. Senior British politicians believed, like Arthur Balfour, that a U.S.-controlled canal would "strengthen our position enormously and . . . with England at Suez and the U.S. at Panama we should hold the world in a pretty strong grip." Soon after the revised treaty was signed, Britain started reducing her costly garrisons and naval squadrons in the Caribbean. The British were beginning to learn how to use American power to their advantage.

With the signing of the second Hay-Pauncefote Treaty on November 18, 1901, which implicitly allowed the fortification of an American canal, the long rise of the United States to local preeminence was complete. As the president of Colombia noted, the treaty "ruptured the dikes placed against so-called American imperialism . . . It changed the face of the question and made the situation for the [Colombian] Government obscure, delicate and complex: action and inaction equally presented great problems and reason for anxiety." Just how "delicate and complex" would soon be illustrated.

The signing of the treaty cleared a significant obstacle from the path toward an American canal. Its location, however, still looked like Nicaragua. The Panama lobby was heading in the wrong direction after the death of McKinley—Roosevelt had not even been considered as a target for their propaganda—and it was believed that the new president would be far less influenced by the carefully "converted" Mark Hanna. In October, Hutin in Paris at last gave Walker an estimate of the value of the New Company's property, set at just over $109 million, albeit open to arbitration. The next month Walker's Commission reported.

Bunau-Varilla and Cromwell had done their work well—the engineers clearly preferred Panama from a technical point of view: the route was much shorter, would need fewer locks, and was hindered by less curvature; a ship could pass through in twelve hours rather than thirty-three; it would also be cheaper to build and maintain. Walker estimated a Panama canal would cost just over $144 million, compared to $190 million for Nicaragua. But when the price of the New Company was factored in, Panama became much more expensive. Therefore the Commission, to the particular dismay of engineer George Morison, plumped for Nicaragua.

The following month the United States signed a canal convention with the Nicaraguan government, and on January 9, 1902, the House of Representatives overwhelmingly backed a new bill from Congressman Hepburn appropriating $180 million for the construction of a Nicaraguan canal and sent it on to the Senate. In Washington the Panama venture was now being described as "a worthless ditch."

In Paris, these developments caused a panic. In December there had been angry scenes at a shareholders' meeting, leading to the police being summoned. Attacks on the board of directors were led by Philippe Bunau-Varilla, who urged the shareholders to sell to the United States at whatever price they could get or see their investment become entirely lost. Hutin was forced to resign and was replaced by Maurice Bô, president of the Crédit Lyonnais bank, who, as a penalized shareholder was not strictly allowed direct involvement with the Company. But he was a friend of Bunau-Varilla and Cromwell, and was happy to take the drastic step now required. On January 4, Bô wired Walker a revised price of $40 million, the Commission's own valuation of the New Company's property.

This news changed everything and set the scene for a decisive intervention by the new president. On December 10, Roosevelt had received a letter from his fellow Harvard graduate George Morison, outlining the engineer's reasons for disagreeing with the majority of the Walker Commission's preference for Nicaragua. Roosevelt may have also been influenced by Mark Hanna, who remained a senior figure in the Republican Party, or by the fear that the unfinished Panama Canal would be completed by a European power if the United States pressed on in Nicaragua. Whatever the reason, Roosevelt now had a fixed idea: he wanted the Panama route. As soon as the news of the revised price came in from Paris, the president summoned the Walker Commission and interviewed them one by one to persuade them to change their verdict. Several protested, but as the price had been the sticking point for Panama, on January 18 they complied with Roosevelt and Morison's wishes and published a revised report recommending Panama. An amendment was drafted that authorized the president to purchase the French Company's Panama property and concessions for $40 million; to acquire from Colombia perpetual control of a Canal Zone at least six miles wide; and to build a Panama canal. If a clear title or a satisfactory agreement with Colombia could not be reached "within a reasonable time," then the president was authorized to proceed with the Nicaragua route. John Coit Spooner, a past master at steering difficult legislation through the Senate, was chosen to introduce the amendment, and thus to face the full fury of Morgan and the Nicaragua party.

But the Panama lobby would be on hand to help. On January 27, Maurice Bô reinstated Cromwell as the New Company's U.S. representative, albeit with an order to stick to "legitimate means." The same day Cromwell met with Bunau-Varilla (they both claim this is the first time they worked together), who had rushed to Washington to prepare for what would be the climax in the Senate of the long "Battle of the Routes."

The astonishing, Roosevelt-led turnaround caused great confusion in the United States press, long accustomed to the American preference for a Nicaragua canal. Much of the concern about Panama was the prospect of dealing with Bogotá. "The Colombians . . . have negro blood enough to make them lazy, and Spanish blood sufficient to make them mean," declared *Harper's Weekly*.

Somewhat prophetically, the *New York World* commented, "Talk about buying a lawsuit—the purchase of the Panama Canal would be buying a revolution."

◀◀◀◀- →▶▶▶▶

Since the beginning of the year, the Hepburn Bill had been in the hands of Morgan's Senate Committee on Interoceanic Canals. After extensive cross-examining of all available experts, the Committee, in spite of the Walker Commission's decision, voted seven to four in favor of Nicaragua. But Hanna, with Cromwell's help, produced a minority report in favor of Panama. The date of June 4 was set for the start of the debate in the Senate over which of these would be adopted.

In the meantime, Bunau-Varilla was as busy as ever, writing to newspapers and politicians, producing pamphlets, and pouring pro-Panama rhetoric into the ears of anyone who would listen. Then the Panama lobby had a stroke of luck. On May 8, the volcano Mount Pelée on the Caribbean island of Martinique exploded with devastating effect. The town of Saint-Pierre in its shadow was utterly destroyed, and more than thirty thousand people were killed. Although Martinique was nowhere near either route, volcanoes were suddenly on everyone's mind. Then, just a week later, the news came in that a volcano in Nicaragua itself had erupted. Friends of Panama in the press had a field day.

Senator Morgan opened the debate in the Senate with a spirited counterattack on the "volcano scare," brandishing a letter from the foreign minister of Nicaragua (who had somehow been persuaded to deny the eruption had taken place), and pointing out that Panama had itself recently experienced an earthquake. But the main thrust of his argument against Panama was political. Its people were "mixed and turbulent"; it was chronically unstable; to build a canal there, the United States would have to take the country by force, an action, predicted the Alabama senator, that would "poison the minds of people against us in every Spanish-American republic in the Western Hemisphere, and set their teeth on edge against us."

The next day, Senator Mark Hanna replied in favor of his minority report. It was to be the greatest speech of his career. Shunning rhetorical flourishes, he spoke in a slow, businesslike way, illustrating his points with an impressive array of visual tools, including a huge map showing active volcanoes in Nicaragua. All this had been prepared for him by Cromwell and Bunau-Varilla. The Panama route was shorter, he pointed out, had less curvature, better ports, a railway, fewer locks, and "was a beaten track in civilization." Furthermore, the engineers wanted Panama, and "there are now done a great many things which fifty years ago were unheard of, never dreamed of, never thought possible, as a product of human intelligence and ingenuity in engineering. It has become a byword today that in the hands of a skillful engineer nothing is impossible."

The speech, over two days, certainly changed votes, although the Panama lobby was not home yet. Pro-Nicaragua senators suggested that the whole effort of the Hanna party was to delay any canal in order to serve the interests of the transcontinental railroads. There still persisted, too, a feeling that Panama was irrevocably stained by corruption and what was seen as the vice of the French years. "It is the certainty of moral defilement," declared Senator John H. Mitchell of Oregon. "Panama cannot be touched with safety by American people."

The volcano argument was also foundering. The Nicaraguans were sticking by their story that there had been no recent eruption in their country, and the whole scare was starting to be seen as an invention of the Panama lobby. On June 6, a cartoon appeared in the influential *Washington Star*, showing Hanna slapping imaginary volcanoes on to a map of Nicaragua aided by a comical Frenchman, Bunau-Varilla, and James J. Hill, head of the Great Northern Railroad. As Bunau-Varilla wrote, "If the vote were to be taken under this impression Panama was done for ever ... Fortunately I had a sudden inspiration."

Over the next few days Bunau-Varilla scoured the philatelists of the capital looking for a certain 1900 one-centavo Nicaraguan stamp, which he had come across the year before. In the foreground of the stamp is pictured a busy wharf while in the background rises the magnificent bulk of Mount Momotombo. In an artistic flourish the illustrator had added smoke to the top of the volcano, which was actually more than a hundred miles from the proposed Nicaragua canal. Just before the vote, every senator was sent this "evidence" of the dangers of the Nicaragua route.

It was almost the last shot, but this went to Senator Morgan, who used his final speech before the vote on the minority report to launch a bitter attack against his enemy Cromwell. The "direct, constant, and offensive intrusion of the Panama Canal Company" into the workings of the U.S. government was, he said, "humiliating" and "repulsive." "I can not neglect Mr. Cromwell," he said. "I trace this man back ... to the beginning of this whole business. He has not failed to appear anywhere in this whole affair." The contagion of Panama, "death's nursery," had through its agent Cromwell poisoned everything it touched.

Everyone knew that the vote on June 19 would be close, and the press and the country, which had followed the fourteen-day debate closely, waited with bated breath. When the result came, it could hardly have been narrower, with Hanna's minority report in favor of Panama winning by just eight votes. "The battle was won," wrote Bunau-Varilla. "Truth at last triumphed."

After this, the passage of the Spooner amendment was a formality, and the House of Representatives was persuaded to back the act as well. In part, the pro-Nicaragua faction assumed that either the French title would prove defective or an agreement with Colombia would not be forthcoming and they would get their preferred option after all. If they had lost a battle, they had not yet lost the war.

CHAPTER FIFTEEN

"I TOOK THE ISTHMUS"

The first potential stumbling block was dealt with quickly. The U.S. attorney general sailed to Paris and exhaustively went through the available books and contracts before pronouncing that the deal with the New Company was legitimate. But on the second issue, of coming to a deal with Colombia, it was not to be so simple.

Since October 1899, Colombia had been in the throes of its longest and most devastating civil war since independence eighty years before. The "War of a Thousand Days," fought between Conservative and Liberal factions, would claim the lives of between 150,000 and 250,000 Colombians.

With Liberal armies threatening Bogotá itself, the administration, led by the elderly Conservative José Manuel Marroquín, was showing signs of confusion, and was having great difficulty staying in contact with its representatives in Washington. Marroquín tried to delay the signing of any deal with the United States until his position was more secure, but amid calls from the Nicaragua party that the "reasonable time," as stipulated by the Spooner Act, had run out, a treaty was signed with the Colombian legation's secretary, Tomás Herrán, on January 22, 1903 (the previous envoy had resigned in disgust at what he saw as the bullying tactics of the U.S. administration). Herrán himself had been concerned that further delays would lead Roosevelt, whom he described as "impetuous [with a] violent disposition," simply to seize the Isthmus.

The terms of the treaty were that in return for an annuity of $250,000, with a $10 million gold onetime payment, the United States would receive a six-mile-wide Canal Zone on a hundred-year lease renewable at the sole option of the United States. Although Colombian sovereignty was specifically recognized, this was something of a fig leaf: the United States was to be allowed to establish its own courts within the proposed Zone and, in an emergency, to land its forces without Colombia's consent to protect the canal.

Morgan did his very best to wreck the treaty in the Senate, proposing a number of amendments, including anti-Catholic measures, which he knew would make the deal unacceptable to Colombia. Along the way, he described the treaty as a compact with "a crowd of French jail-birds, cleverly advised by a New York railroad wrecker . . . and a depraved, priest-ridden people." The Alabama senator successfully filibustered into March, but overplayed his hand. Roosevelt pushed, Morgan broke down, and the treaty was ratified without amendments on March 17. Now the ball was firmly in Colombia's court.

◄◄◄◄ ►►►►

In mid-March 1903, with the civil war at last over, and as the new Colombian Congress was being elected, the *Panama Star and Herald* commented, "Few of the members who will assemble in Bogotá, competent observers say, have ever seen the ocean . . . They are comparatively indifferent to the advantages of the project, while feeling great pride in their soil and sovereignty, and a corresponding fear of the gradual absorption of their territory by the United States. These things count against ratification."

Soon after, Claude Mallet returned to the Isthmus, having served for two years in Bogotá. It was not good to be back. There was "a great deal of illness" in Panama, and yellow fever in Colón. "I have heard of four cases (two deaths) since I arrived on Thursday," he wrote to his Panamanian wife, who had remained in England for the health of their children. More than anything, Mallet reported, there was great depression about the chances of the canal treaty going through. "Religion here has taken an extraordinary hold upon the people," he wrote on June 1. "A few years ago such a scene [a procession of girls carrying an effigy of the virgin] would not have been permitted. The Jesuits are getting in their work and unless the canal is made we shall lapse back to what the place was fifty years ago."

Panama's senator José Agustín Arango, who also worked as a lawyer for the Panama Railroad, believed that the result of the forthcoming debate in Bogotá was a foregone conclusion and refused to attend the opening of the Senate at the beginning of June 1903. Instead, he believed that the best hope for a canal to bring muchneeded prosperity back to his homeland was through secession. By May a small revolutionary group was active, centered on Arango's sons and sons-in-law, all young men educated in the United States. Soon after, Federico Boyd, the son of the founding editor of the *Star and Herald*, and Dr. Manuel Amador Guerrero, the railroad's seventyyear-old, frail-looking head physician, were brought on board. The group met secretly at Amador's house, or at the Panama electric light plant.

Petitions were sent from Panama to Bogotá both for and against the treaty. Liberals were opposed to the "selling" of Panama to the United States. Cromwell helped organize pressure in favor. An open letter from Panama's senior Conservatives to the Colombian president Marroquín warned that rejection of the treaty would "give rise to unpatriotic feelings."

In fact, Marroquín was in a near-impossible situation. In the

United States he was seen and portrayed as an all-powerful dictator, but this was far from the case. His power was extremely fluid, varying from issue to issue, and he had made enemies across the political spectrum. It was imperative to his political survival that he did not alienate any of his fragile support.

Indeed, the canal question carried political high explosive. In Colombia, sovereignty was of prime importance, the chief symbol of national permanence and unity in a land of disordered change. In fact, the constitution specifically forbade the transfer to another power of the sovereignty of any part of the country. It was one thing to give a concession to a private company, quite another to hand one to the voracious power to the north, which had already demonstrated its aggression in Cuba and the Philippines. "Not an atom of our sovereignty nor a stone of our territory," wrote the newspaper *El Correo Naçional,* should be given up, even if it meant "renounc[ing] the honour of a canal across Panama."

Anti-Marroquín newspapers, of which there were many, attacked the treaty as a way of damaging the president. Herrán had sold out, it was stated; the deal was an example of Yankee imperialism; there was still hope of a European country, Britain or Germany, riding to the rescue to build the canal; Morgan's comments in the U.S. Senate debate about "depraved, priest-ridden people" were printed, causing widespread resentment.

Under the aggressive leadership of Roosevelt, the United States had been throwing its weight around in the region. At Guantánamo Bay in Cuba, ideally situated to guard the Windward Passage into the Caribbean and thence to the Isthmus, a U.S. naval base had been established in February 1903. At a speech in Chicago in April, Roosevelt declared that "our nation has insisted that because of its primacy in strength among the nations of the Western hemisphere it has certain duties and responsibilities which oblige it to take a leading part thereon." What would become known as the Roosevelt corollary to the Monroe Doctrine emerged as a policy soon after Roosevelt entered the White House. Not only was the United States committed to excluding European powers from the hemisphere, but it was also taking on the role of "international police power" intervening in cases of "chronic wrongdoing" or "incompetence."

To Colombians, this posture was both frightening and insulting. It is "a warning to our countries," wrote the Bogotá paper *El Porvenir*. "It is the conviction of his irresistible superiority and vigor that makes the Yankee, from Mr. Roosevelt to the rag-picker, treat the turbulent republics of Latin America with haughtiness and contempt." The authority to intervene, said the paper, was "derived from nobody knows where . . . as though the great nation had received from some universal power the mission to put in order those who live in disorder!"

Against this background of distrust and fear, public sentiment on the Hay-Herrán Treaty quickly changed, the U.S. ambassador in Bogotá reported back on April 15, "from approbation to suspicion and from suspicion to decided opposition." The minister, Arthur Beupré, still believed that Marroquín had the power to force the measure through Congress, but that an open vote would see it rejected.

But this would not be put to the test. Marroquín had no intention of acting so vigorously on the canal question. He saw himself in an unwinnable position. "History will say of me," he had written the previous year, "that I ruined the Isthmus and all Colombia, by not permitting the opening of the Panama Canal, or that I permitted it to be done, scandalously injuring the rights of my country." The way out, as he saw it, was to hand over the responsibility for the decision to Congress, a step the constitution demanded anyway.

But the Colombian president was also personally ambivalent about the canal, which, if built, would open up his country as never before. Like U.S. Secretary of State John Hay, he was a novelist. In his 1897 book *Entre Primos*, he used a cultural confrontation between an effete Englishman and an idealized, hardworking Colombian to show the frippery of the outside world and the superiority of the insular Colombian character. During the civil war he had risked ruining his country in order to protect it from the demands of the Liberals—

railroads, foreign influence, and capital. In many ways the canal represented the greatest threat of all to everything he held dear—the sheltered, Catholic, genteel age of nineteenth-century Bogotá, untrammeled by technology, modernism, or Protestant capitalism.

Discussions of the treaty continued through the spring. In April, the Colombians again indicated that, even if they gave in on the sovereignty question, an even greater sticking point was the issue of Colombia's right to a proportion of the money to be paid to the New Company. On this issue, though, Cromwell had engineered his great coup. "We pointed out," the lawyer later wrote, "that Colombia had already pledged herself morally to consent, and that her consent should be imposed on her as being demanded by international good faith." Even Hay asked Cromwell whether, perhaps, some $5 million or so could not be paid over from the $40 million, but Cromwell succeeded in persuading him that this would be tantamount to giving in to blackmail. Cromwell's influence, on behalf of his client, right at the center of the U.S. government, is astonishing.

Then the Colombians hinted at another possible way out of the impasse. If the 1900 extension to the concession, organized by Hutin in the midst of the Colombian civil war, were declared illegal, then they could simply let the original term of the deal with the New Company expire in October 1904, and then sell the lot to the Americans for $25 million. But Cromwell need not have worried. Roosevelt and Hay were appalled by this threat, which confirmed their opinion of the Colombians as shifty and grasping. Hay had strong views on property rights, calling the Colombians "greedy little anthropoids."

The Americans decided that a firm hand was needed. On June 9, eleven days before the debate in the Colombian Senate was due to start, a serious threat was issued from Hay's office: "If Colombia should now reject the treaty or unduly delay its ratification, the friendly understanding between the two countries would be so seriously compromised that action might be taken by the Congress next winter which every friend of Colombia would regret." All efforts by Marroquín to reduce the humiliation of the deal were now met by a firm rejoinder: any amendments or other delays would be "tantamount to a rejection of the treaty."

Behind this browbeating tone was the determination of the president, Theodore Roosevelt. With elections looming in 1904, he was talking up the grandeur and national pride that the construction of the canal would bring to his country. It was, he told an audience in Chicago, the "greatest material feat of the twentieth century—greater than any similar feat in any preceding century." Of course, it "should be done by no foreign nation, but by ourselves."

The Panama lobby was also keeping up the pressure. On June 13, Bunau-Varilla, at huge expense, cabled Marroquín. "The only party that can now build the Panama Canal is the United States," he wrote. "Neither European governments nor private financiers would dare to fight either against the Monroe Doctrine or the American Treasury for building Panama Canal." Failure to ratify, he warned, would lead to either the "construction of a Nicaragua Canal and absolute loss to Colombia of the incalculable advantages resulting from construction on her territory the great artery of universal commerce, or the construction of the Panama Canal after secession and declaration of independence of the Isthmus of Panama under protection of the United States as has happened with Cuba."

Cromwell was busy, too. On June 12 he had paid a public visit to the White House, and the next day a story appeared in a New York newspaper, which turned out to have come from Roger Farnham, Cromwell's press agent. "President Roosevelt is determined to have the Panama Canal Route," the piece read, saying that a combination of "the greed of the Colombian government" and the "frenzy over the alleged relinquishment of sovereignty" made defeat of the measure "probable" in the Colombian Senate. But, the article continued, "the State of Panama will secede if the Colombian congress fails to ratify the canal treaty." Supposedly, Farnham even told the paper's editors the date of the "revolution"—November 3, when U.S. newspapers would be full of returns from the midterm elections.

Indeed, the treaty never stood a chance in the Colombian Senate.

The debate started on June 20, and was dominated by attacks on Marroquín that had little to do with the canal. Two weeks later General Rafael Reyes, back in Bogotá after a period of exile and a firm supporter of the treaty, asked Beupré for an additional $5 million up front from the United States and $10 million out of the $40 million for the New Company to break the deadlock.

Hay replied that the U.S. Senate would not approve it. "Any amendment whatever or unnecessary delay in the ratification of the treaty would greatly imperil its consummation," he told Beupré. A few days later Roosevelt wrote to Hay backing up this firm stand. "Make it as strong as you can ... Those contemptible little creatures in Bogota ought to understand how much they are jeopardizing things and imperiling their own future." In fact, Hay, apart from his improperly close relationship with Cromwell, had his hands tied. The close result of the vote in the Senate on the Hanna minority report meant that any deviation from the strict terms of the Spooner Act could see the treaty fail to make it through the Senate. Thus the intransigence of Morgan and the Nicaragua party doomed the treaty as much as any opposition in Colombia.

The rejection from Bogotá, when it came on August 12, was overwhelming, with 24 voting against, with 3 abstentions. Even Marroquín's son voted against the measure. In the United States, the vote was seen as an attempt to extort more money out of the United States or the French Company. Patience with Bogotá, never extensive, was now at an end. It was time for a new plan.

-◄◄◄◄- ►►►►-

Roosevelt and Hay now weighed the options open to them. The first was to persevere with Colombia and hope that the treaty might be ratified the following year. The second was to push ahead with the Nicaragua option, as the Spooner Act directed. Or the whole question could be handed over to Congress to decide. The fourth option was somehow to proceed with the Panama route without recourse to Bogotá.

The first option was quickly written off. The president wanted a decision before the 1904 elections and was not inclined to continue negotiations with what he now called "the foolish and homicidal corruptionists in Bogota." But to turn to Nicaragua (or see this option chosen by Congress) would for Roosevelt not only represent a personal defeat, but also be "against the advice of the great majority of competent engineers," as the president declared. Furthermore, there was a growing consensus that the great new warships under construction in U.S. yards as part of Roosevelt's naval expansion would struggle with Nicaragua's narrow and winding rivers. Roosevelt was set on Panama. In September the French minister in Washington, Jules Jusserand, sent a dispatch to his government reporting of the president that, "I know, for having heard him say so, how intensely he wants it [the canal at Panama]; he will neglect nothing that may enable his country to perfect this work and be the master thereof."

So nothing was to be ruled out, including seizing the Isthmus by force. In March 1903, U.S. spies had been sent to Panama to obtain information to assist military operations there. Days after Colombia's rejection of the treaty, a paper had been forwarded to Roosevelt by Hay's deputy, Francis B. Loomis, which seemed to offer a fig leaf of respectability for such a move. Written by an expert in international law, Professor John Bassett Moore, the paper argued that under the justification of "universal public utility" Colombia had no right to stand in the way of an improvement that would benefit the entire world.

Such a move carried great political risks, both domestically and internationally. But there was another option. Only two days after the rejection of the treaty (but before the news reached the United States), Senator Shelby Cullom gave a press conference on the canal question. Cullom was the chairman of the Senate Foreign Relations Committee, and had just been conferring with Roosevelt at the president's summer residence at Oyster Bay. Roosevelt was prepared for bad news, said Cullom, but was still determined on a Panama canal. When asked how this would be possible if the treaty failed to be ratified in Bogotá, Cullom replied, "We might make another treaty, not with Colombia, but with Panama." A month later Hay wrote to Roosevelt dismissing the possibility of making a "satisfactory treaty with Colombia," but going on, "It is altogether likely there will be an insurrection on the Isthmus against that government of folly and graft that now rules in Bogota . . . Something we shall be forced to do in case of a serious insurrectionary movement in Panama, [is] to keep the transit clear. Our intervention should not be haphazard, nor, this time, should it be to the profit . . . as heretofore, of Bogota."

⧏⧏⧏⧏⧏ ⧐⧐⧐⧐⧐

*I*n Panama the independence plot had gathered momentum and important friends. Following Arango and Amador, more Panama Railroad employees had been brought on board, including Herbert Prescott, assistant superintendent of the Panama Railroad (whose brother, another plotter, was married to Amador's niece), and James R. Beers, freight agent and port captain for the Pacific terminus of the PRR. Both were United States citizens, and the U.S. consul Arthur Grudger also joined the group. In July 1903 Cromwell, de facto head of the railroad, had summoned Beers to New York, at about the time of his planted story in the *New York World* about Panama's secession. Beers's meeting with Cromwell went well. The lawyer gave Beers a cable code and warned him to keep secret the involvement of the PRR, as it could forfeit its concession from Colombia. Cromwell also suggested a date for the revolution, November 3.

On August 26 Amador was sent by the plotters to New York. They were aware that without U.S. help any move by Panama toward independence could easily be crushed by Colombian forces. Amador sailed on board the *Seguranca*, a Panama Railroad and Steamship Company steamer. He had few funds for his trip, but managed to win a

*S*panish conquistador Vasco Núñez de Balboa discovers the South Sea and that Panama is a tantalizingly narrow isthmus.

*W*illiam Paterson, the Scottish promoter who declared that with possession of the Isthmus "trade will increase trade and money will beget money."

*M*apping the route for the Panama railroad through thick jungle and swamp.

*M*embers of the American Selfridge expedition in the Darién jungle, 1870.

*A*rmand Reclus, the young French naval lieutenant who mapped the route of the French canal and led the de Lesseps effort in its early years.

*T*he hero of the Suez Canal, Ferdinand de Lesseps, depicted as Hercules pushing apart the continents of Africa and Asia.

*F*erdinand de Lesseps with his second wife and some of his many offspring.

A triumphal arch, part of the lavish welcome given to de Lesseps when he descended on Panama at the beginning of 1880, fêted as the "Presiding Genius of the Nineteenth Century."

*C*harles de Lesseps, who urged his father not to take on the challenge of Panama but, seeing that the old man had made up his mind, gave him his unconditional backing.

*C*olón Harbor in 1884. The steamer was king, but much nonperishable freight was still carried by sailing vessel. The following year the town was destroyed by fire after a revolution on the Isthmus.

*T*he beginning of the "big ditch." In spite of the hopes of the leadership, much of the French canal was dug by men rather than machines.

*J*ules Dingler, *Directeur Général* of the canal, 1883–85, who would pay a terrible price for his devotion to the endeavor in Panama.

*T*he execution of Pedro Prestan in Colón on August 18, 1885.

A French ladder excavator. The machines that had triumphed at Suez proved unable to cope with the heavy clays of the Chagres valley.

*P*hilippe Bunau-Varilla, French engineer, lobbyist, and plotter extraordinaire.

*B*ottle Alley in Colón. The small town had nearly 150 bars, with 40 in this one street alone.

*H*uerne, Slaven & Co. dredges at work. Visitors were hugely impressed by these monster machines, but the American contractors were among the most corrupt of all those working for the French Company.

*T*he works in the Culebra Cut in 1888, with Gold Hill on the left.

With the press running for cover, the directors of the Canal Company, led by Ferdinand de Lesseps, are brought to trial. Eiffel brings up the rear.

𝒪n the Isthmus, wreckage from the French effort was everywhere, with the jungle quickly returning.

THE COUP D'ETAT.

New York World, November 9, 1903.

*I*n a cartoon published six days afterward, the *New York World* gives its impression of the "Panama Revolution."

*W*illiam Nelson Cromwell on one of his frequent journeys between Panama, New York, and Paris.

*G*eneral Esteban Huertas in the regalia of the Commander-in-Chief of the Panama Army. Declared a "Hero of the Republic" for his part in the "revolution," he was quickly seen as a threat by the Conservative junta.

$\mathscr{A}$ steamer carrying laborers from Barbados arrives at Colón. The tiny island provided the bulk of the thousands of workers for the American Panama Canal effort.

$\mathscr{A}$n ICC-run mess kitchen for the West Indian workers. No chairs or tables were provided, and the food was often inedible. After a short time, most workers made their own arrangements.

A fumigation squad, carrying ladders, paper, and paste, assembles in Panama City, 1905.

*D*octor William Gorgas near Miraflores.

A cemetery on the western slope of Ancón Hill photographed shortly after the completion of the canal.

*T*he energetic and resourceful chief engineer John Stevens, in boater, surveying work along the line.

*E*mptying spoil cars by means of dragging a metal plow along its surface. Such ingenious devices saved countless man-hours for the American canal effort.

*T*heodore Roosevelt, in white suit, making "a Strenuous Exhibition" on the Isthmus.

A West Indian wedding party at Culebra in 1913.

A commissary store in Balboa, with its separate sections for "Silver" and "Gold."

*C*laude Mallet, with his Panamanian wife, Matilde de Obarrio. Mallet's official reports and private letters give an illuminating view of Panama during the construction period.

*S*panish track workers taking a break in the Culebra Cut. Antonio Sanchez is second from right.

*S*team shovels at work on the bottom of the canal.

*B*lasting rock on Contractors' Hill, January 1912.

*L*oading holes with dynamite to blast the west bank of the Culebra Cut, February 1912.

*A*t 4:30 p.m. on May 20, 1913, workin at the final depth of t canal, shovels No. 22 and No. 230 meet "no to nose" at the cente of the Cut.

slide of 300,000 cubic yards in the Culebra Cut near Empire, August 21, 1912.

𝒢atún Locks under construction, showing the overhead cableway and the huge, rail-mounted structures holding the steel shutters.

𝒲orkers at the base of the lower Gate of Gatún Locks.

The final joining of the ocean being accomplished by pick-and shovel men digging a channel through the Cucaracha slide

The opening of the canal: S.S. *Ancon* passes the remnants of the Cucaracha slide on August 15, 1914.

The U.S.S. *Texas* in Gatún Lock in July 1919, a sight that would have pleased Roosevelt enormously. The military requirements of the United States were instrumental in getting the canal built.

goodly sum playing poker during the voyage. Also on board, on un-
related business, was José Gabriel Duque, the Cuban-American
owner of the *Panama Star and Herald* and the lottery, head of the fire
brigade, and reputedly now the richest man on the Isthmus. Duque,
an American citizen, knew about the plot, but was not part of the
revolutionary junta. He later claimed that much of the money won by
Amador was from him.

The boat arrived in New York on September 1, and Amador saw
Cromwell the next day, receiving "a thousand offers in the direction
of assisting the revolution." But it was José Gabriel Duque who was
met off the boat by Roger Farnham and taken straight to the office
of Cromwell and Sullivan at 41 Wall Street. For Cromwell, Duque
had two distinct advantages over Amador: he was rich, and he had no
awkward connection with the Railroad. The lawyer assured Duque
that there was no chance of Colombia coming to a deal, and that if
Duque lent the revolution $100,000 on Cromwell's security, the
lawyer would arrange for him to become the first president of an independent Panama. Of course, Cromwell went on, Duque should go
to see Hay, and, picking up a phone on his desk, he organized the
meeting there and then. The following evening Duque was on an
overnight train to Washington (to avoid having to register in a hotel),
and met Hay at ten o'clock the next day. The secretary of state all but
told him that the United States would support the revolution: "The
United States would build the Panama Canal and did not propose to
permit Colombia's standing in the way," Hay pronounced. If the revolutionaries took Panama City and Colón, he went on, American warships would prevent Colombian troops from landing under the
justification that they were keeping fighting away from the all-
precious transit.

No sooner had he left Hay's office than Duque was on his way to
see his old friend Tomás Herrán at the Colombian legation. Perhaps
because of some slight from the junta in Panama, from the influence
of his wife, a fiercely patriotic Colombian, or because he still hoped to
shock Bogotá into ratifying the treaty, Duque told Herrán everything.

The next day, September 3, the Colombian minister cabled home: "Revolutionary agents of Panama [are] here. Yesterday the editor of La Estrella de Panama had a long conference with the Secretary of State . . . There is the probability of revolution with American help." Herrán also set detectives on Amador's trail and fired off a warning to Cromwell that the Compagnie Nouvelle and the Railroad would lose their concessions—everything they were hoping to sell for $40 million—if they supported revolutionary activity.

This had Cromwell running scared. The next time Amador went to his office, he was "out." Amador said he would wait, but still the lawyer refused to appear. Eventually Cromwell burst out of his office and physically removed the Panamanian doctor from his premises. Soon after, Cromwell made arrangements to leave the country on business. He knew his card was marked and that someone else would have to take up the challenge of engineering the revolution.

Amador was confused and downhearted, cabling a single-word message—"Desanimado" ("Discouraged")—to his coconspirators in Panama and prepared to sail on the next ship. But then Amador heard that, should he remain in New York a little longer, he would receive help "from another quarter."

Philippe Bunau-Varilla later claimed that his voyage to the United States at the beginning of September 1903 was motivated by the illness of his thirteen-year-old son, who was staying with John Bigelow. In fact, the Frenchman was up to his neck in Cromwell's plot. At the beginning of the month he had written an article for Le Matin, predicting revolution on the Isthmus and naming that same date—November 3. He arrived in New York on September 22—exactly the time it would have taken if Cromwell had summoned him straight after Herrán's warning.

Bunau-Varilla met Amador two days later and found the doctor in a state of fear and indignation. "All is lost," said Amador. "At any moment the conspiracy may be discovered and my friends judged, sentenced to death, and their property confiscated."

The Frenchman reassured him that he, Bunau-Varilla, would handle everything. Just over a week later, Bunau-Varilla, through Hay's deputy Francis Loomis, one of the many Americans he had cultivated as they passed through Paris, secured a meeting with Roosevelt, ostensibly to discuss *Le Matin*'s role in the Dreyfus affair. Of course, the conversation turned to Panama. Bunau-Varilla announced that there was a revolution coming. The president was naturally unable to give overt support, but the Frenchman picked up what was left unsaid. Roosevelt later wrote to John Bigelow of the meeting: "I have no doubt that he was able to make a very accurate guess, and to advise his people accordingly. In fact, he would have been a very dull man had he been unable to make such a guess."

A week later Bunau-Varilla met Hay who agreed that an insurrection was imminent and let him know that U.S. naval units were already standing by to dash to the Isthmus "to keep the transit open." When Bunau-Varilla got together with Amador again shortly before the doctor's return to Panama, he assured him that U.S. help would be forthcoming for the revolution, as long as it happened on November 3. The money—$100,000—needed to bribe the Colombian garrison would come from the Frenchman's own resources, on the condition that Amador agreed to make Bunau-Varilla minister plenipotentiary in Washington for the new republic.

Bunau-Varilla now took total charge. As he wrote, "I held all the threads of a revolution on the Isthmus." The weekend before Amador's departure he spent at the Bigelows' house at Highland Falls writing a declaration of independence, military plans, and a new cipher code—Amador was "Smith," Bunau-Varilla, "Jones"—while his wife and Grace Bigelow sewed together a new flag made out of silk purchased by Bunau-Varilla at Macy's. The whole "revolution kit" was wrapped in the flag and presented to Amador when he left on October 20.

Back in Panama, Amador found his coconspirators unhappy about Bunau-Varilla's demand to be made minister plenipotentiary, the flag (it was much too similar to the Stars and Stripes), the small amount of money promised, and the lack of firm proof of U.S.

military assistance. Where was the signed agreement from Hay or Roosevelt? Who exactly was this Bunau-Varilla, and what authority did he have to offer promises of help? The plotters, for the most part wealthy landowners or professionals, had much to lose. The "revolution" experienced its first serious wobble.

Worse was to come. While Amador had been away in the United States, the junta had been working to bring into the conspiracy key players on the Isthmus. The mayor of Panama City, who happened to be the brother of Amador's young wife, María de la Ossa, was successfully recruited, as was the deputy head of the police force. General Esteban Huertas, the young commander of the local garrison, who was married to a Panamanian, seemed sympathetic although so far uncommitted, but his second in command, when approached, indignantly threatened to reveal the plot. To get rid of him, the state governor José de Obaldía, who lived with Amador and was unofficially in on the conspiracy, had invented an invasion in the north of Panama by Nicaraguan troops and dispatched a force under the man's command to investigate. But Obaldía, to cover his back, also cabled Bogotá on October 25 about the invasion scare. Three days later, Obaldía heard that the Colombian authorities, acting with uncharacteristic haste, had readied a force at Cartagena under the supreme commander of the army, General Tovar, to proceed to Colón to assist in repelling the supposed invasion.

The news caused a renewed panic among the conspirators, who demanded that Amador should rapidly provide proof of American support and the veracity of Bunau-Varilla's promises or the whole project would be abandoned. The next day, October 29, Amador sent the following cable to New York: "Fate News Bad Powerful Tiger Smith," which translated as "For Bunau-Varilla. More than two hundred Colombian troops arriving on the Atlantic side within five days." "Urge vapor colon," Amador went on, abandoning the code. Obviously he hoped that Bunau-Varilla, on his own authority, could order a U.S. Navy steamer to the Caribbean side of the Isthmus.

Of course, Bunau-Varilla had no such power, but he did have

friends in the right places. The same day he rushed to Washington. "It was a test to which I was being submitted," he later wrote. "If I succeeded in this task the Canal was saved. If I failed it was lost." His aim was to make the U.S. government understand that "its duty was to send immediately a cruiser in anticipation of probable events, rather than to wait for their explosion" as it had done in 1885 during the Prestan uprising. In Washington, Bunau-Varilla saw his friend Loomis, who was standing in for the secretary of state while Hay was away on holiday. Loomis agreed that the situation was "really fraught with peril for the city of Colón" and gave the Frenchman to believe that a steamer would be dispatched straightaway.

Bunau-Varilla had been watching the reports of U.S. Navy ships in the newspapers. He knew that the *Nashville* was at Kingston, and, according to his account, guessed that this would be the vessel sent to Panama. Calculating the speed of the craft and the distance to be covered, he estimated when the gunboat would arrive at Colón. The next day he cabled "Smith" in Panama saying a U.S. warship would be with them in two and a half days.

Bunau-Varilla's confident tone gave the conspirators new heart. In a frenzy of activity, the flag was redesigned, a new declaration of independence was penned, and Duque and his fire brigade of some three hundred young men were recruited and armed. Herbert Prescott brought his boss, Colonel James Shaler, into the plot and, realizing the importance of the railway—the only way across the Isthmus—they arranged for all the line's rolling stock to be moved to the Panama side. Shaler, a tall, white-haired seventy-seven-year-old, was a popular figure in Panama, and would later be made a "Hero of the Republic."

As Bunau-Varilla had predicted, the *Nashville* appeared in Colón Harbor late on the afternoon of November 2. The ship's captain, Commander John Hubbard, however, was not yet suspecting anything out of the ordinary. His orders were simply to consult with the U.S. consul and report back on goings-on on the Isthmus. Nor were Colombian loyalists suspicious of the arrival of the two-stacked gunboat—the *Nashville* had been at Colón just two weeks earlier. But to the conspirators here was irrefutable proof that Bunau-Varilla and the Americans were going to deliver on their promises.

At around midnight on the same day, a Colombian gunboat, the *Cartagena*, also arrived in the harbor. On board were three generals and about five hundred *tiradores*, or expert marksmen. The next morning Hubbard went on board to be informed by General Tovar that he was landing his men. Hubbard was determined to play it by the book. He had as yet received no orders to prevent the disembarkation, and there was so far no disturbance onshore to merit his intervention. Thus, shortly after first light on November 3 Generals Tovar, Amaya, and Castro, followed by Colonel Eliseo Torres, the next most senior officer, resplendent in uniforms of yellow, blue, and gold, glittering with medals and braid, stepped ashore onto the wooden wharf at Colón, closely followed by the rest of their men.

It was a bitter blow for the conspirators. Not only was the Colombian force formidable, but the Americans had singularly failed to prevent their landing, as had been promised. Fresh panic swept the group, and even Amador considered calling the whole thing off. However, Señora Amador was made of sterner stuff, rallying the plotters and quickly devising a trap to neutralize the Colombians.

The generals were met by local dignitaries and reassured that all was well to the north and that they should re-embark straightaway. But something made Tovar suspicious, and he demanded to be taken to Panama City. Enter Shaler, to play his part to perfection.

Unfortunately, said the Panama Railroad's superintendent, there were at the moment insufficient cars to transport the troops. However, there was a special luxury carriage available which could ferry the generals and their aides across to Panama. The Colombians protested, but were reassured that their men would be on the very next train.

Once on board the car, Amaya suddenly became jumpy and announced that he was going to stay with the men, but at that moment Shaler pulled the signal cord, jumped off the train, and waved cheerfully at the generals as they steamed out of the station. Soon after, Hubbard received orders from Washington, sent the day before but delayed, instructing him to prevent the landing of any armed force, or its use of the railroad. He therefore ordered Shaler not to transport the Colombian troops at Colón, thus giving the superintendent another excuse to buy time for the plotters at Panama City.

As soon as Amador heard from Prescott that the generals were on the way, he appealed once more to Huertas. "If you will aid us," he said, "we shall reach immortality in the history of the new republic." If he didn't, the elderly doctor warned, Huertas would surely be relieved and sent to some violent interior province of Colombia, far from his friends and family in Panama. At last Huertas agreed to be part of the uprising, his decision helped by the offer of $50 for each of his men, and $65,000 for himself.

The generals' luxury train arrived at Panama at 11:30, to be met by General Huertas, a military band playing patriotic songs, and crowds of children waving Colombian flags. As Tovar later said in his defense, "There was nothing that did not show the greatest cordiality and give me the most complete assurance that peace reigned throughout the department." After a procession through the city, the Colombian generals were taken to a hotel to have a siesta.

Meanwhile Amador and Duque prepared for a mass meeting to take place in the city at 5:00 p.m., with the fire brigade poised to arrest those who might resist the uprising and ready to distribute rifles. But rumors were everywhere, and at 1:30 p.m., the generals were awakened to be told that a demonstration was going to take place. Then a note arrived from a local Panamanian loyal to Colombia warning Tovar to trust no one.

The general roused himself and demanded to know why his men had still not arrived. While Shaler continued to invent excuses as to why the men could not be transported, Huertas took the generals to lunch. All the time, their suspicion was mounting. After lunch, having again ordered the governor, Obaldía, to organize the immediate dispatch of their men, the generals proceeded to the barracks to carry out an inspection. By 5:00 p.m., Tovar had heard reports of a mob gathering and making its way toward them. Huertas suggested that a patrol be sent out and Tovar agreed. But as the men detailed for the patrol proceeded out of the barracks, as if to pass in front of the generals seated on a bench near the seawall, they split into two columns, one marching in front of the seated men and one behind. On a command the men wheeled round and stopped, their fixed bayonets pointing toward the astonished Colombian top brass, who were told that they were now under arrest.

Tovar charged at one of the soldiers but was immediately hemmed in by bayonets. Castro also made a run for it, but was quickly recaptured, having been found hiding in a toilet stall. The prisoners were led away to the jailhouse to cries from the growing crowd of *"Viva el Istmo libre!" "Viva Huertas!" "Viva el Presidente Amador!"*

In order to maintain the fiction of his noninvolvement, Obaldía was arrested. Then U.S. vice-consul Felix Ehrman sent a message to Washington detailing the successful uprising, and at around 6:00 p.m., the leaders of the revolutionary junta proceeded to Cathedral Plaza to be acclaimed by an enthusiastic crowd. Now only the small matter of the five hundred heavily armed soldiers at Colón stood between Panama and independence.

⋘⋙

Colonel Eliseo Torres, the commander of the Colombian force at Colón, had heard nothing of the goings-on in Panama City, but was becoming increasingly aggressive about Shaler's constant refusal to transport his men. Then, early on November 4, he received a letter from Hubbard informing him that the railroad was closed to all troops. At lunchtime the same day, Torres was approached by Porfirio Meléndez, the junta's man in Colón, and told, over a drink at the Astor Hotel on Front Street, about the arrest of the generals and the uprising in Panama City. Meléndez then offered the colonel a bribe if he would remove his men. At first Torres refused to believe the news, but then he flew into a rage at the treachery of the Panamanians and their American friends, threatening to burn Colón to the ground and kill all American citizens in the town if the generals were not released.

Hubbard immediately readied his tiny force on the *Nashville* and started evacuating American and British women and children onto boats in the harbor, while their menfolk were herded into one of the stone buildings belonging to the Panama Railroad. Some forty U.S. sailors and marines were landed to defend the building, which was soon surrounded by Torres's greatly superior force. At this, Hubbard moved the *Nashville* close to the wharf, causing the *Cartagena* quickly to slip away, leaving her troops stranded. The American gunboat then trained her armament on the Colombians, and a tense standoff ensued.

But twenty-four hours later, when told that a U.S. force of five thousand men was on the way to the Isthmus, and satisfied with his brief defiance, Torres agreed to leave for the payment of $8,000. The money for the bribe had to be borrowed from the safe of the U.S.-owned Panama Railroad. There was not enough, however, also to pay for the passage on a steamer, so more money had to be obtained from a local bank. This loan was guaranteed by Hubbard and Shaler, both American citizens. With the departure of the Colombians, the revolution was complete. The following day, to express their gratitude to the United States, an American Army officer, Major William Murray Black, was asked to raise the new Panama flag over the prefecture of Colón. Soon after, an official cable arrived from Hay at the State Department. As the people of Panama had "resumed their independence," it read, the U.S. consuls should "enter into relations with it as the responsible government of the territory." *"Viva La Republica de Panama!"* exclaimed the *Star and Herald*.

◀◀◀◀ ▶▶▶▶

*T*he revolution had succeeded with American connivance, but it still relied on the United States to make it irreversible. The news of the uprising caused a sensation in Colombia, where the initial fury was aimed at Marroquín. His residence was pelted with stones, the police were called in, leading to the wounding of several protestors, and martial law was declared. But soon, as detailed accounts of the events became known, the anger was redirected toward the United States. A heavy guard was thrown around the American embassy and Beupré was told he should leave the country for his own safety. As Ambassador Herrán delivered a formal protest to Secretary of State Hay, thousands of Colombians volunteered to take part in an expedition to recapture Panama. Reyes threatened that unless recognition was withdrawn from the breakaway republic, the United States would have "a second Boer War" on its hands.

But only hours after the declaration of independence American troops had been landed and there were half a dozen U.S. gunboats on either side of the Isthmus. Roosevelt was wielding his "big stick"—naval power—for the first time. The Colombians were forbidden to land soldiers anywhere in Panama. On November 19 Reyes arrived off Colón as head of a commission charged with offering Panama anything short of independence. But he was not even allowed to go ashore, and proceeded to Washington to try his luck there.

Meanwhile, the Colombians equipped a force to try to make it overland to Colón through the Darién jungle. The men started off the following month, exhorted by their general that "it is preferable to see the Colombian race exterminated than to submit to the United States." But Darién proved impenetrable and, ravaged by disease, the troops soon turned back.

Claude Mallet's take on the extraordinary events of earlier in the month is pretty much spot-on: "I have come to the conclusion," he wrote on November 20, "that the scheme for a Republic was planned here, supported financially by persons interested in canal affairs in Paris, and encouraged by the Washington officials." Nor was he unaware of the implications: "The Americans, by their action here, have cast international customs to the winds, and henceforth, a new example has been set how to acquire the territory of your neighbour or friend."

As Cromwell and Bunau-Varilla had anticipated, the U.S. newspapers on the day after the "revolution" were dominated by domestic election news. On November 5, however, Panama was on every front page, and many papers would concur with Mallet's reading of the events. It was, said one, "revolution of the canal, by the canal, for the canal." "It is another step in the imperial policy," said the *Pittsburgh Post*. " 'Might makes right'—steal from the weak." There were many echoes of five years before, when the war with Spain had led to the formation of a widely supported Anti-Imperialism League. For the *Baltimore News*, the "Panama Affair" had, like the U.S. actions in the Philippines and Hawaii, brought the United States down to the sordid level of the land-grabbing European powers. To blame, said another paper, was the "hot-headed and immature" Theodore Roosevelt. "It begins to look as if nobody can touch that Panama ditch without being defiled," concluded the *Salt Lake Herald*.

The criticisms of American aggression, connivance in the revolution, and overhasty recognition of the new republic would be led by the *New York Times*, then a fiercely partisan Democratic paper. To the *Times*, the canal was "stolen property," and it soon focused its guns on the shady role of Cromwell. One of his partners, Edward B. Hill, when approached replied in classic style, "You can quote me to the extent of saying that I have nothing to say."

Others took a more pragmatic line. Even if the policy was wrong, said the *Houston Post*, "The thing is done, there is no way of undoing it, and the least said about it the better." For the *San Francisco Chronicle*, it was a sign of the times, but not therefore a cause for regret: "The world must move on," it wrote. "It is an age of power. The weak will be protected, but they will not be permitted to obstruct, whether upon the continent of America, the isthmus of Panama, the isles of the Pacific, the plains of Manchuria, or the valleys of the Ganges and the Indus. It is manifest destiny."

In all, about two-thirds of the United States' newspapers supported Roosevelt's actions, buying into his theory of "eminent domain" and his portrayal of the Colombians as blackmailers and extortionists. Those opposed tended to be Southern and Democratic-leaning. Certainly, public opinion never quite reached the level of opposition to the action in the Philippines. "The disheartening fact is that the connivance of our administration in the dismemberment of a sister republic is accepted so phlegmatically," wrote a correspondent to the New England Anti-Imperialist League. "The country ought to be ringing with the protests of citizens in mass-meetings assembled." But the man in the street's verdict, as reported by a Yale professor of law, was that "it served Colombia right." With the general acceptance of the U.S. action over Panama, one of the founding principles of the United States passed away forever, and the stage was set for U.S. aggression and expansion throughout the region and, indeed, the world.

⋘ ⋙

Leading the country away from its historical anticolonialism was, of course, Theodore Roosevelt. While many hoped that there had not been direct involvement in the revolution, they also admired the president's "virile" and "strenuous" response to events. One congressman was quoted as saying to Roosevelt, "Mr. President, I am glad you did not start the rabbit to running, but as long as the rabbit was going to run anyhow, it's a good thing we did not have a bow-legged man in the White House who couldn't catch it."

Roosevelt, of course, defended his actions and denied any role in the uprising. "I did not lift a finger to incite the revolutionists," he declared. "I simply ceased to stamp out the different revolutionary fuses that were already burning." His first task after the fait accompli was to bring his cabinet on board, and he gave a long, detailed statement of his position. When he had finished he turned to his secretary of war, Elihu Root. "Well," he asked, "have I answered the charges? Have I defended myself?"

"You certainly have, Mr. President," replied Root in a jokey tone. "You have shown that you were accused of seduction and you have conclusively proved that you were guilty of rape."

But in the changed political climate, it did not matter. On November 10 Roosevelt and his wife went to the opera to see *Barbette* at the National Theater. One of the lines was "What, a diplomat steal? A diplomat never steals. He only annexes!" The entire audience turned toward the president's box, and Roosevelt laughed as heartily as anyone and waved his hand in glee at the admiring crowd.

The next day the French ambassador Jules Jusserand had lunch with the president. When the talk inevitably turned to Panama, Roosevelt declared, "It is reported that we have made the revolution; it is not so, but for months such an occurrence was probable and I was ready for it. It is all for the best . . . Everything goes on there as we would wish; I am about to receive Mr. Bunau-Varilla."

⟨⟨⟨⟨⟨- -⟩⟩⟩⟩⟩

On November 4, when Colonel Torres was still in Colón, Bunau-Varilla had received a cable from Amador asking for the immediate transfer of the promised $100,000 to pay for the bribery of the Colombian troops. No mention, however, had been made of the agreed appointment of the Frenchman as Panama's minister plenipotentiary and envoy extraordinaire. Bunau-Varilla reluctantly released $25,000, which was transferred to a Panama bank for the use of the junta. The next day another cable arrived, again pressing for more money and for Bunau-Varilla to expedite the recognition by the United States of the new republic. But, to Bunau-Varilla's growing suspicion, there was still no mention of the diplomatic appointment. In fact, the junta was preparing to send its own commission to Washington to negotiate a new canal treaty, just as Bunau-Varilla feared.

The Frenchman was determined that only he should have the honor of seeing his name on the canal treaty, and was not about to let anyone else "mess up" the negotiations.

Bunau-Varilla knew very well that the United States could not recognize Panama until the Colombian troops had left Colón, but his reply implied that both the advance of the rest of the money and the recognition from the United States, so crucial to Panama in its first days, depended on his appointment as Panama's minister in Washington. When de facto recognition arrived just after midday on November 6, the Panamanians were under the impression that this had been arranged by Bunau-Varilla and later that day, wanting to keep him on side and secure formal recognition from the United States (which required a reception by the president), the junta at last gave him the appointment he wanted.

But three days later, just as Amador and Federico Boyd were preparing to sail for the United States, Bunau-Varilla was cabled detailed instructions about the sort of treaty Panama wanted. The terms included joint tribunals in the Zone, the reversion to Panama of land leased to the New Company, and powers of raising duties at the terminal ports. The clear implication was that Bunau-Varilla was to start negotiations, but to discuss all matters with Amador and Boyd when they reached Washington.

It is not known whether this cable was ever seen by Bunau-Varilla. By November 9 he was already in Washington, "to begin there," as he puts it, "the last and supreme battle." The same day he lunched with Hay, having informed the secretary of state of his appointment as "envoy extraordinaire" as soon as he had received it. At the meeting Bunau-Varilla urged Hay to organize quickly his official reception by the president. Hay agreed to this, but then asked the Frenchman about reports that a commission was setting off from Panama to come to negotiate a canal treaty. Bunau-Varilla had seen the same newspaper story that morning and had his answer ready: "Mr. Secretary of State, the situation harbors the same fatal germs— perhaps even more virulent ones—as those which caused at Bogota the rejection of the Hay-Herran Treaty." The same "intrigues" of "politicians" were active in Panama, as in Colombia. The situation could only be saved, Bunau-Varilla exclaimed, by "firmness of decision, and lightning rapidity of action. It is necessary to leave the enemy no time to perfect his plans."

The "enemy"—the "fatal germs"—were, it should be stressed, the Panamanians themselves, the leaders of the country he was supposed to be representing. But to Bunau-Varilla, the Commission was a "manoeuvre," an "intrigue . . . Amador was a party to it. I knew his childish desire to sign the Treaty." Bunau-Varilla was determined that such "childish" politicians should not stand in the way of "the last and supreme battle" being fought, and won "for the triumph of the Panama Canal" by Bunau-Varilla himself.

Hay did not miss the urgency, producing for circulation a draft treaty the very next day. He also took on board the Frenchman's tone, and realized that as long as he was dealing with Bunau-Varilla rather than the incoming commission of Amador and Boyd, Panamanian interests could be largely discounted. Both men were also aware that the treaty faced its sternest test at home in Washington, in a Senate that had only narrowly approved the choice of Panama. In addition, the rumors of improper U.S. involvement in the "revolution" had provided ammunition to enemies of the administration and/or the canal, what Bunau-Varilla called "the passions of parties and of contradictory elements." But with Panama prostrate—through its dependence on the U.S. military for its survival, as well as because of its *extraordinaire* representation in Washington—a deal could be rushed through whose terms would be irresistible to the Senate.

This is reflected in the articles of Hay's first draft treaty, produced on November 10. Its basis was the Hay-Herrán Treaty, including the onetime $10 million payment and the annuity, but substantially modified in favor of the United States. Nowhere was Panamanian sovereignty acknowledged, and the proposed Canal Zone was increased in area by 60 percent and included the "terminal" cities of Colón and Panama City. Within this Zone, now to be American "in perpetuity," the United States would have total military and civic control. Every possible objection that the Senate could raise was dealt with head-on. In fact many of the measures echo those amendments proposed to the Hay-Herrán Treaty by Morgan with the explicit purpose of making the deal unacceptable to Colombia.

On the same day that Hay composed this draft, the commission of Amador and Boyd set sail from Panama. They were due to arrive in New York seven days later. With them they carried orders for Bunau-Varilla that he should "adjust" a treaty, but that "all clauses of this Treaty will be discussed previously with the delegates of the Junta, M. Amador and Boyd." That Bunau-Varilla had not been explicitly told this by cable shows how, overestimating his importance, the junta feared antagonizing its "friend" in Washington; and also that they never suspected that he would move with, as he put it, such "lightning rapidity of action."

On Friday, November 13, in a hastily assembled uniform of the official representative of Panama, Bunau-Varilla was presented to Roosevelt. To witness the history in the making, and the de jure recognition of the new republic, the Frenchman's son went along too. After formal statements, Roosevelt took Bunau-Varilla's arm and asked him, "What do you think, Mr. Minister, of those people who print that we have made the Revolution of Panama together?" Bunau-Varilla replied with a rush of satisfactory rhetoric about "calumny" and "the mist of mendacity."

As he left the reception, Bunau-Varilla, aware that Amador was now only four days away, gave Hay another nudge. "For two years you have had difficulties in negotiating with the Colombians," he said. "Remember that ten days ago the Panamanians were still Colombians . . . You have now before you a Frenchman. If you wish to take advantage of a period of clearness in Panaman diplomacy, do it now! When I leave the spirit of Bogota will return."

In fact, Hay was operating at breakneck speed. A week later he would write to his daughter, "As for your poor old dad, they are working him nights and Sundays. I have never, I think, been so constantly and actively employed as during the last fortnight." He rushed his treaty round the departments and had a revised draft with Bunau-Varilla by late on November 15.

Bunau-Varilla was at one with Hay on the need to placate the Morgan party in the Senate—he even vainly tried to "convert" the Alabama senator—but he had to object to the inclusion of the terminal cities in the proposed U.S. zone. Panama City was, after all, the seat of government of the new republic. But he offered instead the right to expropriate property in Panama City or Colón on public health grounds and to enforce sanitary arrangements therein. And to see off any possible objection about the lack of U.S. control, he went even further than Hay had dared, adding this amendment: "The Republic of Panama grants to the United States all the rights, power and authority within the zone mentioned . . . which the United States would possess and exercise if it were the sovereign of the territory . . . to the entire exclusion of the exercise by the Republic of Panama of any such sovereign rights, power or authority." The "inflammatory, unnecessary and offensive" clause goes to show how little Bunau-Varilla weighed Panamanian dignity against pleasing the U.S. Senate.

Within twenty-fours hours, helped by his hired lawyer Frank Pavey, Bunau-Varilla had completed his new draft and was on his way round to Hay's house. But finding it in darkness he returned early the next morning and delivered the treaty. That same morning, November 17, he learned that Amador and Boyd had landed at New York.

Then, yet another happy accident: Boyd and Amador were met off the boat by Cromwell's agent Roger Farnham. Cromwell himself was due back from Paris later that day. Could they wait, as he wanted to speak to them? Aware of the lawyer's power and influence, the Panamanians delayed going straight to Washington, and met Cromwell later that day, and were persuaded to appoint him Panama's financial agent.

By coincidence or not, it gave Bunau-Varilla a precious further twenty-four hours to close the deal. But there was no word from Hay as the Frenchman waited nervously in his hotel suite for the entire day. At last, at 10:00 p.m., Bunau-Varilla sent a note to the secretary of state's house. He would tell the Panamanians to stay in New York, he wrote, but had to sign the treaty the next day. Hay replied immediately, inviting Bunau-Varilla to come that night.

When they met, Bunau-Varilla again urged speed. Hay was happy with Bunau-Varilla's draft, but knew that what looked like a great deal for his country might not look so good to an actual Panamanian. As he would write to Senator Spooner, the new treaty was "very satisfactory, vastly advantageous to the United States, and, we must confess, with what face we can muster, not so advantageous to Panama . . . You and I know too well how many points there are in this treaty to which a Panamanian patriot could object." If the Hay-Herrán deal had been unfair on Colombia, the new treaty was many times worse for Panama, as Hay later admitted.

At lunchtime the next day, Hay consulted with the attorney general and the secretary of war, Elihu Root, and in a frantic afternoon the final drafts were drawn up in the State Department. At 4:30, the two Panamanians, blissfully unaware of what was going on, boarded a train for Washington, but at six o'clock Bunau-Varilla arrived at Hay's office to sign the treaty. To the Frenchman's delight, waiting reporters addressed him as "Your Excellency." At 6:40 p.m., the treaty was signed, with a pen owned by Cromwell and ink from Abraham Lincoln's inkwell. "We separated not without emotion," Bunau-Varilla later wrote, "having fixed the destiny, so long in the balance, of the great French conception."

At 11:00 p.m., Bunau-Varilla was at Union Station in Washington to meet Amador and Boyd. As he later recounted, "I greeted the travellers with the happy news! 'The Republic of Panama is henceforth under the protection of the United States. I have just signed the Canal Treaty.'"

The Panamanians were stunned. According to Bunau-Varilla, "Amador was positively overcome by the ordeal" and nearly fainted. Neither did Boyd respond as he should have done to "a happy event which ought to have filled their hearts with joy." In fact, having been at first disbelieving, the Panamanians were soon furious, all the more so when they learned the terms of the treaty. Reportedly Bunau-Varilla was spat at by Boyd. They realized they had been betrayed. "Cherish no illusion, Mr. Boyd," Bunau-Varilla said when the Panamanian suggested that fresh talks could be had on various points. "The negotiations are closed."

Amador and Boyd did try to reopen talks two days later, but without success. In the meantime, Bunau-Varilla attempted to bully them into ratifying the treaty there and then, without further recourse to Panama, at one point pressing a pen into the hand of Amador, who reacted by angrily hurling it across the room. Bunau-Varilla then cabled Panama offering immediate credits of up to $100,000 from the bank of the House of JP Morgan if they ordered Amador and Boyd to ratify. Everyone knew that General Rafael Reyes would soon be in Washington and would offer pretty much anything to get Panama and the canal back for Colombia. Although Reyes's mission would prove fruitless, in spite of the high-profile support of ex-president Cleveland, it provided Bunau-Varilla the leverage to force super-quick ratification of his treaty by Panama. In fact, the junta agreed to sign on November 26, before they had even seen the treaty, which was on its way by boat, wrapped in a Panama flag and sealed with the family crest of John Bigelow.

At 11:30 on the morning of December 2, less than twenty-four hours after being brought to Panama City, the treaty was ratified. There cannot have been time to make a Spanish translation of the English text or to make copies for distribution to the nine men due to confirm the agreement. The likelihood is that the Hay–Bunau-Varilla Treaty was not even read by the signatories of the ratification decree, though the treaty would reduce their new country to little more than vassalage.

At first, the signing was welcomed in Panama. Then, as the rush and adrenaline of the last month subsided, a new view emerged. "What do you think of the canal treaty?" Mallet wrote to his wife soon afterward. "Here the people are disgusted, and one of the prime movers in the independence movement, was heard to say '*nos han vendido*' ['We've been sold out']. Well, the Yankees have got them at last, and they have been foolish enough here to think those hardened and practical people were governed more by sentiment than by their interests." Soon a view solidified that national rights had been signed away by a foreigner, and that perhaps Panamanians had merely changed an impotent overlord for a powerful and determined one. The brief honeymoon period was over, even before the first spade load of the American canal had been dug.

◄◄◄◄◄─►►►►►

In spite of all the efforts made to contrive a treaty to the liking of the U.S. Senate, the debate and division there were fierce, ironically in part as an embarrassed reaction to the meanness of the deal. The treaty, one senator pointed out, gave the "United States more than anybody in this Chamber ever dreamed of having . . . we have never had a concession so extraordinary in character as this. In fact, it sounds very much like we wrote it ourselves." Most of the opposition, however, was directed at the way Roosevelt had behaved toward Colombia. Some argued that the president had effectively declared war, something only Congress was authorized to do. Democratic senator Thomas Patterson of Colorado declared that the Canal Zone was "stolen in the most bare-faced manner from Colombia." "The president has denied with some heat that he had any complicity in this business," said Senator Edward Carmack. "He does not conceal the fact that he desired this insurrection. He does not conceal the fact that he intended to aid it if it occurred, and he can not conceal the fact that he did aid it." There had been a lot of talk, Carmack continued, about the people of the Isthmus "rising as one man," "but the one man was in the White House."

On the Senate floor Carmack went on to warn that the action against Colombia was "but the beginning of systematic policy of aggression toward the Central and South American states." "I fear," declared another senator, "that we have got too large to be just." An amendment ordering a payment of compensation to Colombia was narrowly defeated.

The Democrats were undecided how to vote on the treaty. They had 33 of the 90 Senate seats, and if united, could have blocked the measure and given Roosevelt a severe setback less than twelve months before the presidential elections. But many were in favor of a canal, which was also popular in the country. One Texas senator explained the dilemma by telling the story of a dog catching a rabbit in violation of its previous teaching: "You might whip the dog, but would you throw away the rabbit?"

In the event, less than half the Democrats voted against the Hay–Bunau-Varilla Treaty, which passed by 66 votes to 14 on February 23. Two days later the treaties were officially exchanged.

It was one of the most important deals in the history of American foreign relations, as it gave the United States absolute control over the future Panama Canal, and thus over the strategic and economic crossroads of the Americas. A contemporary historian, Wolf von Schierbrand, stated that the treaty's importance "to our future political, commercial, and naval expansion, in the Pacific as well as the Caribbean Sea, can scarcely be overestimated. It will be the main pillar of our future strength in those all-important regions." "From the point of view of world politics," said another distinguished commentator, "the construction and operation of the canal as a government undertaking means the extension of the political control of the United States over the Spanish-American nations."

On May 2, 1904, the assets of the Compagnie Nouvelle were signed over to the United States for $40 million. The sale was handled by JP Morgan (thanks to an intervention by Cromwell). Together with the $10 million paid to Panama, the sum dwarfed the purchases of Louisiana ($15 million), Alaska ($7.2 million), and the Philippines ($20 million). The actual physical handover on the Isthmus occurred early on May 4, when a U.S. Army engineer, Second Lieutenant Mark

Brooke, met with a representative of the New Company at the old Grand Hotel. After a few perfunctory words, the Stars and Stripes was hoisted. After all the ceremony of the French years, the amazing razzle-dazzle of Ferdinand de Lesseps, the presentation of the momentous occasion was something of a disappointment to the Panamanians.

The $40 million converted to 206 million francs, of which 128 million went to the credit of the Old Company and 77.4 million to the New Company. None of the shareholders of the Old Company got anything. The 226,296 who put in a claim as bondholders got on average 650 francs, or $156, approximately ten cents on the dollar for their investment. The New Company shareholders received 129.78 francs per 100-franc share, which worked out at an interest rate of less than 3 percent per annum, but must have been much more than they expected. Thus not only had Bunau-Varilla got his name on the treaty, but he also got back the money he had forcibly invested more than ten years before.

The Frenchman had resigned as Panama's minister on March 2, 1904, his job, "The Resurrection of the Panama Canal," complete. Cabling the decision to Panama City, he asked for his remuneration (which at $1,000 per month was in total less than $5,000) to be put toward the cost of erecting a statue of Ferdinand de Lesseps, "the great Frenchman, whose genius has consecrated the Isthmus to the progress of the world." As he crossed the hotel lobby to take the message to the telegraph office, he reports, "somebody unexpectedly seized my hands to express to me his congratulations. It was the lawyer Cromwell."

⤛⤜ ⤛⤜

Roosevelt, never one for self-doubt, conceded in a private letter that there was "great uneasiness caused among my friends by my action," but in reality he had few qualms about the path taken. "The one thing for which I deserved most credit in my entire administration," he would write, "was my action in seizing the psychological moment to get complete control of Panama." "It was a good thing for Egypt and the Sudan, and for the world, when England took Egypt and the Sudan," he wrote to his old friend Cecil Spring Rice at the British Foreign Office. "It is a good thing for India that England should control it. And so it is a good thing, a very good thing, for Cuba and for Panama and for the world that the United States has acted as it has actually done during the last six years. The people of the United States and the people of the Isthmus and the rest of mankind will all be the better because we dig the Panama canal and keep order in its neighborhood. And the politicians and revolutionists at Bogota are entitled to precisely the amount of sympathy we extend to other inefficient bandits."

In the November 1904 election Roosevelt saw the canal as a benefit, rather than a hindrance to his campaign, even though Henry Davis, the Democratic vice-presidential candidate, criticized Roosevelt's actions over Panama as belonging "more to an empire than a Republic." "Tell our speakers to dwell more on the Panama Canal," Roosevelt told an aide during the campaign. "We have not a stronger card." It had become a symbol for his active, vigorous leadership.

On November 8, 1904, Roosevelt got 7.5 million votes to his opponent's 5 million. The victory was attributed to Roosevelt's personal appeal, but also to the popularity of his activist Panama policies. A dismayed member of the New England Anti-Imperialist League commented, "We stand today, apparently in the shadow of a great defeat. Theodore Roosevelt represents today the temper and point of view of the American people, as to armies, navies, world power, Panama republics and American police duty on the Western Hemisphere."

But in spite of this victory, some of the Panama mud stuck. More dirt would be dug up in the years to come, leading to continued press and congressional investigations. Most important, the events leading up to the start of the U.S. construction effort would put the canal on the defensive in terms of domestic politics. After all the intrigue and politicking, huge pressure would now be bearing down on the canal effort to "make the dirt fly," with disastrous consequences.

Internationally, the secession and subsequent treaty locked the United States into a cycle of expansion in the region, and its long-range cost in bad feeling and ill will was immense. Had more attention been paid to the legitimacy of many of the Colombian concerns and to the reality of the political situation in Bogotá, rather than to the interests of a private, foreign-owned corporation, a deal could have been hammered out. Once this failed, it was poor diplomacy by Hay to sign a treaty with the new Republic of Panama so patently unfair that it was bound to store up trouble for the future. But as Roosevelt would later point out, while the arguments went on, at least now the canal was being built.

CHAPTER SIXTEEN

"MAKE THE DIRT FLY"

I"In America, anything is possible," Jan van Hardeveld would proclaim to his wife, Rose, and their two small daughters whenever he learned of some modern miracle of enterprise in his new country. The family lived on a homestead in a remote part of western Wyoming, where Jan worked as the foreman of a gang of largely Japanese workers on the Union Pacific Railroad. A recently naturalized Hollander, he had particular admiration for President Roosevelt's Dutch blood. When he heard about the start of the American canal, he was determined to be part of "the mighty march of progress." "The French gave up . . . but we will finish!" Jan proclaimed. "With Teddy Roosevelt, *anything* is possible."

George Martin, a carpenter's apprentice living in Barbados, was eighteen when he wrote, "A voice from a great people" invited him to help build the Panama Canal. "With the others I accepted . . . so I leave father and mother, brothers and relatives, away in the land of the Indies, in the west, and came to this strange land . . ."

As early as January 1904, while the Senate was still debating the Hay–Bunau-Varilla Treaty, journalists from the "great people" were on the Isthmus reporting back that there "is nothing in the nature of the work . . . to daunt an American. The building of the canal will be a comparatively easy task for knowing, enterprising and energetic Americans." Many were confident that it would be a splendid showcase of the ever-growing industrial and technological might of the United States, and the country's new superiority over the old powers of Europe.

With hindsight, the American project might seem to have a "solid inevitability" compared to the tragically doomed de Lesseps adventure. In fact, the construction was beset by very serious difficulties throughout, but particularly in the first three years, and on several occasions came close to disaster. When the Americans started work they replicated almost all the mistakes made by the de Lesseps company: they favored a sea-level canal; they split authority for the job, as the French had done up until the arrival of Dingler in 1883; their initial site investigation was patchy, leading to unpleasant surprises later on; and more than anything, they understimated or misunderstood the dangers of disease and the simply vast scale of the construction challenge.

On March 3, 1904, a week after the formal exchange of treaties with Panama, Roosevelt appointed a seven-man Isthmian Canal Commission (ICC). Their order from the president was simply that "the results be achieved." The chairman was the veteran Admiral Walker, known to many as the "Old Man of the Sea," who had led previous canal bodies. Although in this respect experienced, he was an old-fashioned figure and had not overseen any really large construction projects. The next most senior appointee, and the only member of the Commission who would actually reside on the Isthmus, was another military man, Major General George W. Davis, who was to be governor of the Canal Zone. The emphasis for the other five appointments was on engineering experience, rather than familiarity with heading up such an immense logistical project. Davis, for his part, had been involved with one of the Nicaragua private canal companies, but was first and foremost a colonial administrator—he had played a part in the organization of the U.S. military governments of Cuba, Puerto Rico, and the Philippines. As in the other newly acquired territories, the government of the Canal Zone, indeed, the entire commission and canal effort, would report to the new secretary of war, William Howard Taft.

Before the Isthmian Canal Commission was appointed, Roosevelt had been lobbied by delegations of prominent U.S. doctors urging him to give the medical challenge in Panama top priority. They seem to have been preaching to the converted. Roosevelt had been shocked by the death rate from yellow fever among U.S. soldiers in Cuba—five times more men had been killed by illness than by enemy action—and had himself, before he became president, publicized these terrible statistics in Washington. As early as February 1904 he wrote to Admiral Walker, "I feel that the sanitary and hygiene problems . . . on the Isthmus are those which are literally of the first importance, coming even before the engineering . . ."

Nevertheless, there was no medical representation on the first Commission, effectively the board of directors of the canal effort. But the American Society of Doctors did get their recommended man, Colonel William Crawford Gorgas, appointed chief medical officer. Gorgas was well respected for his work attacking the yellow fever epidemic in Cuba and was the country's leading expert on tropical diseases.

In early April the grandees of the Commission descended on Panama, accompanied by Gorgas and another sanitary officer and fellow veteran of Cuba, Louis La Garde. The doctors wasted no time in diagnosing malaria as an even greater threat to the canal builders than the dreaded yellow fever. Gorgas visited the marine barracks at Bas Obispo, a seemingly healthy, breezy spot, and was told that 170 of the 450 men had caught malaria since the beginning of the year. The source of the infection was not difficult to find. When Gorgas and La Garde examined the inhabitants of the nearby "native" village, they discovered that some 70 percent had the enlarged spleen of the malaria carrier.

The engineers of the ICC were accompanied by Roger Farnham, the press agent of the ubiquitous William Nelson Cromwell. As well as getting himself appointed Panama's U.S. counsel, Cromwell had become an "all-purpose trouble-shooter for the Republican Party." He did not need to be told what failure in Panama would do to the party's fortunes in the forthcoming presidential elections and was determined to keep an eye on the canal effort. Mallet did his best during the Commission's two-week stay to discover what he could about the Americans' plans. One of the commissioners told him that "he was sure every member of the Commission hoped that a sea-level canal would be built if it be practicable."

In fact, nothing concrete was decided by the trip. The question of the design of the canal hinged on the suitability of a variety of sites for the construction of dams and/or locks, namely Gamboa, Bohío, and Gatún. Until proper, deep borings were made, all the engineers could propose in the meantime in the way of "making the dirt fly" were harbor improvements at Colón and designs for waterworks for the two terminal cities.

On May 6, two days after the official handing over of the French properties to the United States and the raising of the Stars and Stripes on Ancón Hill, John Findlay Wallace was appointed to the job of chief engineer, in charge of all canal construction work, although without a seat on the Commission. Wallace, a Midwestern-railroad veteran and first-rate engineer, had been tempted to Panama by $25,000 a year, a salary larger than that of any other government employee except the president.

The new governor of the Zone, Major General Davis, arrived to stay on May 17. A man of few words or courtesies, he soon found that what could be got away with in Cuba or the Philippines would not do in Panama. Davis threw himself into the work, issuing orders and rushing about, but failed to call on President Amador for several days and even refused to attend the many ceremonies inevitably arranged in his honor by the Panamanians. Complaints reached Washington and eventually Davis was ordered to change his attitude. There was further bad feeling as the marking out of the new U.S. Canal Zone boundaries was begun and the reality of the Hay–Bunau-Varilla Treaty sunk in. "They have taken all the meat and left the bone," one "disgusted" Panamanian complained to the British consul.

"The canal employees are coming," Mallet wrote to his wife on June 2. "The Isthmus is swarming with Yankees already," he reported a week later. "From ocean to ocean you see them everywhere and American flags hoisted on all sides." Most excitement was attached to the arrival—at the end of the month—of Wallace and Gorgas to take up permanent residence. "The medical board declares that not one mosquito shall survive," wrote Mallet. "Panama without mosquitoes? What a blessing . . ."

⫷⫷⫷⫸⫸⫸

On June 21 the steamer the *Allianca* sailed from New York. As well as Wallace and Gorgas, on board was William Karner, a colleague of Wallace from Chicago who had been appointed assistant engineer; two other senior sanitary officers; a new head nurse, Eugenie Hibbard, with two other nurses; and about a dozen clerks and sanitary inspectors. Karner, who would later play a crucial role as the chief recruiter of labor for the canal, had taken the job out of loyalty to his old boss, in spite of the fact, he wrote, that the "proposition [of the job] and a residence in Panama was not very alluring to me." Eugenie Hibbard, a Canadian, had made her name in hospital and training-school administration. Forty-eight in 1904, she had served in Cuba—and survived an attack of yellow fever. In spite of her great experience of difficult postings, Hibbard reports that she was quite daunted by the prospect of Panama. Her friends had asked her why she would want to go to "such a God forsaken place where the French have so finally failed!" "We felt," she wrote of herself and two fellow nurses, Miss Markham and Miss McGowan, "that we were going to a country of swamp and jungle, filled with crawling and flying death, where any white woman was sure of destruction."

After a rough and uncomfortable voyage, the *Allianca* arrived at Colón on the morning of June 28. "The rainy season had just commenced," William Karner remembered, "and a shower that morning had left the streets of Colón and Cristóbal in thick, impassable mud. It was not a pleasant introduction to a strange country and city, both of which we knew had a bad reputation as to health and sanitation." The party was met by Governor Davis and piled onto a train to Panama City.

The outskirts of Colón made their customary shocking impression on the new arrivals. The conditions, Hibbard remembered, "beggar description, the houses being huts of wood built on piles 2 or 3 feet above the most filthy water, foul smelling and covered with green slime filled with most objectionable refuse . . . Leaving Colón behind," she continued, "we saw for quite a distance alongside the Canal long neglected and broken and abandoned machinery, with here and there many graves surrounded by small railings (wooden) and marked with a rough white wooden cross impressed one forcibly of what had taken place. Soon we began to climb the mountains and the remarkable beauty of the country, the hills and foliage thrust itself upon us. I had never seen such luxuriant growth of trees and shrubs . . . flowering plants and many beautiful orchids growing at random."

The transit completed, the nurses were conveyed to the French-built hospital at Ancón. Once the pride of the tropics, the grounds had reverted to jungle, and the buildings were in a woeful state of decay and dilapidation. The nurses were shown to their quarters, "a strange and unattractive abode," said Hibbard, "the first night passed in these quarters was sufficient to have broken down the courage that has brought us here. The following day, I asked the Commanding Officer for something to guard ourselves with and he gave me a pistol (a Colt revolver) too heavy for me to handle in one hand. I placed it on a chair at my bedside at night and looked lovingly upon it as a possible protector."

The wards, in which about thirty patients, mostly incurables, were being cared for by the French Sisters of Charity, were filthy by Eugenie Hibbard's standards. The task of cleaning them up, and clearing out the ancient, bug-infested horsehair mattresses, fell to the nurses. "There was, I realized, a stupendous piece of work before us," Hibbard wrote, "and so it proved to be."

The day after the arrival of the *Allianca*, Joseph Le Prince, one of Gorgas's sanitary inspectors, carried out a check on potential mosquito breeding sites near the Ancón wards. The bottom of the hill, he discovered, was continually soggy, and adjacent pasture had hoofprints full of water. Nearby drainage ditches were choked with weeds, which retarded the water flow and provided the environment mosquitoes needed to lay their eggs. In fact, he concluded, "A more prolific source would be hard to imagine." The result was that the hospital was swarming. "The *Anopheles* [malaria-carrying mosquitoes] were so numerous," wrote Le Prince, "that night work had to be done in relays; one set of men using fans to protect those working." No fewer than fifty-four *Anopheles* were noted on the upper panel of a single screen door. Furthermore, the patients in the wards were located according to nationality rather than the nature of their illness. "Had it been intended," said Le Prince, "to spread yellow fever and malaria with the greatest rapidity among the patients as soon as they arrived, no better plan could have been adopted." Within just weeks, all but a couple of the small hospital staff had come down with malaria, Gorgas included.

⫷⫷⫸⫸

*T*he engineers among the first arrivals would find a similarly melancholy scene. According to Wallace, there was "only jungle and chaos from one end of the Isthmus to the other." Panama was a gigantic scrap heap. All along the line of the old French canal, abandoned excavators and dredges, some of huge size, slumped lopsidedly, half submerged in swamp or stream. Over everything the voracious returning jungle had draped a thick web of vines. Discarded locomotives and spoil cars were piled in huge mounds of rust and twisted metal. Materials lay scattered everywhere, as if abandoned by a hastily retreating army. The buildings, which at one time had housed more than twenty thousand canal workers, had been reclaimed by termites, rot, or vegetation. Inside one building, where the rafters had decayed and the roof had collapsed, Joseph Le Prince found several trees growing with trunks more than ten inches in diameter. In one place, an entire village had been completely buried by the returning jungle.

Although the wreckage of the French effort scattered everywhere had an unnerving effect on the first American canal builders, once they started to go systematically through their inheritance, the picture brightened considerably. Many of the two thousand buildings would be repairable. Six working machine shops provided a nucleus for later expansion. The French had left their successors maps and surveys, "excellently recorded [which] proved to be of great use." According to Wallace, there was a significant amount of materials and supplies safely stored in warehouses and unissued, which were in "a fairly good condition, and were systematically stored, arranged, tabulated and properly cared for." Vital spare parts and machine tools had been liberally coated in grease against the corroding warmth and damp of the climate. "Splendid workmanship was shown on these machines," one American engineer conceded, "and good material was used in their construction." Although, "obsolete," he went on, "they were good appliances of their date."

On second glance, the actual digging achieved was impressive also. As well as an eleven-mile passage from Colón to Bohío, there were vast excavations where Eiffel's locks were to have gone. On the Pacific side a passage had been dredged from La Boca to deep water, and "considerable work had been done on the channel from La Boca to Miraflores." In addition, over thirty miles of diversion channels had been created for the Chagres River. There had clearly been a lot of very hard work. After everything they had heard, most new arrivals were surprised by the "magnificence of the French failure." The Europeans had achieved, it was apparent, "vastly more than the popular impression." How much of this immense excavation—nearly 50 million cubic meters (73 million cubic yards)—would be useful would, of course, only be determined when a definite plan for the American canal emerged.

Wallace himself wrote that his approach to deciding the type of canal that should be built was determined by the "great amount of work already performed by the old and new Panama Canal companies" as well as "the tentative plans developed by the former Isthmian Canal Commission." The Walker Commission of 1899–1901 had been heavily influenced by the French New Company plan put together in 1898 to increase the saleability of the canal concern. The French proposal had allowed for a dam and locks at Bohío, some fifteen miles upriver from where the Chagres meets the Atlantic. This, it was planned, would create an artificial lake at 68 feet above sea level. With a surface area of just over 13,500 acres (5,500 hectares), this would stretch for thirteen miles through the Culebra Cut, at the Pacific end of which would be built at Pedro Miguel further dams and locks to return shipping to sea level. The lake would provide water for the locks and also, it was hoped, absorb the seasonal floods of the Chagres. Alternatively, a further raised section could be created through the Continental Divide at 96 feet above sea level between Obispo and Paraíso. Clearly the thinking of the French was in part shaped by the sacrifices made in the 1880s. Both of these options had the merit of avoiding "the loss of any work already performed." The idea of a plan that would render much of the French digging superfluous, as eventually adopted, was, for now, too ghastly to contemplate.

Although the Walker Commission had dispensed with the high-level option—feeding the top level of the canal from the upper Chagres would have been too difficult—they had remained wedded to the idea of the main dam at Bohío, albeit with a lake of the higher elevation of 85 feet above sea level. This is what the influential engineer Morison had argued for and defended at the Senate hearings before the Spooner debate. But the Spooner Act had not specified the type of canal except that it should "afford convenient passage for vessels of the largest tonnage and greatest draft now in use, and such as may be reasonably anticipated" and should use "as far as practicable the work heretofore done by the New Panama Canal Company, of France, and its predecessor company." Indeed, during the "Battle of the Routes" in the Senate, one of Mark Hanna's arguments in favor of Panama had been that only there was a sea-level canal possible. In fact, de Lesseps's dream of an "Ocean Bosporus" still held a great appeal, even after the disasters of the 1880s.

The upshot was that Wallace and the ICC members went to Panama with the most basic specifications of the canal—lock or sea-level—undecided. Nothing could be ruled out, and therefore there was much work to be done investigating all the possible options.

When the New Company was handed over to the Americans on May 4, they took over a skeleton workforce of about five hundred men, most of whom were employed in the Culebra Cut, where two French ladder excavators were carrying out intermittent work. Others were maintaining such machinery as had been stored away. At the beginning of June, five different U.S.-led parties were established and set to work: one to survey Colón Harbor; another to start planning waterworks for Panama City. The three other parties were instructed to carry out the deeper borings demanded by the ICC to test for the suitability of various sites for dams and started work at Gatún, Bohío, and Gamboa. Although Gatún had not been mentioned by Walker as a possible dam site, there had been several recent papers published in U.S. engineering journals that had suggested it. The Gamboa group was also charged with mapping the routes of spillways to carry the floodwaters of the Chagres away from the line of the canal, as would be required for a sea-level canal. In July a base camp was established at Bas Obispo and the twelve Americans, accompanied by two dozen locals recruited to do the machete work, started to search for a route to link the upper Chagres with a small river that flowed from the heights of the Continental Divide into the Pacific.

Effectively, they were recrossing the ground covered by Henri Cermoise back in 1881–82, and the same conditions prevailed. But the laboriously cut *tranches* had long disappeared. "It was not possible to advance a foot without hacking one's way through a tangle of creepers," an engineer wrote of the expedition. "Lizards and gaudy snakes crawled and scuttled everywhere . . . insect pests were super-abundant." At the end of each day a space was cleared in the jungle and a makeshift shelter was improvised using poles with canvas or palm fronds for a roof. Nighttime was a torment of itching and scratching at the festering sores caused by ticks, "red-bugs," "jiggers," and other parasitic insects that specialized in laying eggs under the skin of their victims. Supplies were carried by canoe upriver to the surveyors, but once in a while a monkey was cooked and eaten.

As fieldwork continued, three of the old French excavators were overhauled and set to work in the Culebra Cut, both to provide visible proof that they were "making the dirt fly" and also to provide data on the effectiveness and unit costs of different types of machine.

At the ocean termini of the line, a new divisional head engineer, Frank Maltby, had started work on dredging the harbors. Maltby was originally from Pittsburgh, but had worked for three years as head of dredging operations on the Mississippi. He got the job through a friend of his on the Commission. He had never been to sea before and was sick for the entire seven-day voyage to Colón. He found the town "indescribably filthy" but was given lodging in the old "De Lesseps Palace," an imposing residence built at Cristóbal for *Le Grand Français*'s 1886 visit. Within two days he was hospitalized for a week with diarrhea, but once at work he quickly demonstrated that what-ever its outward appearance, much of the supposedly "obsolete" French plant was eminently usable, even machines that had spent the last fifteen years semi- or entirely submerged underwater. "As the use of cheap steel had not become the practice at the time of their creation," explained one U.S. engineer, "they were built of a superior class of iron—a much better metal to withstand the ravages of time and sea water." Within a couple of months Maltby had six of the old Scottish-built ladder dredges back working, crewed in the main, as during the French years, by Greeks. The locomotives that lay abandoned all around were also found to be "built like a watch in workmanship, of splendid material," and were similarly pressed back into service.

But there were also numerous frustrations. Soon after his arrival, Maltby tried to organize the building of a short length of railway track. For some reason there seemed to be plenty of ties lying around. Rails could be picked up from abandoned track, and spikes could be pulled out of rotten ties. But as there was no spike maul to be had, his men had to bang in the spikes with axes.

In fact, it was just as well that so much equipment was suitable to put back to work, as precious little was arriving from the United States. In Washington the Isthmian Canal Commission was from the outset in a state of paranoid ineptitude. The sensational events of the "Panama Affair" in France in 1890–92 had been watched around the world. So, however unfairly, the French had left behind in Panama, along with everything else, the taint of waste, extravagance, and corruption. The instinct of the U.S. Commission, therefore, was to query and triple-check every requisition. "When this whole thing is finished," Commission chairman Walker announced, "I intend that those fellows on the hill shall not find that a single dollar has been misspent." As well as critics in Congress, Walker was acutely aware that the anti-canal or anti-Roosevelt press was waiting to pounce on any example of "waste" in the French style. Therefore, everything had to be cleared by all seven members of the Commission, each of whom felt personally responsible that no "graft" would be tolerated on their watch.

The result was chaos and deadlock. A system of purchases was created that required a nightmare of forms in triplicate. The work on the Panama sewers was hampered by the fact that it took the filling in of six vouchers for the hire of a single horse and cart. That meant that the engineer in charge had to spend his Saturday night filling in no fewer than 1,200 such forms. There was a further, more serious setback to this work when it emerged that the pipes for the job had been sent in the wrong order. Then it was discovered that some vital equipment had been sent, for economy's sake, by sailing schooner and would not arrive for months. When Wallace cabled Washington to protest the lack of equipment coming through, he was sharply reprimanded by one of the commissioners that sending cables cost money.

Among an ever-thickening blizzard of paper, orders became duplicated or lost. Alternatively they were pared down or simply filed away. When Walker left his job the following year, over 160 requisitions were found stuffed into drawers in his desk, some many months old. Those on the Isthmus responded by attempting to predict their needs far into the future or simply bumped up their orders, expecting them to be adjusted downward. On one occasion, Wallace's chief architect, his twenty-nine-year-old nephew O. M. Johnson, calculated that he would eventually require 15,000 doors, for which he needed 15,000 pairs of hinges. He might have expected to receive a fraction of that, but somewhere in the paper storm in the Washington office the order took on monstrous proportions and, soon after, 240,000 perfectly made hinges turned up at Colón.

The architect's office was one of the many bottlenecks in the initial organization. There was a great deal of work involved in repairing the French quarters, let alone designing and building new accommodations. But it was a chicken-and-egg situation. As Wallace complained, "Suitable quarters and accommodations could not be provided without organization, supervision, plans and material, which of course, rendered a large force necessary almost at the commencement of the work, which had to be provided with suitable quarters and accommodation."

Demand for labor was acute while the need for quarters massively outstripped the available supply. Cities of tents were created on the slopes of Ancón Hill and elsewhere, but these were soon full as the workforce expanded to thirty-five hundred by November 1904. To "make the dirt fly," the Washington office was sending hundreds of men to the Isthmus every week, "before there was any way to care for them properly, or any tools or material to work with," as Frank Maltby complained.

Soon after her husband's departure for the canal project, Rose van Hardeveld received her first letter from Jan, who had given up his post on the Union Pacific Railroad to accept a job with the Commission and thus become part of Teddy Roosevelt's "great march of progress." Having sailed from San Deigo, van Hardeveld arrived at Panama City and made his way to Culebra. "A heavy suitcase in each hand, no light anywhere, the sweat rolling down my face, I stumbled along the wet slippery track, which I had been told to follow until I found a place to turn off," he wrote. "I could sense that the water was on both sides. If my foot slipped from the ties, it landed in soft mud. In the deep darkness I seemed to have walked miles, and I never dreamed there could be such unearthly noises as came to my ears from all around. Thick croaking, hoarse bellowing, and strange squeaks and whines leaped at me from the blackness. I have learned since that these swamp noises are made by lizards, frogs and alligators, but to me they sounded like the howling of demons. Well, I decided that turning back looked almost as hard as going on, so here I am." As she read the letter, remembered Rose, "tears stood in my eyes . . . My Jan was not a man to contemplate turning back from any goal he had elected to pursue—unless obstacles loomed virtually insurmountable."

His accommodation turned out to be "a big bare lumber barn, not quite so well constructed as the horse stables on the ranches at home," divided into cubicles just big enough for two men to share. A week later another letter arrived. "The food is awful," Jan wrote, "and cooked in such a way that no civilized white man can stand it for more than a week or two . . . Almost all the food is fried. They feed us fried green bananas, boiled rice, and foul-smelling salt fish. It rains so much that honest to goodness my hat is getting mouldy on my head . . . I haven't had on a pair of dry shoes in weeks." In the next letter, he reported that disease was rife. Rose's parents started raising objections to her plan for the rest of the family to join Jan in Panama.

There are numerous such examples of the shock and instant de-moralization experienced by new arrivals during this early period. Some, however, greeted these challenges with a cheerful determina-tion resonant of the early French period. Jessie Murdoch landed at Colón along with a party of other young nurses in mid-1904 feeling, she admitted, a mixture of "apprehension," "homesickness," and "dread of what the future might hold." Colón was alarming with its "narrow, dirty, half deserted streets, with the native element running about half clothed," and at Ancón Hospital, in spite of the warm welcome from Eugenie Hibbard, she was dismayed by the "old rusted iron French beds, with mildewed mattresses." On her first night she ventured outside, only to be "eaten alive" by mosquitoes. Retreating to bed, "Each had a candle, but it was soon found that it was not wise to keep these burning, as they attracted moths and all sorts of flying insects." "Yet in spite of these many difficulties," she would write later, "we were not disheartened, but thoroughly enjoyed the novel experiences." "We found upon our arrival here," wrote young engineer James Williams, "the wreck of the French companies, a foreign language, strange people, poor food, no ice, no lights, no drinking water, no amusements, or decent living quarters . . ." But more important for Williams was the "thrill and the knowledge that we were working for Uncle Sam, accomplishing something that the eyes of the world were focused upon and something that every citi-zen of the United States [was] interested in."

Others employed in the United States by the Washington office were less impressed with the patently yawning chasm between what they found and what they had been led to expect. "We were supposed to have furniture issued to us, my allotment being nominally six chairs, a bed, three tables, washstand and tin pitcher, and a clothes rack," explained John Meehan, who arrived in early December 1904. "What we really got was a cot, and a dynamite box." Meehan, like van Hardeveld, was living in Culebra, which consisted of several laborers' bunkhouses and a smattering of cantinas and "chino shops," which sold canned food at high prices. Everyone lived on tins of sardines and soggy crackers. The only two-story building was a "hotel" run by "Cuban Mary," a "disorderly place, very dirty, crude in every way." There was one muddy main street; "chickens walked about inside the stores and native shacks, a few pigs and a million goats wandered about the streets." Reading in the evening was impossible, Meehan complained, because of the "army of bugs." The only thing to do was to go to bed or to one of the bars.

Meehan would remain on the project for many years. Others took one look around and simply headed back home again. Charles L. Carroll, a graduate from Pittsburgh, arrived in Panama in August 1904. A month later he wrote to his mother: "I am thoroughly sick of this country and everything to do with the canal ... Everyone is afflicted with running sores. We are compelled to sleep in an old shed, six to a room ... The meals would sicken a dog ... Tell the boys at home to stay there, even if they get no more than a dollar a day." Weeks later Carroll left the Isthmus for good.

In October 1904, the Italian minister in Panama reported back to his government on the dismal start to the U.S. canal effort: "The managers are said to be dishonest and incompetent," he wrote. "There have been many errors and much wastage and pilfering of money. The workers of all nationalities are treated inhumanely. As a consequence of all this, most people look back on the French administration, with all its defects, as more capable, more honest and more just towards the workers."

⫷⫷⫷‑⫸⫸⫸

*W*allace would complain that the delays in sorting out the problems in accommodation were down to "supplies taking for ever to arrive" and the labor "immediately available and who could be secured from the surrounding countries [being] incompetent, shiftless and lazy." But much of the intake from the United States was also seriously below standard. A request was posted for twenty-five track foremen, and when they arrived there were only two who could drive a railroad spike. In further echoes of Blanchet's experience with his new arrivals in 1881, William Karner complained that recruits employed by the Washington office "were not examined at all." One young man presented himself to Karner as a rodman. It was quickly realized that he was nothing of the kind, having no training or experience at all. It was then established that he had received his appointment through the efforts of his member of Congress.

In spite of all the worries about corruption or graft, this was the origin of many of the Panama appointments not just in the early years but throughout the American period. The Swinehart family were typical. At the end of 1904 Swinehart Senior, the chair of a local Republican group in Steamboat Springs, Colorado, wrote to his congressman: "I have two sons who wish to go to Panama to work on the Canal ... I will consider it a great favor if you will see some member of Canal Com." Less than a month later, the congressman delivered two plum appointments. "Please place my name on your list of working Republicans and command me at any time," responded the delighted father.

Along with idealists, professionals, and the beneficiaries of political favors, the Isthmus was also drawing in "railroad men who were blacklisted on the American railroads, drunks, and what we called tropical tramps, American drifters in Latin America." U.S. diplomat William Franklin Sands sailed for Panama in early October 1904. On his ship, a British Royal Mail Packet Company steamer, he was taken aback to read a notice outside the dining room which ordered: "Americans will put their coats on for meals." Why pick on Americans? Then he discovered that the captain had frequently had to arrest U.S. mechanics on the way to the Isthmus for drunkenness, gambling, and even leading mutinies against the officers.

As in the days of the gold rush, such new arrivals inevitably caused friction and difficulties with the Panamanians. One British journalist reported that "the people of Panama look upon Americans as noisy, grabbing bullies." In return, admitted a senior American administrator, "The average American has the utmost contempt for a Panaman and never loses an opportunity, especially when drunk, to show it." In fact by the autumn of 1904 relations between Americans and Panamanians were strained at every level. This had led to dangerous, potentially violent fractures within the new Panamanian political establishment, as well as dissent between senior U.S. Zone officials. It was to report on the origins of this mess, and to suggest solutions, that diplomatic "troubleshooter" William Sands—only twenty-nine but a veteran of diplomatic posts in the Far East—was sent by Taft to the Isthmus in October 1904. His mission was to ensure that nothing in the Panamanian political firmament got in the way of the building of the canal.

After independence at the beginning of November 1903, the leaders of the plot who were Panamanian nationals, rather than Americans, had formed themselves into a temporary ruling junta. Led by Arango and Amador, the junta contained several token Liberals but was otherwise firmly Conservative. The Panamanians had been given a firm warning by U.S. officials in the Zone: the civilized world had determined to enforce order and peace; "Panama must conduct itself as a civilized nation or it will cease to exist as an independent country."

This threat did much to keep tension between the Conservative administration and its Liberal enemies in check, and a national assembly was elected which, although Conservative-led, included an almost equal number of Liberals. Nevertheless, the Conservatives set about removing potential enemies. Several senior Liberals were offered plum diplomatic postings to get them out of the country; General Huertas, a Hero of the Republic for his part in the events of November 1903, was now seen, because of his popularity and Liberal sympathies, as a threat and was sent on a lengthy fact-finding mission to the United States and Europe.

But as soon as one potential enemy was removed, another emerged. The undisputed leader of the Liberals was Dr. Belisario Porras, an archenemy of Amador, described by the American consul in Panama as a "revolutionary firebrand" and "notorious hater of foreigners." Porras, who had worked as a lawyer for the French Company, had opposed the Hay-Herrán Treaty as giving too much control to the United States, and was appalled by the terms of the subsequent Hay–Bunau-Varilla Treaty. Panama, he said, had been "swallowed up" by the United States; national sovereignty had been sacrificed for the benefit of a few wealthy Conservative Panama merchants. In June 1904, he returned to Panama City from exile abroad to be greeted by a huge crowd in Santa Ana Square. Although he admired, he said, the "greatness and harmony of North American institutions," he believed that "any Latin American nation who fused her destiny with that of the United States would suffer greatly and rue the day of their alliance."

In the meantime, the Americans themselves had been providing plenty of fuel for anti-U.S. sentiment on the Isthmus. In May 1904, the Zone authorities successfully demanded that an American doctor be allowed to inspect all ships arriving at Colón and Panama. The man appointed did not even speak Spanish. The following month it was announced that the domestic tariff laws of the United States would be applied to the Zone. This meant that goods from the United States arrived free of duty, while imports from other countries, including Panama, were forced to pay very high rates. As it was simple to smuggle merchandise from the Zone to the Republic, the measure would slash the Panama government's vital customs revenue at the same time as infuriating the country's merchants. Then ports were opened at La Boca and Cristóbal, both adjacent to the terminal cities but within the Zone. As well as threatening to ruin Panama City and Colón, this seemed to be contrary to the terms of the Hay–

Bunau-Varilla Treaty, which had specifically excluded the "terminal cities and the harbours adjacent to said cities" from the U.S.-controlled area.

These measures provoked furious clashes between Amador and his Liberal first *designado*, or vice president, Pablo Arosemena, and gave many the impression that the annexation of the terminal cities, and indeed, the entire republic, was imminent. "I look upon the Republic of Panama as doomed," Mallet wrote to his wife at the end of June. "The Yankees are playing the same tricks here as they did with Colombia in regard to the canal question . . . The U.S. Government are behaving here like highway robbers; they neither respect treaties or persons." A month later he reported, "Opinion here amongst the natives is spreading, and they now think the bargain with the Americans has been a bad one for them and their country; they would prefer, I think, to return to Colombia than continue this way."

At this time the U.S. ambassador to Panama was John Barrett, who was attempting to negotiate a way out of the impasse. Then Governor Davis became involved, which, as he was not an accredited diplomat, the Panamanians saw as a further slight. The negotiations did not go well. For one thing, Davis was intensely unpopular, and Barrett was not much better, variously described as "very loud spoken," "vulgar," and "full of self-assurance." Furthermore, the two Americans both felt that they should be the leading U.S. voice on the matter, and relations between them broke down completely.

In August, the United States published a letter, reportedly written by Bunau-Varilla to Hay back in January, that clarified the "ports question" in his treaty in favor of the Americans. The Frenchman was no longer in the employ of Panama, so he seemed an ideal candidate for taking the blame. But then other correspondence emerged, showing that the provisional government, specifically the archconservative Tomás Arias, had authorized Bunau-Varilla's concession. Soon after, an anonymous flyer was distributed in the streets, accusing Arias of having sold the country's interests, and ordering him to resign or be assassinated.

The following month Hero of the Republic General Huertas returned to Panama, having cut short his trip after hearing that Amador planned to replace him. On October 28, Huertas wrote to Amador demanding the removal of Arias, and of another ultraright minister. Arias resigned, but Amador refused to release the second man. Then the president learned that Huertas, with the backing of Belisario Porras, planned to arrest him at a forthcoming military function. A severely rattled Amador appealed directly to Roosevelt for help in avoiding a military coup, and Huertas and other opposition leaders were sent a firm message from the U.S. legation saying that revolutionary changes would not be tolerated. At the same time, a detachment of marines was moved from their barracks to Ancón Hill. The military function went ahead without incident; Amador stayed at home.

Fortified by U.S. support, the president then made his move against Huertas, demanding his resignation. The general held out for a while, but threw in the towel on November 18. After consulting with Barrett, Amador then decided that a standing army, albeit of only 250 men, was not needed by the tiny republic, and the Panamanian Army was disbanded.

The United States was subsequently blamed for the loss of the army and the national prestige that went with it. But while no doubt demonstrating the ruling elite's dependence on U.S. support, the move was orchestrated by Amador and his Conservative allies. They had worried about the power of the army even in the heady days of November 1903. Now, with the assistance of the United States, the only force in the land that could eject them from power was no more.

※※※

William Sands arrived in the aftermath of the failed coup, and found Panama "festering with intrigue," the American canal officials and diplomats at loggerheads, and growing anti-Americanism in many quarters. The existence of the Canal Zone, Sands would write, "made for an ambiguous and most delicate diplomatic situation. Canal affairs and interests were constantly overlapping or overshadowing the Republic's affairs." To many Panamanians, the Americans seemed determined to tell them what to do, and there was deep concern about "whither Theodore Roosevelt and his 'Yankee imperialism' might be tending." Sands likened the position of the U.S. minister in Panama with that of a resident minister from Great Britain in India, where the threat of being "incorporated into the Raj" was ever present. Nevertheless, he was shocked at how much the Americans were disliked on the Isthmus.

One of Sands's first actions was to meet the new secretary for foreign affairs, Santiago de la Guardia, to request that the position of the governor and the U.S. minister to Panama might be combined in one person. In marked contrast to Davis, Sands was careful to adhere to proper formalities, donning full diplomatic garb, top hat included, and hiring the best two-horse carriage he could find for the one-block journey between the legation and the secretary's office. The approach worked, with the Panamanian happy to allow Sands's request, although de la Guardia did confide to Sands his fears about future relations between their two countries. "Don Santiago was aware," wrote Sands, "that a new North America had come into being since the Spanish War, one that was not very well understood as yet even by the North Americans themselves."

Meanwhile other Panamanians had taken the arguments, particularly about customs revenues, out into the open. A delegation was sent to Washington, and articles by prominent Isthmians started appearing in New York newspapers. Then, in October 1904 a leading Panamanian liberal, Dr. Eusabio Morales, secured a commission from the influential *North American Review* for an article critical of the Hay–Bunau-Varilla Treaty. When word of this got to the Republican Party, Morales was approached by men representing the treasurer of the party and offered a bribe to spike the piece. It was just before the presidential election and there was concern that revelations about Roosevelt's connection with the independence of Panama might come out. Morales declined the money but withdrew the article when Roosevelt publicly instructed Taft to go to Panama and settle the tolls question.

The secretary of war, accompanied by Cromwell, arrived in Colón at the end of November. The highest-ranking American to set foot on the Isthmus so far, Taft was a good choice to mollify the Panamanians, in spite of the fact that, privately, he referred to their country as "a kind of Opera Bouffe republic and nation." At over three hundred pounds, Taft was hugely, disarmingly fat and jovial-looking. Sands would call him "a cold man, despite the legend which grew up about him . . . his geniality was wholly of the surface," but most people found Taft charming. On December 1 he used a speech at a welcoming banquet to assure his audience that the United States had no imperialistic designs on the republic, and then over the next ten days he combined touring the works with negotiating with the Panamanians over the points in dispute. Every evening there were banquets or balls, where Taft entered heartily into the spirit, amazing the Panamanians with his enthusiastic dancing. "Though the heaviest man, in weight, in the room," remembered William Karner, "he was as buoyant and light on his feet as a feather or a rubber ball."

Over the negotiating table, similarly light-footed, Taft managed to placate the Panamanians without actually conceding too much. A controversy over postage rates was settled in Panama's favor; imports from Panama to the Zone were to be duty-free; there was a pledge of money for a stretch of road and a new hospital in Panama City. Taft promised that only essentials for the canal would be imported tariff-free from the United States. Also included in what became known as the "Taft Agreement" was an assurance that employees of the ICC from tropical countries would not be allowed to purchase food from ICC shops. Loopholes in the deal ensured that canal business would not suffer from any of these concessions, but it was the spirit of the Taft Agreement that was important. In the Philippines, despite the defeat of the main pro-independence forces outside Manila in 1902, an insurgency had arisen in the Muslim south that was daily claiming

American lives. For the moment at least, the United States felt that its best policy in Panama was to save the face of the incumbent, pro-American leadership and project a stance of compromise and respect.

◀◀◀◀◀ ▶▶▶▶▶

Taft's next stop was Jamaica. Taking consul Mallet with him as a go-between as well as Chief Engineer Wallace, the secretary met Governor Sir James Swettenham to ask permission to recruit workers for the canal.

The labor problem was among the most serious facing the first American canal builders. In spite of the stream of new arrivals, many soon left or turned out to be unsuitable, and by the autumn of 1904 departments had taken to offering inducements for men to leave one sector of the work to join another. One shipment of laborers was met by agents of the Municipal Engineering Division and others from the Building Department "and so keen a competition developed to obtain the men that there ensued a street fight and the subsequent arrest and jailing over night of the principals." There was also a longer-term question: who was going to build the American Panama Canal?

The leaders of the project, of course, like the new machinery to be deployed, would be American. It was also "recognized" that "most of the superintendents, foremen, and the higher grades of skilled labor would have to be brought from the United States." According to the canal's quartermaster, Major R. E. Wood, "there was no surplus throughout Central or South America" for this sort of work, and "in many classes there were no men at all available" locally.

It was initially hoped that the American canal effort would be characterized by machines rather than men. Early plans estimated that some eight to ten thousand workers would be required, and Wallace told Taft that he wanted to restrict the number to ten to fifteen thousand. A gross underestimate, as it turned out—at one point there would be more than fifty thousand on the payroll—but still a sizable force to be found.

White workers from the United States were ruled out from the unskilled jobs early on as too expensive, too unionized, and vulnerable to tropical diseases. It would be "useless to discuss the question of utilizing the white race for heavy out-of-door work with pick and shovel in the mud and rain," wrote Governor Davis in November 1904. "American working men have no call to Panama," suggested a U.S. commentator, "any more than English working men have to the plains of India."

Characteristically for the time, the question was seen in terms of the fitness of different races for the job ahead. As chief recruiter William Karner would write, "It has been an interesting job—experimenting in racial types." Brigadier Peter C. Hains, who served on the Walker Commission of 1899 and would become a canal commissioner in 1905, laid out official thinking on labor in a 1904 article for the *North American Review*: "Where will the labour come from? . . . The native Isthmian will not work. He is naturally indolent; not over strong; has no ambition; his wants are few in number and easily satisfied. He can live for a few cents a day, and he prefers to take it easy, swinging in a hammock and smoking cigarettes. The native population is wholly unavailable." The "Chinese coolie," who had built railroads all over the United States, was considered able to cope with the climate, "industrious," and easy to manage, but could rarely speak English, and "as soon as he gets a few dollars," wrote Hains, "he wants to keep a store."

Hains's preference was for black workers from the British West Indies, whom he characterized as "fairly industrious; not addicted to drink; can speak English . . . he is willing to work, [and] not deficient in intelligence." There were other advantages: the islands were reasonably nearby and well served by steamer services; education levels were relatively high; the Antilleans had some immunity to some tropical diseases. But more than anything else they were cheap—wages and conditions on the islands were such that virtually anything the

Americans offered would be an improvement. To Taft, there was another great advantage to the West Indian worker. Despite his being "lazy," he had been taught by the British respect for discipline and authority. "He does loaf about a good deal," the secretary of state wrote, "but he is amenable to law, and it does not take a large police force to keep him in order."

Thus Taft chose Jamaica as the nearest and largest of these "natural markets for unskilled labor" to visit in person. But the meeting with the governor did not go according to plan for the Americans. Swettenham remained immune to Taft's charm; in fact, he seemed rather anti-American. The United States party got the distinct impression that he would quite happily see the U.S. canal effort fail. It probably did not help that Admiral Walker, chairman of the ICC, had been musing, according to Mallet, that Jamaica should be taken over by the United States as part of the canal's outer defenses.

To the Americans Swettenham stressed the negatives of the Jamaican experience in Panama during the French period: the "able-bodied emigrants returned enfeebled, sick, infirm, or maimed [who] had to be kept alive at the expense of the parish"; the huge cost to the Jamaican government of repatriating workers after the de Lesseps Company failed. He may have also had in mind the destablizing effects of mass migration—serious worker unrest had been bloodily suppressed only two years before. Then there were the powerful planter interests on the island, ever reluctant to see their pool of cheap labor reduced. The upshot was that the governor announced he would only give permission for recruiting if the U.S. government deposited in the Jamaican Treasury £5 for each laborer shipped to Colón, against the possible costs of repatriating him. Taft, as expected, was appalled at these terms. He called the meetings to a close and returned to the United States.

Wallace arrived back on the Isthmus and, after his customary two days of prostration from seasickness, summoned William Karner and ordered him to get on the next boat to Barbados and to set up a recruiting office there as quickly as possible.

Barbados, although the most distant of the "natural markets for unskilled labor," had several advantages over the other British West Indian islands. The Windwards and Leewards had relatively low populations and were considered to be ruled directly from the Colonial Office. Barbados, though, seemed to have more sympathetic and independent officials and was massively overpopulated, with two hundred thousand people living on just two hundred square miles. With the economy utterly dependent on a near-worthless sugar crop, there was desperate poverty and malnutrition among the black population. "The island has always been and still is run for the whites," wrote an American journalist who visited Barbados at this time. "It is a heavenly place to live for the white man who can ignore the frightful misery of the negroes." It looked like fertile recruiting ground for the Americans.

Karner arrived at Carlisle Bay, near Bridgetown, on December 31 and soon after was introduced by the U.S. consul to the colonial secretary, who told him that the government had been looking at setting up an agency themselves to aid work abroad, as there was a "large surplus" of laborers on the island. In turn, the secretary took Karner to meet the governor, Sir Gilbert Carter. Carter was keen that there should not be a repetition of the situation two years earlier when Barbadians working on a railroad project in Brazil had become stranded and had to be brought home at the government's expense, but otherwise he was far more open to the ICC than had been Swettenham. Karner reckoned that the fact that Lady Carter was an American was helpful.

Karner then arranged for transportation through the Royal Mail Steam Packet Company, which had a large office on the island, employed a local agent, S. E. Brewster, and had medical and contract forms printed up. The contract, agreed with the government, was that each laborer would be employed for five hundred days at a rate of ten cents U.S. an hour. This was about half the minimum that would have been acceptable to a North American laborer but generous by the standards of Barbados, where wages had fallen to as low as a shilling (25 cents) a day. Work was ten hours a day, six days a week, with time and a half paid for overtime and Sundays. Passage to Colón was paid for—with food for the voyage provided—and "medical attendance, medicine, and quarters without furniture, [were] to be furnished free to the laborer, while in the employ of the Commission." At the end of the contract, or if the worker was incapacitated while employed by the ICC, repatriation would be free.

Eventually some twenty thousand Barbadians—the engine room of the canal effort—would be employed under this same contract, with only small modifications. The initial results were disappointing, however. It seems that the memories of the French period, when over a thousand Barbadians had traveled to Panama, the bad political reputation of Central America generally, and the recent experience in Brazil combined to create suspicion of the new canal project. These fears were fanned by stories of unemployment and hardship on the Isthmus spread by planters and managers not keen to see their all-important labor surplus disappearing.

"There was no rush and on the steamer sailing for Colón, January 26th 1905," wrote Karner, "I shipped only sixteen laborers." It would have been seventeen, but at the last moment "one man got stage fright, shouted that I was sending him into slavery and that he would rather kill himself there than to go to the Isthmus and die in slavery." The next shipment had a few more after Brewster "did some hustling in the adjoining parish." But Karner was hindered in his efforts by a loss of contact with Wallace in Panama due to a broken cable. When he did receive a message from his boss his orders were vague. Then there was a problem cashing the ICC's checks and further administrative hurdles. Karner estimated that he needed a full-time employee just to fill out his myriad requisition and expenses forms. The frustration was similar to that being suffered on the Isthmus.

Those first Karner recruits arriving right at the beginning of 1905 joined a canal project mired in confusion and disillusionment. In Panama City, the job of installing running water and sewers was supposed to have been completed by January 1905, but was still months away. Much important equipment had not arrived. The Americans tried to make do with reconditioned French tools and "scrap." The building department was having the same difficulties. When materials were reluctantly supplied, they were often held up by the inadequate facilities at Colón for unloading, storage, and distribution. Building and dock workers were in short supply as the majority were taken up with "actual canal work."

What this meant was "making the dirt fly" in the Culebra Cut. This is what journalists from the United States came to see, and they wanted to report back that the canal was being dug. But the effort from an engineering point of view was an almost total waste of time. In August, by which time three old French excavators had been chugging away for about a month, Gold Hill began to slide into the trench below it, and work was suspended for four weeks. In November the first American-built excavator arrived. This was a ninety-five-ton Bucyrus steam shovel, which could scoop up nearly 5 cubic meters of spoil at a time. Wallace was off the Isthmus, so it was William Karner

Bucyrus steam shovel

as acting chief engineer who ordered the new shovel into action in the Cut. "Ambitious to 'make the dirt fly,'" wrote Karner, "I came near to a mortifying and embarrassing failure, for the night after starting the shovel at work there was a slide in the cut which nearly buried the shovel from sight." The Bucyrus shovel, three times as powerful as any equivalent used by the French, would become the workhorse of the canal, but it was an inauspicious start.

The following month there were six of the old French ladder excavators at work together with an increasing number of resurrected Belgian locomotives and French dump cars. But for all the sound and fury, an engineer reported, "the impression made on the soil in comparison with the entire mass of earth to be handled" was mere "hen scratches." On wet days, the locomotives could pull only four cars at a time, and there were frequent derailments, blamed on the "long and rigid wheel base of the French and Belgian engines," as well as the "poorly ballasted," largely improvised, tracks. As there were also inadequate traction and dumping facilities, the excavators were often idle for lack of spoil cars.

The results of the test borings along the line had also provided disappointment. At Bohío, where the Walker Commission had planned a dam for the lock-canal option, drilling teams had discovered a deep geological gorge, the original bed of the Chagres River. Thus the bedrock on which the dam would have to be anchored was a seemingly unworkable 168 feet below sea level. Above the bedrock was a porous mixture of gravel and other alluvial detritus. Wallace concluded that "there is little probability of finding a satisfactory location for a high dam in this vicinity." There were borings also at Gatún, which had been suggested as a possible site for a dam in spite of the great width of the valley at this point. But here there were two underground gorges even deeper than at Bohío. The Americans drilled to 200 feet below sea level and still did not reach bedrock. "As 200 feet was considered in excess of the practicable depth at which it was advisable to construct a foundation for a dam," Wallace reported, "it was not considered necessary to go deeper." For him, the test results precluded "the economical or safe construction of a dam in [the] general vicinity" of Gatún. Ominously, other scattered borings along the canal line offered only geological confusion: "Practically no regular stratification exists," Wallace reported.

In the absence of an obvious site for a dam along the line of the canal on the Atlantic side, Wallace reported that he favored the adoption of a sea-level canal plan. This was, he wrote, "self-evidently" "the most desirable in economy of maintenance, operation, time of passage through it, and simplicity of design, plan and execution . . . the deterrent factors being time and cost." But more than anything he wanted a decision, to "remove the principal elements of uncertainty now existing in regard to the project as a whole."

Hampered by more than just uncertainty, the effort was on the brink of petering out, strangled by red tape, bickering, and incompetence. Wallace had underestimated the Isthmus. Under pressure to "make the dirt fly," he neglected proper preparatory work. He also failed to provide leadership. His idea of management was to delegate. When he employed Frank Maltby, he told him: "I want you to build up an organization so complete and efficient that you won't have to do anything but sit on the veranda and smoke good cigars." Wallace himself was hardly ever seen out on the line; he rarely left his office, and every small suggestion from one of his subordinates would be demanded in writing. Soon his desk was as covered in chaotic mounds of paper as that of Admiral Walker in Washington.

With no improvement in sight in the grim living conditions, discontent was spreading all along the line of the canal. Then at the end of 1904 it got dramatically worse: yellow fever broke out on the Isthmus.

CHAPTER SEVENTEEN

YELLOW JACK

The American doctors and sanitary inspectors had arrived in Panama full of confidence. They might have felt underappreciated by the engineers among the first arrivals, but they were sure they had the knowledge and experience to rid the Isthmus of disease-carrying mosquitoes. Before departing for the tropics Gorgas and Le Prince had met a senior U.S. entomologist, who had asked them to send back samples of Panamanian mosquitoes. "I will have to do it soon, Doctor," Le Prince had exclaimed, "for in a year or so there will be no mosquitoes there!"

Gorgas had been to Paris to study the medical records of the French companies. He knew the story of the Dingler family, of the massive losses and demoralization from disease during the 1880s. But he was not downhearted, as he was aware that the Americans had a crucial advantage over de Lesseps's men. For between the time of the French on the Isthmus and the start of the American canal effort, a massive advance had occurred in the control of malaria, and, even more so, yellow fever: the miracle of Havana.

As in the fields of technology and engineering, the twenty years after the beginning of the French canal saw astounding advances in medical science. In 1880 the germ theory of disease—pioneered by Pasteur, Koch, and Lister—was still the subject of debate in the medical profession and derision by the public. But by 1900 a revolution had occurred. The new world discovered under the microscope had ushered in fresh understanding of diseases that had baffled man for centuries. For the U.S. effort in Panama no advance was more important than the understanding of the mosquito transmission of malaria and yellow fever.

The entire idea of an insect vector was quite new. In 1878 a Scottish doctor, Patrick Manson, working in southern China, had discovered that mosquitoes carried the developmental stage of a parasitic worm that caused elephantiasis. It was the first proof that a bloodsucking insect could harbor, and presumably transmit, organisms of human disease. Then in 1881, in Havana, the Western Hemisphere's "yellow jack" capital, an article was published in a medical journal that not only identified the mosquito as the yellow fever's carrier, but also the particular species, *Aëdes aegypti*. Its author was French-Scottish doctor Carlos Finlay, who had worked in Cuba for twenty years. He had studied the literature of yellow fever epidemics and had noted that they all mentioned the unusually high prevalence of mosquitoes. He then identified the particular species by analyzing the factors the sites of the epidemics had in common—temperature, elevation above sea level—and matching them to a mosquito that thrived only in these conditions.

But the theory—with hindsight a stroke of genius—was either ignored or ridiculed. The problem was not just resistance to a new idea; Finlay himself carried out numerous experiments the results of which seemed to disprove his own theory. Countless times he attempted to infect a patient using a mosquito that had bitten someone with yellow fever, but no one ever got ill as a result. Finlay, soon disparagingly known as "the Mosquito Man," was written off as a crank.

More than fifteen years later, by which time the Isthmian mosquito had seen off de Lesseps and his French canal dream, an obscure English army physician, Ronald Ross, stationed at a remote field hospital in India, worked out the life cycle of the malaria parasite. In the summer of 1897 he dissected an *Anopheles* mosquito that was known to have bitten a malaria sufferer. Under a microscope he found in the insect's stomach the same circular cells identified as the malaria parasite *Plasmodium falciparum* by a French doctor Alphonse Laveran, in Algeria in 1880. The following year Ross located the mosquito's salivary gland and found the parasite there, confirming that the insect vector passed the disease on with a subsequent bite. Thus to control the disease, which at the time took a million lives a year in India, it was necessary to prevent mosquitoes biting an infected patient as well as keeping them away from healthy humans.

In the same year, 1898, Henry Rose Carter, a maritime doctor with experience of yellow fever quarantines, made an observation that offered to come to the rescue of old Dr. Finlay's theory. While working in a small Mississippi town during an outbreak of yellow fever, he noticed a strange pattern: there was usually a period of twelve days to three weeks between the appearance of the first case of yellow fever in a community, and subsequent cases apparently derived from it. This led him to carry out case studies on dwellings where a patient had become infected. By carefully noting visitors to the house, he established that those who came in the first two weeks were fine, but thereafter, and even when the original patient was removed, there was a risk of infection. Not only did this point to an insect vector, but it also established that the virus needed a period of "extrinsic incubation" inside the mosquito before it became dangerous. This neatly explained the failure of Finlay's experiments.

After the end of fighting in Cuba in August 1898, some fifty thousand U.S. military remained on the island for "pacification." Their continued losses from disease highlighted the fact that yellow fever probably presented the single greatest threat to U.S. expansion in the tropics. For almost everyone there was little doubt as to what was to blame—the filthy streets of Havana. In January 1899, William Crawford Gorgas, who had worked in a yellow fever camp during the war, was charged with cleaning up the city.

Gorgas, the son of a Confederate general, had become a doctor as the only way to secure an army commission after his rejection by West Point. Posted all around the frontier areas of the United States, Gorgas was on the Río Grande near the border of Mexico in August 1882. It was, wrote his wife whom he met that year, "yellow fever's first encounter with one who became its implacable foe, and whose life was to be concentrated on its extermination." Gorgas caught the disease but survived and was therefore subsequently immune. Thereafter yellow fever epidemics became his specialty.

But for now, Gorgas was firmly with the majority about the cause of the disease: rotting rubbish and filth, together with "fomites"—everything the patient had touched while infected. Gorgas met and befriended Finlay in Havana but, he later wrote, "we were rather inclined to make light of his ideas, and none more so than I."

Backed to the hilt by the city's military governor, he went to work. Streets were swept clear of dead animals and rubbish. Every house was cleaned and disinfected with "chlorinated lime," essentially bleach. The exhaustive sanitation campaign was closely followed by the U.S. press. With plenty of "before and after" pictures the work made good copy and showed the American intervention in a good light. The cleanup also slashed the previously high rates of illnesses such as typhoid and dysentery. Furthermore, the yellow fever epidemic of the previous year showed no signs of returning.

But in August 1899 some 12,000 nonimmune Spanish workers arrived on the island. Within weeks yellow fever was back. It seemed that all Gorgas's hard work had not made the slightest difference. Worst of all, the disease seemed to hit hardest in the smarter "expatriate" areas of Havana (where, of course, the highest proportion of nonimmunes were living). The deaths of high-profile members of the U.S. community caused widespread panic.

Governor Leonard Wood ordered Gorgas to redouble his sanitation effort and made $50,000 available for the purpose. But the renewed round of sweeping and scrubbing had no effect. It was time for a new approach.

In June 1900, a special Yellow Fever Commission was appointed by Washington. Dr. Walter Reed, an expert bacteriologist as well as an experienced "frontier doctor" like Gorgas, was in charge, assisted by Drs. James Carroll, Aristides Agramonte, and Jesse W. Lazear.

Reed seems to have landed in Havana with an open mind, amenable to persuasion by observed fact. The questions facing the Commission were simple: What agent causes yellow fever? How is it spread? How can it be stopped? On the first of these, the doctors drew a blank early on. They looked through the microscope at the blood of yellow fever patients but could not find the "germ" or "bacteria." Viruses, of course, were unseen and unknown in 1900. On the second question, however, there was an early breakthrough. Soon after his arrival Reed was presented with a curious case. A soldier at the nearby military base had been locked in a cell following a disciplinary infringement. A month after having been imprisoned, he had come down with yellow fever and died six days later. But none of his eight cellmates had contracted the disease, even the one who had subsequently slept in the dead man's bunk. The men had remained sealed in the cell, but it did have a window. Reed concluded that something must have carried the infection in through the window, passed it to a single subject, and then departed: it had to be an insect.

The Commission turned to Doctor Finlay, whose theories were suddenly in favor at last. Finlay was happy to provide *Aëdes aegypti* eggs so that specimens could be bred for experiments. While several of the doctors tried to find out all they could about the insect's habits and life cycle, others attempted to achieve the demonstration of the theory that Finlay's experiments had failed to provide. For this volunteers were needed who were prepared to be bitten by infected insects. Although those selected would, of course, be the strongest and healthiest specimens, and the best care available would be ready for them, they would still run a heavy risk of death. Five hundred dollars was offered as an incentive, although the first U.S. Army volunteers nobly refused the reward, setting a precedent that was followed throughout the experiments. Reed's team of doctors also subjected themselves to the same tests.

Early results were disappointing, but after belatedly taking into account Carter's findings on "extrinsic incubation," yellow fever was successfully transferred from one patient to another. Along the way both Carroll and Lazear became infected. Carroll narrowly survived, but Lazear, with what Gorgas called the worst case of yellow fever he had ever seen, died an agonizing death on September 25.

Reed was much chastened by the gruesome sacrifice of Lazear, a hugely popular member of the team, but was convinced that his experiments had yielded up yellow fever's secret. However, when Reed presented the mosquito theory to a Public Health Association meeting in Minneapolis in November 1900 he was greeted by a stony silence, followed by scathing criticism. The *Washington Post* was condemning in its report of the new theory: "Of all the silly and nonsensical rigmarole about yellow fever that has yet found its way into print—and there has been enough of it to load a fleet—the silliest beyond compare is to be found in the mosquito hypothesis." The centuries-old, "common-sense" theory that yellow fever was caused by dirt was not to be moved.

Reed returned to Havana and set up a new base, named Camp Lazear, in an isolated spot outside Havana. Here it was possible to achieve a far higher level of control and scientific rigor over experiments. Reed was determined to provide data that even the most diehard believer in the filth theory would have to accept. At the end of November an experiment was started wherein a doctor and three volunteer soldiers were confined for twenty days to a mosquito-proof wooden shack. Inside, they slept on the soiled and *vomito negro*—

plastered bedding of previous yellow fever victims. No one got ill, and the "fomites" theory, which had governed quarantine law for centuries, was demolished forever.

Other meticulous tests demonstrated again that *Aëdes aegypti* was the vector of the disease, but there remained doubters. One was Gorgas himself. Even if the insect did spread the disease, what was to say that this was the sole method of transmission, or even the most common one? The only way to demonstrate the theory for sure was to take it out into the field: to get Gorgas's sanitation squads to destroy the *Aëdes aegypti* of Havana and see what happened.

This Herculean task was something of a last resort. But tests with inoculations had ended when a young American nurse died from her injection, and to screen all yellow fever patients—to keep the mosquitoes from becoming infected—was impossible as many cases went unreported. Therefore the only option left was to take on the mosquitoes themselves.

Called the "aristocrat of mosquitoes," *Aëdes aegypti* is distinctly marked. Its body has a series of silvery half moons, its legs are alternately black and white, and it has four brilliant stripes on its thorax. Only the female of the species is a bloodsucker—she needs blood to mature her eggs—and she has a marked preference for human blood to the extent that she knows where to attack a person: under the wrist or on the ankles, where the skin is thinnest, and never on the face or top of the hand as these places are easily slapped. Also, she is only very rarely found away from human habitation and always lays her eggs near a ready supply of human blood.

The researchers in Havana also discovered that she is very meticulous, preferring to lay her eggs in clean water in man-made containers, such as earthenware jugs or water butts. And this, they concluded, was her great weakness. So when Gorgas went to work in February 1901 on his new campaign directed entirely against *Aëdes aegypti*, he started by directing that all such containers should be removed or screened. Where this was impossible, a layer of oil was poured on the surface of the water to suffocate any larvae, or "wrigglers" as they were commonly known, that might be lurking inside. At the same time, the entire city was divided into districts and meticulously fumigated by burning sulphur or pyrethrum, a dried flower used as an insecticide. The results were truly spectacular—a dramatic reduction in yellow fever from 1,400 known cases in 1900, to only 37 in 1901, none of them after October. The eradication procedures didn't just kill off *Aëdes aegypti*, but reduced the *Anopheles* population as well, thus decreasing malaria cases by more than half.

Havana had suffered some five hundred deaths a year from yellow fever for as long as anyone could remember. Now, quite suddenly, it was over. Furthermore, a controversial and important new theory had been proved correct, and the methods selected to exterminate the disease vector had worked. When the scale of the triumph began to sink in, Gorgas wrote to Reed, "When I think of the absence of yellow fever from Havana for a period of fifty days, I begin to feel like rejoicing that I was ever born!"

All of this hard-won knowledge and expertise was brought by Gorgas to his task in Panama. Indeed, most of the doctors who arrived with him in June 1904 were also veterans of the miracle in Havana. Yet by September, Gorgas would be utterly frustrated, despondent, and full of dread. "The Commission have their own ideas about sanitation, and do not seem much impressed with mine," he wrote. Gorgas accurately predicted what was to come: "I fear an epidemic is inevitable. If only we could convince them! If only they knew!"

⊰⊰⊰⊰⊱⊱⊱⊱

*G*orgas had been confronted by many medical challenges at the start of the American effort in Panama. On his reconnaissance mission in April 1904 he had noted the filthy streets and the extraordinary prevalence of malaria. But he had selected yellow fever as the first of his enemies to be attacked. For a start, the defeat of the disease was an achievable goal; Gorgas had demonstrated in Havana that a spectacular and very press-friendly victory could be won. He had also seen enough yellow fever epidemics to know the disproportionate panic they could cause and how they were ignited by an influx of nonimmune personnel, just as was about to happen in Panama. Furthermore, yellow fever attacked the bosses and spared the workers, affecting in the main white outsiders, perceived to be the most valuable and least expendable of the canal workers. The health of this group would remain Gorgas's top priority. Writing in an American medical journal in 1909, and sounding more than a little like Alfred Mahan, he boasted, "our work in Cuba and Panama will be looked upon as the earliest demonstration that the white man could flourish in the tropics and as the starting point of the effective settlement of these regions by the Caucasian."

Gorgas got to work within two weeks of his arrival, dividing Panama City up into districts and beginning house-to-house inspections, as he had done in Havana. But from the very start his efforts were severely hampered. The problem was that the gentlemen of the Commission simply did not believe the mosquito theory. The year before, a scientific congress in Paris had reviewed Reed's yellow fever work and proclaimed it "scientifically determined fact," and Ronald Ross had received a Nobel Prize for his work on the mosquito transmission of malaria. Ross even visited Panama in mid-1904 and pronounced Gorgas's plans sound. Nevertheless, to Walker, the theory was "the veriest balderdash." Gorgas should concentrate on cleaning up the filth and smells, the chairman of the Commission pronounced. The Zone governor, General Davis, concurred, saying to the doctor in a fatherly tone, "I'm your friend, Gorgas, and I'm trying to set you right. On the mosquito you are simply wild. All who agree with you are wild. Get the idea out of your head. Yellow fever, as we all know, is caused by filth."

Ross himself wrote, "The world requires at least ten years to understand a new idea, however important or simple it may be." Nevertheless, it is not hard to sympathize with Gorgas's frustration. Wallace was no better, sounding like old Jules Dingler when he announced that "clean, healthy, moral Americans" would not contract the disease.

So the Commission believed that Gorgas's efforts were a waste of time and money, and his requisitions for supplies suffered even worse than anyone else's, despite Roosevelt's express order that the medical effort be given top priority. Vital copper screening and medical supplies ordered in October 1904 had still not arrived the following April. Gorgas's department was also given the workers that no one else wanted and ordered to pay the lowest wages. "Consequently," Joseph Le Prince complains, "only poor and unintelligent labour could be obtained . . . some of them could not even climb a ladder. This was the only class of labor allowed the sanitary department. We had to use it, and succeed or fail."

The fumigation squad visited Claude Mallet's house on July 27, 1904. His rooms were swept clean and his yard cleared of anything that might hold water. His tanks were covered with wire netting and taps installed, and he was shown how to pour oil on the surface of the water. He was pleased with the result, writing to his wife that he was now able to read "without having to wipe the mosquitoes off every second," and pronounced himself "a convert to the mosquito theory." But he also reported the more than slightly haphazard way in which the house was fumigated—windows and doors were left open—and that *Aëdes aegypti* larvae were still found in his water tanks on another inspection a week later.

Gorgas had taken on a huge task. Unlike in Havana, in Panama mosquitoes bred all year round. The first inspection showed *Aëdes aegypti* larvae "existed at practically every house in town." There was no running water, and, with ice expensive, locals cooled water by keeping a supply indoors in earthenware vessels, called *tinajas*. "In these," reported Joseph Le Prince, "larvae thrived in great numbers." Gorgas simply did not have sufficient men and materials to carry out the job as thoroughly as required.

Some Panama City residents like Mallet welcomed the chance to have their homes cleaned out at the expense of the U.S. government. The British consul even tried to get the gang to paint his house while they were about it. But the measure was not compulsory. At the beginning of July a fine of five dollars was introduced for anyone who bred larvae in their house, but there were hardly any prosecutions, and usually tenants simply emptied water vessels at the back door while the inspector was entering at the front. Alternatively, the offending containers were hidden away. As most Panamanians were immune to yellow fever, they felt little compulsion to assist in the eradication program, and many did not believe it was possible anyway. "To attempt it is a dream, an illusion, perhaps simply a case of American boasting," wrote the local Liberal newspaper, the *Diaro de Panama*. It was very different from Havana, where Gorgas's squads had had a sympathetic governor and martial law to back them up.

Not that the Americans, who were most at risk, were much more helpful. Visits to Panama City were strongly discouraged, but this was widely ignored, particularly after the banning of gambling in the Zone in August 1904 and the subsequent steep reduction in liquor licenses. Most of the United States personnel on the ground shared the Commission's skepticism about the mosquito theory. A particular concern of the Sanitary Department was the Administration Building, where some three hundred nonimmunes, mostly young Americans, were working. Screen doors were left propped open, and many rooms were unscreened altogether. But when Joseph Le Prince pointed this out to Wallace's nephew O. M. Johnson, the young supervising architect, and alerted him to the fact that the bowls of water used to dampen the architects' copying brushes were ideal places for mosquitoes to breed in, he was laughed at. "Le Prince," Johnson said, "you're off on the upper story!"

"But suppose," the inspector argued, "we have twenty deaths here. Who'll be responsible?"

The architect laughed. "I'll stand the responsibility," he said.

The yellow fever onslaught, as predicted by Gorgas, began at the end of the year. In November an unemployed Italian laborer was brought into the San Tomás hospital in Panama City with a serious case of the disease. He survived, but then news came that two other Italians, members of an opera troupe that had been touring the line of the works, had died from yellow fever on the boat home. The following month Gorgas was forced to suspend his fumigation program in Panama City due to lack of supplies, and six new cases emerged, several from the areas left untreated. "Some yellow fever cases exist in the San Tomas hospital and the Yankees are much scared," wrote Mallet to his wife. Indeed, with the first yellow fever death in December, the Americans were getting jittery. In August, U.S. minister John Barrett had been making plans to bring his mother to live with him in Panama. But on December 20 he wrote to her that he had changed his mind: "If you should be unwell here or if anything should happen to you I could never forgive myself for bringing you to Panama." Wallace tried to calm the workforce by ostentatiously riding around town in the company of his wife, newly arrived from the United States. But his efforts were undermined when it became known that the couple, fearing the worst, had imported two smart metal coffins.

The sense of impending doom deepened with the appearance in mid-January of six cases on the U.S. cruiser the *Boston*, anchored in Panama Bay. An inspection "revealed a dishpan of water standing outside the cook's headquarters. The thing was so thick with mosquito larvae that it was practically a purée." On January 16 the recently arrived young wife of Wallace's secretary John Seager died after a short and very sharp attack of the disease. She had only been married for two months and her death caused deep shock to the expatriate community. Governor Davis called it "the saddest incident in the history of the American colony . . . I attended the funeral this afternoon in the chapel of the Hospital, and as I looked at young Seager overcome with grief at the loss of his wife, I had great difficulty in restraining sympathetic tears. Nearly all the eyes in the room were moist . . . Naturally this death among those that are so well known has almost caused a panic in the ranks of the American employees of the Canal Commission." There were further high-profile deaths, and by the end of January, after nearly twenty cases had been identified that month, it was clear that an epidemic was under way. "How glad I am that I did not bring you down to Panama," Barrett wrote to his mother on January 30. "With malaria and yellow fever rife . . . not knowing who will be the next victim. I am glad that you are safe in 'God's Country' . . . About the only subject of conversation here in Panama is yellow fever."

Everyone had seen the cemetery on the hill outside Colón, "one of the saddest graveyards in the world, acres of little white crosses falling over and rotting under the jungle of tropical growth." Now the shadow of Monkey Hill, where the dead from the French period lay buried, "darkened the whole Isthmus." "The rush to get away," wrote Gorgas's wife, Marie, now with him in Panama, "quickly assumed the proportions of a panic. The canal force—labourers, engineers and office men alike—seemed possessed of one single view: 'Let's get out of this hell hole,' . . . and men arriving one day would take their departure the next, frequently on the same boat." Inevitably the news of the exodus reached the United States, where a newspaper dubbed Panama "the place where the 'ghost walks' . . . it seems that almost everybody is at a standstill down at Panama save the paymaster." The *Panama Star and Herald* concurred: "Unless something is done and done quickly," the paper wrote in late February, "all hopes of building a canal across the Isthmus of Panama may be set aside."

⫷⫷⫷⫷◆⫸⫸⫸⫸

At Ancón hospital cleaning and painting of the wards had, according to Eugenie Hibbard, "advanced quite rapidly." The water guards around the bed legs were removed, and the grounds cleared, revealing the statues of saints scattered around the garden, previously hidden by dense undergrowth. The French nurses were shipped out as well. For all their compassion they were untrained and hindered in their effectiveness by the vows they had taken. Even if instructed not to feed men awaiting surgery, they would ignore the order as it went against their vow to give food to the sick. The nuns also had little time for the mosquito theory. American nurses would put mosquito nets in place around the beds at night, only to find in the morning that they had been tied back by the nuns with bows of brightly colored ribbon.

The hospital staff was suffering from the same frustrations as the rest of the sanitary department. The nurses complained about the poor salaries and lack of quarters. Jessie Murdoch was still having to sleep wrapped in citronella-soaked blankets to deter the mosquitoes. According to Hibbard, "In the early days the securing of absolutely necessary articles was difficult and tedious." As everywhere on the Isthmus, she was forced to "make the best use of the materials left by the French."

The beginning of the year saw a "steadily increasing number of patients." The epidemic had spread from Panama City to Colón and along the line of the works. Soon two wards and several private rooms were given over to yellow fever patients. Each had a wire cage built around his or her bed to prevent them from infecting mosquitoes, and the wards themselves were protected by three screened doors, with pyrethrum powder burning continually between them and a guard outside to see that they were kept closed. With a tripling of yellow fever cases from December to January, "death seemed to dominate the situation," Jessie Murdoch remembered, "almost causing panic . . . [yet] no one showed the white feather but all stood faithfully to their tasks."

Then the epidemic stuttered: there were fewer cases in March than in February, and for the first two weeks of April there were none at all. On April 18 Gorgas wrote, for a piece to be published by *Harper's Magazine*, "I personally believe that we have seen the last case of yellow fever in Panama."

The following day, Gorgas was summoned to the bedside of O. M. Johnson, the architect who had laughed at the warnings of sanitary inspector Joseph Le Prince. The symptoms—the headaches, back pain, terrible thirst, and then the *vomito negro*—were unmistakable. Gorgas personally supervised his care, but there was little he could do apart from make the patient as comfortable as possible. In the meantime, there was a stream of new yellow fever cases in the Administration Building. As Gorgas had feared, the disease had struck at the heart of the American project. In ten days, twenty-one cases were carried out of the U.S. canal headquarters. Johnson died on April 25 and was buried in one of the Wallaces' metal coffins. It was, wrote Governor Davis, like "the ending of many a bright young man I have seen on the battlefield."

But few of the Americans shared the martial, patriotic determination of the young French engineers twenty years earlier. "Everybody here seems to be sitting on a tack," one engineer wrote home. When yet another case was announced in the Administration Building, a young stenographer "rose from his chair and shrieked, 'I want you to understand now that if Tabor dies, I'm going home.'" Many were already on their way as "yellow fever . . . completely filled the atmosphere." Panama City was abandoned as white Commission staff were moved out to Ancón Hill, but in less than two weeks two hundred resigned. One returning nurse told the *New York Tribune* that, bafflingly, yellow fever was even killing "well set-up, clean boys with good principles." "We were taxed to the utmost in the effort to care for the sick and keep hope and encouragement alive," writes Frank Maltby, who was still laboring away dredging the ends of the canal. It didn't help that Chief Engineer Wallace was off the Isthmus in Washington, pressing his case to be given more control over the project.

"Many resigned," read that year's ICC annual report, "while those who remained became possessed with a feeling of lethargy or fatalism." In all, some five hundred U.S. employees fled the Isthmus during April, May, and June 1905, about three-quarters of the white workforce after what was, in historical terms, a fairly mild flare-up of yellow fever. Amid the chaos came a reluctant reappraisal of the French effort, as, in the early summer of 1905, the work came to a virtual halt.

✦✦✦✦✦✦

*I*n Washington the wheels had been turning, albeit slowly. After his visit to Panama in November, Taft had reported to Roosevelt that the Commission under Walker and Davis seemed unwieldy and obstructive. As an engineer on the ground put it: "The military regime in Panama, in so far as the furtherance of engineering efficiency is concerned, is a failure; in so far as the maintenance of official orthodoxy is concerned, it is a great success." This was backed up by Wallace, who requested that the Commission be reduced to three men: governor and chief engineer in Panama, with a chairman in Washington. In January the president requested that Congress amend the Spooner Act to make this possible, and the following month sent an eminent U.S. surgeon to investigate what was seen as Gorgas's failure to control disease on the Isthmus.

The surgeon, Dr. Charles A. L. Reed, toured the works during February, and his report was leaked to the U.S. press. One particular example he gave of the nightmare of red tape afflicting the medical department caught the eye and was reproduced across the country: a newborn baby needed a nursing bottle; the nurse applied to her superior, Major La Garde, who, finding the requisition of the previous September still unfulfilled, then made out another order, which had to be endorsed by Gorgas himself as well as the chief of the bureau for materials and supply, Mr. Tobey. Then the order was copied and at last a messenger was permitted to go to a chemist and buy the nursing bottle, which finally reached the infant two days after the necessity for its use had arisen. The bottle should have cost no more than thirty cents, but counting the money value of the time of the nurse, of Major La Garde, of his clerical help, of Colonel Gorgas, of Mr. Tobey, of Mr. Tobey's clerks and of the messenger, the cost to the government of the United States, Reed calculated, was around $6.75. For all Walker's parsimony, it seemed the waste of the French canal period had never gone away.

Roosevelt was furious at the leak, but even angrier about the blow to the prestige of his canal project. When the Senate refused to agree to the change in the Commission, the president, acting by executive decree, demanded the resignation of Walker and his six colleagues. On April 1 he announced a new governing body for the canal, composed, as Wallace had suggested, of an executive committee of chief engineer, chairman, and governor, with four essentially sleeping partners added in to pretend compliance with the terms of the Spooner Act. Wallace, still highly thought of in the press, remained as chief engineer, and now had a seat on the Commission. Theodore Shonts, a "gruff, domineering" Pennsylvanian who had built, run, and owned a number of Midwestern railroads, was made chairman; and Charles Magoon the new governor. Magoon had made his name as a lawyer specializing in colonial administration and had served as legal counsel to the first Commission. He had helped Davis set up the Zone government, and had visited the Isthmus with Taft the previous November. While in Panama he had made a very favorable impression on the American chargé d'affaires William Sands, who had recommended him for the new dual role of governor and American minister to Panama.

Wallace was summoned to Washington for the first meeting of the new executive committee on April 10. Inevitably the recent yellow fever outbreak was discussed. It seems that there was little confidence in Gorgas. Shonts suggested that he be replaced with a friend of his, an osteopath with no experience of tropical medicine. Magoon agreed that a more "practical doctor" was required, one who would deal with the "smells and filth." This suggestion was passed on to Taft, who approved it and sent it to the president.

But Roosevelt consulted medical authorities in the United States, all of whom backed Gorgas as the best man for the job. Finally the president sought the advice of a close friend and hunting companion, Dr. Alexander Lambert. The Commission and the secretary of war, Roosevelt told Lambert, were complaining that Gorgas spent all his time trying to kill mosquitoes while Colón and Panama were as dirty and stinking as ever. "Smells and filth, Mr. President," Lambert replied, "have nothing to do with either malaria or yellow fever. You are facing one of the greatest decisions of your career. You must choose between Shonts and Gorgas. If you fall back on the old methods of sanitation, you will fail, just as the French failed. If you back up Gorgas and his ideas and let him pursue his campaign against the mosquitoes, you will get your canal."

It was a bold step to go against the advice of his own Commission and secretary of war, but Roosevelt overruled their recommendation and ordered Magoon, who was about to leave for Panama, to give Gorgas all the backing he could.

Accompanied by Wallace, the new governor arrived at Colón on May 24, replacing Davis and Barrett, both of whom had already left the Isthmus, the former in the throes of severe malaria. Magoon was an immediate improvement on his predecessors. Sands described him as "huge in all three dimensions . . . and he had the gentle nature which so often accompanies vast bulk." At 230 pounds, he was about as far from Roosevelt's vision of the new "strenuous" American as you could imagine. But he was immensely clubbable, from the very first ceremony in honor of his arrival, Magoon "displayed great interest in the people," and, according to the *Star and Herald*, won the confidence of the Panamanians more than any other American had done so far. This helped immensely in his diplomatic task, defined by Sands as achieving "a truce among the personally jealous political leaders and between the racially hostile political parties long enough to get the Panamanian Republic in working order."

In his role as governor of the Canal Zone, he had an even harder job ahead. Publicly he oozed confidence and optimism, but he reported in private that conditions were deplorable. Earlier that month the *Star and Herald* had written, "It would perhaps be difficult to find any spot on earth where discontent reigns so supreme as on the Isthmus of Panama." Magoon wrote to Shonts back in Washington that he found the men working on the canal "ill-paid, over-worked, ill-housed, ill-fed, and subjected to the hazards of yellow fever, malarial fever," and other diseases. Whatever exuberance had fired the first Americans in Panama, it was now long gone, replaced by bickering and demoralization.

One of Magoon's first acts was to listen to Gorgas about the problems he had been having with requisitions. The governor then cabled through to Washington the doctor's demands, and within forty-eight hours long-denied supplies were on their way. It looked as if Gorgas would at last have the tools he needed to complete the job. Magoon also made speeches promising that schools and churches would be built, and families encouraged to move out to the Isthmus.

Then, after only two weeks back in Panama, Wallace applied for urgent leave to attend to personal affairs in the United States. He also requested a private interview with Taft. Although Wallace had professed himself pleased with the recent changes to the Commission, it appears that it irked him that he had to answer to Shonts. He believed that the canal effort would be best served by concentrating all power in one man, namely himself. He also confided to Magoon that he had been offered a job with a salary of some $50,000 to 60,000 back in the United States. Wallace told Magoon that as he considered himself essential to the canal effort, he was going to try to squeeze Taft for a higher salary. In fact he wanted to be both chairman and chief engineer with the right to come and go between Washington and Panama as he wished. Failing this, he would be happy to leave the "godforsaken" yellow-fever-ridden Isthmus for good and take the money offered at home. All of this Magoon promptly cabled to Taft.

So the usually genial secretary of war was in a black temper when Wallace arrived to meet him at the Manhattan Hotel in New York on June 25. At the request of Taft, William Nelson Cromwell was present as a witness, much to Wallace's annoyance—one of the complaints he wanted to make was against the lawyer's disproportionate influence on canal affairs. Taft bluntly asked Wallace what could be so important to cause him to leave the Isthmus again at such a crucial time. Wallace replied that he wanted to resign as he had been offered another job with none of the risks of living in Panama. Perhaps Wallace expected Taft to offer him the top job to keep him in the organization, but if so he misjudged the secretary of war. Taft exploded: "For mere lucre you change your position overnight without thought of the embarrassing position in which you place your government by this action. By every principle of honour and duty you were bound to treat this subject differently . . . Great fame attached to your office, but also equal responsibility, and now you desert them in an hour . . . I am exceedingly sorry that you cannot see what a dreadful, dreadful mistake you are making. It pains me more than I can tell." Wallace offered to stay on in some capacity to minimize the upset to the construction effort, but Taft ordered him to resign and have nothing more to do with the canal.

Wallace's resignation sparked fresh panic in Panama. "We felt like an army deserted by its general," Frank Maltby would write. The rainy season had started, and yellow fever cases in June had nearly doubled over the month before. Men started frantically checking themselves every morning for signs of the illness. According to Marie Gorgas, "the effect [of Wallace's resignation] upon the workers at the Isthmus was deplorable. It seemed to inspire the labouring and the executive forces with one ambition: a determination to scuttle. There was only one reason why they did not get away en masse, and that was the lack of shipping space to carry them."

CHAPTER EIGHTEEN

RESTART

The arrival, in July 1905, of Wallace's replacement, the rugged and ingenious John Stevens, marks a turn in fortunes for the beleaguered canal. Stevens had built the Great Northern Railroad across the Pacific Northwest. The foremost railway man of his day, he had proven his tenacity in rough territory from Canada to Mexico, surviving attacks by wolves and hostile Indians along the way. Although he would leave under a cloud two years later, his new plan of action would ultimately save the canal.

Initially Stevens, who had been about to leave for the Philippines for a railway construction job, turned down the offer to become chief engineer in Panama. "Then I was asked to meet...Cromwell," Stevens wrote. The lawyer "seemed to have a deep and heartfelt interest in the success of the proposed work . . . after listening an hour or two to his silver-tongued arguments I consented . . . with conditions." Stevens laid these out when he met President Roosevelt. There could be no interference from above or below, and he could not promise to stay on the job beyond the time "I had made its success certain, or had proved it to be a failure."

Stevens sailed from New York accompanied by Theodore Shonts, the new Commission chairman. Shonts remembers being shocked at discovering that there were more canal employees booked on the steamer's return journey than were on the outward trip. Little fanfare greeted their arrival on July 24, and Stevens straightaway started assessing the situation. For all his experience, what he discovered was profoundly shocking. "The condition of affairs on the Isthmus," he would later write, "can truly be described as desperate; even by many well-wishers it was regarded as hopeless." Hungry men were foraging the swamps for sugarcane and the jungle for bananas, and in the faces of office workers and laborers alike he saw fear and disillusion. According to Stevens they were "scared out of their boots, afraid of yellow fever and afraid of everything." Many believed the "history of the Americans on the Isthmus would be a repetition of the De Lesseps failure." It was widely rumored that Shonts had been sent down to tell them to pack up and go home.

Stevens found "no organization worthy of the name," he said, and "no cooperation existing between what might charitably be called the departments." In the Culebra Cut, Wallace had been pushing the work ahead in order to satisfy what Stevens would call "the idiotic howl about 'making the dirt fly.' " But when Stevens surveyed the work from a hill above *la grande tranchée*, he saw all seven steam shovels idle for want of spoil trains. There were seven locomotives, but they were all derailed. "I believe I faced about as discouraging a proposition as was ever presented to a construction engineer," Stevens would write.

The first meeting between Stevens, Shonts, Magoon, and Gorgas was a chance for a fresh look at the problems facing the enterprise. Magoon explained that just about everyone who could get off the Isthmus had left. The governor reckoned the main difficulty was with food supply—shortages caused by crop failures and an exodus of men from the countryside to work on the canal had driven prices to

levels twice that of New York. On two recent occasions wages had
been raised for the American workers, and both times the Panamanian merchants had increased their prices to match them. Magoon
reckoned some of them were making profits of up to 100 percent.
Shonts's reaction was to order the establishment of "commissary,"
ICC-run shops along the line, free to sell to anyone, even though, as
Magoon quickly pointed out, this was against the agreement made
with the Panamanian merchants by Taft. Shonts, who clearly thought
that Magoon had become a little too friendly with the locals, brushed
this aside, telling the governor to "keep his eye on the ball . . . Our
sole purpose on this Isthmus is to build the canal."

The other priorities identified during this meeting were to improve the accommodation available to the workforce and to confront
the specter of fever. "There are three diseases in Panama," Stevens
proclaimed to the assembled white staff the next day. "They are yellow fever, malaria and cold feet; and the greatest of these is cold
feet." From the start the new chief engineer projected a hardy image.
"I have had as much or more actual personal experience in manual labor than any one here—surveys, hardships, railroad construction in
all its details and operation," he announced, calling on his subordinates to display "dogged determination and steady, persistent, intelligent work." According to Frank Maltby, he was "enthusiastically
cheered; the men looked at each other appreciatively as if to say,
'That's the man to follow.' "

Stevens canceled the plan to build him a large official residence at
Ancón, and ordered the removal of the canal headquarters to Culebra, right on top of the work and away from the temptations of
Panama City. In his battered hat and rubber boots and overalls, and
with an ever-present cigar, Stevens trudged up and down the works,
assessing equipment and personnel, trying all the time to spread calm
and determination among the workforce. The evenings were spent
dealing with the administrative mess left by Wallace and hammering
some sort of organization out of the chaos.

Frank Maltby fully expected to be replaced by a new man, but heard nothing from Stevens for a week after his arrival. Then he had a brisk summons by telegram: "Come to Panama on the first train. Stevens." "We sat out on the veranda under a full tropical moon and among the magnificent Royal Palms of Ancon Hill," Maltby wrote of their meeting. "Everyone else disappeared. Mr. Stevens did not talk much but asked questions—and could that man ask questions! He found out everything I knew. He turned me inside out and shook out the last drop of information I had." Maltby learned subsequently that Stevens had had someone waiting in Washington to take his place, but, uniquely among Wallace's department heads, he kept his job. Maltby, in turn, was impressed by Stevens—the fact that he had gone through "the hardships of a pioneer in the rugged West" and his quick grasp of the issues at stake. "His desk was always clear," Maltby wrote; "one could get a quick decision." It was a great improvement on Wallace.

Stevens's first major decision came after only a week on the Isthmus. In the full knowledge that it would not play well to the press and his political bosses back in the States, on August 1 he ordered a stop to the excavation work in the Cut. No more dirt would fly until proper preparations had been made. In the Cut, half of the steam shovels were shut down, and the free workforce transferred to sanitation and accommodation.

Stevens thought little of the French machinery, however well restored. "I cannot conceive how they did the work they did with the plant they had," he wrote of the de Lesseps effort. In its place he put in huge orders for new American machines. Wallace had been planning to try out various different designs of excavators, spoil cars, and locomotives, but Stevens just trusted to his experience and went ahead and ordered what he wanted. Stevens respected Wallace as an engineer and put his failure down not just to the "severe case of fright" from yellow fever that had precipitated his departure, but also to his unwillingness to take on his superiors. Stevens, unlike Wallace, had no seat (for now) on the Commission, but expected, and got, whatever he demanded. "I determined from the start," he would write, "that the only line of policy that promised success was one of going ahead and doing things on my own initiative, without waiting for orders or approval."

To be fair to Wallace his experimentation with excavation had provided useful experience. The Bucyrus shovels had proved to be strong and reliable, and now Stevens ordered dozens more, including several state-of-the-art 105-ton monsters. Where early models had gone wrong, changes were made, with speed and strength the primary requisites. Steel replaced iron, and parts liable to break were enlarged and strengthened. The result, according to Stevens, was "a machine in every way superior to any in existence."

Stevens also ordered 120 locomotives and 800 cars to carry away the spoil, as well as new drills, vastly superior to those used by Wallace and the French. A compressed air pipeline was planned for the length of the Cut to power them. Stevens had by now seen enough to identify the bottleneck in the excavation effort. As he put it, "The problem was simply one of transportation." To maximize the effectiveness of any excavator, it had to be serviced efficiently by spoil removal trains. Thus, for Stevens, the railway, the Panama Railroad, was the key to success on the Isthmus, something never fully appreciated by the French.

Stevens's first impression of the Panama Railroad had not been favorable. He described it in July 1905 as "two streaks of rust and a right of way." Its management was "thirty years behind the times." Most of it was still single-track, there were practically no sidings, and the rolling stock had been obsolete for years. In the summer of 1905 traffic was almost at a standstill with thousands of tons of freight piled in cars, on docks, and in warehouses, some of which had not moved for eighteen months. Even shipping papers and other records had been lost. Stevens was told the good news that there had been no collisions on the line for a year, but replied dismissively, "A collision has its good points as well as its bad ones—it indicates there is something moving on the railroad."

Stevens brought in a new manager, W. G. Bierd, and laid plans for the double-tracking of the whole line, the installation of a new tele-graph line, and for the rebuilding of culverts and bridges. At the ter-mini he ordered that new sidings and yards be started, along with extra warehouses, docks, and new coaling plants.

All this would need a massive influx of labor. While he was still in New York, Stevens had met William Karner and instructed him to re-turn to Barbados and to keep the recruits flowing to the Isthmus (al-though Stevens did warn that he was a "crank" for Chinese labor). In addition, recruiting agents in Martinique and Cartagena were told to step up their work.

Since the disappointing first shipment in January, the attitude to working in Panama had been transformed in Barbados. Karner puts this down to an incident in early May 1905. On the return trip of a Royal Mail steamer from Colón to Bridgetown, "two colored men stepped from a rowboat to the landing," he wrote, "almost in front of the window in my office . . . They attracted considerable attention from the men working on and around the landing. It was quite un-usual to see a negro laborer riding in a cab, and when these two men, who were smoking, got into a cab and started uptown, the crowd of colored men and women stood aghast and wondered. They soon learned that the two men were in the first shipment I made, January 26th. They had saved money, paid their return passage and still had money for a good time at their home-coming . . . From that time on there was a steady increase in numbers in our shipments." "Colón Man" had arrived in Barbados.

The "Panama Craze" that suddenly took hold of the island led to a repeat of the scenes witnessed at Kingston docks a generation earlier. On one recruiting day, described by American journalist Arthur Bullard, more than two thousand people crowded into Bridgetown's Trafalgar Square, where the police could barely control the crush. "I wanted to go and do you know the reason why?" asks Barbadian Benjamin Jordan, who was nineteen in 1905. "In Barbados they wasn't paying you nothing. Even getting ten cents an hour to come to Panama was better than staying in Barbados." Another canal old-timer, interviewed for a television documentary in 1984, simply wanted to be part of the great project: "one of the greatest engineering feats the world has ever undertaken." Soon groups of young men wearing their best suits and heading on foot for Bridgetown docks became a familiar sight all over the island. Panama offered excitement, adventure, an escape from the tiny, claustrophobic country with its poverty and rigid social and racial stratification. It was almost an act of rebellion. One group of young men on the way to Bridgetown, it was reported in the Legislative Council, passed a field where a gang of sugar estate workers was being supervised by the plantation manager. One of the young men in the Panama-bound crowd shouted: "Why you don't hit de manager in de head, and come along wid we!" It may have been meant in jest, but it sent a shiver of anxiety through the island's white elite.

According to Arthur Bullard the men waiting in Trafalgar Square were ushered a hundred at a time into a large warehouse where they were given a medical examination. Benjamin Jordan had passed all the medical checks, but had a final question to answer: "The doctor was examining us ten in a row," he remembered. "He said he wasn't sending anyone to Panama under twenty. I was the smallest one in the bunch. When he came to this fella, he said, 'How old are you boy?' 'Twenty.' 'How old are you boy?' 'Twenty.' Everyone was twenty. When he come to me, I was the youngest of the group, you know. All of the other nine were twenty. I was the smallest. I was only nineteen and had got to put on a couple more years. 'I am twenty-three, doctor.' 'No, boy, you're not twenty-three years old, but you'd like to go to Panama, wouldn't you?' 'Yes, doc.' 'Well I'll send you. But you nine, go home.' Well I had to get out of the city fast," says Jordan. "They were going to break my this that and the other to prevent the doctor sending me. I had to hurry up and get out of the town."

Loading the steamer to Colón started at nine in the morning and took most of the day, as the men's contracts were checked and possessions carted on to the deck. Huge crowds gathered to see the men off and wish them good luck. "I never saw so many negro women in all my life," wrote Bullard of the sailing day he witnessed. "All of them in their gayest Sunday clothes, and all wailing at the top of their voices." Bullard was taking the same steamer to Colón. Onboard were seven ship's officers and more than seven hundred blacks. "Every square inch of deck space was utilized. Some had trunks, but most only bags like that which Dick Whittington had carried into London. There was a fair sprinkling of guitars and accordions." As the boat got under way the singing of hymns started, with one side of the deck Church of England and the other nonconformist. "There was only one song, a secular one, on which they united," writes Bullard: "Fever and ague all day long/At Panama, at Panama,/Wish you were dead before very long/At Panama, at Panama."

The journey to Colón took about twelve days, and all the time the passengers remained on deck, in rain and sun with not enough room each to even stretch themselves out. On Bullard's ship, he writes, the decks were often hot enough to fry an egg, and the passengers had to be hosed down to keep them cool. Even so, in the heat tempers flared and on one occasion the captain had to threaten a man with his revolver to break up a fight. Seven men were clapped in irons and put in the baking-hot brig.

Young Benjamin Jordan got off the steamer at Colón in October 1905. "They brought me here, put me down in the Cut, put a pick and shovel in my hand. I had never seen a pick and shovel before. I started to cry." His boss took away his tools and gave him a job as a waterboy, fetching drinks for the other workers. Jordan was not the only new arrival to find the confusion, noise, and mass of unfamiliar machinery overwhelming and frightening. "On the appearance of the place, I thought I'd go straight home," remembered one digger who arrived at the end of 1906. "Everything looked so strange, so different to home. I felt that I would go back home. But it wasn't so easy to do that, you know, so I continued."

Karner in Bridgetown continued to increase his shipments dramatically. During the first nine months of 1905, fifteen steamer loads carried some three thousand Barbadians to the Isthmus under contract. Recruitment was halted in September due to a lack of accommodation for the workers, but was restarted at the beginning of 1906, during which twenty-one steamer voyages carried over sixty-five hundred new recruits. In March 1906 Karner even chartered a steamer, the *Solent*, to be engaged in nothing but carrying workers from Bridgetown to Colón.

There were Barbadians traveling to the Isthmus under their own steam as well, in roughly equal numbers to those going from the island under contract. This included those who did not like the idea of signing themselves up for nearly two years or had been rejected on medical grounds, as well as men who hoped to get better terms than the basic unskilled labor deal Karner was offering. Harrigan Austin was an experienced carpenter, and arrived in Panama on Sunday, October 9, 1905, having paid his own steamer fare. Austin was one of about a hundred men and women—nearly all West Indians—who responded to a competition staged in 1963 for "the best true stories of life and work on the Isthmus of Panama during the construction of the Panama canal." The initiator was the Isthmian Historical Society, run by American Zonians. The competition was publicized in newspapers in Panama, Central America, and the Caribbean islands, and offered a first prize of $50. Although some respondents might have tailored their accounts to suit the purpose of winning the money, the large collection contains many diverse attitudes and opinions as well as a wealth of detail.

Harrigan Austin's Panama adventure did not start well. To raise the fare of £2 10s. (US$14) for the passage, he had to pool the savings of his extended family, and took virtually nothing with him apart from his carpentry tools. He landed at Colón, "having had a hazardous trip, of thirteen days in bad weather, poor accommodation in general with sparing meals on a crowded ship, we were all more or less hungry. We saw after landing on the dock, a pile of bags of brown sugar. And the whole crowd of us like ants fed ourselves on that sugar."

Austin was taken on straightaway and loaded with the other men into one of the freight cars, which were then "hurried off, and distributed at various Stations. My lot happened to be Las Cascadas." The men were led to a camp of tents, and each was assigned an army-style cot. The next morning he was put to work repairing old French quarters at Bas Obispo. His foreman was a white man, but he appointed one of the experienced West Indians as subforeman "as really the only thing he knew to do was to watch us but really very little about handling or directing a carpenters' gang."

Other West Indians were less cynical about their American bosses. John Butcher arrived from Barbados on January 12, 1906, and, like Austin and some two thousand more workers, was employed on assembling and renovating buildings, a Stevens priority. His first assignment was as a plumber's helper. He instantly got on with his immediate boss, a young American, Edward T. Nolan (they were still in touch with each other by letter in 1963). Nolan's superior, the assistant quartermaster, was "a real pusher," Butcher remembered. "He always promised permanent work to the better workmen. Hearing this, I tried my best to work harder and more than anyone else. Carpenters, plumbers, electricians, painters—all accepted this challenge but of course, as far as plumbers were concerned there were none better than the Nolan-Butcher team. Through hard work, we excelled in whatever jobs we were assigned . . . As a husky, strong, active young man who was never afraid of work, I was always in demand. I still have the joy of just knowing that there are so few of those early houses on which I did not work."

Many of the accounts written by West Indians show similar pride in their work and participation in the Panama project. Others took pleasure in the new skills they were rapidly forced to acquire—operating tools such as hammers and drills that they had never even seen before. But Harrigan Austin, already an artisan when he arrived, was deeply disappointed when he was put on the same wage level as the unskilled labor: "We were often forced to work in the rain," he wrote, because if they stopped, their wages were cut. "Indeed to some degree life was some sort of semi-slavery, and there was none to appeal to, for we were strangers and actually compelled to accept what we got." In the case of an argument, says Austin, "the bosses and policemen right or wrong would always win the game, and those men who had the chances filling such position were generally of the dominating type who tried to bring others into subjection for their fame."

The police of the Isthmus had given the massive influx of West Indians, or "Chombos" as they derogatorily called them, the same sort of welcome afforded to the arrivals of a generation before. There was particular dislike of their presence in Panama City, where large gangs were at work for the whole of 1905 building sewers and waterworks, and paving the main streets. On one occasion at the end of April a group of about 150 men staged a sit-in when their American foreman ordered them back to work before most had eaten their lunch. The demonstration grew more heated, with loud complaints about low wages and their late payment. The foreman summoned the local police, who charged the strikers and then chased them across the square in front of the old Administration Building. In the ensuing mêlée twenty-one workers were seriously enough injured by bayonet stabs and rifle butt blows to require hospital treatment.

"The disgraceful scenes of yesterday will live long in the memory of those who witnessed them," wrote the *Star and Herald* on April 29. "The senseless attacks upon inoffensive persons was enough to make anyone's blood boil... Carelessness and utter indifference to the wants of the men who are brought here to do the actual work of digging the Canal is silently, but nevertheless, surely breeding trouble. Who is responsible? There is no denying the fact that the men have been brought here under false pretenses and misrepresentations and have been badly paid and underfed... and in many cases put to work under incompetent men possessing an inherent hatred and contempt of the colored races." The *Colón Independent*, a triweekly founded in 1899 by a Barbadian, Clifford Bynoe, would write a year later of this time, "One could scarcely breathe God's free air without being clubbed and kicked... The American occupation then was a terror and a disgrace."

Consul Mallet, whose job it was to try to protect British citizens from such attacks and to seek redress from those responsible, blamed both the Americans and the Panamanians for the incident. Writing to the foreign secretary about the "serious disturbance," he explained: "the majority of Americans here—I refer particularly to those who hold subordinate positions—exhibit an extraordinary contempt for the Jamaican negro, and most of the trouble so far has been due to the blustering behaviour of the foremen in charge of the gangs." But he wrote too about the "intense dislike and jealousy felt by the police towards the coloured natives of Jamaica on the Isthmus." There had been increasing complaints, he reported, about the violent methods resorted to by the native police when making an arrest for some trivial offense. "In fact," he ended, "their arbitrary conduct is no better to-day than it was during the worst period of the Colombian regime on the Isthmus of Panama."

After much prevarication Mallet at last extracted an official apology from the Panamanian secretary for foreign affairs. Magoon, of whom Mallet had a high opinion, made conciliatory noises, but the canal authorities asked the Panamanian police to arrest Jamaican Charles Schuar, who was seen as the leader of the workers' action. He was promptly imprisoned and then deported.

There did follow, however, a reorganization of the police by an American instructor, and, on Mallet's suggestion, some West Indian constables were taken on to help police their own neighborhoods. But the West Indians remained wary. "In Jamaica a constable is a peacemaker," one told an American journalist. "Here he just hits a man with a stick."

From the very start, and for much of the construction period, the question of food would remain a leading catalyst for dissent and dissatisfaction among the West Indians. While prices rose fast to "Klondike" levels, wages had stayed the same for the workers. In November 1904, the PRR had actually lowered its minimum wage to bring it into line with the canal's pay rate. The money saved was spent on increases for the white skilled railroad employees. Further pay hikes for the Americans on the Isthmus had not been matched for the West Indians, many of whom now found themselves in a desperate situation. "Instead of the canal bringing with it those good old times it is bringing hard work and starvation pay for the majority and fortunes for the few," complained the *Colón Independent* at the end of 1904.

On a wage of seldom more than a dollar a day, the West Indians were being asked to pay seventy-five cents for a dozen eggs and sixty cents for a chicken. Coffee and bread brought to the works by West Indian women cost an hour's wages. In their desperation, many were surviving on a diet of sugarcane and were becoming seriously malnourished. At the beginning of 1906, two American journalists from the New York magazine the *Independent* interviewed a man they described as of "unusual intelligence." He declined to be named in the article, and is referred to only as a "Jamaican carpenter." But he is of particular interest as he had been on the Isthmus since 1894, and had worked for the French at the height of the activity of the New Company. "Things were very different in those days," he told the interviewers. "The workmen are more afraid of the Americans than of the French . . . there are no loafing jobs now, such as there used to be. It is like running a race all the time. You don't mind it for a day, but you can't keep it up." Although the basic pay, he said, was better from the Americans, there were no longer chances to increase this through piecework. "Besides," he went on, "the blacks had more chance of promotion under the French. They could get to be timekeepers or checkers then, but they can't now."

The biggest difference for him was the cost of living. Yams used to be sixty for a dollar, but now you only got sixteen. "If they starve themselves," he said of the West Indian laborers, "they can save a good deal. If they are well fed they don't save. Out of 80 cents a day it takes 50 to buy food, and then there are washing, clothing etc., besides. Some of the men try hard to save; buy 2 cents bread, 2 cents sugar, and go to work all trembly and can't lift a thing."

William Karner backs this up. "In their anxiety to save money to send back home," he wrote of the Barbadians, "they were literally starving themselves." An American journalist, John Foster Carr, who visited the Isthmus in mid-1905, investigated this for himself: "I have looked into hundreds of their pots boiling over bonfires, as they crouched beside them," he wrote. "A very large number contained nothing but rice, or a piece of yam, or some plantains. Others had added a small piece of salt pork, beef, or codfish. In the rainy season, when with damp wood their primitive fires fail them, they tell me that they have often to choose between half-cooked yams and rice—which the doctors say is not digestible—and biscuits . . . weak and anaemic are these poorly fed laborers. They fall easy victim to malaria, and on this account alone, the Chief Sanitary Officer maintains, pneumonia with seventy to ninety percent of fatal cases is prevalent among them, when the better-fed white man is nearly immune."

After a steady average of four pneumonia cases a month, suddenly in October 1905 there were twenty-six, all West Indians. On December 13 the headline in the *Colón Independent* read: "Pneumonia Rampant On the Isthmus. Has taken an epidemic form. Fatal Among Colored People." A doctor was asked by the newspaper for the attribution of the disease. "A severe cold," he replied. "The laborers are generally wet with perspiration and will sit in the wind to cool off. Very often they go to bed in their wet clothes and when the chilly part of the night comes on the body becomes cold." With the return of the wet season in spring 1906, the rate would jump again. Because viral pneumonia was almost unknown on the islands, the new arrivals were particularly vulnerable.

In November 1905, journalist Poultney Bigelow made his famous trip to Colón. An experienced reporter (and former law-school classmate of Theodore Roosevelt), Bigelow had made his name with stories on labor conditions in South Africa and the Far East. His father was John Bigelow, who had visited the Isthmus in 1886 together with de Lesseps and remained a lifelong supporter of the canal. Poultney Bigelow, however, seems to have been drawn to the story by the increasing rumors back in the United States that the project was in trouble from labor strife, confusion, and corruption.

In Colón, whose condition he described as worse than anything he had ever seen, even in the "slums of Canton," Bigelow wandered the streets, unescorted by any official, interviewing those he came across. One Barbadian he met he described as wearing "a clean collar, a black derby hat and a good suit of clothes—an educated and prosperous example of his race." From him he heard complaints about the high cost of living and the late payment of wages. "But his main grievance was that as a man of color he received no encouragement for his work; no one seemed to care whether he got good work out of his men or not—all the white men about him were trying to see how little they could do, each for himself." Others reported that they received unequal justice and were treated with rudeness by the American bosses.

Worst of all, however, was the sickness. "Throughout my pestiferous excursion up and down this filthy city," Bigelow wrote, "I could not find a single man or woman who had not suffered or was not suffering from fever of some kind." One worker he met was "a splendid specimen of manhood, a negro such as would have been recruited with pride into the Tenth United States Cavalry." But the man was sick and could only walk with difficulty. He felt he had been deceived, Bigelow reports. The place was "unfit to live in." He was trying to get back to Jamaica but the next steamer was already full, taking away "400 negroes, all returning to Jamaica in disgust."

The journalist's own steamer from Colón carried the same number of returnees, and when Bigelow met Swettenham and the chief justice of Jamaica they confirmed to him "what is denied by official authority in Washington" that "negroes are returning from the canal in portentous numbers" and that the men "were not honestly or humanely treated."

In mid-December, Stevens wrote to Shonts: "Notwithstanding nearly six thousand new laborers were brought in between August 15 and November 15, our force shows little or no increase . . . our forces are being constantly depleted by departure from the Isthmus . . . The Jamaicans are returning almost universally."

⫸⫷⫸⫷

The West Indian workers, hampered by disease and malnutrition, were criticized by the American canal authorities as weak and idle. Official ICC reports wrote of their lack of vitality and frail "disposition to labor." "The West Indian's every movement is slow and bungling," wrote one American journalist, echoing the prevailing sentiment. "Every small object a subject for debate; anything at all a sufficient excuse for all hands to stop work." But, as the writer went on, there was a "certain and unjustified cruelty" in forcing "poor half-fed fellows" to work eight to ten hours in such heat. "Until you have tried to do a good fifteen minutes' work with a pick and shovel during the rainy season . . . you can have no idea of the exhaustion that tropical heat brings even to the laborer who is used to it."

Stevens declared that the value of the West Indians as laborers was low under any conditions, but admitted, "They were not getting proper food in sufficient and regular amounts to give them strength for continuous work." The situation was improved a little with the gradual opening up of ICC-run "commissary" stores along the line, where, using coupons issued against pay, employees could buy food imported from the United States at "cost price," or at any rate cheaper than prevailing locally. There was much praise in some quarters for the fact that the Commission, through bulk buying, could ship goods two thousand miles and still sell them at prices comparable to those in New York City. This may have been a great boon for the well-paid white workers, but the wages of the West Indians, although generous by Barbados or Jamaica standards, would not have gone far in the United States. It did not help either that cooking was forbidden in the workers' barracks.

Construction had been ongoing on several hotels, where the white employees were served meals. Soon after taking over, Stevens decided to offer the West Indians cooked food as well in a bid to improve their productivity. Originally the entire catering operation was farmed out to a private company, but when the contractor calculated that he needed to charge $30 a month per white employee and $12 a month for a laborer, the Commission decided to set up and run the operation themselves.

While more "hotels" were built for the American workforce, for the blacks there were "messes," kitchens established near the work sites. No tables or chairs were provided in these, so the diners were forced to squat or stand with their food. By February 1906, there were over fifty in operation, feeding 7,000 to 8,000 workers a day. Breakfast invariably consisted of coffee, bread, and porridge; lunch was usually bread, beans, and rice; supper was more bread with potatoes, soup, coffee, and perhaps some meat.

But if malnutrition declined, grumbling continued. The food served seems to have been indescribably awful. One sympathetic American called it "the leavings from the hotels . . . [which] are not fit to eat before they are leavings." Barbadian John Butcher, who otherwise generally speaks well of his treatment on the Isthmus, described the rice he was given as "hard enough to shoot deers." When they had meat, "many men spent an hour trying to chew or eventually threw [it] away because it was too hard." Harrigan Austin remembered the food as "poorly prepared, almost raw." But anyone who protested was arrested for bad behavior by the policemen sent to keep order in the kitchens at mealtimes.

In order to maximize the efficiency of their workers, the Commission sought to take more and more control over the lives of the West Indians. When he arrived at Colón at the beginning of 1906, Jules LeCurrieux was, at sixteen, even younger than Harrigan Austin. Although born in French Guiana, LeCurrieux's family had emigrated to Barbados, so he came under a Karner contract from Bridgetown. Straight off the steamer, the men were piled into railway freight trains for distribution along the line. "To our surprise," wrote LeCurrieux, "we were unloaded off the train as animals and not men, and almost under strict guard to camps."

These "camps" might have been of tents, like Harrigan Austin's, or simply boxcars from the railways, but LeCurrieux was deposited in one of the newly assembled workers' barracks. This consisted of a separate toilet and a hut of about fifty by thirty feet. Into this space were crowded seventy-two men. No furniture, sheets, or pillows were provided. Jamaican journalist Henry de Lisser visited one of the barracks later that same year: "Inside the houses themselves you find groups of men seated round a box and playing cards; you find some listening to one of their number playing softly on a flute; you find others in bed," he wrote. "These beds are canvas cots fixed onto iron standees which can open and shut as required. Each standee is about seven feet high, and has three cots hung on either side of it, each cot being six-and-a-half feet long by two-and-a-half feet wide . . . when they were all occupied the room cannot be the most pleasant place in the world to sleep in." According to the "Jamaican carpenter," "There is no privacy or quiet in the bachelor buildings . . . Some of the men are noisy at night and have no sense of decency . . ."

"We were taken to a kitchen," continued Jules LeCurrieux, "and each of us were given 1 plate, 1 cup, 1 spoon, and a meal, then those utensils were ours—the price to be taken out of our first pay." That same afternoon LeCurrieux was put to work with a gang in the Cut. His job was to drill twenty-foot-deep holes at the top of Gold Hill to be stuffed with dynamite to "tear the old hill down."

When work finished for the day LeCurrieux was given a thirty-cent ticket, the value of which was taken from his pay. This entitled him to three meals and accommodation in the barracks. After two weeks he got his first wages, which he used to buy a pillow and blanket "and a few cakes of soap to wash our dishes and clothes." "The discipline maintained in the labour camps is severe," reported Mallet back to London. LeCurrieux remembers that at 9:00 p.m. an old piece of rail was knocked with a metal bar, signaling "go to bed, no sound."

At 5:00 a.m., they were awakened by more loud knocking, and after a hurried breakfast they were on a labor train by six. To keep the men at work, they were denied food or shelter if they could not produce the ticket that said they had labored that day. "This rule worked well and tended to drive out the undesirable class," reported Stevens. No one was allowed in the barracks during working hours—you had to be on the job or in a hospital. Those who broke this rule were arrested and fined three days' wages.

Furthermore, about once a week there were spot checks on those sleeping in the barracks, as the *Colón Independent* complained: "At midnight when everyone is asleep, suddenly the cry of 'tickets' is heard. The laborer, frightened out of his sleep, very often cannot remember at the moment what he has done with his ticket, and is hustled off to prison." "This system has been adopted to keep loafers out of the camps," continued the paper, "but it would be better to allow a few loafers to get in than that so many innocent men should suffer. The system is a rotten one and must be changed."

<hr />

"*I* grew careless last week," wrote Jan van Hardeveld to his wife, Rose, in August 1905. "Before I realised it I was one sick hombre—stomach out of order and my blood full of malaria bugs." There was better news—he had met a fellow Dutchman, Jan Milliery, who had been in South Africa during the Boer War and had subsequently worked as a track foreman. Milliery was experienced in life in the tropics and was a good cook. The two men were rooming together and had become firm friends.

Against the advice of her family, Rose had decided to take herself and her daughters out to Panama to join her husband. In the meantime, while they waited for quarters to become available, she had been reading up about the history of the canal dream, and the more she learned, the more she began to share her husband's enthusiasm. In his letters, Jan was frank about the difficulties—there had been little headway with the "real work," the men were "dissatisfied," the labor problems were "acute." The resignation of Wallace had thrown everybody. But Jan had clearly not lost his faith: "The slowness of the work would be discouraging," he wrote home in September, "if I were not certain that our Government can and will accomplish whatever it sets out to do. You know what I always say—in America, anything is possible..." In the same letter he told Rose that the quartermaster had at last assigned him married quarters. Two weeks later the family were on their way to Panama.

The voyage for Rose was accompanied by a mixture of seasickness, "deep foreboding," and great excitement—at seeing Jan again and at the prospect of joining the canal effort. Everyone saved their best outfits for the landing at Colón. Jan was waiting for them and climbed aboard the ship to gather his family into his arms. "The children were shy," remembered Rose. "They scarcely knew him at first. He was so very thin and burned to a deep brown."

To the new arrivals Colón was as shocking and overwhelming as ever. The waving, feathery palm trees were as beautiful as Rose had imagined they would be, and the flowers "larger and brighter" than anything she had seen before. But the horses that drew the carriage to the railway station were "unbelievably mangy-looking," there was a "foul smell" cloaking everything, and "naked brown children" playing on islands in a sea of rubbish, sewage, and greenish, filthy water. Once on the train Jan confessed that their intended house was not yet ready and they would be camping out for a few days in another one nearby.

Leaving the train at Las Cascadas, Rose found herself in the "blackest, darkest place I had ever been in. Not one flicker of light shone anywhere. We stumbled over a number of wet, slippery tracks and walked along a board walk until we reached the steps of the house," obviously long unoccupied. Inside, furniture had been thrust through the door and left, and a large number of bats were living in the rafters. They had clearly been in residence for some years: "a penetrating stench, so vile it was almost unbearable" hit them as soon as they went inside. Black lizards with bright yellow heads scurried for cover. The first priority was to get the children to sleep. Jan and Rose assembled two beds, and covered them with a mosquito net as the house was unscreened. "By the time I had undressed Janey and Sister," wrote Rose, "they were both sobbing forlornly."

The next morning, as Jan ran for the labor train to take him to his post in the Cut building track for the excavators and spoil trains, Rose set about finding something to give the children to eat. Venturing out of the house, she was confronted with the sprawl of "dingy, nondescript houses" that constituted Las Cascadas, and was instantly "hot and uncomfortable . . . as though I was being smothered between wet, evil-smelling sponges." She identified a shop run by a "bald-pated Chinese," but he seemed to have little to sell except tinned butter, plantain, yams, and soggy, stale English biscuits. At a nearby meat stall, Rose turned away in disgust at the flyblown ribbons of beef. They ended up having fruit for breakfast, bought from a West Indian woman hawking from house to house a tray of oranges and bananas she carried on her head.

At lunchtime, Rose's husband returned accompanied by his Dutch friend Jan, who had been renamed "Jantje"—"Little Jan"—to avoid confusion. Rose learned that as Jantje was not an American citizen he had to find his own living quarters, and was still trying to find something suitable after three months on the Isthmus. His plan was to bring his new wife and their son, born the previous November, out to live with him in Panama, and he had already started the process of getting U.S. citizenship.

Jantje Milliery had arrived at Ellis Island at the end of 1902, having briefly lived in Brussels after leaving South Africa. He married a Dutch woman, Martina Korver, from Rotterdam, the following year and they lived in Jersey City Heights. He had applied to the ICC on June 26, 1905, enclosing a reference from the Dutch consul general of Orange Free State: "Applicant is apparently a steady reliable man," it reads. "He is conversant with track repair methods, and speaks English very well." On July 5 he received an appointment, and sailed for

Panama on the tenth. The money was not that good—he started on $1,000 a year (van Hardeveld, five years older and already a U.S. citizen, was on $1,700)—but being part of the canal meant more to Milliery than the money: it was a means to becoming an American.

That evening Jan van Hardeveld returned exhausted from his day's work. Rose and the girls had spent the afternoon trying to establish which was worse—the soggy heat of outside or the eye-watering stench of the interior of the house. Rose begged him to take some time to help her sort out the mess, but he was "so absorbed in his work that he could not see what overwhelming difficulties confronted me in trying to care for the family." "You don't know what you are asking," Jan replied impatiently. He could not leave his unreliable West Indian laborers for a minute, he said. "We're here to dig this canal."

Jantje stepped in to help Rose in the business of rapid acclimatization, showing her how to hold a damp matchbox at a certain angle to strike and get a light. The local plantains, he explained, could be fried or roasted in their skins. It was all right to buy beef, but it should be cooked for a long time and then only the broth used.

Soon after her arrival Rose was taken to a local party, where she felt very out of place as the only "white" woman in the room. "The people of the new Republic of Panama considered us an uncouth race," she soon learned. There was at that time only one other white American woman in Las Cascadas, an old tropical hand with an alarmingly pinched and yellow face. It was very much a frontier town. Going to and fro, Rose had noticed "dingy places bearing across the front the word *Cantina*... by the smells around the places, and the conditions of the men and women coming out of them, I knew they must be saloons. It worried me to see the little black children running in and out, freely, to see the black women staggering, laughing, cursing, and to watch our own men going in for drinks." She had quickly discovered that Jan and Jantje carried a demijohn of rum beside their workplace icebox—"and that bothered me too." Soon Rose found herself involuntarily averting her eyes when she passed the cantina near her house. "A brown woman sat there looking out," Rose remembered. "She reminded me of a fat spider waiting for someone to devour. She often smiled and nodded at me in a friendly way, but I hated her."

Then at last their proper house was ready, or ready enough for them to move in. The first building erected on the site by the French, it was known as House Number One. Despite the grand name, it was small and dingy, with only one bedroom and a tiny kitchen. But from its high position it offered a view all along the line of the canal as far as the Pacific Ocean to the south and Bas Obispo in the north, where, "the good old Star Spangled Banner, doubly beautiful and precious in this strange country, flew from the pole on top of the hill in Camp Elliott, the United States Marine Corps station." And just below, indeed virtually under the house, was the Cut, where, Rose writes, "the French had made a noticeable beginning." Immediately below the house lay "pieces of machinery overturned, strings of cars, engines, and twisted rails, all covered with growing vines and brush. Large trees had grown up through the couplings of a string of cars at the foot of the hill." Farther down, however, the Americans were at work, and Jan was able to point out to the children the Bucyrus shovel served by his track-shifting gang.

For the children it was thrilling to be so close to their father at work and to the most spectacular section of the canal. According to Rose they "quickly assumed something of their father's proprietary feeling" about the project. They were also making the most of being virtually the only American children among many homesick adults. At the new house ice was delivered every day and in November an ICC-operated food store opened at Empire, two miles away. Even so, day after day was the same meal: "beans, soggy crackers, Danish butter, and fruit. Occasionally a chicken relieved the monotony." On one occasion Rose took the train to Panama City, where she found that anything could be obtained but at exhorbitant prices. She was also unimpressed by the "crooked gambling houses, filthy saloons and brothels. The well-known 'American sucker' had come to the Isthmus and was being properly fleeced by those who knew how."

Toward the end of the year, a trickle of wives started arriving. One in Las Cascadas had a fright on her first day when she mistook an iguana for a crocodile, and "remained in a permanent state of terror . . . every little bug made her hysterical." Rose did her best to help the newcomers become oriented, and, doing so, she wrote, "I sometimes succeeded in bolstering my own failing morale." Meanwhile her husband was becoming increasingly tired and grumpy, endlessly complaining about the standard of work of his West Indian laborers. "There was little I could say or do to make him relax," wrote Rose. "The Canal about which he was so intensely, feverishly concerned might have been his own personal project—his and Teddy Roosevelt's."

Other Americans needed more than the belief in Roosevelt's "great march of progress" to induce them to come to the Isthmus and stay there for any length of time. The first step was to offer exceptional wages. Soon after taking over, Stevens established four recruiting agents, one in New York, one in New Orleans, and two roving. These interviewed candidates and promised anything up to double his current salary in the United States. They also offered free transportation to Panama, free furnished accommodation and medical care, and long, six-week annual paid holidays. According to a senior American administrator on the Isthmus, "Special inducements were added one after another, until an established system was developed which contained perquisites and gratuities which in number and value far exceeded anything of the kind bestowed upon a working force anywhere on the face of the globe." But the initial results were disappointing. Jobs were easy to come by in the United States at that time. More than anything else, though, the shadow of fever still darkened Panama's reputation.

CHAPTER NINETEEN

THE RAILROAD ERA

Crossing the Isthmus by railroad during his first week in Panama, Stevens's fellow passengers had pointed out Gorgas's sanitation squads draining pools, fumigating houses, and oiling waterways. Each spotting was cause for new "ridicule, not only of Colonel Gorgas but also of the mosquito theory, some of these comments reflecting very severely upon the quality of the Colonel's mental equipment. My attention," Stevens later wrote, "was repeatedly called to the great waste of money and the utter futility of the whole procedure."

Since the arrival of Magoon, Gorgas had at last started receiving supplies, and Stevens and Shonts, with Roosevelt's instructions ringing in their ears, had further upped the backing for the Sanitation Department. Shonts, although still skeptical about the mosquito theory, had in July 1905 increased Gorgas's workforce from two hundred to over two thousand. Stevens initially shared Shonts's doubts. But he was so impressed both with the urgent need to combat the fearful disease and by Gorgas's conviction that he could do it, that he decided to provide full support and funding.

So began, in July 1905, one of the most famous sanitary campaigns in history. Mosquito brigades were formed for every district of Panama and Colón. Panamanian doctors were recruited at the local level, responsible for daily house-to-house inspections. A combination of respect for Magoon and Gorgas's charm and tact produced new compliance from the residents of Panama City, who were offered a $50 reward for reporting a case of yellow fever. For each one—and there were forty-two cases in July—their movements during the days before the appearance of the first symptoms were painstakingly traced to find the source of infection.

But nothing was left to chance. Every dwelling, from the grandest *palacio* to the tiniest shack, was now meticulously fumigated. Teams were sent out through the streets, with each man carrying a ladder and a gallon of glue. On their shoulders they had strips of paper 6 feet long and 3 inches wide to stick over doors, windows, holes, and openings in the wall to prevent the smoke or the insects escaping when the pans containing sulphur or pyrethrum and alcohol were lit inside. If it was a large building, once it was sealed the sulphur smoke was pumped in from outside, through a tube inserted into the door through the keyhole. In a year, 330 tons of sulphur and 120 tons of pyrethrum—the entire annual output of the United States—were used up. "The fumigation campaign was so intense," remembered one sanitary squad worker, "that there was a big, thick white cloud of smoke from the sulphur hanging over the Zone and Panama City, and even the leaves on the trees curled up."

At the same time other teams checked on the water that people kept in barrels for everyday use, unwittingly providing breeding grounds for the next generation of *Aëdes aegypti*. In early July 1905 running water had at last been connected for Panama City, which was of great assistance to the efforts of the sanitary squads. So with households in the city largely clear of water containers, the squads could concentrate on potential breeding sites among rubbish and elsewhere. "An empty tin can was the special aversion of the Sanitary Squad," wrote Frank Maltby. "We became so clean, orderly, and 'dried out' that it was painful." Where water could not be removed—in cesspools, cisterns, puddles, or potholes—other teams arrived to spray the surface of the water with kerosene to smother the "wrigglers." In a year, over two and a half million gallons of oil was used in this way. Success demanded total thoroughness. Gorgas even had the holy water in the font of the cathedral changed every day once it was found that mosquitoes were breeding there.

Indeed, with most households dispensing with domestic water containers, the yellow fever mosquitoes started laying their eggs wherever they could find pools of water—in hollowed-out stones and even in the leaves of trees, in particular that of the *calocasia*, which grew in weedlike profusion around the houses. As well as clearing all vegetation from the vicinity of living quarters, Gorgas's squads started laying traps. Such is the fastidiousness of the female *Aëdes aegypti* that the bowls of sweet clean water now left out by the sanitarians proved far more tempting for ovipositing than a dirty puddle. Every day the water in the traps was simply emptied on to the dry ground and replaced. "They eagerly accepted the much cleaner tin pans placed out for their particular benefit," writes Joseph Le Prince, "and thus involuntarily committed race suicide."

As well as aiming to exterminate the *Aëdes aegypti* by attacking its larval stage, Gorgas sought to prevent any adult survivors from coming into contact with humans, or more precisely, vulnerable white Americans. The U.S. workforce now found itself thoroughly protected by metal screens. Because of the warm, salty, and damp climate of the Isthmus only very pure copper would resist rapid corrosion (even so, the screens on every American home or dwelling place had to be checked by yet another team every week). It was all astronomically expensive. One order for high-grade copper screening, signed off by Stevens in the autumn of 1905, came to $90,000, nearly double the entire Sanitary Department budget for the previous year. Orders also went in for three thousand rubbish bins, four thousand buckets, a thousand brooms, and 5,000 pounds of common soap. Alongside the specific antimosquito measures came a massive expansion of the medical facilities. A second hospital at Colón belonging to the Panama Railroad was taken over and the capacity of Ancón hospital was extended to 1,500 beds and the staff to 470. Twenty district hospitals were opened the length of the line, along with forty smaller field hospitals, as work started on refurbishing the old French sanatorium on Taboga. In his first twelve months Gorgas had been allowed to spend $50,000. For the next year, his expenditure topped $2 million.

If this was throwing money at the problem, it worked. In August cases of yellow fever fell by nearly a half to twenty-seven, with nine deaths. The following month there were only seven cases and four deaths. The last death from yellow fever was reported in Panama City on November 11, 1905. As they gathered in the autopsy room, Gorgas instructed his staff to take a good look at the man: he was, said Gorgas, the last yellow fever corpse they would see.

And so it proved. It may have taken twice the eight months required in Havana, but now Panama was free of yellow fever, for the first time, and forever. It was a massive breakthrough for the American canal.

⫷⫸

The following year, 1906, would be one of the most difficult for the project: even if the terrible fear caused by yellow fever had faded, the death rate among the workers and technicians—from malaria, pneumonia, typhoid, and accidents—would actually increase to its highest for the whole U.S. construction period. But at the end of 1905 the project's leaders could congratulate themselves on a number of achievements to add to Gorgas's yellow fever victory. Problems with the water supply for Panama City had been corrected, so that Mallet could write to his wife in September that at last "the strong smell of decomposed fish has gone." Sewers were in operation and much of the city had been paved. In the six months since Stevens's arrival over six hundred of the old French buildings had been repaired, twice the number Wallace managed in a year. Stevens's other priority, food supply, although not solved, was certainly being addressed. Refrigerated trucks were now carrying ice and perishables along the line to the growing number of commissary stores, hotels, and messes. Several of the Panama Railroad's steamers had been fitted out with cold compartments, so that fresh food could arrive in pristine condition from the United States. At the end of the year Stevens started plans for a cold-storage plant and bakery at Cristóbal.

The white, largely American canal community was changing, and the project was beginning to lose its frontier town feel. When American journalist John Foster Carr visited the Isthmus at the beginning of 1906, six months after his first trip there, he found that "the day of the good-for-nothing tropical tramp had nearly passed." Certainly Stevens had set about, as he put it, "weeding out the faint-hearted and incompetent," but for Carr, the Isthmus itself had also carried out some sort of selection. "The men themselves," he wrote, "have distinctive virtues as a body that are easily accounted for. Most of them are plucky, for it took pluck to come to the Isthmus and stay when yellow fever was in the land. They are mostly decent, healthy fellows, for the climate is severe on vices of over-indulgence in a northerner. Of those who will not heed the warning many are invalided home; a certain number die. Something like a real moral selection is the result."

Six months before, Carr had found the young Americans on the project simply surviving. At the end of the day, "they were too tired to talk. They sat about silently and went to bed at nine o'clock. On Sunday there was nowhere to go, because the jungle hemmed them in as if it were a thousand leagues of ocean." The one day off would be spent "on the hotel verandas, smoking, lazily watching the vultures floating high up in the air, 'talking shop,' and telling tales of Cuba and the Philippines, where scores of them have been." But now some of the rough edges were disappearing. Food was plentiful and relatively cheap; screens on windows and doors meant that lights could be burned after dark; the shock of the climate and the work ahead wore off; the fear of "yellow jack" was gone. "The last six months have seen a great change," wrote Carr at the beginning of 1906. "New habits are forming and life is rapidly approaching the normal."

Carr was something of a drumbeater for the canal project; other journalists give a more nuanced view of the emerging new community. "Normal family life is becoming established and society is developing peculiar forms," reported the *New York Independent* magazine in March 1906. "In some places it resembles official life in India. At the balls married women reign supreme, with abundance of admirers and no debutante rivals . . . After the novelty . . . wears off, life . . . is barren and dull for most of the men . . . It is more from ennui than from viciousness that many of the employees seek for solace in the cocktail and the jackpot."

Some of the Americans did take things into their own hands. Frank Maltby, still living in the old "De Lesseps Palace" where every room was now full of young engineers, used trips back to the United States to bring to Panama a pool table, card tables, and a piano. He also subscribed to every paper he could think of. So was established "Maltby's Mess," a mini-community remembered fondly by many. Others started a baseball league and bridge clubs.

But for most, particularly the young bachelors, there was little more variety of diversion than had been available for Henri Cermoise twenty years before. "Most of the young men on the Isthmus have absolutely no places of amusement, recreation, and rendezvous except the saloons and gambling places," complained a U.S. diplomat. For all Carr's "moral selection," over six hundred bars were kept busy on the Isthmus, arrests for drunkenness far surpassed any other cause, and a huge number of prostitutes made a good living in the terminal cities.

The corrupting influence of life in the tropics, and of life in Panama in particular, on fine young upstanding Americans was of constant concern and interest to the public at home. Apart from anything else, it made for good copy. Thus the challenge for Stevens and Magoon in finding respectable diversion for their workers became a question not just of protecting the men from their worst impulses, but also, and perhaps more important, of nullifying dangerous domestic criticism. In early 1905, a YMCA representative, touring the Isthmus, had written, in a widely reproduced report, that "positive forces for evil" were "wide open in . . . Panama and Colón." At fault was the legal lottery in the republic, "saloons and drinking places in large numbers . . . dispensing a most inferior and highly injurious quality of liquor," the popular sports of bullfighting and cockfighting, and prostitution, which, he said, was "as bad as might be expected in a country of loose marriage relations, lax laws etc." The solution to the moral crisis was identified as the creation of "libraries and reading rooms . . . reputable places of amusement, grounds for outdoor games . . . [and] clubs for mental, moral or physical culture."

This measure had been backed by Wallace and other senior Americans on the Isthmus, but the Commission under Walker, although "heartily approving of the plan," had not felt that the law gave them the authority to "use money appropriated for the construction of the Canal for the amusement of the Canal employees." The forceful Stevens had more luck and in November 1905 the ICC decision was overruled by presidential decree, and work started on a clubhouse at Cristóbal, complete with dance hall, card room, bowling alleys, gymnasium, showers, and a writing room. Three more were earmarked for Empire, Gorgona, and Culebra. At the same time, sports pitches, "opportunities for wholesome open-air exercise," were planned and started.

But women were considered the key. To break down the all-male, army-camp atmosphere in which "immoral" behavior was considered acceptable, Stevens, Magoon, and Shonts went out of their way to encourage men to bring their wives to the Isthmus. A heavily subsidized steamer fare was offered, along with superior accommodation and commissary rights. By autumn 1905 work was under way on a number of schools for Zone children, the first of which opened in January 1906.

All this municipal work occupied much of the labor force in Stevens's first six months, but there were important improvements on the engineering side as well. Deeper borings with state-of-the-art drills had at last found bedrock deep under Gatún; at Colón, the docks were overhauled and vast warehouses constructed. The backlog on the all-important railway was cleared by the end of the year. Maltby's coastal division had dug an underwater channel out to sea for large ships to use the port, and the old French canal had been dredged as far as Gatún so that supplies could be brought inland. All this, which involved the removal during 1905 of well over a million cubic yards of underwater material, was achieved by the old, inherited machinery. There would not be an American dredge at work until mid-1907.

In the Cut, a pipeline had been laid carrying compressed air to power the drills, and by December 1905 there were nineteen shovels at work in the "big ditch." Not that "dirt" was "flying"—the floor of the French diggings had not been lowered by an inch. Instead, patience was still the watchword as the shovels carefully widened and prepared the site to Stevens's exact specifications. Terraces were built for further excavators to work on, as teams such as Jan van Hardeveld's laid miles of heavy track for the spoil trains to come.

All the while, the chief engineer took pains to remain visible and accessible. Mallet reported to his wife in September 1905 that "Stevens lives on the line." The chief engineer also put aside three hours every Sunday morning to hear complaints from the workforce and continued to tour the works, dropping in unannounced for lunch with the shovel operators or engineers. According to William Sands, "Stevens' sturdy, competent presence gradually put new heart" into the workforce.

But whatever public image he projected, Stevens had a number of grave concerns at the end of his first six months in charge, in particular with that selfsame workforce. Stevens had asked his recruiters in the United States to send south some five thousand technicians, mainly railroad men. They had managed to produce only a little more than three thousand, and clearly some barrels had been scraped. On one occasion a consignment of eighteen track foremen reported for work only for it to be discovered that only two had any sort of track experience at all. The rest were sent back on the next steamer. "I am not running a training school to teach boys engineering and construction," wrote Stevens angrily to Commission chairman Theodore Shonts. "What I want is men who can go to work when they get here." In Washington, Shonts had his own problems. For political reasons he was already trying to juggle the lucrative contracts for canal machinery around various states. Now he was being steadily lobbied by politicians on behalf of their constituents wanting jobs on the Panama gravy train.

This was immediately apparent to stenographer Mary Chatfield, a formidable looking spinster in her midforties, who arrived at Panama City from San Francisco on November 30, 1905. Chatfield would spend sixteen months on the Isthmus, during the course of which she wrote numerous letters to her ladies' literary club in her home city of New York. One of her first letters sets the tone for her reports from Panama: "I am not running things. If I were there would be some changes, for I never saw such a state of affairs."

Her most immediate complaint was about the quality of the "skilled" workforce. Starting her first job in the Hydrography Department, she soon discovered that it was almost impossible to find good recruits to man the gauging stations that measured the velocity and flow of the numerous streams in the canal's path. "So many men sent down here drink to excess," she reported back to her literary society. "I am informed that the Isthmian Canal Commission send numbers of such people down here at the request of senators, congressmen and heads of departments."

Her own boss, the chief clerk of the department, a Scotsman, comes in for particular criticism. "Like many other people here in positions of authority," she wrote, he was "lacking in training and experience for such a position." A young graduate engineer under the man ended up teaching him his job, "an everyday state of affairs on the Isthmus," wrote Chatfield. An American journalist with far less of an ax to grind backs this up, recounting the story of a well-connected clerk starting work on a salary of $2,500, more than twice that of his overall supervisor. Good workmen were arriving, Chatfield writes, but "finding they have not a fair chance against the favourites," they were leaving just as quickly.

⋘⋙

*H*appily for Stevens the beginning of 1906 saw the West Indian workers arriving far faster than they were departing. Much of this was due to Karner's renewed recruitment drive in Barbados, and the fact that the West Indians on the Isthmus could now report more regular wages and less police harassment. At the end of 1905, there had been about eighteen thousand on the payroll, compared to thirty-five hundred twelve months before. Of the fifteen thousand nonwhites, about half were Barbadians.

Such was the exodus of labor from Barbados that by early 1906 it was hardly possible to go ahead with the sugar crop in the St. James and St. Peter parishes because men "have returned [from Panama] with money which they are spending in sight of those who did not go," who promptly took off themselves. But if Panama now drew in Barbadians in unprecedented numbers, Stevens was less than happy with the results. Although he applauded the West Indians' "innate respect for authority," the improved food supply seemed to have had little impact on their productivity or ability to resist diseases. So he started looking elsewhere, seeing the problem, as always, as one of racial characteristics. His first preference was for Japanese or Chinese labor, but a delegation from Tokyo had toured the works in May 1905 and described conditions as "unsatisfactory." The Chinese were also unwilling to help, still stunned by the appalling treatment of "coolies" by the British in the Transvaal. Furthermore, Stevens was aware that the importation of thousands of Chinese would cause political problems at home in the United States, where indentured labor was frowned on by public opinion, and in Panama. One of the government's first new laws, introduced at the end of 1904, had been a measure to prevent Chinese immigration.

In Cuba the quality of the large influx of Spanish labor at the end of the war had impressed the Americans, and Stevens saw this as a possible answer to his problems. For him, they had the advantage, unlike the blacks, of "a capacity to develop into subforemen . . . they are white men, tractable, and capable of development and assimilation," he wrote to Shonts in December 1905. Certainly something had to be done. "I have about made up my mind," he went on, "that it is useless to think of building the Panama Canal with native West Indian labor . . . I do not believe that the average West Indian nigger is more than equivalent to one-third of an ordinary white northern laborer . . . I regard the situation as critical, as the success or failure of our plans rests wholly upon the labor proposition."

It was all getting the best of John Stevens. He was now working eighteen hours a day and suffering from insomnia, so frustrations about the lack of expertise in his organization, the high rate of sickness, or delays in progress became ever more overwhelming. "No one will ever know," he later wrote, "no one can realize, the call on mind and body which was made upon a few for weary months while all the necessary preliminary work was being planned and carried forward . . . and the only gleams of light and encouragement were the weekly arrivals of newspapers from the States, criticizing and complaining because the dirt was not flying."

And it was not just the lack of visible, photogenic progress that fueled newspaper attacks on the canal. Still under scrutiny by the partisan Democratic press was Roosevelt's precise part in the "revolution" of November 1903. Then, as men returned from Panama sacked or otherwise embittered by the canal leadership, stories starting circulating of out-of-control extravagance and corruption on the Isthmus. The oil supply business, it was alleged, had been given to the

Union Oil Company in controversial circumstances. Under the direction of Cromwell, the Panama Railroad had made an undoubtedly illegal bond issue, which afterward had to be recalled. Some higher-ups on the Isthmus were receiving inflated salaries, it was suggested.

But it was the secrets of "the lawyer Cromwell," still ever present in Panama's affairs, that most interested the canal's enemies. Ever since the signing of the Hay–Bunau-Varilla Treaty, some sections of the press had put forward the theory that the entire revolution had been a ploy by a Wall Street syndicate, a "Stock Gambler's Plan to Make Millions!" as a *New York World* headline put it. Roosevelt's partners in the "theft" of the canal, the *New York Times* suggested, were "a group of canal promoters and speculators and lobbyists who came into their money through the rebellion we encouraged, made safe, and effectuated." Soon after, the same paper reported that the president of a large French bank had said that roughly half the money paid to the New Company had stayed in the United States. Maurice Hutin, when interviewed, said that the payment had never reached French shareholders, "as the United States naively thought." Instead, it was suggested, a syndicate set up by Cromwell had secretly bought up shares in the New Company at rock-bottom prices, and then, having persuaded the U.S. government to pay $40 million for them, had pocketed a huge profit.

Alongside the investigation of this story, reports of extravagance on the Isthmus became more and more common in the U.S. press, endlessly conjuring up the ghost of the famously wasteful French effort. At the end of 1905, therefore, a special Senate inquiry was authorized to carry out a full "investigation of salaries, supplies, contracts, and the general conduct of the commission." The Senate Committee on Interoceanic Canals, the *Panama Star and Herald* reported on January 1, 1906, was going to "raise the canal lid."

Three days later, on January 4, came the publication of Poultney Bigelow's report from his Colón trip in November. Carried by the prestigious *New York Independent* magazine, and provocatively titled "Our Mismanagement in Panama," the article caused a sensation. As well as telling of his meetings with ill, disgruntled, and departing West Indian workers, Bigelow was scathing about the filthy state of Colón, faulty work on the sewers in Panama, and the shortcomings of the American workforce. "Our Panama patriots are kept busy," he wrote, "finding occupation" for "flabby young men" with "political protection . . . who amuse themselves playing the doctor or the engineer." In all, he found "jobbery flourishing" and the system in Panama showing "ominous signs of rottenness."

The response in Panama was mixed. One engineer exclaimed, "I do not think there is a place on the face of the globe more lied about than the Isthmus of Panama. But the American people don't want to believe anything good of it, or of those who see fit to undertake the battles down here. However, we are going ahead regardless." Others, like Mary Chatfield, found that Bigelow had echoed a lot of her own complaints. "I have heard all those things and many more since I have been on the Isthmus," she wrote home about his criticisms. It could have been even worse; "he could not find out much," she explained. "People were afraid to tell him."

The reaction in Washington, however, was swift and ruthless. Bigelow was hauled before the Senate committee, but not before his report had been viciously rubbished by Taft and several of his sources uncovered and discredited (one, it emerged, had been the veteran American journalist and businessman Tracy Robinson). Bigelow had only been on the Isthmus twenty-eight hours, Taft pointed out, he hadn't left Colón, and the West Indians he saw leaving in "disgust" were simply going home for the Christmas holidays. The committee followed this line with Bigelow, but in other ways they were less sympathetic to the canal leadership. Magoon and Stevens were summoned from Panama to be interrogated. This particularly irked the chief engineer, who despised politicians and suffered terrible seasickness. Shonts was hauled in as well. Why was Colonel Gorgas, the senators asked, receiving $10,000 a year, far in excess of the salary due to his rank? The careful, diplomatic answers of Magoon alone to the barrage of questions stretch to nearly three hundred pages of published minutes.

Although no longer the committee chairman, Alabama senator John Tyler Morgan, now in his eighty-first year, was the driving force behind the questioning. And his main target was not so much the alleged extravagance, but the role of his archenemy, the man who now referred to Panama as "my canal," William Nelson Cromwell. Determined to find out the truth of the lawyer's role in the Panama "revolution" and the rumored syndicate, Morgan summoned Cromwell before the committee. But Cromwell was saying nothing, refusing to answer questions that might affect the privacy of his ex-client, the New Company. Morgan, incensed, brought a resolution before Congress forcing Cromwell to testify. The measure passed, but Cromwell was out of the country in France at the time. Soon after, Morgan died, and without his leadership the Senate committee stuttered and then dropped the investigation. For now, the question of "Who Got the Money?" remained unanswered. But the story would not go away for long.

For its part, Bigelow's article would cast a long shadow over the next months on the Isthmus, dividing opinion while contributing to an air of uneasiness and crisis. In fact, while the piece contained justifiable criticism, its tone was undoubtedly slanted against the canal project. Although difficult, conditions were simply not as bad as he had made out. A British naval officer, Charles Townley, visited the Isthmus at the end of April 1906, and, considering the press coverage he had seen, was agreeably surprised by what had been achieved. "Many of the prominent American newspapers have sent representatives to Panama to inquire into the true state of affairs there," he reported to the British Foreign Office. "Some of these men have been imbued with an honest desire to tell the truth, but the majority would seem to have realized that criticism of weak spots is more likely to attract readers and increase the demand for their paper than an impartial setting forth of all that has been accomplished. This carping newspaper attitude is beginning to make an impression on public opinion."

There was one more serious problem identified by Townley, however. In January 1906 Stevens had complained to Morgan about how his efforts were being held back by the lack of a definite plan for the canal. The "principal elements of uncertainty" in the "project as a whole," complained of by Wallace over a year earlier, were still painfully unresolved. It was as if, Stevens explained, "I had been told to build a house without being informed whether it was a tollhouse or a capital." As Townley reported on May 3, 1906, "At the present moment the hesitation of Congress to finally decide upon the type of canal to be constructed is hampering the entire labour organization on the isthmus." Before Ferdinand de Lesseps had even been to Panama, his 1879 Congress had opted for a sea-level canal, with disastrous consequences. Two years into their canal building effort, it was now time for the Americans, in turn, to make their own "fatal decision."

CHAPTER TWENTY

THE DIGGING MACHINE

For a long while the momentum was with the proponents of an American sea-level canal. In June 1905 Roosevelt had appointed a board of consulting engineers, composed, as in the old French days, of international engineers of undisputed eminence. Of the thirteen members of the board, five were European. The eight Americans included General Davis, erstwhile governor of the Canal Zone (between attacks of malaria), along with old hands from the various U.S. canal bodies, and one engineer who had helped draft the New Company plans of 1898. The most significant of the three newcomers was Joseph Ripley, who was then working as chief engineer of the Sault Sainte Marie Canals, better known as the Soo Canals.

The board did not meet until September 1905, when they were entertained by Roosevelt at Oyster Bay. "I hope that ultimately it will prove possible to build a sea-level canal," the president told the assembled engineering grandees. "Such a canal would undoubtedly be the best in the end if feasible; and I feel," he added, echoing the late

Mark Hanna's arguments during the "Battle of the Routes," "that one of the chief advantages of the Panama route is that ultimately a sea-level canal will be a possibility." But at the same time the president demanded a canal "in the shortest possible time."

In the meantime, the engineering leadership on the canal could only speculate about what would be decided. There were plenty of proposals, however, to fill the official vacuum of ideas. According to Stevens, all sorts of plans were "showered" on him during 1905: "One genius proposed to wash the entire cut into the oceans by forcing water from a plant on Panama Bay; another to erect a big compressed air plant at Culebra to blow all the material through pipes out to sea [both technologies were seen, at the time, as the coming thing] . . . such schemes provided plenty of amusement to afford relaxation," Stevens wrote.

There were blasts, as it were, from the past as well. Soon after the Oyster Bay meeting, Roosevelt received a letter from Philippe Bunau-Varilla, who, like Cromwell, had clearly been unable to let go of his Panama baby. The great Frenchman announced to the president that he had "discovered an unknown way through this mysterious labyrinth" that was the finding of the best plan for the canal. It was a repetition of his much-cherished "excavating in the wet" theory, whereby the canal could be operative on a locks basis while being lowered to an open, sea-level channel, the old de Lesseps dream. The sending of the letter coincided with Bunau-Varilla's usual careful attention to publicity.

Getting nothing but polite brush-offs from the president, Bunau-Varilla focused his attention on one of the newcomers among the Board's experts, Isham Randolph, who had been chief engineer of the Chicago Sanitary and Ship Canal, completed in 1900. But Bunau-Varilla's plan came with estimates of cost and time whose optimism rated with the finest moments of the old de Lesseps propaganda sheet, the *Bulletin*. Bunau-Varilla continued to pester away in his own inimitable style, but on November 7 he received back from Randolph his latest missive with the following note attached: "Mr. Randolph . . .

advises M. P. Buneau Varilla [sic] that he is not seeking professional advice from him: and further that he deprecates the persistent generosity with which that advice is being urged. He returns herewith unread, the treatise which accompanied M. Varilla's note of the 6th inst."

Aside from distractions, the sea-level plan seems to have made the early running. Wallace, interviewed by the board, was a firm proponent. Taft, too, had pronounced himself in favor of a sea-level canal while on the Isthmus at the end of 1904. Stevens, also, he said, had taken on the job expecting it to mean digging all the way down. On October 4, the board of engineers arrived in Panama. It was unusually pleasant weather for the week they spent there, dry with blue skies.

Three months later, the results of the board's deliberations, an enormous report, was handed in to the Isthmian Canal Commission. The *Engineering Record* called it "the most important document in the engineering history of the Panama Canal to date." The experts had failed to agree unanimously, but had voted 8–5 in favor of the sea-level plan. In the majority group were all the Europeans, along with ex-governor Davis and two other Americans.

To comply with the instruction of the Spooner Act that the canal had to accommodate the largest ships then afloat or being planned would need locks of such size, they argued, as to be "beyond the limits of prudent design [and] safe and efficient administration." Even so, however big the locks, they were bound to become obsolete at some time in the future. A sea-level canal, on the other hand, would be "easily expandable" in the future, and thus would "endure for all time."

The plan put forward is close to that of the Old French Company of the early 1880s, with a tidal lock at Ancón and a large dam at Gamboa to regulate the flow of the Chagres, along with some nineteen miles of permanent diversion channels to restrict rivers that would otherwise flow into the canal prism. Even with the numerous levees and embankments envisaged, it was accepted that most of the volume of the Chagres would still have to use the canal to get to the sea: "The de Lesseps idea of a still water canal is thus replaced by a regulated river." To build this canal, it was estimated, would cost $250 million and take twelve to thirteen years.

Virtually every element of this plan was sharply criticized by the proponents of the minority report, submitted to the ICC at the same time. Because of the immense depth of excavation needed at the Continental Divide, even with the steep sides the sea-level plan envisaged, the waterway at the bottom of the great gorge would be only 150 feet wide at its surface. Ships would be unable to pass each other, but would have to moor, as at Suez.

Some eighteen streams or rivers, it was calculated, would pour their waters into this deep and narrow chasm, creating currents of some 2.6 miles an hour as well as eroding banks and depositing silt. Even without the crosscurrents, the "narrow gorge" would be "tortuous." For nineteen miles, a large ship would have to be continuously changing direction in channel with a width only from one quarter to one-fifth her own length. "Such a waterway," wrote one of the minority report authors, "is far from meeting the conception of free and unobstructed passage popularly associated with a sea-level canal." The danger of landslides—with hindsight the unconquerable obstacle to a sea-level plan—was alluded to, but not stressed. The nightmare of slides in the Cut was still largely to come for the Americans.

The minority report, largely the work of Joseph Ripley and distinguished U.S. engineer Alfred Noble (who had helped build the Weitzel Lock on the Soo Canals), was in favor of a lock canal. To satisfy the requirements of the Spooner Act, the locks would be 900 feet long and 95 feet wide, big enough to handle "the largest ships now existing or under construction"—the *Mauritania* and the ill-fated *Lusitania*, of the Cunard Line, both over 760 feet long with a beam of 88 feet. In comparison, Eiffel's locks had been under 600 feet long and about 60 feet wide. These new locks might be bigger than anything so far attempted, but they were not, Ripley and Noble argued, "beyond the limits of prudent design." The example of Ripley's Soo Canal, where a huge volume of traffic between Lake Huron and Lake Superior had been handled without mishap since the 1850s, gave them confidence that such locks could provide "safe and efficient administration."

The main difference between this lock-canal plan and everything that went before it was not just the scale of the locks, but the location of the "controlling feature" of the scheme, the great dam for the Chagres. This the minority reported shifted from Bohío to Gatún. It had been accepted that neither offered ideal situations for a dam, with their bedrock in places far below sea level. But Gatún had several important advantages, in spite of the fact that the dam there would need to be immense—a mile and a half long and 100 feet high, an unprecedented size. Because Gatún was downstream of Bohío, and rivers tend to deposit large and coarse material upstream and finer and denser material near the river mouth, the alluvial deposits that sat above the bedrock at Gatún would, it was hoped, be less permeable. But more important was the site of the dam. A far bigger expanse of water would be created than by blocking the river at Bohío—a new lake of some 164 square miles was envisaged stretching all the way through the Cut, drowning several villages and settlements as well as much of the existing Panama Railroad. It would be, if completed, bigger than any man-made lake before. And this additional size was the key: not only would the lake provide simple navigation for a large part of the transcontinental route and, because of its size, nullify problems of silting and currents; it would also tame forever the volatile Chagres. Unlike the previously mooted Lake Bohío, Lake Gatún would be wide enough so that the greatest floods would only raise its level a few inches, easily coped with by a spillway, whereby the Chagres would resume its route to the sea at San Lorenzo. At the same time, the proposed lake would provide, even in the dry season, enough water for the huge locks for twenty-six transits a day, or some

30 to 40 million tons of traffic annually. When and if this limit was reached, further control could be imposed on the water supply by the construction of a second dam upriver above Gamboa.

The ICC spent just under a month considering these two different proposals, then, on February 5, they opted to give their backing to the minority lock-canal plan. Stevens's influence seems to have been important. Although initially in favor of a sea-level canal, by October 1905 and the consulting board's trip to Panama, he had declared himself undecided. The following month, having carried out a "personal study of the conditions," he was urging the ICC not to back the "impractical futility" of a canal à niveau. According to Stevens, he also talked round President Roosevelt, during a trip to Washington in January 1906. So when the matter was handed over to Congress to decide, the pro-sea-level board majority report was accompanied by the ICC's decision for locks, as well as a letter from the president backing up this decision. Taft had also changed his mind since the year before. So there was a letter from him in the package as well, in which he upped the time and money estimate of the majority report considerably, as well as warning of "the difficulties and dangers of navigation" the sea-level plan threatened. "We may well concede that if we could have a sea-level canal with a prism from 300 to 400 feet wide," he wrote, "with the curves that must now exist reduced, it would be preferable to the plan of the minority. But the time and the cost of constructing such a canal are in effect prohibitory."

To the frustration of everyone, especially those on the Isthmus, the decision was tied up in committee for several months. Almost anyone ever connected with the canal was wheeled out to give their opinion. Then, on May 17 the committee chose, by the margin of just one vote, to reject the advice of the ICC, Roosevelt, and Taft, and recommed to the Senate that they adopt the sea-level plan.

Drastic action was called for. Stevens was summoned again from Panama, to endure once more the sea-crossing and the machinations of political Washington. He had seen the Chagres in flood that month, and was more convinced than ever that the river would wreck a sea-level canal within a year. He hammered away at the House Committee on Interstate and Foreign Commerce about the problem of the Chagres, and put together a compelling speech in favor of the lock canal to be made in the Senate. This was delivered on June 19, by Philander Knox, previously Roosevelt's attorney general and now a senator from Pittsburgh, where, happily for his constituents, the massive steel lock structures would most likely be built.

But it was a good speech, well delivered, and just enough to do the job. Two days later the Senate voted 36 to 31 to back Stevens's judgment and on June 27, the House followed suit. Thus only a handful of votes determined the United States' choice between a lock canal and a sea-level attempt that, in all likelihood, would have ended in failure.

So at last the decision was made, and the aimed-for canal had a definite shape for the first time. Starting at Limón Bay, a ship would take a short sea-level passage to Gatún, where it would find three tiers of double locks. These would raise the ship to the level of the new lake—85 feet above sea level. The vessel would cross the lake, which continued, like the spout of a funnel, through the Culebra Cut to Pedro Miguel. There, a much smaller dam would be encountered, containing a single tier of locks that would lower the boat to a small, intermediate lake at 55 feet above sea level. This would continue through to the gap between Ancón and Sosa Hills, where another small dam would hold two locks to lower the ship back to sea level and out into the Pacific. As the locks were to be in tandem, simultaneous two-way traffic would be possible. With some modification, this was the plan followed to the very end. Thus in place of de Lesseps's dream of an "Ocean Bosporus," the Panama Canal would be instead a "bridge of water" between the two oceans. Instead of requiring the moving of the mountain, the waterway would go over it. And with the drowning of much of the French diggings in the Chagres valley under the new lake, millions of cubic yards of excavation, for which so many engineers and workers had suffered and died, were at a cruel stroke rendered irrelevant.

As soon as the decision was announced, the critics swung into action. The majority report of the board of consulting engineers had judged that a dam at Gatún would be a "vast and doubtful experiment." "It is nothing short of monstrous to jauntily rest this national enterprise upon untried methods vastly beyond the range of experience and past success," they had argued. Subsequent criticism remained focused on the dam, a "simply preposterous piece of work," wrote one expert. In 1889 a large dam at Johnstown in Pennsylvania, similar in design to that mooted at Gatún, had collapsed; an entire city had been washed away and over two thousand lives lost. There were no proper foundations at the chosen site, argued a contributor to the *North American Review*: "To base any scheme on a work like the Gatún Dam, is to build a house on sand."

Next in the firing line were the plans for the massive locks, the safety of which one engineer, Lindon Bates, called "the greatest engineering conflict of the canal." The terrible danger was that a ship would ram the Gatún lock gates and thus cause the entire lake to pour out through the breach. "Every vessel in the waiting basin and every building and structure between Gatún and the sea in its path would be swept to utter annihilation," wrote Bates in late June 1906. "The damage to the canal and locks could not be repaired for years. To refill Lake Gatún would consume nearly a year of itself. The adoption of the lock flight arrangement, which puts so fearful a premium upon an accident, cannot be characterized as other than a most colossal and disastrous mistake."

Just before the time of Bates's writing, there had been a bad accident on the Manchester Ship Canal when a ship had failed to slow down and broken through a lock. As the *Manchester Guardian* reported on June 22: "In the Irlam lock the water is sixteen feet below the normal level; the muddy bottom is in many places exposed; and an abominable stench fills the air." Bates concluded that "accidents are therefore at the Isthmus certain and inevitable," particularly under tropical conditions where, he wrote, "the vitality of men is reduced, alertness and initiative are at their lowest."

In fact, on the Isthmus, Stevens and his engineers had shown considerable initiative. Gambling on the lock-canal version being adopted, they had laid plans to start right away. Twenty-four hours after the decision, work began on clearing the site at Gatún and laying rails to bring spoil from Culebra to start the process of building the biggest dam ever seen.

⧸⧸⧸⧸⧸ ⟶⟫⟫⟫⟩

If the metaphorical clouds cleared when the final plan for the canal was at last decided, on the Isthmus the wet season in mid-1906 was all too real. "Heavy rain day and night," remembered one West Indian. Every worker recalls his clothes permanently soaked. "Hard rains had set in by this time," wrote Rose van Hardeveld. "Everything smelled of mold and decay. Water fell from the sky in great drenching sheets. The house and everything in it was sticky and wet." Her husband, working with his friend Jantje in the Cut, seldom had a dry shirt or a pair of dry shoes. Every night, exhausted, he would come home with mud and water squishing in his shoes and his shirt and trousers wringing wet. Rose's iron cookstove and kerosene lamps were little help in getting the clothes dry.

"Never patient, Jan was now decidedly irritable," remembered Rose. "His thin face grew thinner, his prominent nose larger, it seemed to me. His cheeks were gaunt and hollow. He ate very little, and I felt sure he had malaria . . . All he thought of night and day was the Canal." Then, in mid-May 1906, Jantje "came bounding up the steps three at a time one evening, shouting that his wife and baby were coming on the boat tomorrow morning!" The next day, before they had even had a chance to unpack, Jantje, carrying his baby boy on his shoulder, brought the new arrivals to meet Rose, Jan, and the girls. It seems to have given Rose a great lift. "I looked upon her at once as a close friend—closer than I could ever hope to feel to any of the native women," she wrote of Jantje's "pretty young wife," Martina. The young couple, as they moved into Las Cascadas House

Number Seven, were full of plans for saving their money, and moving to the United States, "so that their boy might grow up in America." Above all, "they were very happy just to be together."

All the while, everyday life seemed to be slowly improving for the white workforce, or at least for those who remained healthy. Las Cascadas was expanding as new homes were being erected nearby. There was ice aplenty, and better food was reaching the new commissaries. In late June, Jantje made a trip to Panama City and came back with "something wonderful." In a wholesale importers he had found them unpacking the first consignment of Edison phonographs to arrive on the Isthmus. He bought two and a half dozen records for each. "We had not realized how starved we were for music and entertainment until we heard the first strains of 'Silver Threads Among the Gold' floating from the big tin horn," remembered Rose. They all sat entranced, playing the records over and over, and then Jantje—or "Teddy" as he was called by his wife (his middle name, fittingly, was Theodore)—took his son Jack in his arms and danced around to the music of "Hungarian Rhapsody." "Supper, rain, canal, everything was forgotten for the time being," Rose remembered fondly.

⫷⫸

*E*ven after the decision on the canal finally came through, Stevens still had the majority of his workforce assembling and repairing buildings—quarters, clubhouses, hotels, warehouses, schools, churches, or commissaries. In two years, 85 million feet of board was used on new buildings, and by June 1906 over a thousand—nearly half—of the old French quarters were in use.

For John Meehan, who had arrived back in 1904, a turning point had been reached when, in late 1905, a new hotel opened that had different sections for those wearing coats and those not. "The rule," he wrote, "marked the first definite break in the community of interest that had existed up to this time among construction men, engineers, artisans, and office men."

In other ways, too, the white community became more stratified as the facilities improved. A policy was adopted by the new head of the Quarters and Labor Department, Jackson Smith, whereby white workers were assigned homes exactly linked to their position in the canal hierarchy—one square foot of floor space for each dollar of monthly salary. This, according to Stevens, "proved a strong incentive to encourage individual ambition. A promotion in rank meant not only a better wage, but more commodious living accommodations, and a certain rise in the social scale. Distinctive social lines were drawn on the Isthmus," he went on, "as sharply as they are elsewhere."

Not everyone was happy. It was widely believed that Jackson "Square-foot" Smith, as he became known, tended still to give the best accommodations to his own friends. Mary Chatfield was living in one of the resurrected French dwellings. She complained that the large verandas let the rain in, and, sleeping up near the roof, she would be awakened by the storms, which "sounded as though some one was throwing boulders and trying to tear the boards off of the roof."

Her fiercest criticism was for the food served by the new ICC hotels. "The meat served is almost always beef, and such beef! It does not taste like anything," she wrote to her literary ladies in June. "Tho' the waters abound in fish, there is *never* any fish served . . . the vegetables are all canned and very poor quality. The soup always tasteless as hot water." She concludes that part of the problem must be widespread pilfering. Her letters do, however, give evidence of the increasing amount of organized activity available to the U.S. workforce. For the July 4 celebrations, she reports, there were tug-of-wars, obstacle races, horse and mule races, pole vaulting, and dancing competitions, with first prizes of $25. There were a couple of sour notes, however. The food served "was *worse than usual*, which was only just possible," and another incident upset her: "A few colored people tried to watch the games at Cristóbal and were chased off by mounted policemen. A very unpleasant sight."

Mary Chatfield was also less than impressed with the typical

American attitude to the Panamanians, whom many referred to dismissively as "Spiggoties," from the familiar cry of Panama City peddlers and pimps: "Speak de English?" While working in the Hydrography Department, Chatfield actually had a Panamanian boss, a Mr. Arango, the only local to occupy a senior position in the canal setup. "I was angry at first to find that I had been placed under a Panamanian engineer," she writes. "But presently discovered him to be a gentleman, and an educated man, which I hear cannot be said of many from the States."

In the many bars and gambling dens of the terminal cities there was constant tension between locals and Americans, particularly the seemingly ever-present U.S. military personnel. In early June 1906, an incident in Colón's red-light district led to the arrest by Panamanian police of two U.S. Marine Corps officers and a midshipman from a gunboat in the bay. They were subsequently "severely manhandled" by the Panamanians. Magoon blamed both sides. The U.S. citizenry encountered by the Panamanians were largely from the South, he explained in a letter to Taft on June 5, "and [made] no distinction between Panamanians and negroes." The Latin Americans, for their part, were "liable to these quick and furious exhibitions of uncontrollable rage."

Aside from cultural or racial friction, there were also political and economic issues that were giving the locals cause for complaint. Panamanians remained wary of American intentions, particularly toward the anarchic terminal cities, seen by Zone authorities as a threat to the increasingly orderly nature of life in the U.S. enclave. Local merchants, who had hoped for a return of the glory days of the de Lesseps era, were furious about the rapid expansion of ICC commissaries and restaurants.

The Americans, for their part, were concerned above all with political stability and the rule of law. The volatile history of the Isthmus had been a powerful argument against Panama being selected as the canal's location. The project's backers, such as Roosevelt and Cromwell, did not need telling how damaging headlines in U.S. newspapers about political violence in Panama would be to the canal effort.

This was all about to get much more difficult. In July there were to be two important elections in the new Republic—for the municipal councils and the National Assembly. Tension between the two opposing parties, the incumbent Conservatives and the opposition Liberals, had been growing for some months. In October 1905, Magoon, at the request of Amador, had put marines and Zone police on alert when a Liberal rally in Panama City had threatened to turn violent. The following month, when Taft was on the Isthmus, the Liberals had presented him with a "Memorial." In it they asked whether during the forthcoming elections U.S. forces would be used to "guarantee public order and constitutional succession in the Republic." If so, did this include supervising the polling stations and ensuring a fair election?

The role that the United States would play was of vital importance to the opposition. They knew that without American intervention in the polling process, government leaders, who controlled all the electoral machinery, would not allow themselves to lose a national vote, however small their real popular support. This was, of course, long established: the way real political change came to Panama was through intrigue or revolution, rarely the ballot box. So if the poll was going to go ahead without U.S. supervision, wondered the Liberals, and thus deliver an inevitable Conservative victory, how would the United States react if they took the traditional step and tried to gain power through a coup?

The response from Elihu Root, now U.S. secretary of state, communicated to Magoon at the beginning of December, was a careful exercise in tact. The United States earnestly wished for "fair, free and honest" elections, he said, but would not take direct control of the voting process. Root knew how that would look to other already fearful Latin American countries and he had his hands full dealing with problems in Cuba. The United States, said Root, would exercise its rights to maintain order in the terminal cities and the Zone, or "in that territory [in] which [disorder] can be prevented by the exercise of its treaty rights, and will not go beyond those treaty rights."

The Liberals pronounced themselves satisfied, but interpreting Root's response to mean that U.S. troops would not intervene in Panama's rural areas (in fact, treaty rights and the Constitution permitted intervention anywhere), they started preparing for an armed uprising in the countryside, their traditional stronghold.

Two days after the receipt of the Root reply, Amador reported to Magoon that armed bands were assembling in the interior, with red ribbons around their hats, the traditional symbol of revolution, warning that without U.S. intervention he would be forced to re-form the army, something neither man wanted. Magoon reported to Washington that "party feeling is very bitter, and serious disorder during the elections in June and July should constitute no cause for surprise." The Conservatives were accused by their domestic enemies of being traitors and sellouts. The official Liberal newspaper the *Diario de Panama* described the choice for the voters as between electing the Liberal Party or seeing Panama being annexed by the United States. In reply, a senior Conservative declared that he would sooner see the nation under U.S. control than have it fall into the hands of the "niggers."

On the urging of Magoon, at the end of April came the clarification of Root's reply: the United States would move to "suppress any insurrection in any part of the Republic." The uprising was dead in the water, and the continuance of the rule of Amador and the Conservatives was assured. As Mallet explained to his superiors in London, because it was "customary" for government candidates to win elections, the defeat of the opposition was a safe prediction. At the same time he passed on a report from the *Star and Herald* that "explicit directions have been given to the police to prevent by every means in their power the success of the Liberals, who, in a fair election, would overthrow the Amador government by one hundred to one."

Thus by refusing to supervise the elections and at the same time banning revolution from the Isthmus, the United States' actions were decisive in maintaining in power an unrepresentative, undemocratic government. Mallet put this down to American dislike for the Liberals' racially mixed constituency. Certainly, for now, the United States felt more at ease with the Conservative faction. Taft had reported to Roosevelt after his trip to the Isthmus that the Liberals were much less trustworthy and that if they came to power they would bring an injection of unwanted "Negro influence" into Panamanian politics.

Amador's party, as predicted, won both elections with ease, but not before requesting, and receiving, a cache of arms from the Americans, as well as the deployment of three hundred marines just outside Panama City. During the municipal voting on June 24 there was sporadic violence leading to four dead and over twenty injured. Widespread fraud was evident: thousands of Liberals arrived to vote only to find that their names had disappeared from the list. William Sands, the U.S. chargé d'affaires, reported, "The police [who owed their jobs to the ruling government] voted the first time in uniform and the second time in civilian clothing, returning again to the polls with their rifles 'to preserve order.'" There was a week until the National Assembly elections, during which Magoon hauled the party leaders before him and appealed for calm. With the Marine presence and U.S. gunboats in the harbors at both ends of the line, the election went off peacefully with the result never in doubt. Therefore, as in the defeat of the Huertas coup plot, Amador was in power thanks to American support, and the United States found itself by the end of 1906, as much through events as by design, in almost complete control of Panamanian affairs.

❖❖❖❖❖——❖❖❖❖❖

As the painstaking work to prepare the "canal-digging machine" continued, the leadership of the project sought to take control in other ways as well, to create the best, the most efficient environment for the enormous task undertaken. Stevens's argument with West Indian workers was not just that they were slow and incompetent but also that they were part of a "prevailing clannishness" that needed to be broken up. In fact, the black workers—usually lumped together as "Jamaicans"—were far from being the homogeneous body that Stevens feared, consisting instead of a great variety of nationalities and cultures. And even among the British West Indians, as opposed to those from French-, Dutch-, or Spanish-speaking areas, there was little fellow feeling among the nationals from the various islands; instead there was competitiveness and distrust. One of the complaints of the "Jamaican Carpenter" about the ICC barracks was the mixing they had to put up with: "There is no sense in putting so many different races together—Jamaicans and Bims [Barbadians] and Martiniques in the same room. It is not right."

But to the American leadership they were all just a collective black mass, and one, furthermore, that felt itself indispensable to the canal effort. According to Stevens, "some sort of hazy idea had gotten into their heads" that they "controlled the labor market." To put them in their place (as well as to find better-working men), Stevens decided to carry through his idea, mooted at the end of 1905, to bring in "laborers of other races and different characteristics." In February 1906, nearly three hundred Galicians and other Spaniards were shipped to Panama from Cuba, where they had been working on railway construction. Thus they brought the track-laying skills that were vital for Stevens's transport revolution on the Isthmus. The chief engineer monitored the new men carefully, deciding that "one of them will do and is doing, as much work as three of our West Indian negro laborers." So, although Karner was to keep his work going in Barbados as well as in other islands, in mid-1906 the ICC set up recruiting agencies in Madrid and Rome and started importing European laborers. Spaniards were the first preference, but Stevens had decided that he wanted at least "three separate nationalities of laborers . . . so that none of them will get the idea that they are the sole source of supply on earth."

Over the next two years, some 12,000 Europeans were brought in on ICC contracts: 8,200 from Spain, 2,000 from Italy (largely from impoverished Sicily and Sardinia), and 1,100 from Greece, where another agency was set up in 1907. Typically, the men were contracted for three-year tours. Unlike the West Indians, the Europeans were expected to pay their own passage. The fare—a whopping $45—was deducted from their pay and there was no guaranteed repatriation. However, they were offered twenty cents an hour, as opposed to the ten-cent rate of the Karner contract. The reasoning went that it was worth paying twice as much for workers who were three times more productive.

For some in Madrid it was an illustration of how far the nation's fortunes had fallen that Spanish men were to return as lowly workers to a country once the crossroads of their great empire. The indignity was almost too much to bear: "If America needed common laborers, let her seek [them] among her own people," wrote one national newspaper. "The American is too proud to work with his hands! He must work with his head, and Spain must be her hands! Spain refuses to be the hands of an American head!"

Nonetheless, there were plenty of takers for the chance of leaving Spain behind. The country had seen some of the worst anarchist violence in Europe, and with industry and agriculture depressed, there were widespread unemployment and hardship, made worse by a string of influenza epidemics. There had been large-scale recent emigration from Spain to Cuba and elsewhere, and now, the stories went, the best money to be made was in Panama. Antonio Sanchez was different from the typical emigrant in that at thirty-five he was older than most, and had once been reasonably well off. He still owned a fruit and olive farm at Valero de la Sierra, in the province of Salamanca, but prices had fallen too low to make the business viable. When disease and famine carried away his wife and two daughters, Sanchez decided to leave his surviving nine-year-old son behind with grandparents and take his chances in Panama, where, he had heard, "everything was gold and all things were as sweet as honey." "Everybody in his area was so scared of disease," Sanchez's stepson explained. "His farm was worthless; he just had to try his luck somewhere else. He had to leave." With about a dozen friends from Salamanca, Sanchez sailed from the port of Vigo; he would never return to Spain nor see his son again.

Sanchez's first impression of Panama was that he had exchanged one site of *"peste"* for another. "It was not a livable place," he explained to his stepson years later. But the Americans, determined to avoid the problems they had suffered with the West Indians, had pulled out all the stops for the new arrivals. Relatively comfortable barracks had been built of similar size to the West Indians' but housing only twenty-five people each, rather than seventy-two. Castilian Spanish were carefully kept separate from Galicians as, Sanchez explained, "they hated each other." Special kitchens were constructed for them. Unlike the West Indians, the Europeans got chairs and tables. Most important, every effort had been made to provide familiar food such as potatoes and spicy Spanish sausage. They were even given wine at lunch in the European manner.

For now, all this looked justified, as the Americans assessed their new workers. "Not only are they more than twice as efficient as the negroes, but they cope better with the climate," gushed the 1906 ICC annual report. "The Spaniard is certainly the more intelligent and better worker," wrote a visiting journalist. Furthermore, the influx seemed to have fulfilled its other purpose as well: "It did exactly what was expected in changing the self-confidence of the negroes," Stevens later wrote. "From an amusing but embarrassing attitude of self-complacency, they soon exhibited the aspect of men who were afraid of losing their jobs, and their value increased accordingly."

According to Antonio Sanchez there was mutual respect and affection between the Americans and the Europeans during the construction period. Relations with the blacks, however, were strained from the outset. "The Europeans hated them," Sanchez remembered. It was partly the language problem: "Every time one of them said something the other would take it as an insult, and vice versa.

There were a lot of fights. With fists, shovels . . ." Stevens's plan to divide and rule the workforce seems to have succeeded.

⫸⫷

*J*n May 1906, an American journalist, told of the decision to recruit Europeans based on the success of the first shipment from Cuba in early February, went to investigate these paragons of efficiency himself. Assigned to track work in the Cut, the Spaniards had been quartered nearby in unscreened barracks close to marshland. "Toward the end of the first fortnight, they began to fall ill," the journalist discovered. After four weeks, 165 of the 270 had been hospitalized, over 60 percent, "practically all with malaria."

During the headline-grabbing yellow fever epidemic of May to August 1905, 48 people had died of the disease. But during the same period twice as many had died of malaria, 49 from pneumonia, 57 from chronic diarrhea, and 46 from dysentery. The mortality rate for the year, not including accidents, was 24.3 per thousand. In 1906, this number would jump to 39.29, the highest level of the U.S. construction era. This is nothing like the 70-per-thousand rate suffered by the French during their annus horribilis of 1885, but it is still higher than anything under the New Company in the 1890s.

The dry start to the year gave no indication of what was to come. But with the onset of the rains in mid-May, and the transformation once again of the Isthmus into, as Mary Chatfield wrote to a friend, "driving rain and muddy, muddy, much muddy, mud," both malaria and pneumonia struck hard. In June, of the three hundred marines deployed near Panama City for the Panamanian election, more than half came down with malaria. By the end of the month, Ancón hospital was admitting seventy-five people a day with the disease. "This rainy season has been a heavy trial on the canal builders, the railroad and the sanitarians," read a dispatch from Panama to the *New York Daily Herald.* "There has been a riot of malaria, all departments being hampered by having so many men in the hospital." In July, the black workers suddenly started dying from pneumonia at a rate of eighty a month. By November, there had been nearly four hundred fatalities from the disease, along with two hundred from malaria.

But the number of deaths from malaria does not tell the whole story. Although debilitating, the disease was rarely fatal, at least on its first attack, but in 1906 the cases that came to the attention of the medical system numbered nearly twenty-two thousand. Joseph Le Prince estimated that an astonishing 80 percent of the overall workforce was hospitalized at some point during the one year for malaria alone. The fallout rate of the Spanish pioneers from Cuba was not so bad after all.

This sort of rate of attrition meant that life in the field, out on the mosquito-ridden works, was a desperate, bewildering struggle. "You turn up to work in the morning with a gang about 125 men and by Eleven clock you will find about 40 men all the others fall down with malaria," remembered West Indian Rufus Forde. "They spin all around like a top before they fall and that get you so frighten that at some times you don't come back after dinner." Benjamin Jordan, the Barbadian who had lied about his age to get selected for an ICC contract, contracted malaria within weeks of arriving on the Isthmus. "I can't describe them," he says of the mosquitoes. "I hear 'woo' and they are into you." Malaria, he says, "took me at night . . . in the morning when I woke I couldn't get out of bed. But I did manage it, I got out, and my neighbour advised me to go to hospital. When I was discharged was deaf as bat . . . Malaria and the mosquito brother were top."

A number of the West Indian accounts are full of praise for the hospital care they received once they had, almost inevitably, come down with one of the prevalent diseases. Jamaican James Williams, in his early teens, worked in a kitchen at San Pablo, on the banks of the Chagres River, "where mosquitoes were frequent, especially at nights. Consequently I began to get fever." The following day a doctor was visiting and someone told him that Williams was ill. "The doctor immediately advanced to me and felt my pulse. I could remember he said to me 'You are going to be sick, boy, go up to the hospital right a way.' He further asked me, 'Are you a God fearing man?' I replied, 'Yes,' " recalled Williams. "He said to me 'You are going to die.' "

Williams was put on a train to Ancón hospital, where, fearing malaria, he was given two-hourly doses of quinine and an ice bed bath. He had never been in the hospital before, and it was a "fretting" and alarming experience. The next day, parched with thirst, he drank a bowl of water left out near his bed. This turned out to be poison to kill flies and mosquitoes and brought on severe vomiting in young Williams. That night his blood was tested and he was shortly afterward moved to the typhoid fever ward, where he made a slow but steady recovery. He remembered the staff who cared for him with great affection: "I can truthfully say those American nurses—my own dear mother could not be more kind and tender to me." After a couple of weeks, Williams was eating again and being given "eggnog twice a day also real American Whiskey every day."

But other accounts tell, as in the bad old French days, of men released from the hospital before fully well or able to return to work—and thus qualify for further free hospital care. Other men were sacked when they started to look ill. Saint Lucian Charles Thomas worked at the iron foundry at La Boca: "I was fired after two days," he said. "I remember the foreman call to me & said to me you are fired, you are looking tired. I was not exactly tired but I was feeling quite sick & just trying to make a week so I could get a commissary book for $2.50 to get something to eat and drink." As the West Indians, unlike the white Americans, had no paid sick leave, some, unwilling or unable to forfeit their wages, would work on to the point of dropping. One account, redolent of the worst horror stories of the railroad or French era, explains how men suffering the dysentery which often hit those weakened by malaria would sometimes just disappear, never to make it to the hospital (or onto the official casualty figures). Said Barbadian Clifford Hunt: "Men in my gang, tell the Boss I am going out to ease my bowels and they die in the bush and nobody look for you."

Pneumonia may have been the biggest single killer in 1906, but malaria, it was judged, offered the greatest threat to the success and efficiency of the project. Pneumonia was almost unknown among the white workforce, and dead black workers were easily replaced, such was the glut of labor in the islands. Malaria, on the other hand, also affected the whites, and, because rarely fatal, usually resulted in expensive hospital treatment for the black worker. Virtually nothing would be done to counter pneumonia, while the campaign against malaria was on an undreamt-of scale, far surpassing even that against yellow fever.

◄◄◄◄— ►►►►

"The question of controlling malaria appeared at first sight to be utterly hopeless," wrote Joseph Le Prince. Part of the reason that malaria was a greater challenge than yellow fever was in the different nature of the two diseases. Those unlucky enough to contract yellow fever either survived and were free of the virus and immune forever or were dead. Either way, they were no longer a source for the infection. If someone caught malaria, on the other hand, they were far more likely to live, but the disease seldom went away for good. Usually the patient would remain both a recurrent sufferer and, for about three years, an ongoing source for the continued propagation of the bacterial parasite. Gorgas's very earliest tests in 1904 had shown that some 70 percent of Panamanians carried the infection in some form. So the approach of keeping the mosquito away from the disease, successfully followed in the yellow fever campaign, was a nonstarter.

The only point of attack had to be the *Anopheles* mosquito itself. To an extent, the species was the same everywhere, and as such, it was accepted, was going to be a much more formidable enemy than its yellow fever–carrying cousin, the fastidious, house-dwelling *Aëdes aegypti*. The *Anopheles* was, in contrast, omnipresent in the deepest bush as well as the backyard. For Gorgas eradicating the *Aëdes aegypti* was "making war on the family cat," while a campaign against the malaria-carrying *Anopheles* was "like fighting all the beasts of the jungle."

July 1904 had seen Joseph Le Prince, one day off the boat from New York, poking about in hoofprints below Ancón Hill looking for *Anopheles* larvae, and thereafter, although the yellow fever mosquito enemy had first priority, investigations continued into the "Isthmian *Anopheles*." The researchers started by determining the local species most responsible for malaria transmission. Thousands of mosquitoes were captured and analyzed, and their behavior studied. Tests included getting human volunteers to sit in a mosquito-filled net. As Le Prince explained, "Very patient negroes were necessary . . . Conditions soon became unbearable even to those persons who were accustomed to be bitten frequently."

By the end of the first year, it had been established that the insect most responsible for malaria on the Isthmus was the "white-footed" *Anopheles albimanus*. Unfortunately this was not only the most abundant, but also the species most determined to enter inhabited buildings. One of its tricks was to cling to dark clothing and thus gain entry to houses even if they were screened.

Thousands of eggs were collected, hatched, and observed at every stage. Adult specimens were dyed using an atomizer so that tests could be conducted on their flying distances and habits. When it was established that the mosquito could not fly far without alighting on some sort of vegetation, work started on clearing 200-yard-wide areas around where people lived and worked. Tests showed that *Anopheles* preferred to rest on a dark surface on the leeward side of buildings, so black bands 2 feet wide were painted on sheltered walls at a convenient height for mosquito catchers to collect them. When it was noticed that certain species of spiders and lizards started congregating there to feed, these were bred in great numbers and released to wage war on the enemy.

Analysis of the larval stage showed that, disappointingly, it was far hardier than that of *Aëdes aegypti*, able to survive in water only a fraction of an inch deep, or even in mud once the puddle had dried. It had no particular preference for clean or dirty water and would still be alive after up to two hours under a film of oil. Nevertheless, the larval stage was still the mosquito's most vulnerable time, so the challenge was to deal with the breeding grounds.

It was a massive, almost hopeless, task. During the wet season, when at Culebra, for example, it averaged twenty-four rainy days a month, there was simply water everywhere. But even during the short dry season, there were swamps, springs, or seepage outcrops near every settlement in the Zone. Fast-growing vegetation clogged streams, protecting the larva from its natural predators and providing still pools for egg laying. The ongoing engineering work made it difficult, too. Badly placed spoil dumps blocked natural drainage, and excavations constantly filled with water. Every time a railroad tie was moved, it left an indent in the ground that could collect water and therefore mosquito larvae.

Thus Gorgas was never going to defeat malaria in the way he had yellow fever. But he believed he could control it by reducing the *Anopheles* population of the Zone. Swamps were drained using hundreds of miles of ditches, or filled with spoil from the works. Elsewhere, further natural predators were encouraged or introduced, including a top-feeding minnow from Barbados. According to Le Prince, "larvae of dragon flies and water beetles were of great value." But above all, vast quantities of poison and oil were deployed across the Isthmus. A special plant was built at Ancón to manufacture a larvicide consisting of carbolic acid, resin, and caustic soda. Some two hundred barrels were applied monthly around the edges of pools and streams. Vegetation that clogged up running water was cleared by burning or with phenol or copper sulphate. To smother the "wrigglers," crude oil, mixed with kerosene to increase its spreading qualities, was sprayed everywhere. At its peak in early 1907, the campaign was getting through sixty-five thousand gallons of crude in a month. Unsurprisingly, visitors to the Isthmus started commenting on the pervasive smell of petroleum.

-《《《-》》》-

*R*esults would come, but for the men in the field, particularly those near the jungle, work at the end of 1906 meant swarms of mosquitoes. Some took to rubbing exposed parts of their bodies with a mixture of kerosene and coconut oil, but they still got bitten and they still got malaria. The only treatment was quinine, either in a pill—"the size of a quarter and twice as thick"—or as a sickeningly bitter liquid. Mallet reckoned that quinine was "the cause of many break downs in the constitution, it ruins the stomach and digestive organs." John Prescod, who arrived from Barbados in June 1906, described another nasty side effect: "Malaria fever have me so bad I has to drink plenty of quine tonic tell I heard singing in my ears murder murder going to quits drinking quine was getting me deaf."

"The prevailing illness is malaria," wrote Mary Chatfield in a letter home dated June 30, 1906. "Many and many are the corpses I see carried past the office . . . the majority of the victims of malaria are the negro laborers." "I went to the Cristóbal dispensary this morning to get some tonic," she wrote a month later. "It was a pitiful sight to see the sick coloured laborers. Many of them were so weak they could not sit up while their medicine was being prepared, but lay on the benches and the floor."

Albert Peters, who reached the Isthmus in August that year, "eager for some adventure and experience," caught malaria within a week. He survived, but there was a daily reminder of those who did not. "Every evening around 4:30," he wrote, "one could see No. 5 engine with a box car and the rough brown coffins stacked one upon the other bound for Mt. Hope [cemetery] which was called Monkey Hill in those days. The death rate was high . . . If you had a friend that you always see and missed him for a week or two, don't wonder, he's either in the hospital or at Monkey Hill resting in peace."

"That's the reason we all used to go to Church more regular than today," said Barbadian Amos Parks, "because in those days, you see today and tomorrow you are a dead man. You had to pray everyday for God to carry you safe, and bring you back."

Rose van Hardeveld had from the outset found "the horrible and unfamiliar noise at night" in Panama more nerve-racking than any other "trials and tribulations." As well as the strange, unearthly sounds made by alligators, bats, night birds, or insects, "the very worst of all was the wailing for the dead that came from the labor camp below us." "When one of their number died," she continued, "the friends and kindred of the deceased would gather in the room where the corpse lay. All night long they would drink rum and wail and sing Old English Gospel hymns in the flattest, most unmusical way imaginable . . . These tones would sway and swing in the air like the dance of witches." It would leave her sleepless and "utterly unnerved and filled with a vague, mounting dread."

By July 1906, as malaria and pneumonia hit hard, "The wailing and singing at the labor camp went on so often that there was hardly a night when the camp was silent . . . Slowly but surely my natural fortitude was giving way, and I was becoming a nervous, fearful woman. I believe it was the consciousness of what would happen to the children that kept me from going to pieces."

But then their youngest daughter, Sister, fell seriously ill with a combination of malaria and dysentery. She became, Rose wrote, "a limp, feverish little bundle, crying night and day." She was told to give her quinine, but the young girl could not keep it down. "All the time I was becoming lower in spirits and less able to cope," Rose remembered. "The thought of putting my baby in a strange hospital was the last straw. That night I gave way to old-fashioned screaming hysterics, outside beside the roaring cataract. Poor little Janey clung to me, her frightened eyes searching mine for the cause of such carryings on! After that when I sat through the long nights, comforting my whimpering child in my arms, the howling and moaning from the labor camp no longer grated so shatteringly on my nerves. I knew what it was to seek relief in wailing. Though for me, such yielding to hysterics was a matter for private shame, never to be regarded as an accepted social custom, I could concede to the black people whatever gratification they might find that way."

Sister recovered and Rose found that she could now sleep through the nightly din from the labor camp. Martina Milliery's improved English meant that she was a real support and help for her friend. Rose's spirits were also lifted when she started helping out her husband by writing out Sunday passes for his team of Spanish workers. "With this little job to do for my husband, for the Canal Commission, for President Teddy Roosevelt, and for my country, I was in my glory," she wrote. "I sometime had difficulty writing those strange Spanish names, but still I liked doing it for these black-eyed and very deferential men."

⧽⧽⧽⧽

*M*ost of the new Spanish arrivals, like van Hardeveld and Jantje Milliery's gang, had been put to work on track construction and repair. The basic work on the Panama Railroad main line had been slow going. It was not entirely double-tracked until well into 1907, but a maze of sidings, branch, and service lines had been constructed—some 350 miles by June 1906. Most of this track, however, was in the Cut. Here, readying completion by late that year, in spite of all the prevailing sickness, was Stevens's great digging machine, perhaps his era's most important contribution to the American canal.

The lock-canal plan adopted that summer would still require, it was originally (under)estimated, the digging out and removal of more than 50 million cubic yards of rock and soil. For this to be achieved as quickly and cheaply as possible would require, first, the greatest possible number of steam shovels in operation in the space available. Therefore the excavation was planned to proceed along a series of horizontal benches, or terraces across the valley in the making, each wide enough to carry two parallel rail tracks. Thus, in places, up to seven shovels could work on the same hillside almost stacked on top of each other up the terraced slope. Next, it was crucial that the shovels be working at maximum efficiency. Under normal conditions, tests had shown, it took about a minute and a half (seven bucket loads) for a shovel to fill a single spoil car; about forty-five minutes for an entire train. In the case of the smaller French trains and cars, it was much less. Thus, Stevens calculated, if it were never to be idle, each shovel required the service of a virtual conveyor belt of three to five entire spoil trains so that there would be at least one in attendance at all times. To run this sort of traffic in the narrow confines of the Cut required an enormous and highly intricate track system the likes of which probably no one else in the United States had the expertise to design and build.

But Stevens went further. To put it simply, by starting the work at the two ends of the nine-mile Cut and working inward toward its highest point, the site could, in the main, be organized so that there was a small but significant upward gradient on the terraces. This meant that empty spoil trains would be climbing up to their shovels, but then, when fully loaded, had a downhill journey to the dump sites. The scheme had the added advantage that water in the ditch, a constant annoyance for the French, naturally flowed away to both ends where it was easily disposed of with giant pumps. If Stevens's track system was fantastically skillful and intricate, like the assembly line in one of the new mechanized U.S. factories, the use of the gradient—whereby nature was made a helper rather than an enemy—was engineering at its simplest and most brilliant.

A surprising number of the "moving" parts of this system were still from the French era. At the end of 1906, over half the locomotives in the Cut were old Belgian machines, able, in dry weather, to pull about thirteen small 9-cubic-yard cars. But as fast as the new American models arrived, they replaced the old plant. The U.S. locomotives could haul four or five times the volume of dirt. In the same way, the new American spoil cars were also on a different scale, of a different age, immensely strong and able to hold at least three times more weight than the old French models. On one occasion a single rock weighing some thirty-four tons was loaded onto a single one of these new cars without mishap.

There was another important innovation: instead of individual cars self-tipping when wet soil or clay stuck and had to be removed by shovel, the American cars were one-sided only and linked together with panels, making a single long surface, like a giant conveyor belt. This not only meant a greater area was available, but also brought into play at the dump sites an ingenious invention. At the end of each of the new trains was a wagon holding what looked like a giant, one-sided snowplow, linked to the locomotive at the other end by a thick chain. When the spoil arrived at the dumping site—whether it be a marsh fill, a dam, or a causeway—the open side of the cars faced where the soil was required, and the plow, its blade at an angle of about forty-five degrees, was pulled from one end of the "belt" to the other, scraping the mud and rocks over the side. The empty spoil car departed, followed along the dumping site track by another specially adapted locomotive with armlike blades at ground level. These flattened the soil, making room for the next load. When a new and firm terrace had been thus created, the rails were simply moved across to the edge and the process repeated. The contrast with the French period, when much of the spoil had to be unloaded by hand, is sharp. The saving in man-hours was immense.

The most labor-intensive aspect of the process was now moving track, either at the dump sites or in the Cut, where teams would have to update the intricate system as the site constantly changed shape and dimensions. Then, at the end of 1906, the general manager of the Panama Railroad, W. G. Bierd, came up with an ingenious invention, a swinging boom mounted on a flatcar that lifted extant track and moved it nearby without the need for disassembly. It was a slow process, but not nearly as slow as doing it by hand. Like the other innovations, it was just the sort of miracle machine that de Lesseps had hoped in vain would come to the rescue of his own canal effort.

As well as heavier, stronger, and cleverer machinery, the railroad-era American canal builders had more useful experience than their French forebears. The railway boom in the United States had provided an invaluable training ground for hundreds of American engineers, whose expertise was far in excess of anything available to the de Lesseps effort. It was not just Stevens and Bierd, but a host of switchmen, signalmen, locomotive drivers and mechanics, electrical engineers, and railroad foremen. If transportation, the railway, was the key to building the canal, as Stevens had decided, then he had a depth of talent to call on.

The Americans also had the luxury of time. Stevens may have had a tightfisted Congress and, in parts, suspicious domestic press to contend with, but that was nothing compared to the pressure on a private company watching the bourse every day and with its life in the hands of volatile "confidence" and the "folly and gullibility of Capital." It helped that Stevens was not easily thrown by advice or instructions from above. But, crucially, largely freed of direct money-raising concerns, he had the freedom to do what was right for the engineering of the canal rather than for its public relations. So instead of having to feed the *Bulletin* monthly excavation figures, he was able to concentrate on the painstaking, unglamorous preparatory work, without which the canal project would not have succeeded.

The long delay between the stopping of "making the dirt fly" in August 1905 and the resumption of excavation in earnest at the beginning of 1907 turned out to be time very well spent. In spite of the terrible rates of sickness among the workforce, the digging machine was now ready, and excavation records were about to be shattered.

-◀◀◀◀-▶▶▶▶-

The massively increased traffic on the railroad, serving not just the engineering part of the project but the houses, shops, and restaurants of the employees as well, did have its downside. There were virtually no roads on the Isthmus, and often the only way to get somewhere was to walk along the tracks. As the line got busier, it became more dangerous, and railroad accidents started becoming an almost daily fact of life. Often, amid the shouts, blasts, and din of the works, and partially deafened by the side effects of quinine, men simply did not hear the danger in time. In mid-August, after she had spent "a very pleasant day in Gorgona," the train carrying Mary Chatfield back to Panama City "ran over a colored man, cutting off one leg far above his knee, and I think, killing him—I hope so—he was so mutilated. A fearful sight," she wrote home. "The school teacher at Cristóbal and a nurse from Ancón were in the car with me. The nurse went right out to see what she could do, but I sat still and shuddered."

Although West Indians were most at risk, especially soon after they arrived, due to their lack of familiarity with locomotives and track, the danger affected everyone, particularly in the Cut, where a bewildering network of tracks, in constant use, now covered almost every flat surface. On September 17, Jantje "Teddy" Milliery had lunch at home as usual, before returning to his work site just below their House Number Seven. He stepped over the first two tracks across his route, but then, just as he reached a third track, he turned to wave to his wife and baby son watching him from the doorway of their house. At that moment he was hit by ICC Locomotive No. 215, an empty spoil train that was reversing without the customary look-out in place on the end car. According to his official file, his "pelvis and both lower extremities [were] completely crushed." "I saw the accident and reached Jantje before he died," Jan would tell Rose. "I tried to tell him we would look after his wife and baby. I hope he understood me. He had such an awful time dying . . ."

During the weeks that followed, Rose spent her days with Martina, "helping her in any way I could to bear up under her grief and start planning her life anew." But her nights she spent "pacing the floors of our little house atop the hill, wringing my hands and trying desperately, futilely, to unknot my nerves." Martina was now no longer entitled to live in House Number Seven, and had to earn a living. For a couple of weeks she tried setting up a laundry, but then decided to return to Holland. "I went with her to the Dutch Consul in Panama," wrote Rose, "to arrange for passport and passage. After a last sad pilgrimage to the damp grave of her husband, she went back across the ocean, a mournful figure in black."*

With Martina no longer relying on her, Rose began to break down again. She talked with Jan about quitting Panama. He had been badly shaken, too, but responded by "hurling his energies with renewed determination into the job at hand." Rose, however, found herself, she wrote, "drifting closer and closer to the yawning chasm of panic into which I had fallen once before, during the height of Sister's bout with the fever. And finally, much to my own disgust, I was put to bed with another spell of hysteria. The children haunted the bedside like frightened little shadows. I realized that I must pull myself together."

Then there was a much-needed and very welcome boost: "news came to us of the expected arrival, soon, of a visitor who—Jan triumphantly told us—had the welfare of all of us at heart: Theodore Roosevelt." It appeared that the man for whom "anything was possible" was coming to see his canal.

---

*Martina Milliery, née Korver, remarried and had another child in about 1912. This son emigrated to South Africa in 1930 but the rest of the family moved to Dutch-controlled Indonesia. During the Second World War they were interned by the Japanese. Jantje's son Jack died in the camp in 1945, shortly after his stepfather. Martina survived, but was blind from malnutrition. She returned to Holland and died in 1958, impoverished, in a home for the blind.

SEGREGATION

Roosevelt's visit to the Isthmus can only really be compared with the two much-celebrated visits of "the Presiding Genius of the Nineteenth Century," Ferdinand de Lesseps. The authorities in Panama had heard about the impending presidential descent back in July, and from that moment on thousands of workers had beavered away preparing the Isthmus for Roosevelt's November inspection. According to Mallet, Panama had never before been so thoroughly scrubbed, swept, and cleaned. A wing of the new hotel, the Tivoli, was rapidly completed to house the honored guest, and a new railway station built nearby. An elaborate schedule was prepared, replete with ceremonies, speeches, and dinners.

Roosevelt sailed on November 9 on board the 16,000-ton *Louisiana*, the largest battleship of the now rapidly growing U.S. fleet, with two cruisers in attendance. It was an unprecedented moment. Never before had a serving U.S. president left the country. Of course, there were some on the Isthmus who were cynical about the "momentous visit." Mary Chatfield had written home in September: "There is much talk about the anticipated visit of the president. All agree that if he wants to find out how things are he will have to come in disguise."

To be fair to Roosevelt, from the moment of his arrival he went to great pains to throw the canal leadership on the Isthmus off balance, to dig beneath the prepared façade. Frank Maltby wrote that Roosevelt "seemed obsessed with the idea that someone was trying to hide something from him." For his landing on November 15, schoolchildren had been lined up to sing "The Star-Spangled Banner" and a cannon procured for an official salute. But the president arrived onshore an hour early, much to the consternation of the official greeting party, which included the president of Panama, who were still at breakfast in the Washington Hotel.

On the first of his three days in Panama, Roosevelt excused himself after lunch at the new Tivoli Hotel, saying he was retiring to his room. "Instead," writes Maltby, "he bolted out the back door, rushed up the hill to Ancón Hospital and into the wards, where he began talking to the patients as to their treatment and care." Thereafter, Roosevelt continually evaded his official schedule to drop in on messrooms and kitchens, to interview passing workers, or to ferret around in ICC barracks and lodgings. Canal officials were thrown into confusion. Mary Chatfield reports that "when the president was at Cristóbal they were in a panic at the Cristóbal Hotel, hurrying off the filthy table clothes and replacing them with clean ones, fearful he might come bounding in."

Roosevelt, in contrast to de Lesseps, deliberately came to Panama at the height of the rainy season. He wanted to see conditions at their worst. And it rained. On the second day of his visit, three inches fell in two hours, a new record even for Panama. Roosevelt took it all in his stride, rushing about or posing in a downpour sitting at the controls of one of the huge Bucyrus steam shovels, all the time making what a *Washington Post* headline called "A Strenuous Exhibition on the

Isthmus." "He was intensely energetic," remembered Frank Maltby. "He seemed to be able to carry on a conversation with me and dictate a cablegram to his secretary at the same time. He reveled in the publicity and commotion his visit created. He would make a speech at the slightest opportunity and without any preliminaries." Everywhere he went, addressing the white workers as "the pick of American manhood," he urged them to "play their part like men among men."

After two days, Stevens was exhausted. "I have blisters on both my feet and am worn out," he told Maltby. "Shonts is knocked out completely." On the last day, Maltby showed the president the site of the controversial Gatún dam. To get a better overall view it was suggested they climb a nearby hill. "We, together with three or four Secret Service men, charged up the hill as if we were taking a fort by storm," Maltby reports.

On the evening of his departure, a mass reception for President Roosevelt was held in the great building that covered the largest wharf of the Commission at Cristóbal. Virtually the entire American canal force was present, crowding the immense structure, which was decorated with flags and lanterns. Roosevelt then made an impromptu speech, which captures the martial heroism of his vision of the great enterprise: "Whoever you are, if you are doing your duty, the balance of the country is placed under obligation to you, just as it is to a soldier in a great war," he proclaimed. "As I have looked at you and seen you work, seen what you have done and are doing, I have felt just exactly as I would feel to see the big men of our country carrying on a great war."

The visit went down well with the press at home, even among those papers that were most critical of the canal, and provided a significant morale boost on the Isthmus. Rose van Hardeveld remembers the effect it had on her. "We saw him once, on the end of a train," she wrote. Jan had got hold of small flags for the children, and told them when the president would be passing their house, "so we were standing on the steps. Mr. Roosevelt flashed us one of his well-known toothy smiles and waved his hat at the children as though he wanted to come up the hill and say 'Hello!' I caught some of Jan's confidence in the man. Maybe this ditch will get dug after all, I thought. And I was more certain than ever that we ourselves would not leave until it was finished." Two months later a visiting English journalist noted the "energy" and "optimistic spirit" of the Americans working on the canal. "Every man," he wrote, "seems animated with the idea that he is doing a necessary part of the canal, and a feeling of pride prevails everywhere."

Roosevelt reported back to Congress on December 17. There was impressive progress to outline. In spite of the rainy season, and the thousands of men still employed putting up buildings, the month before his visit had seen a new record for excavation—325,000 cubic yards. The long period of preparation was at last coming to an end, and the actual digging was under way. At Gatún over a hundred new borings had been made on the dam site and excavation had started on the lock basins. At Cristóbal he had seen the new bakery in action, churning out 24,000 loaves a day, as well as the nearly completed coal depot and cold storage plant. The workforce had topped twenty thousand, and the supply from the West Indies and Spain seemed secure.

But the bulk of his message to Congress concerned what he must have judged to be the two interlinked problems that posed the greatest threat to the success of the canal: the high turnover of skilled men (still running at nearly 100 percent a year) and negative publicity at home. A new reward for long service—the Roosevelt medal—was announced. And the canal effort was described in unmistakably patriotic terms—"something which will redound immeasurably to the credit of America." The sanitation effort of Gorgas was praised to the rooftops. Among the Americans, including dependents, there had not been a single death from disease in three months, a very impressive record, Roosevelt pointed out, even by mainland United States standards. On numerous occasions direct reference was made to Poultney Bigelow and his report rubbished, which gives an indication of the great and lasting effect it had had. It was almost as though Roosevelt went to Panama specifically to erase the stain that his law school classmate had put on the enterprise. It was simply unpatriotic to criticize the canal effort, the president exclaimed. For detractors, he said, he felt "the heartiest contempt and indignation; because, in a spirit of wanton dishonesty and malice, they are trying to interfere with, and hamper the execution of, the greatest work of the kind ever attempted, and are seeking to bring to naught the efforts of their countrymen to put to the credit of America one of the giant feats of the ages."

However, Roosevelt himself had seen that all was not rosy on the Isthmus. On his return to Washington he wrote to Shonts: "The least satisfactory feature of the entire work to my mind was the arrangement for feeding the Negroes. Those cooking sheds with their muddy floors and with the unclean pot which each man had in which he cooked everything, are certainly not what they should be." And while the health of the white workers was indeed impressive, "the very large sick rates among the negroes, compared with the whites," was alarming. In fact, as Roosevelt's own figures acknowledge, the black workers were three times as likely to die of disease. In the ten months of 1906 before the presidential visit, thirty-four white workers had died, compared with nearly seven hundred West Indians. Roosevelt suggested that "a resolute effort should be made to teach the negro some of the principles of personal hygiene."

Gorgas had concluded, in his health report of July 1906, that the black workers were dying at three times the rate of the whites because, contrary to the earlier belief, their race could not stand the climate as well as their American employers. "We do not agree with the doctor," countered the *Colón Independent* angrily. "The higher death rate is, in our opinion, due to circumstances. The white employers are better housed, better paid, and therefore live better; they do the bossing while the blacks do the actual labor, such as work in mud, and water and rain. Change conditions with the two races and see if there would not be triple the amount of deaths."

Mary Chatfield, soon to leave the Isthmus having, she felt, "done one citizen's duty towards the building of the Panama Canal," gives a vivid description of what conditions were like for the black workers. Riding on a train near Mount Hope, she spotted some laborers' quarters near the railroad:

> Wretched little houses rest on stilts, and now during the rainy season the water is constantly on the level with the floors . . . When I left the office at 5 o'clock the negro laborers were returning to their quarters and were getting their suppers on little charcoal braziers outdoors. It was a sad sight to me . . . How could they get their suppers with rain pouring in torrents for an hour? They are not allowed to cook in their quarters for fear of fire and no covered place is provided for them in which to cook, so these poor men exist under difficulties. Consider the brilliant criticisms some of the authors of magazine articles make on "The lazy, worthless, Jamaican laborer." They sleep all night on a strip of canvas but little wider than their bodies, they must get up in the morning and cook their breakfasts out of doors in the tropical rain or shine, as it happens. They must be at work at 7 o'clock A.M., they get their noon meals under the same weather conditions as other meals. They receive the splendid wage of 10 cents, U.S. currency, an hour. They are obliged to pay at the government commissary as high prices for food as are charged at the grocery stores in the City of New York, whose proprietors have high rents to pay and are doing business for profit.

The West Indians, often unfamiliar with modern machinery, and given the most dangerous jobs, were also suffering from accidents at twice the rate of the white employees. At Ancón hospital, detailed autopsies were carried out on West Indians, which included the measurement of brain weight, skull thickness, and skull shape. The doctors' conclusion was that the large number of accidents befalling the black workers indicated "a striking lack of appreciation for a dangerous environment [in] the negro's mental processes."

If accidents and disease were deemed to be the West Indians' own fault, or as a result of their inherent weaknesses, this reflects deeply held ideas about race. These, in turn, would shape every aspect of life in the Canal Zone, and nowhere more so than in the division of the workforce into the Gold and Silver Rolls, described by one canal historian as a "notorious" example of "racial and ethnic discrimination by the U.S. Government." Harry Franck, a travel writer who worked in the Zone as a policeman for three months in 1912, remembers his surprise at seeing notices everywhere stipulating whether a shop, railway car, toilet, or drinking fountain was for Gold or Silver Roll employees. But he quickly worked it out. "The ICC has very dexterously dodged the necessity of lining the Zone with the offensive signs 'Black' and 'White,'" he wrote. "Hence the line has been drawn between 'Gold' and 'Silver' employees. The first division, paid in gold coin, is made up, with a few exceptions, of white American citizens. To the second belong any of the darker shade, and all common laborers of whatever color, these receiving their wages in Panamanian silver. 'Tis a deep and sharp-drawn line." For Franck, there was little doubt as to the model being followed. "Panama is below the Mason and Dixon Line," he concluded.

It has often been noted that U.S. imperialist expansion went hand in hand with rising racism. Influential thinkers such as Alfred Mahan and politicians such as Senator Albert Beveridge of Indiana had used a social Darwinist doctrine of Anglo-Saxon superiority and the "civilizing mission" to justify U.S. imperialism in the Philippines, Hawaii, and Cuba. It was not long before people started applying this theory to race issues closer to home. "If the stronger and cleverer race is free to impose its will upon 'new-caught sullen people' on the other side of the globe," asked the *Atlantic Monthly*, "why not in South Carolina and Mississippi?"

Indeed, the closing years of the nineteenth century saw the abandonment of the Southern blacks by Northern liberals, and as the "white man's burden" was shouldered overseas, the Southern states began a process of disenfranchisement and officially sanctioned discrimination against their black populations. In 1896 Louisiana had contained 130,000 black voters. Four years later, there were only 13,000. And what became known as Jim Crow laws spread across the South, officially segregating whites and blacks, with the best facilities always reserved for the former. What had previously been unspoken and unenforced was, by the time of the beginning of the U.S. canal effort, rigid and backed up by the law.

This system—with the euphemisms "Gold" for Anglo-Saxon whites and "Silver" for everyone else—was imported into the Canal Zone in Panama by the U.S. authorities and would survive in various forms for nearly a hundred years. But it was not imposed, as is often believed, en bloc, but was rather a gradual and complex process that parallels the other ways in which the Commission sought to impose itself on the lives of the canal builders of all backgrounds. It started with the decision made at the outset of the project to pay some workers in U.S. gold currency and others with local silver money. Attached to the Gold Roll from the beginning were privileges such as paid sick leave and holidays and better accommodation (basically the generous deal needed to lure workers from the United States). Who got what was decided by an amalgam of precedents—the PRR had always paid its U.S. workers in gold and the rest in silver, while the French companies had paid almost everyone in local currency but had divided its workers from all backgrounds into skilled and unskilled grades. The early Gold-Silver system merged these two approaches (a U.S. government report in 1908 would describe the distinction in terms of skills, but noted that the Gold Roll was "nearly all Americans"). Either way, white American citizens in the Zone, all in theory skilled workers, were almost always on the Gold Roll, and as the vast majority of the earliest unskilled workers were West Indians, the terms "Gold" and "Silver" quickly took on racial connotations.

Initially, however, it was not that simple—a relatively large number of West Indians, approaching a thousand, were put on the Gold Roll as skilled workers. These included foremen, office clerks, and teachers. This was considered a good way to co-opt potential leaders of the "Jamaican" community, and also to incentivize workers to train in useful skills and thus gain promotion to the higher-status Gold Roll.

Then, with the arrival of Stevens and the building of Commission hotels, restaurants, additional hospital facilities, and shops, it was discovered that by limiting access to parts of these establishments to Gold Roll employees, it was possible to keep undesirables away from the elite white sector of the workforce. Supposedly, it all began with a pay car. When two separate windows were used, one marked "Silver" the other "Gold," it was found to provide the "solution to troubles growing out of the intermingling of the races." Thereafter this practice was widely adopted, and no commissary or post office was built without separate sections for Gold and Silver. In everything, there was a premium service for the Gold employees.

But with the distinction now being used to prevent "intermingling of the races" on the Zone, the blacks on the Gold Roll presented a problem. In September 1905 Stevens closed the door to the Gold Roll for West Indians by ending both direct recruitment to the Gold Roll and promotion from the Silver Roll. At the end of the following year he started removing blacks from the Gold Roll, even if they were skilled and valuable employees. There was the occasional protest. The manager of the commissary at Cristóbal wrote to Stevens, "It would, I think, be very impolitic to separate all of the Commissary employees by color putting all the colored men on the silver roll. They would naturally feel it to be in a measure a humiliation. We have a number of colored men in charge of Departments . . . We also have two or three colored clerks in our Shipping office, who are very valuable men and draw larger salaries than some of our white clerks." Nevertheless by mid-1907 only a tiny handful of blacks, mainly postmasters and teachers, remained on the Gold Roll, and they would be gone by the following year.

The arrival of the Spanish and other southern European workers from mid-1906 onward might have had an unsettling effect on this rapidly solidifying racial system. But although southern Europeans were thought higher up the evolutionary pecking order than the blacks, they were certainly beneath the Anglo-Saxons and were in coloring, it was suggested, somewhere in between white and black. Thus they formed an intermediate layer—paid in Silver, but with better food, accommodation, and general treatment along with some Gold Roll privileges.

The education system in the Zone provides a microcosm of the development of this system of inequality based on race. Some of the earliest Canal Zone schools had a mixed intake of West Indians, Panamanians, and a few whites. As more families came out from the United States and the West Indies to live, the classrooms were segregated, and then the white and black children were separated into entirely different schools. Light-skinned Panamanian children from good families as well as the children of white European laborers enrolled in the white schools, the latter only under sufferance.

The white schools, housed in new buildings and well staffed and equipped, performed at a level at least equal to that back at home in the States. The nonwhite schools, however, were less than second-class. In 1909 there were about seventeen children per teacher in the white schools; in the others, it was 115 pupils per teacher, an astonishing disparity. Furthermore, the black schools were usually housed in dilapidated buildings, staffed by less well trained teachers and had to make do with textbooks discarded by the white schools. There was no question of pretending to provide separate but equal facilities.

The West Indian children were taught American history, discipline, orations, manners, the three Rs, and subjects such as carpentry and gardening that would equip them for unskilled work on the Zone. In 1911 a secondary school was opened for white children, but for the black students there were only advanced classes in agriculture, sewing, and domestic service.

This official sanction of racism nourished and legitimized racist behavior on a day-to-day basis. Harry Franck commented that a "new amalgamated" national "type" was being created in the Zone: "Any northerner can say 'nigger' as glibly as a Carolinian, and growl if any of them steps on his shadow," he wrote. So prevalent were the attitudes associated with "South of the Mason-Dixon line" that newcomers assumed that most of the Americans were Southerners, although in fact Northerners were in the majority. Even the nursing staff, who mostly cared very well for their black patients, were not immune to prejudice. Among three nurses arriving in November 1905 was Miss Emma M. Jeffries, a black American. On the steamer from the States, Miss Jeffries, according to the *Colón Independent*, "was made to feel the prejudice against her color, as one of the white nurses refused to occupy the same state room with her." It got worse when she was taken to Ancón hospital. "Miss Jeffries was informed at the nurses' reception room that she had made a great mistake in coming here, as all of the other nurses were white and had decided to go on strike if forced to work with a Negro. They even refused to sit with her at the same table for meals." Jeffries returned to New York in disgust.

Others also found the way color dominated life in the Zone too odious to cope with. "My father read of Panama and thought it a wonderful place to come to because he saw progress in Panama," an Antiguan lady told a researcher in the 1970s. But he did not work for long in the Zone. "He just could not take it—the life was so different. We were not accustomed to be told so much about your colour or to have to think about it often, black and white. He couldn't stand it so he left the Canal Zone and came to Panama [City]."

For black laborers out on the works, "some of the foremen were very polite, while some were very rough and impolite," as one West Indian recalled. Edward White, from Jamaica, remembered being very lonely when he first reached Panama, but found himself made to feel part of a family by his American foreman and timekeeper.

"The lonely feeling started to leave me, as these men treated me like their own. Mr Arthur, Mr Chambers, and I were so knitted together, I felt as if I was their own son."

This tone tends to be the exception in the West Indian accounts, however. Most are at best mixed about their treatment. Jeremiah Waisome was born in Nicaragua, but had lived in Panama since he was a baby. When he was twelve or thirteen, proud of his ability to read and write, he applied for work on the canal: "Unknown to my mother one morning instead of going to school, I went to Balboa to look myself a job. I approach a boss one morning for a water boy job. 'Good Morning, boss.' I said. 'Good morning, boy,' he retorted. At this time he was chewing a big wad of tobacco. I ask him if he needs a water boy, he said yes. He ask me 'What is your name?' I told him. Then I noticed that my name did not spell correctly, so I said, 'Excuse me, boss, my name do not spell that way.' He gave me a cow look, and spit and big splash, and look back at me and said: 'You little nigger! You need a job?' 'Yes, sir.' 'You never try to dictate to a white man.' "

An American journalist sympathetic to the U.S. canal authorities reported in 1906 that he had "often seen the threat of the slave-driver in the foreman's eye—the menace of brute force." Occasionally, this was more than a threat. "Among the white employees on the 'gold roll' some times an employee would use his hands or foot on one of the 'silver employees,' " admitted a steam shovel engineer. On March 23, 1906, the *Colón Independent* ran a story about how a man at Bas Matachín Machine Shop "by the name of Bryan was thoroughly clubbed and kicked by Master Mechanic Cummings because he refused to lift up a bucket of metal which was beyond his strength." When the accusation was taken to court, it was the victim Bryan in the dock, with his attacker Cummings demanding that the West Indian be punished for insolence.

The very worst foremen were dismissed, and treatment improved as the Americans learned that shouting and hitting were not the best ways to get results from their gangs. However, actual physical aggression against the blacks continued. After the death of Jantje Milliery,

Rose and Jan van Hardeveld had made a new best friend, Charles Swinehart, the mining engineer given a job through his father's connections with the local Republican Party at Steamboat Springs, Colorado. According to Rose, Swinehart was very much "the he-man type" and one evening at dinner a "troublesome" West Indian discharged from his gang "elected to place himself under the veranda and shout abuses at the house and Americans in general. He cursed and swore, while everyone at the table tried to act as though nothing were happening. Suddenly Charley, his lips set and his face white, politely excused himself. He left the table, went into the bedroom, and then we heard him go down the steps. In a moment there was silence below. We heard the young man coming back up the steps. He entered the bedroom, came out, and reseated himself at the table. The conversation and the meal continued. A few days later Charley was summoned to appear before the judge at Empire to answer the charge of knocking a British subject over the head with the butt of a revolver. He pleaded guilty, and was fined twenty-five dollars. 'Was it worth the money?' asked the judge with a twinkle in his eye. 'Yes, indeed, sir,' answered the aggressor gravely."

A journalist visiting the Isthmus in 1908 was advised that "it cost twenty-five dollars to lick a Jamaican negro and if I did it be sure and get my money's worth."

⫷⫷⫷ ⫸⫸⫸

𝒯he standard response of the black worker to bullying or abuse, according to virtually every American account of the construction period, was to "straighten himself up and say to the foreman 'I wish you to understand, sir, that I am a British subject, and if we can not arrange this matter amicably we will talk to our Consul about it.' " In fact, Mallet had his work cut out caring for those denied wages or hospital care and utterly desperate. There was no way he could deal with complaints from over twenty thousand British citizens on the Isthmus, as he frequently pointed out to the unresponsive Foreign

Office. Nevertheless, pride in being British seems to have sustained the self-respect of the West Indian workers in often very difficult circumstances. Guyanese novelist Eric Walrond, who moved to Panama as a fourteen-year-old in 1911, would write in 1935, by that stage a committed Garveyite, that the West Indians had "developed an excessive regard for the English." But in his 1926 short story "Panama Gold," the protagonist, returned from the Isthmus to Barbados, triumphantly explains how he came to be given compensation for a lost leg: " 'Pay me,' I says, 'or I'll stick de British bulldog on all yo' Omericans!' . . . Man, I wuz ready to stick Nelson heself 'pon dem . . . I let dem understand quick enough dat I wuz a Englishman and not a bleddy American nigger!"

"As British subjects," William Karner wrote of the Barbadians he recruited, "they think they are close to royalty and quite superior to white laborers from the United States." In fact, the West Indians *did* consider themselves superior to Americans. After all the British Empire was still the most powerful in the world, as they would point out, and they were as much a part of it as anyone. The Americans thought this was hilarious.

In other ways, too, the West Indians resisted the Commission's attempts to dehumanize and control them. In early 1907 there were nearly 12,500 workers in the ICC's austere, heavily regimented military-style barracks. Two years later there were less than 3,500. The others preferred to pay the exorbitant rents of the terminal cities or simply put up a hut of flattened tin cans and old dynamite boxes in the bush. Either way, the move reclaimed independence and dignity. In the same way the attendance at the ICC-run kitchens collapsed, with 80 percent making their own arrangements by the end of 1909.

In the workplace there was little point in complaining. "You couldn't talk back," remembered Constantine Parkinson. "It would get you fired if you talked back." Young Jules LeCurrieux, who had done a variety of jobs since starting work on dynamiting Gold Hill, protested on behalf of his gang when they found work unloading cement impossible because of the choking dust. He was promptly fired.

So the workers simply voted with their feet, walking away from the worst jobs or the worst bosses. On other occasions, as in the French days, they would move about the line looking for the best pay or to be with their friends, taking on a new name each time so that they could be reemployed. In both cases it was bad news for the efficiency of the canal effort: the dispersal of the workforce in "private" accommodations made the control of malaria and other diseases much more difficult, and the moving about of the workers from job to job caused frequent delays to the construction program.

The Spanish workers were always treated better than the West Indians, but by the beginning of 1907 they too were beginning to cause difficulties for the authorities. For one thing, their impressive initial energy and zeal had not lasted. If they did not succumb to disease, they soon adjusted their work rate to a more realistic tropical pace. By the middle of 1907 a divisional engineer at Culebra was even requesting that his Spanish workers be replaced by West Indians. The Europeans, he argued, were "little better than the West Indian negro," and as they were paid twice as much they were a waste of money. Even Stevens was forced to admit that while the introduction of the Europeans might have improved the work rate of the blacks, "the efficiency of the Spaniards did not hold up to the standard first developed."

For another thing, they were breaking their contracts and leaving in large numbers, mainly to move on to better-paid railway or mining work in South America. The Chilean consul was among those actively recruiting among the ICC's Spaniards, to the fury of the American authorities. Consul Mallet estimated that nearly half of those recruited during 1906 were gone by the beginning of the following year. The main impetus was money—although the Spaniards accepted that they were well paid by the Commission, the cost of living in Panama was such that they would struggle to earn the steamer fare home, let alone the riches they had anticipated. Antonio Sanchez tells of how his group "were deeply disappointed when they realized they would not be able to save enough money for the return trip to the land of their birth." And if any of them "became a victim of misfortune," he says, they were in real trouble.

In late January 1907, the thousand or more Spaniards working in the Cut went on strike demanding an increase in pay from $1.60 to $2.50 a day. The West Indian workers were not supportive, however, and had to be protected by the police. After a tense standoff, fighting erupted that led to several deaths and serious injuries among Spaniards and Zone police. The strike's ringleaders were rounded up and the protest quelled. Stevens later ascribed the violence of the repression to the need to give a "severe lesson" to prevent future demands endangering the project. But clashes between Spaniards and police continued for the rest of the year.

Around this time letters and articles started appearing in Madrid newspapers reporting that all was not well on the Isthmus for the expatriate workers. A letter from three workers, printed in *El Socialista* at the end of December 1906, complains about the high expenses in Panama, the retention of a proportion of their wages to repay their outward fare, and poor food and accommodations. Furthermore, the letter said, "People are falling ill the whole time . . . Many are leaving." The letter ended by warning others not to be deceived by the "siren songs." A Spanish journalist sent out to Panama noted, "The labourers' lives are not highly valued, so there are frequent accidents."

Toward the end of 1906 worrying news also began to reach Italy about the fate of the thousand or so workers recruited to work in Panama. It was said they had to labor eight hours a day in a swamp with water up to their knees, under the sun in torrid heat, exposed to torrential rain, and suffering from dreadful illnesses. A Naples paper claimed that most of the workers had died, and there were thousands of corpses on the streets. In both countries, the governments began to come under pressure to prevent further migration to the Isthmus.

To Stevens this was simply petulance. "My own private opinion," he wrote to Shonts in mid-January 1907, "is that no European nation is favourable to the building of the Panama Canal: that they do not want it built; will do anything they can possibly short of open hostility in the shape of force to prevent the consummation of the project, and will, if the movement of laborers from their countries assumes large proportions, take steps directly or indirectly, to prevent such movements." Stevens, however, was about to become yesterday's man.

◄◄◄◄-►►►►

The chief engineer was in Washington in December 1906 and those who saw him were shocked at how weary and sour he had become. It appears he had fallen out with Gorgas, whose starring role in Roosevelt's congressional message would have irked Stevens. The following month ICC chairman Theodore Shonts resigned to take up a lucrative post in New York, about which the president could have no complaint. Shonts had told Roosevelt that he would depart the project once the preparatory phase was completed. This resignation should have pleased Stevens. Relations between the two men, never good, had deteriorated of late, and Shonts's departure also cleared the way for Stevens to take absolute control over the project, on the Isthmus at least, as he had requested for so long.

In other ways Stevens had no cause for gloom. The heavy rains experienced by Roosevelt had continued, leading to flooding of the works in December, but in January, with the return of dry weather and the deployment of no less than sixty-three Bucyrus shovels, over half a million cubic yards had been excavated. This monthly figure would grow steadily thereafter, proving that Stevens's machine was working well.

But at the end of January, Stevens sat down and wrote an extraordinary letter to Roosevelt. Six pages long, it revealed the depths of his exhaustion and bitterness. Although he appreciated the support the president had given him, Stevens wrote, he had never sought the Panama job and did not like it. The "honour" of being the canal's builder meant nothing to him. He had been endlessly attacked by "enemies in the rear." Even the level of his salary had been questioned, when, in fact, he could have returned to the States and secured any of a number of far more lucrative and less stressful jobs, some of which, he wrote, "I would prefer to hold, if you pardon my candor, than the Presidency of the United States."

Roosevelt received the letter on February 12. He did not "pardon the candor." Only two months before, he had told the canal workforce that they were like an army in the field. Now their general, to whom Roosevelt had given almost unqualified backing, was looking to desert his troops in a most unmartial way. The letter was sent on to Taft with a note from the president attached: "Stevens must get out at once." Then he telegraphed Stevens to tell him that his resignation had been accepted, effective April 1.

Stevens never spoke or wrote about his real reasons for quitting, leaving the field open for a miasma of speculation. He had fallen out with the president, it was alleged; he had found that the Gatún dam plan was unworkable; he had discovered something about the role of Cromwell in the sale of the New Company so explosive that it would "blow up the Republican Party."

Many felt that he had not actually meant to resign, but was either letting off steam or flexing his muscles. Mallet reported to London that Stevens's resignation was never formally tendered and that "an immoderate amount of adulation over the success of Mr. Stevens' organization and management led him to imagine his services were indispensable to the successful prosecution of the works."

Stevens, like Shonts, had secured on his hiring the promise that he would be allowed to leave the project once it was up and running. His career before and after Panama shows a succession of departures to take on new challenges, and perhaps Stevens felt that his job was done on the Isthmus. By his own reckoning he handed on a "well-planned and well-built machine." Whoever came after him would merely have to "turn the crank," he said. But perhaps he also realized that the nature of the task had fundamentally changed with the firm adoption of the lock-canal plan. From being an unprecedented but essentially low-tech canal, it had become an equally huge, but also technically complex project. There is little doubt that Stevens was the best man to design and build the transportation system for the excavation of the canal, but he had little experience of hydraulics, lock design, or dam construction. Perhaps he understood that it was time for a man with different skills to step up to the plate.

But probably the greatest factor leading to Stevens's departure was mental and physical exhaustion. Stevens once said to Maltby, "I know you pretty well now and without raising the question of your competence, if you were chief engineer you wouldn't last thirty minutes." Working twelve to fourteen hours a day, suffering from insomnia, endlessly dragged to Washington to be hauled before "idiotic" congressmen, he had had enough.

On the Isthmus the news came as a severe blow—"astonishing" wrote the *Star and Herald* on February 28. Over the following weeks the paper traces the surprise, sadness, and then anger of the canal workforce. "Unless this step has been forced upon Mr. Stevens, a supposition which is scarcely likely," the paper wrote on March 2, "his action in retiring from the canal work looks suspiciously like an abandonment of a trust, and unless it be his desire to lay himself open to the same scathing rebuke which was heaped on Mr. Wallace his obvious course is to at once withdraw his resignation . . . we think that in his place a strong sense of loyalty, we might even say of devotion to an ideal, should have outweighed mere personal considerations." No one really knew what these "personal considerations" were. When asked, Stevens merely growled back, "Don't talk, dig."

A petition was organized, begging him to stay, and promising to work even harder for him in the future, but to no avail. After numerous farewell functions, the chief engineer sailed from the Isthmus for the last time at noon on Sunday, April 1. There was a huge crowd on the wharf to see him off. Other vessels in the harbor, reported the *Star and Herald*, "whistled their salutes, the crowd waved hats and handkerchiefs, and many shed tears while the I.C.C. band played Auld Lang Syne. Mr. Stevens stood at the rail, and as long as he could be recognized his face was pale and sad."

Roosevelt had rated Stevens highly—he was his sort of "strenuous man"—and he was grieved as well as angered by his departure. He also knew full well that the canal would never be built if it kept losing its chief engineers. So he now decided to place the work "in the charge of men who will stay on the job until I get tired of having them there, or till I say they may abandon it . . . I shall turn it over to the army."

"THE ARMY OF PANAMA"

To an extent, then, the project had come full circle. After all, the military needs of the United States had been of primary importance in starting the American canal. It was as a conduit for a sea power that the canal's supporters had successfully sold the idea to the U.S. Congress and public. But the all-new Isthmian Canal Commission, ordered to take over on April 1, 1907, was not entirely military. Its new chairman was Lieutenant Colonel (later Major General) George Washington Goethals, one of the army's finest engineers, with particular expertise in lock construction. There were two further Engineer Corps officers, a Navy man, and Colonel Gorgas was given a seat on the Commission for the first time. But there were also two civilians—an ex-senator from Kentucky and Jackson "Square-foot" Smith, like Gorgas promoted to the Commission. Furthermore, the military men were detached from their usual chains of command, reporting to Goethals, who himself dealt directly with Taft. All the Commission members were required to live on the Isthmus, where they would work as heads of departments.

There was no question, however, of the seven commissioners having equal say, as envisaged by the Spooner Act. Each man was summoned before Roosevelt and told in no uncertain terms that there would be only one boss. "Colonel Goethals here is to be chairman," said the president. "He is to have complete authority. If at any time you do not agree with his policies, do not bother to tell me about it—your disagreement with him will constitute your resignation." As well as chairman, Goethals was appointed chief engineer, head of the PRR, and would wield total control over the government of the Canal Zone. The new arrangement made Goethals, in the words of his biographer, "most absolute despot in the world . . . [who] could command the removal of a mountain from the landscape, or of a man from his dominions, or of a salt-cellar from that man's table." It was the "one-man proposition" demanded by Stevens, and there would be only one end in view. As Goethals himself explained: "It was asserted that the Department of Government, generally, regarded the construction of the canal as of secondary importance and seemed to consider that the main purpose and object of the work on the Isthmus was to set up a model of American government in the heart of Central America as an object lesson to the South and Central American republics." Governor Magoon had left the Isthmus the previous September to help out with the crisis in Cuba and was now told that he would not be returning to Panama. Henceforth, as Goethals wrote, "everything should be subordinated to the construction of the canal, even the government."

Goethals himself told a New York friend that his taking the job was "a case of just plain straight duty. I am ordered down—there was no alternative." He landed on the Isthmus in mid-March, for a two-week handover period with John Stevens. It was an awkward time for the new man. Stevens's popularity was everywhere apparent, along with deep unease among the civilian engineers about the nature of the new army regime and the inevitable changes in personnel that the new leadership would bring. On March 18 there was a reception in Goethals's honor at Corozal. Stevens was not there, but every time his name was mentioned in a speech a loud cheer rang out. When it was Goethals's turn to speak, he tried to reassure the men. There would be no military uniforms or saluting on the Isthmus, he said. "I expect to be chief of the division of engineers, while the heads of the various departments are going to be the colonels, the foremen are going to be the captains, and the men who do the labour are going to be the privates . . . I am no longer a commander in the United States Army. I now consider that I am commanding the Army of Panama, and the enemy we are going to combat is the Culebra Cut and the locks and dams at both ends of the canal, and any man here on the work who does his duty will never have any cause to complain of militarism."

Goethals had been on the Isthmus before. In November 1905, early in the Stevens regime, he had accompanied Taft to Panama as part of a group of army experts looking at the fortification requirements for the canal. At the time he had commented on the chaos and hysteria, but now, starting to look around, he was agreeably surprised. "The magnitude of the work grows and grows on me; it seems to get bigger all the time," he wrote to his son on March 17. "But Mr. Stevens has perfected such an organization so far as the RR [railroad] part of the proposition is concerned, that there is nothing left for us to do but to just have the organization continue in the good work it has done and is doing." The Stevens system was operating well. In March over 800,000 cubic yards had been excavated, and the following month would see this rise again to nearly 900,000, with five hundred trainloads of spoil being dumped every day. Eighty percent of the necessary machinery was in place, and, although there were still nearly four thousand men employed on building work, 70 percent of the required Gold Roll accommodations were completed. About a fifth of the workforce of nearly thirty thousand was off sick at any one time, but infection rates for malaria were falling as Gorgas's two thousand sanitarians continued and extended their campaign against the *Anopheles* mosquito, meticulously draining hundreds of square miles of swampland.

Goethals's main concern was the more technical parts of the project, the locks and dams, areas outside Stevens's expertise. "The hydraulic part of the propositions is not so good and is a way behind," he wrote to his son on March 22. Goethals quickly judged that some of the department heads did not have the necessary experience for the new tasks ahead. Maltby, for instance, although "an excellent man at dredging," "had no work on foundations and locks and is therefore of no account." Reorganization was needed, "and yet not to demoralize the other branches of the work we have to be careful in making changes." Such was the new man's confidence in Stevens's system for the Cut that he judged that the canal's completion date now depended not on *la grande tranchée* as everybody had always assumed, but on the creation of Gatún Dam and Lake, and the necessary prior relocation of large parts of the railway. That said, excavation in the Cut was still in its infancy—it had been widened by over a hundred feet but hardly lowered at all. The terrible setbacks that would accompany deeper excavation were still, for now, in the future and unanticipated.

Goethals took official charge on April 1, 1907. He immediately threw himself into the job, spending the mornings on office work and the afternoons inspecting the line, propelled along the railroad in a gasoline-driven railway car, known as the "brain wagon" or the "Yellow Peril." He would frequently dismount to talk to a foreman or manager. He was, a contemporary writes, "a tall, long-legged man with a rounded, bronzed face and snow-white hair. His moustache was also white, but stained with nicotine, for he smoked many cigarettes . . . He wore civilian clothes with the usual awkwardness of a man who has spent most of his lifetime clothed in the uniform of his country." Every day the role of "Czar of Panama," which included leadership of civil government, courts, schools, post offices, the police, and the battalion of U.S. marines in addition to the canal work, seemed to grow in size. "The strenuous existence of the past seems like mere child's play to the 5 past days," he wrote to his son on April 4.

There was no mass purging of the Railroad-era men, but changes were inevitable. Soon after Goethals's arrival, Frank Maltby left Panama, although he would return as a private contractor later. The excellent head of the railway, W. G. Bierd, the inventor of the track-shifter, resigned as well, supposedly because of ill health, but, Goethals noticed, he cropped up soon after working for Stevens in the latter's new job as head of the New Haven Railroad. Then, at the beginning of May, the steam-shovel men decided to test out their new boss, requesting a steep pay increase with the threat of a strike if their demands were not met. As one of the new commissioners, Major William Sibert commented, "the President, in his talks, praised the men for their patriotism and enlarged upon their hardships to such an extent that . . . after the visit the steam-shovel men asked for a rise in wages."

Goethals, still finding his feet and assessing the extent of his power on the Isthmus, acted cautiously, referring the matter to Taft, who was paying a visit to the Isthmus. Taft heard the men's demands, and then consulted with Roosevelt in Washington. "Things are unsettled here," wrote Goethals in a private letter on May 7. In Washington, it was decided that as the steam-shovel men, on $210 a month, were already the best paid of the mechanics, their hoped-for $300 a month could not be granted. Instead Taft offered a 5 percent pay increase. But the steam-shovel men remained determined. The increase was rejected and the men came out. The next day all but thirteen of the sixty-eight shovels were idle. It was the most serious strike on the canal so far.

But Goethals did not panic, even as the stoppage continued, reducing excavation to a quarter of its previous level. Handling it slowly, he gradually recruited strikebreakers until he had replaced the original workers. When the strikers gave in and asked for their jobs back, they were told that they would have to start again at the most junior level. By July, all the shovels were back in action, and excavation was once again at full tilt, with just over a million cubic yards extracted, a new record. It was an unmistakable victory for Goethals, and for the rest of the construction period there would be no stoppage on anything like the same scale. And the "Czar of Panama" had not even had to use the most potent weapon at his disposal. Under the original terms of Roosevelt's Executive Order setting up the first Commission, the chairman had the right to expel from the Zone anybody, who, in his opinion, "was not necessary to the work of building the canal, or was objectionable for any reason." With his power enhanced by his defeat of the steam-shovel men, Goethals dealt ruthlessly with a small stoppage in November by boilermakers at two large machine shops. Replacement workers were quickly in place and the strikers found themselves deported on steamers back to the United States. Thereafter, his response to any strike threat was simple: be back at work tomorrow morning or be expelled instantly from the country.

The European Silver Roll workers were dealt with even more firmly. They were continuing to leave the Isthmus for better work opportunities elsewhere, thus depriving the ICC of the repayment of their steamer fare. In response, Goethals banned the solicitation of labor within the Zone, and placed guards at the ports to prevent contracted workers from leaving. "I have no complaint of any kind against the Isthmian Canal Commission," stated Spanish worker F. Olario when hauled off a Chile-bound steamer in May 1907. "I was always well treated, liked the wages I used to get, but could not understand the orders of the foreman, and besides, I was most of the time sick, out of the four months that I have been a laborer on the Isthmus."

Early in his tenure, Goethals had set up a routine that he would hear complaints from Gold Roll employees every Sunday morning, just as Stevens had done. Silver Roll employees had the same chance to air their grievances, but only with Joseph Bucklin Bishop, the unctuous secretary to the Commission, who, among other things, acted as Roosevelt's eyes and ears on the Isthmus. Bishop recruited a Spanish-speaking Italian, Joseph Garibaldi, grandson of the famous independence leader, to deal with the southern Europeans. In a 1907 labor report Garibaldi explained the genesis of the problems the Spanish labor seemed to be presenting. "Supposed ill treatment in most cases was simply due to a misunderstanding between the men and the employees in charge, because of different languages," he wrote. Hardly any of the Americans spoke Spanish. "In some cases the laborer," Garibaldi continued, "failing to understand the order and not complying with it immediately, has been discharged. If the discharged man resented this action and made some comment in his native language, accompanying his remarks with gestures—as most Europeans do—the foreman, failing to understand the man, and thinking himself insulted, would in some cases use violence. The result of this would be a strike by the whole gang, and sometimes by the entire camp."

Garibaldi tactfully pointed out that the foreman "was not always to blame, this owing to the rather turbulent character of the imported laborer," but in July and August 1907 such small-scale strikes were happening all along the line among the European laborers. The ICC response was to try to identify the "ring-leaders" and swiftly deport them as "professional agitators."

Although the measure brought success on the Isthmus—strikes fell away from the end of 1907—the reluctant returnees further fueled to the clamor in the Spanish press to outlaw the ICC recruitment agents. After a spate of newspaper stories detailing the violence of the "Yankee police," the arrival of a liberal government in Madrid in early 1909 saw the representatives of the canal finally banned from Spain. The Italian government followed suit, even though their official investigator had found very few of his countrymen still at work on the Isthmus when he visited in late 1908.

Goethals was unconcerned. The attitude was: we do not want you anyway. "At the present time all of our superintendents and foremen are unanimously of the opinion that the efficiency of our 20-cent (40 cents silver) contract labor is much less now than it was a year ago," he wrote to the Spanish chargé d'affaires in Panama City. "In addition, several instances have been reported to me which indicate that the conduct of our contract laborers, as a whole, verges on insubordination; that the orders of foremen and others in authority are not received with respect and executed as the necessities of the work require." Thereafter, although there were still some twenty-five hundred Spaniards working on the canal at the end of the construction period, the numbers steadily dwindled. For various reasons, Stevens's experiment had failed. In the main, then, it would still be British West Indians who would do the bulk of the work building the American Panama Canal.

⫷⫷⫷⫸⫸⫸

In spite of the problems with the Spanish laborers, the work continued steadily through 1907. Surveying parties were hacking through the jungle to map the contours of the new lake basin. In July work started on digging the lock basins on the Pacific side, and August saw a new, fresh record for excavation. By the end of the year, the workforce had grown by 15,000 to nearly 46,000, twice the peak number under de Lesseps. The year delivered a total excavation figure of nearly 16 million cubic yards, more than the entire American total up to December 1906.

Goethals divided the work into three divisions, as the French had done. The Atlantic Division stretched from Limón Bay to Gatún. To protect the entrance of the canal from "northers," the French had dug their canal in the shelter of the bay's eastern shore. The Americans opted to head directly into the center of the bay, and protect the entrance to the waterway from storms and silting through the construction of breakwaters out into the harbor. While these were being planned, dredges were scooping and sucking out a channel 41 feet deep and 500 feet wide from deep water three and a half miles offshore to the site of the planned dam, three and a half miles inland.

This key structure was also the responsibility of this division. By the end of the year the dam site was clear of vegetation and the lock basin excavation proceeding well.

The Central Division ran from Gatún to Pedro Miguel and included the preparation of the new lake basin as well as the excavation in the Cut. The Pacific Division ran from deep water in Panama Bay up the valley of the Río Grande to the foot of the mountains of the Continental Divide at Pedro Miguel. As on the Atlantic side, dredges and steam shovels worked their way upward from the coast.

Inevitably, there were some changes to the original plan. After 2 million cubic yards of spoil had already been removed from the site of the Sosa locks, it was decided in December 1907, for a variety of reasons, to move them three miles inland to Miraflores. For one thing, Miraflores offered a more stable site for locks and dam, but, most important, it was safe from naval bombardment.

In line with the military requirements of the canal, and prompted by the U.S. Navy, the width of the locks was increased from 100 to 110 feet, in part because of the extra compartments around naval vessels' hulls needed to combat the new threat of submarine attack. The largest Navy battleship on the drawing boards, the *Pennsylvanian*, had a beam of 98 feet. (The *Titanic*, then under construction, was 94 feet wide.) The locks designed by Eiffel, when de Lesseps finally conceded to the lock plan, were little more than half this size. The width of the rest of the canal was increased as well from 200 to 300 feet at the bottom, making it four times as broad as the projected French canal. It was becoming increasingly apparent that the de Lesseps canal, had it been completed, would have been almost immediately obsolete.

These changes obviously increased the massive excavation still ahead for Goethals and his army regime. But for now this held no fear. By the beginning of 1908, the majority of the workforce was at last engaged in actual excavation, rather than building or sanitation work. "The biggest boss is King Yardage," wrote an American journalist who visited in February 1908. "A toiling, moiling, delving potentate to whom all make obeisance, and who imperiously demands results every minute of the day." And the results were spectacular. In 1908, 37 million cubic yards were removed, more than double the previous record year and about half of what the two French companies had achieved in seventeen years. The era of the "solid inevitability" of the American canal seemed at last to have arrived.

-◄◄◄◄◄-►►►►►-

But the turnover of skilled American staff, still running at a rate of nearly 100 percent a year, remained a concern of the canal leadership. During 1907, more than three thousand new skilled workers had to be recruited in the States to keep up a Gold Roll force that in the middle of the year numbered only 4,400. The response was to accelerate the process, started by Stevens and Magoon, of providing for the white workers every possible convenience and luxury.

Each morning a supply train of twelve cars left Cristóbal for the line, containing five of ice and cold storage provisions, two of bread, one of vegetables, and four of staple commissary supplies. Starting in April 1908 the bakery started producing pies and pastry in huge quantities, and the cold storage facility was expanded to include an ice-cream factory and a coffee-grinding plant. Laundries and drying rooms were constructed for the Gold Roll employees. More and more stores were opened, to the dismay of the Panamanian merchants and the delight of house-and-home runners like Rose van Hardeveld. When a commissary at last opened in Las Cascadas the vegetables might have been thin on the ground, she reports, but the staples were plentiful. And if you got there at eight in the morning, as most tried to do, you might even find something new to break the monotony. Rose felt that a corner had been turned: "I realized . . . that the last vestige of fear and uncertainty seemed to have left us when our children were able to buy ice cream cones and soda pop at the clubhouse . . . we now felt thoroughly at home, truly, now, a transplanted bit of the United States." Jessie Murdoch, the Ancón nurse who had arrived back in 1904, expressed a similar sentiment. By mid-1908, she wrote, "we were surrounded by all the modern comforts and conveniences. Telephones buzzed, electric lights were flashed on, and we recognized ourselves as a part of an ideal community."

For Rose van Hardeveld, even more important than home comforts was the growing number of families in the Zone. Roosevelt's visit had helped improve the image of Panama, and the ICC offered strong inducements, mainly in the form of superior housing for married workers. By May 1908 there were well over a thousand families in the Zone, and a riot of weddings. On one steamer ten brides arrived from the United States and were all married on the dock within twelve minutes of disembarking. The bachelors on the Isthmus who could not persuade their sweethearts to join them had to look closer to home. This meant the nurses of Ancón hospital, who consequently could take their pick.

Once assigned married quarters, the young couples found that virtually everything was provided free by the ICC, including rent, light, janitor service, ice, distilled water, and fuel, as well as hospital and medical care. All the bride and groom need buy was bedclothes and china. As the Zone policeman Harry Franck pointed out, "It is doubtful, to be sure, whether one-fourth of the 'Zoners' of any class ever lived as well before or since. The shovelman's wife who gives five-o'clock teas and keeps two servants will find life different when the canal is opened and she moves back to the smoky little factory cottage and learns again to do her own washing."

In the summer of 1908 the van Hardevelds were told that a new house was ready for them nearby. Before moving out of House Number One, they took a holiday back in Nebraska, returning in November with a new addition to the family, a son. Their new dwelling was "one of the brand new cottages over the hill . . . painted battleship grey." Although the mold and insects soon moved in as well, Rose professed herself very pleased. The house had modern plumbing and electric light, and was "clean and comfortable, just about the type of home a man in the States would try to provide for his family."

There were now nearly forty families in Las Cascadas, a far cry from how it was when the van Hardevelds first arrived. Families had been encouraged, of course, to give stability to the workforce, and as a way of keeping the men on the straight and narrow. According to Rose, this was working. With the arrival of the wives, "attendance in the saloons fell off to a considerable degree, and normal social patterns became possible."

"Our friendships with neighbours deepened," Rose wrote. "We drew together in a sort of compact clique. How we worried together and laughed together." The main meeting place was their old House Number One. This had been taken over by their friend Charley Swinehart. His father had died, and so his mother and two teenage sisters had come out to join him and his brother in Panama. Dakota, or "Cote," Swinehart seems to have become something of a matriarch of the Las Cascadas community. Rose described her as "a fragile little person who suffered a great deal from the heat and humidity, but who maintained a cheerful outlook and a brisk efficiency that inspired and reassured us younger women."

Jan remained obsessed with the canal and would spend his evenings talking to Charley Swinehart about yardage excavated, the best dynamiting techniques, and the challenges still ahead. The shared canal-building task—vast, historic, epic—united and inspired many of the Americans on the Zone. "Nothing else seemed quite so important as this immense project moving gradually and steadily to completion," wrote Rose. "Nearly all the women and children felt the same way . . . This was our life. All other things were subordinate."

But not everyone was so motivated. According to an official report it was "not until the business depression . . . in the United States, in the winter of 1907–1908, [that] was there a lessening of the numbers leaving the Isthmus for the States." Even in 1909–10 the turnover of skilled workers was nearly 60 percent. "Anyone who stays here through a year of it becomes depressed," wrote an engineer on the project, "and visions of the home country, with its bracing weather, its familiar scenes and its fond ties, begin to float out on the curling wreaths of smoke from pipe or cigarette." A journalist who visited in early 1909 found a few Americans who unreservedly loved the country and climate, but in most he discovered "a certain pathetic note of exile from all that is dear."

To address this homesickness, it was decided to try to keep the men occupied as much as possible. Two and a half million dollars were allocated each year to entertainments and recreation, some $750 per white employee. Churches and Sunday schools were constructed, and more playing fields laid out. Most important, however, were the Gold Roll clubs, run by the YMCA. By late 1907, there were four in operation, at Cristóbal, Culebra, Empire, and Gorgona. Each had bowling alleys, a billiard room, a library, and a gymnasium. They also provided the location or focus for a bewildering array of organized activities: sponsored hikes and horse rides through the jungle, amateur theatricals, boat trips to Portobelo, athletic competitions, sightseeing trips on labor trains to the Cut or the locks areas. Lecturers and professional entertainers were also brought in. There were numerous clubs for games including chess, checkers, and bridge. Orchestras, bands, and glee clubs were formed, and lessons offered in everything from Spanish to first aid to Bible study. Over two thousand books were provided in the libraries, where more than eighty U.S. newspapers and periodicals were also available. When the clubs were inspected in early 1908, the visitors were impressed, commending the clubs "without reservation." "They fill a necessary place in the somewhat artificial life on the canal zone," it was concluded, "where a body of loyal Americans, far removed from the uplifting influence of home and friends, are performing with genuine enthusiasm a work of great importance to their country, in a climate demoralizing to the white man."

The white community also had its own ICC-produced newspaper, the *Canal Record,* first published in September 1907, and free to anyone on the Gold Roll. It was determined that this should not replicate the French *Bulletin*—praise of department heads was expressly forbidden—but the *Record* charted the excavation and building work week by week, keeping the community abreast of progress and making people feel involved. By printing the excavation figures of particular divisions or even steam shovels, the paper helped fuel competition among the shovel men and train drivers, thereby increasing productivity. But the *Record* was also the social "notice board" of the Gold Roll Americans, and as such offers a fascinating glimpse of community life. "Zonians" seem to have been, on the whole, great "joiners." By this time there was a plethora of societies, many based on place of origin or trade. One issue in mid-September 1907 mentions a new baseball team organized at Culebra composed entirely of men from Georgia. There is a notice about a forthcoming entertainment "to be furnished by Sidney Landon, character delineator." The results of a recent bowling competition between teams from Empire and Culebra are printed. Chess, checkers, and billiard tournaments were, it appears, in progress at two of the clubs.

It was all wonderfully wholesome, just as American domestic opinion demanded. To many it seemed that the impossible had been achieved—proper society had been created two thousand miles from home in the middle of jungle and depraved natives. In early 1909 Rose van Hardeveld's family moved to Empire. She was impressed. There was "a really active American community . . . Here were nicely dressed, pretty young teachers and office workers. Clean, fine-looking, bronze-faced young chaps escorted them in the evenings to a dance or to the band concerts."

One such office worker was Courtney Lindsay, whose long and detailed letters home have survived and offer a picture of everyday life on the Isthmus during the Goethals era. Lindsay arrived at the beginning of June 1907, about a month after Goethals took over. He was just short of his twentieth birthday. He had been working in his hometown of Savannah, Georgia, for the local railway company when he met someone recently returned from the Isthmus on holiday. "He says it is not home, but on the order of a boarding school," he wrote to his mother about the encounter. "The fare is not Delmonico's, but he says it is eatable and that if you want you can save half your salary."

Thus encouraged, Lindsay secured a position in Panama paying $125 a month. His mother was a friend of Major David Gaillard, ICC commissioner and head of the Central Division, so this might have helped. Lindsay's job was the same as Mary Chatfield's first position—stenographer in Arango's department of meteorology and river hydraulics, based in Panama City. So like Chatfield, Lindsay would be part of the "B-echelon" of canal personnel, working far from the construction and excavation "front line." He wouldn't even see the canal, apart from the view from the train, until eighteen months after his arrival. His letters show none of the heroic motivation of someone like Jan van Hardeveld.

His first impressions were favorable, however. "Every day I am better pleased that I came," he wrote to his mother a week after his landing. He had quickly judged the ICC-provided food—"things are not always very clean"—and made alternative arrangements, eating lunch at the house of a Jamaican woman. "I have adapted myself pretty well to the climate and conditions," he wrote home a week later. He had even put on weight, and was, he reported, taking three grains of quinine every morning.

He was also agreeably surprised by the social life in the city. His boss tended to hand on invitations to gala occasions to his employees. "The Tivoli is giving a reception and dance tonight to the Vice-President," he wrote home excitedly at the beginning of July. "So I am having my dress suit pressed for the occasion. This is the second time I had used it in the month I have been here. I never wore it once in Savannah." His younger sister wrote to him, asking about the pineapples and her brother's romantic prospects.

Pineapples are only fifteen cents "spickity," he wrote back. "Yes, there are a great many American ladies, not so many girls. This is a very 'marrying' place, and nearly all the good looking girls are Mrs. There are a few exception among the nurses however."

But it did not take long for Lindsay to adopt some of Chatfield's cynicism about the actual work. Less than a month in, he wrote that as the department boss was away, "things have already begun to slack up. This job is like plenty of Gov't places in the States. There are one and a half men to do one man's work." His immediate superior was an Englishman, Vince, "who seems to have caught the 'manana fever.'" He was dismissive, too, of the endless congressional committes visiting the Isthmus, assessing the works while being treated to a round of dances and parties. "Now what can they tell about it?" he asked in a letter in November. "Seems to me it is a trip on Uncle Sam." The following month he reported that "the novelty has worn off and nothing ever happens." There was a friend of his, Hugh Wills, due out soon to join him, but for now he felt homesick, left out of his life at home ("I'm doomed to bachelor hood"), and sad about being away for Christmas.

His first Christmas Day on the Isthmus turned out to be all right. He went fishing in the Bay of Panama, had dinner at the Tivoli, and then went to a party at the Corrozal Club, where there was singing, stories, music, and boxing bouts. Soon after, he took a week's sick leave at the sanatorium on beautiful Taboga. All Gold Roll employees were entitled to fifteen days' paid sick leave per six months of work. For many, this was just a nice extra holiday. Lindsay says that while he was on Taboga "I've never felt better in my life." In the New Year his hometown friend arrived and Lindsay began to feel settled in. His bachelor residence was refurbished and electric lighting installed. There were trips to Portobelo and to Old Panama, the city up the coast destroyed by Sir Henry Morgan back in 1671, now a picturesque ruin. In March he reported that a show he had attended, the "Empire Lady Minstrels" was "the best amateur entertainment I've seen in a long while." All the while he was learning Spanish, and was proud to report that he could now say, "I have neither one nor the other but I have the trunk which the sailor from the ship of the Captain gave me."

In August 1908 he returned home for his annual leave, and when he came back he found himself posted to Culebra. It was a bit of a comedown after Panama City. "Nothing ever happens here," he complained in a letter to his father. "The only thing worth mentioning since I came on the 20th of last month has been the repair of the YMCA phonograph." But he soon adjusted. "Am beginning to like Culebra better," he wrote home the following month. "The YMCA is an oasis in the desert. I enjoy the bowling, indoor baseball and gymnasium very much." In January, he reported, he "broke into Culebra society" by attending a dance at the club. "The hall is small, and the floor not near so good. Still it is rather livelier than the Tivoli,—it's more like a country town where everybody knows everybody else."

His only health scare came at the end of this year. He spent Christmas in the hospital, thinking he had malaria. But no "bugs" were found in his blood, and although he was given quinine "steadily," he was discharged after a week. The following year saw the young American acting in a farce called *Facing the Music* and learning bridge; there were moments when he really felt in love with Panama. "It seems to me," he wrote to his mother in October 1910, "that a dry season night down here, with a moon, is about as near perfection as this world ever gets."

The following year, it would get even better. In May his friend Hugh became engaged to one of the Ancón nurses, a Miss Dequine. Before the end of the year, Lindsay had followed suit, having met an English nurse, Olive. "She's just about the nicest thing in the girl line there is," he told his parents. As soon as family quarters became available, they married at the small Colón Episcopal Church, Christchurch-by-the-Sea, built back in the 1860s by the Panama Railroad.

⋘⋘— ⟫⟩⟩⟩

The majority of Gold Roll employees accepted the way in which the canal authorities dominated and organized their lives. Visiting journalists, however, were fascinated by the white society that had been created. Everything, all the essentials of life, were supplied by the "state." What was this system? they asked. Was it some form of "military paternalism"? Or "welfare socialism"? Certainly life in the Zone had little in common with the ideas of the capitalist democracy at home. No one was allowed to own meaningful property or vote for the Zone government. And it seemed to work. "The commissary is an assured success," reported one journalist in early 1909. "It has shown the absurdity of the ancient superstition that organized society, the state, cannot attend to the needs of a people as economically and with as efficient service as can an individual or a corporation."

American journalist Arthur Bullard, who had been in Barbados to watch Karner recruit laborers, actually tracked down a member of the U.S. Socialist Party among the Gold Roll workforce. He asked him whether he was living in his ideal state. "First of all, there ain't any democracy down here," Bullard was told. "It's a Bureaucracy that's got Russia backed off the map ... Government ownership don't mean anything to us working men unless we own the Government. We don't here—this is the sort of thing Bismarck dreamed of."

The concentration of power in one man, the "Czar of Panama" George Goethals, had resulted, one journalist wrote, in "the establishment of an autocratic form of government for the Canal Zone ... not in accord with the principles of democracy." Zone policeman Harry Franck described the regime as "enlightened despotism." According to him, it seems to have succeeded through the character of Goethals himself, whom he describes as "an Omnipotent, Omniscient, Omnipresent ruler." This is echoed in many other accounts. Rose van Hardeveld also calls Goethals "omnipresent." "The Old Man" as he became known, "was so constantly on the job that we never thought of him as being at home or eating or sleeping." "Goethals dominates over everybody and everything," Mallet reported to London. To anyone in Panama, this was unmistakable.

"You can't realize what the Chief Engineer is until you live on the Isthmus," wrote Courtney Lindsay home. "His power is as near absolute as any man's can get."

Goethals himself was uneasy about the nature of his regime but believed it was the only way to get the canal built. But there is more than a hint of Big Brother in some of his methods. Officials, known as "spotters," toured the works and the terminal cities in disguise, not only to punish "loafing," but also to weed out potential troublemakers. The spotters had the power to deport "undesirables." "The system is one that would be very repugnant to Englishmen," reported a London journalist. "Employés dismissed are given no notice nor granted any compensation." "The men complain of the savage rigor with which even petty misdemeanours are punished all along the Zone," wrote an American journalist in an article published in April 1909. Two men who attacked the Zone government in a New Orleans newspaper made the mistake of remaining on the Isthmus. They were arrested, prosecuted for criminal libel, and imprisoned. A watching journalist described the sentences as "judicial terrorism . . . the kind of justice dealt out in some, if not most, of the courts is not the sort that would be tolerated long in a democracy."

But on the whole, more subtle pressures were sufficient to keep criticism at bay. Those who complained were labeled "kickers." As one perceptive American journalist explained: "there has grown up in Panama circles somewhat of a tendency to monopolize patriotism, and identify it with official designs, means, methods, and management. Dissent or a different viewpoint is too often hailed with cries of 'Enemies of the Canal.' " To criticize the leadership, then, was un-American, as many Zonians believed. One of the first resolutions of the new Women's Club in Panama was "that every club-woman in the Canal Zone constitute herself a committee of one to foster favourable instead of adverse criticism of the conditions of the Zone and of the Isthmus of Panama."

Goethals sat at the top of a rigid hierarchical structure. There was a racial "ladder," of course, with the Americans and the hundred or so British at the top; next came the Panamanian and Spanish "almost-whites"; at the bottom were the blacks, with the West Indians beneath the locals in status. But within the small white community there was also an obvious pecking order. "Caste lines are as sharply drawn as in India," wrote Harry Franck. "The Brahmins are the 'gold' employees ... But—and herein we out-Hindu the Hindus—the Brahmin caste itself is divided and subdivided into infinitesimal gradations. Every rank and shade of man has a different salary, and exactly in accordance with that salary he is housed, furnished, and treated down to the least item,—number of electric lights, candle-power, size of bed, size of bookcase." Such differences in status felt immensely important. "D, who is a quartermaster at $225, may be on 'How-are-you-old-man?' terms with G, who is a station agent and draws $175. But Mrs. D never thinks of calling on Mrs. G socially," Franck continued.

But if the Zone had become, as the diplomat William Sands complained, a "drearily efficient state," the terminal cities remained, in comparison, anarchic and chaotic. Panama City had more than 200 bars, Colón 131, including 40 in one street. Every Saturday night special trains were put into service, bringing in hundreds of canal workers. For Harry Franck, Panama and Colón acted "as a sort of safety valve, where a man can ... blow off steam; get rid of the bad internal vapors that might cause explosion in a ventless society."

It was, then, a less than ideal setting for the fostering of understanding and respect between Americans and their Panamanian hosts. The Americans "blowing off steam" seemed to the locals loud, rude, and drunk. Harry Franck describes an American "type" "grown so painfully prevalent": "a chestless youth ... whose proofs of manhood are cigarettes and impudence and discordant noise, and whose national superiority is demonstrated by the maltreating of all other races." Clashes continued, often centered on the notorious Cocoa Grove brothel in Colón. In September 1908, in Panama City, an American was killed and another seriously wounded in an altercation between citizens and U.S. sailors. The Zone authorities demanded and received permission to patrol the terminal cities to prevent a recurrence of fighting, and the Panamanian government, protesting that the fault was with the drunkenness of the Americans, was forced to pay an indemnity of nearly half a million dollars to the United States.

Many Americans considered the Panamanians backward, deluded about their own importance, and lacking in gratitude for everything the United States had done for them. In March 1908 an article appeared in the Philadelphia *Saturday Evening Post* entitled "Life in Spigotty Land: The Cohorts of King Yardage." Its author, Samuel G. Blythe, described the "scores of clear-eyed, broad-shouldered and hard-headed Americans who are carrying out their part of the work without hope of fame, but as Americans, doing an American job in an American way." Little heed was paid to the Panamanians, he wrote, "who are funny little people, vainglorious and, thinking they achieved their own liberty, have an idea the canal is being dug for their especial benefit." In fact, the truth was "the republic was made for our convenience and it is held up by the scruff of its neck by this Government."

Indeed, neither of the republic's political parties could afford to antagonize Uncle Sam. The Conservatives, many still favoring annexation by the United States, saw American power as the best defense of their interests. The Liberals needed the Americans as well. Unless the forthcoming 1908 presidential elections were supervised by the United States, there would be an inevitable repeat of the fixed municipal and National Assembly votes of two years previously. The government candidate, backed by the outgoing Amador, was Ricardo Arias, brother of Tomás, and an ultrarightist. The Liberal Party, thinking its own candidate would never stand a chance, backed José de Obaldía for the presidency. Obaldía had been a popular vice president and was also close to the Americans, having served as ambassador in Washington.

It proved a shrewd move. Taft considered Arias corrupt and utterly lacking in scruples, while Obaldía was seen as the best guarantee of a smooth succession. Predicting that Arias, with Amador's help, would so blatantly fix the vote that an uprising would result, he decided to acquiesce in Liberal demands that the United States supervise the election. In the meantime, William Nelson Cromwell popped up again helping run Obaldía's campaign. Realizing he was fatally out of favor with the Americans, Arias withdrew and Obaldía was elected unopposed.

Clearly the Liberal Party no longer seemed a threat to American interests in Panama. Taft affirmed, "We have such control in Panama that no Government elected by them will feel a desire to antagonize the American Government." Indebted to the United States for its 1908 election victory, the party under Obaldía's presidency would make no trouble for Goethals. But then, at the beginning of 1910, the president died. His successor as first designate was Carlos Mendoza, who had been a leader of the revolution in Colón back in November 1903. According to Mallet, Mendoza was "extremely tactful and friendly towards everybody," but for the Americans there was a problem. Mendoza was a mulatto. Not only would having a nonwhite Panamanian president contrast a little too sharply with the racial hierarchy in the Zone, but Mendoza, according to Sands's replacement as U.S. chargé d'affaires, possessed "a racial inability to refrain long from abuse of power."

Mallet reports that on the prompting of Goethals, a junior officer in the U.S. legation, Richard O. Marsh, "put it about to the most notorious babblers in the city that the United States Government would regard the election of Senor Mendoza as unconstitutional, and that if the National Assembly persisted in his election a military occupation of Panama would be the inevitable result." Mendoza formally withdrew his candidacy and an elderly white Liberal patrician was installed as president. "It is really farcical to talk of Panama as an independent state," wrote Mallet to the Foreign Office. "It is really simply an annex of the Canal Zone." The United States' grip on the republic would last until the end of the construction period (and, of course, beyond). Mallet reported in 1913, after the election the previous year of Belisario Porras, the erstwhile "notorious hater of foreigners," that it was now impossible to be president without being "docile to American wishes."

◄◄◄◄-►►►►

In the United States, the end of 1908 saw a presidential election campaign between Taft and William Jennings Bryan. Roosevelt had publicly backed his secretary of war. But then, a month before the vote, Panama was once again front-page news. The story had been reignited in September of the previous year when Cromwell's claim for payment from the New Company, being arbitrated in Paris, was leaked to the New York press. Undoubtedly the lawyer had put a favorable gloss on his description of work performed for his client, but the extent of influence he claimed in the heart of U.S. government was deeply unsettling. Then, in October 1908, the *New York World* published a story that accused Taft's influential brother Charles, and Roosevelt's brother-in-law, Douglas Robinson, of being members and beneficiaries of the syndicate supposedly set up to profit from the sale of the New Company to the U.S. government. Further allegations were made during the campaign as the Democrats saw a way to attack the Republicans. Cromwell, the *World* claimed, was "practically the Secretary of War as far as the Panama Canal was concerned," and his "law offices at No. 41 Wall Street were even regarded by many as the real executive offices of the Panama Canal."

Roosevelt, furious that what he considered to be the greatest foreign policy achievement of his administration was once again mired in scandal, brought a prosecution for criminal libel against Joseph Pulitzer, owner of the *World*, two of his editors, and two publishers of the *Indianapolis News*, which had picked up the story. To prepare his defense, Pulitzer sent two of his best investigative reporters to Washington, Paris, Panama, and Bogotá to get the "Untold Story of Panama." Followed everywhere by Secret Service agents, they found obstruction at every turn. In Paris they were told that the details of shareholders were in a sealed vault. When their lawyers eventually got access, they found the records virtually nonexistent. The paper's British counsel commented, "I have never known in my lengthy experience in company matters any public corporation, much less one of such vast importance, having so completely disappeared and removed all traces of its existence as the New Panama Canal Company." In Panama, the journalists found vital cable evidence destroyed and the "revolutionaries"—unwilling to lose the trust and support of the United States—good at keeping political secrets. They denied everything, even meeting Cromwell.

But by now the cases had become more about freedom of speech and federal versus state government than about specific allegations. When the trial started in 1909, it was deemed unconstitutional for the government to "drag citizens from distant States to the capital to be tried." Judge Anderson dismissed the case, and the evidence of the syndicate and of United States collusion in the "revolution" was never put to the test. The judge did, however, have one final comment to make on the case: "There are many peculiar circumstances about the Panama canal business," he said. "Rather suddenly it became known that it could be procured for $40,000,000. There were a number of people who thought there was something not just exactly right about that transaction, and I will say for myself that I have a curiosity to know what the real truth was . . . I am suspicious about it now."

❦❦❦❦~➤➤➤➤

On the Isthmus, however, the "Army of Panama," now numbering nearly fifty thousand, kept up 1908's high excavation total during the following year, as fatalities, particularly from disease, continued to fall. The largest cause of death, for the first time, was in 1909 from accidents on the works. On the Atlantic Division huge amounts of silt and sand were being sucked from the channel from coast to deep water, the old French canal from the bay to the site of the Gatún

Dam and locks had been effectively redredged to carry materials to the construction side, and old French-era dredges, many twenty-five years old, were making progress in the channel from the bay to the locks.

On the Pacific Division there had also been steady progress, working in from the sea, shifting material with dredge, shovel, or hydraulic jet. In the harbor, an 11,000-foot-long breakwater was under construction to guard against submarines, and to prevent the channel from silting up. It was proving slow work as the dumped rock either disappeared into the mud of the bay or pushed up other sandbanks nearby. Eventually over ten times the originally estimated quantity of spoil would be required. But in the Central Division, the infamous Culebra Cut, *la grande tranchée*, had shown itself once more to be the biggest challenge of all.

"HELL'S GORGE"

In Culebra, the mountains were on the move. Work on deepening the Cut had begun in earnest with the end of the steam-shovel men's strike in July 1907. But as the gorge grew in size, it was as if the land was fighting back. On the night of October 2, after particularly heavy rain, a great mass of earth and rock plunged down into the Cut from the slope just south of Gold Hill at Cucaracha. Two steam shovels were overturned and nearly buried, track and piping carrying water and compressed air were destroyed, and the drainage system was wrecked. Horrified engineers then noticed that the slide was continuing. An area of about fifty acres continued to move for the next ten days, sliding into the canal prism at a speed of about fourteen feet a day. Gaillard, the engineer in charge of the Cut, described it as being "a tropical glacier—of mud instead of ice." Goethals reported that "it required night and day work to save our equipment." By the time the equilibrium of that particular part of the mountain had been restored and the movement stopped, over half a million cubic yards had entered the Cut. In his end-of-year report for the Foreign Office, Mallet wrote, "the magnitude of the task is much greater than was at first thought." "There is less disposition," he went on, "to under-rate the French failure." Certainly Goethals quickly revised his earlier view—the job in the Cut was now deemed the "most formidable of the canal enterprise."

The first great Cucaracha slide was just the beginning. As the ditch was lowered foot by foot, there followed numerous similar "gravity slides." In many places along the walls of the Cut, a layer of semi-porous clay sat on top of a stratum of impervious rock. Rainwater seeped through the clay to form a soapy, greasy layer on top of the harder rock. When this rock sloped toward the Cut, there would come a point when the friction between the two layers became so reduced that the top layer slipped into the Cut, "like snow off a roof." The following year, 1908, saw slides of this type at Paraíso, near Gold Hill, and at Culebra.

But such was the baffling geology of the Cut, with rocks of all different types in bewildering combinations, that gravity slides, most usual during the wet season, were not the only problem. Some of the strata, previously long-buried, reacted to the air in a way that caused them to become unstable and unable to support material lying above. Other harder rock, depending on its lines of fracture, would collapse into the Cut when its lateral support was removed, bringing down upper layers as well.

Spaniard Antonio Sanchez, who worked in the Cut for four and a half years, told of a curse going back to French times. The ground itself, he said, would take revenge against those who sought to "dissect nature's creation." Most vivid in his memory was the shrill sound of whistles from an accident site. If they were not at work, foremen would appear at their camp to demand that they come to help dig out men and equipment buried by slides. But while they were attempting to rescue the buried men, they too were subject to the danger of further slides. Sometimes the deep mud they worked in would prevent them from getting out of the way quickly enough if there was another earth movement. The majority of the time, he reports, they would only manage to dig out disfigured and broken bodies.

Most of the slides, however, were slower, although more substantial than these sorts of avalanches. But even if a slope moved toward the Cut at only a few inches a day, it still required the re-laying of miles and miles of track. And as soon as a slide was cleared, an engineer remembers, "the old hill politely slid back again, completely filling the canal." As a West Indian worker put it, "Today you dig and tomorrow it slides."

The slides made Culebra an unpredictable enemy for the "Army of Panama." The deep gorge, wrote a senior U.S. administrator, "was a land of the fantastic and the unexpected. No one could say when the sun went down at night what the condition of the Cut would be when the sun arose the next morning. The work of months or even years might be blotted out by an avalanche of earth." At the end of 1907 Goethals had to refuse to set a completion date for the canal as, he said, "The difficulties we are liable to encounter are unknown to ourselves and uncertain." Another senior engineer confessed that it was impossible to plan for the final shape of the ditch as "this material has or will ultimately make its own design as to slopes." In other ways as well, the Cut was "fantastic and unexpected." Such was the geological chaos of the ground that dynamiters and steam shovel operatives, as Goethals explained, "found themselves handling hard rock one hour, while the next hour they might be working in earth or clay." In some places the downward pressure of the unsupported rock faces would push up the comparatively soft strata of the canal floor, sometimes as much as thirty feet. On one occasion, Gaillard himself was standing at the bottom of the Cut when the ground he was standing on rose six feet in five minutes. Just as uncanny for the diggers were the cracks that appeared at the bottom of the Cut, spewing out stinking sulphurous fumes or boiling water. Blasts hot enough to char wood were emitted from the ground, caused by the oxidation of iron pyrites in the soil or by the vaporization of water in the intense heat of friction as the despoiled ground writhed and slipped.

To prevent the slides Goethals tried all the techniques then available. Shovels worked at the top of the slopes to reduce the weight of material pushing down on the lower levels. Long "nails" were driven into the sides of the trench to bind the porous layer to the rock beneath; slopes were plastered in concrete. Such measures were being used with success at the time by the British in Hong Kong, but the scale and complexity of the Cut would doom all to failure. To keep water from the slopes, large diversion channels were built near the crests to carry away moisture that might otherwise saturate the sides of the Cut. But this approach failed as well. The only option left was simply to dig it all out again.

Unlike the French, Goethals had the muscle to do it. The massive steam shovels, by now personalized with female names, were removing huge amounts of dirt. On average over the construction period they dug out a million cubic yards each, a testament to their sound construction and efficient maintenance. In the peak month of March 1909, there were sixty-eight shovels at work in the Cut excavating an astonishing 2 million cubic yards. In the same month seven hundred thousand pounds of powder was exploded. Thanks to the system set up by Stevens, 160 trains, carefully controlled from the construction headquarters at Culebra, ran in and out of the gorge every day, pulling thousands of flatcars to and from the dumps; in the Cut's nine miles there were now seventy-six miles of construction track.

The work never stopped. At the end of the day, the track shifters, dynamite gangs, and steam-shovel operators were replaced by coaling trains and maintenance crews who worked through the night so that nothing should delay progress the next day. And although about a quarter of the effort involved digging out material from slides, the Cut still got deeper and deeper and more and more spectacular.

The Cut was the "special wonder of the canal," "one of the great spectacles of the ages." Over 70 percent of the vast total canal excavation came from its nine miles. For the increasing number of tourists, gazing down into the great man-made canyon from its edge high above, it was an inspiring sight. "The Cut is a tremendous demonstration of human and mechanical energy," wrote a British visitor. "It is simply the transformation of a mountain into a valley." It was more than "heroic human endeavour," said another. It was a "geological event." The scale was overwhelming. "From the crest," wrote an American tourist, "you looked down upon a mighty rift in the earth's crust, at the base of which pygmy engines and antlike forms were rushing to and fro without seeming plan or reason. Through the murky atmosphere strange sounds rose up and smote the ear of the onlooker with resounding clamor." These included the "strident clink, clink, clink of the drills . . . the shrill whistles of the locomotives . . . the constant and uninterrupted rumble" of the ever-moving dirt trains, the "clanking of chains" of the shovels, "the cries of men, and the booming of blasts. Collectively the sounds were harsh, deafening, brutal such as we might fancy would arise from hell."

William Baxter started work as an official guide in 1911. In that year there were fifteen thousand tourists. "They are generally comfortable men and women of 50 or more," he wrote. The English tended to wear cork hats, though "some American men dress as if for a trip through the jungle when they go out on a sightseeing train. Most women wear heavy ugly shoes. All tourists carry umbrellas." "Patriotic tourists, or perhaps it would be better to say 'chauvinistic tourists,' are rather common," he continues. "They have two great topics: 'The French Failure' and 'The Cost.' It is futile to explain to them that a private company of Americans would have failed as the French company did, under the same conditions. 'We have done it, and they failed,' is always the answer."

For the "antlike" figures working far down below, the Cut was known as "Hell's Gorge." The noise alone is hard to imagine. On a typical day there would be more than three hundred rock drills in operation, as well as the steam shovels, trains, and the blasting of some six hundred holes, with all the booming and crashing reflected and amplified by the walls of the "big ditch." But that was only a part of it. As a Barbadian dynamite carrier, Arnold Small, remembered, "There was no shelter from the sun or the rain. There were no trees, then, just a bare place. When the sun shine, you get it, when it rain fall, you get it. When the wind blow, you get it." Ten feet of rain fell in the Cut during 1909, converting it to a muddy nightmare. John Prescod was working at Bas Obispo "at the steam shovel in mud and water. One pair of boots last me one day. In the afternoon walk to the camp barefoot." "I had never saw so much rain in all my life as I see in the Cut," says another digger. "You had to work all through the rain, I remember when I was in the drilling gang, the boss allway say keep the drills agoing so as to keep your body warm sometimes, you are so cold that your teeth keep rocking together, in the morning you had to put your clothes on damp no sun to dry them."

In the dry season the perpetual wet was replaced by 120-degree heat, and clouds of choking dust. "For the first couple of days or weeks, you are always out of breath," says Arnold Small.

Harry Franck vividly remembered the day he spent during 1912 traversing the Cut enrolling workers in a census he was conducting. "The different levels varied from ten to twenty feet one above the other, each with a railroad on it, back and forth along which incessantly rumbled and screeched dirt-trains full or empty, halting before the steam-shovels, that shivered and spouted thick black smoke as they ate away the rocky hills and cast them in great giant handfuls on the train of one-sided flat cars that moved forward bit by bit at the flourish of the conductor's yellow flag. Steam-shovels that seemed human in all except their mammoth fearless strength tore up the solid rock with snorts of rage and the panting of industry, now and then flinging some troublesome, stubborn boulder angrily upon the cars ... Each was run by two white Americans ... the craneman far out on the shovel arm, the engineer within the machine itself with a labyrinth of levels demanding his unbroken attention. Then there was of course a gang of negroes, firemen and the like, attached to each shovel."

All around, scores of drills were "pounding and grinding and jamming holes in the living rock." Anywhere near them was "such a roaring and jangling that I must bellow at the top of my voice to be heard at all. The entire gamut of sound-waves surrounds and enfolds me." There were gangs everywhere, on the floor of the canal and on the terraces and "stretching away in either direction till those far off look like upright bands of the leaf-cutting ants of Panamanian jungles." And over it all hung heavy clouds of coal dust from the trains and shovels.

With so many men and machines crowded into this narrow space, almost nowhere was work more dangerous or life cheaper. "There were so many engines at a time in the Cut," remembers Rufus Forde, "that most every month, a man lost his leg or badly damage. When any thing like that happen one engineer will turn to next engineer, one just grease the wheel. In those days a fowl life was more valuable than our lives." One Panama-born West Indian remembered seeing a man cut cleanly in two, with his legs carried away by the train, which did not bother to stop. "Billy had been the engineer. He will stop his train on the tracks for a horse or a cow, but not for a human. Those were his words always."

Tales of serious danger from accidents dominate the accounts of the West Indian workers. One remembered seeing a Spanish track layer hit by a locomotive and pushed for about twenty feet along the track. "He was still alive, with mostly all his skin was stripped off like a piece of ham bone. All I could hear him say was 'Mi madre, mi madre!'" Harry Franck reckoned you needed "eyes and ears both in front and behind, not merely for trains but for a hundred hidden and unknown dangers to keep the nerves taut." Scores of men were killed by being hit by the swinging boom of a steam shovel. Jan van Hardeveld narrowly escaped being crushed trying to right an overturned shovel, but soon after had his leg badly injured by a flying spike maul. Antonio Sanchez worked several months of 310 hours, the overtime being night work on track relocation when "the mud and slime was always present as well as the danger of the various spoil trains and rolling stock in dark and rainy nights." In March 1909 he was disabled for three months when his foot was crushed by the wheel of a train.

Even worse than the traffic and machinery was the vast amount of dynamite being deployed to break up the rock so that it could be handled by the shovels. Accidents were numerous. Goethals blamed the incompetence of the workers, but some of the explosives became unstable from exposure to the Panamanian climate. On other occasions the subterranean heat in the Cut ignited the charges before the men were safely clear. Once, a premature explosion was caused by a bolt of lightning during a storm, killing seven men. The most common danger, however, was when excavating machinery hit unexploded charges. "It was a very awful sight to see how they dig out the bodies," remembered Constantine Parkinson, "but it did not mean nothing in construction days people get killed and injured almost every day and all the bosses want is to get the canal built."

The worst such accident occurred in December 1908, at Bas Obispo at the north end of the Cut. "Preparation was made to shoot down a high Hill in the center of the waterway on Sunday A.M.," said Jamaican Z. McKenzie. "Unfortunately on Saturday about 12.30 P.M. the blast went off. I just leave the Gang to eat my lunch. I ran to the Spot & Saw what happened. Oh, it was a day of Sorrow for the living." The accidental ignition of 22 tons of dynamite, in two separate explosions, was heard three miles away and left 60 injured and 23 men dead, 17 West Indians, 3 Spaniards, and 3 Americans. West Indian Amos Clarke remembered seeing "flesh hanging on the faraway trees. It was something terrible and awful to look at."

Antonio Sanchez described going to work every day in the Cut as like "going to a battlefield . . . we had to sweat and be brave." Even at a supposedly safe distance from the great explosions, bits of rock would be flung into the air for hundreds of feet. "Many times the rocks would hit laborers with such impact that they would fall unconscious on the spot," he said. "As there were no other means for our protection, we used our shovels to cover our heads from the impact of the flying projectiles." Harry Franck noticed that the track switchmen, or "switcheroos," built sheet-iron wigwams, not as shelter from the sun, but as protection from flying rocks.

John Prescod was in a drilling gang near Empire in mid-April 1913. In one "difficult place," at the bottom of a steep and unstable cliff, it was impossible to set up the drills due to rocks falling from above. His foreman was Charley Swinehart, the friend of the van Hardevelds. "General foreman came to spot," Prescod wrote, "say your all don't started up yet no boss rock falling down un us. Say if I go up and set up a drill God dam it I going to fire the whole bunch of you I am sorry to say sad accident occurred. Rock fall from the bank knock Mr. Swinehart down in the canal Put him on a flatcar rush him to Ancón Hospital die the same day." According to his official record, thirty-two-year-old Swinehart, an old-timer having been in Panama since April 1905, died of a fractured skull. Rose van Hardeveld says that he was still breathing as the hospital car rushed him to Ancón, but he passed away before his mother could reach his bedside. "Two days later, all of us who had become such close friends gathered in the hospital chapel to weep with the bereaved mother and sisters," Rose writes. The surviving family returned, "brokenhearted," to the States.

◀◀◀◀◀◀━▶▶▶▶▶▶

To stop the flooding Chagres from flowing into the Cut as the trench deepend, a huge earth dike was built across the north end at Gamboa. But as in French times, frequent flash floods caused delays and damage to equipment. Still the work was pushed on, even when, in 1910, the Cucaracha slide started up again. By 1912, it had deposited over three million cubic yards into the canal prism. And now the other side of the trench had come to life. At Culebra a huge crack appeared about a hundred yards away from the crest of the Cut. The new club-house was disassembled and moved away, as were some thirty other buildings in the town. But still the crack widened as the edge started to slip inexorably downward. Eventually seventy-five acres of what had been the town fell away into the canal. The mass dumped was twice that of the Cucaracha slide.

Goethals simply ordered it dug out again, but Gaillard was distraught. Then in January 1913 Cucaracha slid again, this time completely blocking the end of the Cut. For Gaillard, this seems to have been something of a final straw. He appeared to suffer a breakdown and left the Isthmus. Back in the United States he was diagnosed with a brain tumor and died before the end of the year. Everyone assumed that it had been the pressure of digging the Cut that had killed him. His fellow engineer and friend William Sibert wrote of his death: "at the end of long years of patient, exacting work, of terrific responsibility, the tragic end has come . . . just as much a direct result of the struggle itself as if it were the work of a hostile bullet."

Even as the shovels lowered the floor of the canal scoop by scoop, there were many who believed that the Cut could never be finished, that it would continue to fight back until it had defeated its despoiler. For their lock-canal plan the French had estimated that 23 million cubic yards had to be moved from the Cut. The Americans initially upped this to 53 million cubic yards, but the estimate rose to 78 million cubic yards in 1908, 84 million cubic yards in 1909, 89 million cubic yards in 1911, then to 100 million cubic yards in 1913. This was partly because of the widening of the bottom width but also due to breaks and slides. George Martin, who had been on the Isthmus since 1909, remembers when working in the Cut in 1911, his bosses' "encouraging talk. 'Boys, are you saving your money? It won't be long now, we will see water into the Cut.' But we just take it for a joke," he wrote. "I personally would say to my fellow men, that could never happen. My children would come and have children, and their children would come and do the same, before you would see water in the Cut, and most all of us agree on the same."

<del>━━◄◄◄◄- ➤➤➤➤━━</del>

George Martin, an apprentice carpenter, had been eighteen when he arrived in Panama from Barbados. He had heard, he wrote, "A voice from a great people" inviting him to help build the Panama Canal. His first job was on the relocation of the Panama Railroad, identified by Goethals as a priority. The line had to be moved to high ground to avoid the area of the proposed Lake Gatún. The job was far bigger than the original railroad construction of 1850–55, requiring either fills, cuts, or bridges for most of its length. The work took Martin deep into the jungle, where spiders and snakes abounded, as well as what he called the "Goosyana Fly"—"when he stings, he leaves worms in the flesh." There were also swarms of *Anopheles* mosquitoes. "The fever lashed good and plenty," Martin writes. "In those days you watch men shake, you think they would shake to pieces." As it was impractical to carry out antimosquito measures in the temporary camps along the new line, Gorgas's department was reduced to catching them in traps, one of which netted 1,800 specimens in a week. But Martin had a good boss who "did not order or compelled, he only pleaded, so we obeyed." Martin worked on a culvert, and, when it was completed, on laying the tracks on it. "We took the spiking of the rail, to the pulling, like a merry-go-round," said Martin. "This were a sight to watch us work along this line; the work was hard but we did it cheerful . . . Every man with an iron bar about five feet long, one would sing, and while he sings, you watch the track line move. The white bosses stand off and laugh. The Songster had a song, goes this way, he would sing the first part, and we comes in with the second part, it goes:

Nattie oh, Nattie O—first
2nd   Gone to Colón
Nattie O Nattie O
2nd   Gone to Colón

1st	Nattie buy sweet powder
2nd	Powder her—— — —<u>you know</u>
1st	Nattie buy sweet powder
2nd	Powder her—— —same

And so he would sing this song over and over, gentlemen watch track line move, the work appeared sweet, the white foremen enjoyed the singing they laugh and did laughed."

Martin's is perhaps the most positive of all the hundred or so accounts in the "Competition for the Best True Stories of Life and Work . . ." collected in 1963 (he received the second prize of $30). He writes of the incessant rain and constantly wet clothes but adds, "We worked joyfully in these days." The food he was given was good, and the boxcars they were first billeted in were "like palaces." Martin worked for the canal for nearly forty-six years until the mid-fifties. Looking back at the construction days he saw them as a time of excitement, and also comparatively low prices. "$2.50 [commissary] book was plenty in those days," he wrote. "Construction days were better days, never to be seen again, the money was paid small, but we live big." On one occasion he was accidentally given two $5.00 books for the price of one. "What to do with $10 in those days? . . . I bought a ham, at that time it look as big as I were . . . real lean, I took ham to work every day in order to have it finish, my associate and I ate ham for days. I don't think about ham these days it's too high in price, now it is for the other fellow." Best of all though was "our ice-cream, I am saying here it was refreshing. We worked hard, but cheerful, I can assure you," he went on. "Our boss never had any worries, he only says what he wanted, and it was done."

Mallet reported in early 1913 that the West Indians had become a "fine body of disciplined and skilled workmen." Many of the Americans were beginning to agree. The secretary to the Commission, Joseph Bishop, would later write that the work of the West Indian artisans "proved very satisfactory." Overall, he continued, the West Indians were "quiet, usually honest, as a general rule well and

respectfully spoken, demonstrating an aptitude to learn the rudi-
ments of the various sorts of work for which they were contracted."
Another engineer declared that the West Indian laborer had lived
down his bad reputation and developed into a good workman, "and
pretty certain always to make a fair return to the United States on
the money it paid him in wages . . . The American republic always
must stand indebted to these easy-going, carefree black men who
supplied the brawn to break the giant back of Culebra." Unlike the
Spaniards, wrote Harry Franck, "the negroes from the British West
Indies . . . could almost invariably read and write; many of those
shoveling in the 'cut' have been trained in trigonometry." (Not that
any of this was reflected in their pay. A black West Indian would
have to be skilled and to have served for a number of years to earn
as much as the minimum for a European laborer—US$0.20 an hour.
By September 1909 fewer than a thousand had qualified.)

As a rule, the West Indians were sober, industrious, and religious.
Harry Franck remembers frequently coming across "young negro
men of the age and type that in white skins would have been loafing
on pool-room corners, reading to themselves in loud and solemn
voices from the Bible." "What was the black culture that the West Indians brought to Panama?" asks poet, social historian, and "silver-
man" descendant Carlos Russell. "An amalgam of European customs
and ideals with a decidedly British (Anglo-Saxon) veneer imposed on
a fragmented African base, weakened, but not eradicated by centuries
of slavery. It was a culture with a distinct penchant for things and
ways British. Proper spoken English, conservative dress, a black suit,
stiff collar and tie in the tropics, proper deportment and a loyalty and
dedication to a job which demanded much and paid little." And life
and culture were changing as the construction years passed. "Now
here comes a little improvement," writes Jules LeCurrieux. "The West
Indian Negro woman began to immigrate here, then the poor old
bastards found themselves wives of their tribes and began to live like
human beings and not beasts, or slaves, they found someone to cook
them a decent meal, to wash their clothes, some one to be a compan-

ion." Although the authorities approved of the increasing arrival of West Indian women and children, as they had for the whites, there were precious few ICC-provided accommodations for families, so most lived in expensive rented flats in the terminal cities. Harry Franck, while taking the census of the Zone in 1912, went into many of these. "They lived chiefly in windowless, six-by-eight rooms," he wrote, "always a cheap, dirty calico curtain dividing the three-foot parlour in front from the five-foot bedroom behind, the former cluttered with a van-load of useless junk . . . a black baby squirming naked in a basket of rags . . . Every inch of the walls was 'decorated' . . . With pages of illustrated magazines or newspapers . . . Outside, before each room, a tin fireplace for cooking precariously bestrided the veranda rail."

Not only was the black workforce ruthlessly excluded from Gold Roll facilities, but also virtually nothing was provided for their amusement, edification, or recreation. In one year, the ICC actually spent fourteen times more per person on "extras" for the white personnel than for the blacks, who, of course, made up the large majority of the employed numbers. So the West Indians were largely left to their own devices.

The church provided the center for the developing West Indian communities. "The men are kept hard at work full six days a week," wrote a visiting American journalist. "On Sunday morning every religious community is busy—you would think a great revival was in progress." By 1910, nearly forty "black" churches were in operation in the Zone, almost all established without any material assistance from the ICC. The majority were Anglican but there were also Methodists, Baptists, Pentecostals, and Episcopalians, as well as more "charismatic" congregations. For one of the leading black Panamanian historians, the church was "a forum for expression on many issues. It preserved the self-respect of the workers, and stimulated their pride." Others were more cynical, seeing the white-dominated Anglican Church in particular as a tool to "tame them and provide a relief valve." The loud singing, extravagant dress, and general exuberance of the low-church black congregations was commented on by Americans, with approval as well as condescension. As far as they were concerned, emotion and energies were being worked out that could otherwise be directed against them.

But the Christian churches of various denominations did not have a monopoly on the spirituality of the imported black workers. As in the islands, their influence was leavened by other traditions that took in "obeah," or sorcery, herbal medicine, and rituals of spirit possession, all of which survived from their African inheritance.

Other carryovers from Africa via the Caribbean islands were the Mutual and Friendly societies, designed to protect those injured or bereaved. As during the French era, "Burial clubs" or "su-sus" became widespread in Panama, whereby small sums were deposited every month against the cost of one's funeral. This was not only because of the high death rate, but also because of the social importance of funerals to the West Indian community. Within the separate island communities—Barbadians tended to stick with Barbadians and Jamaicans with Jamaicans—there was in general a high degree of communal and interdependent living. Harry Franck comments that while West Indians seemed to know everything about their neighbors down to the most intimate detail, the Americans he came across would often not even be aware of their neighbors' names. In the absence of any ICC-organized activities, the West Indians put together their own cricket teams, as well as card or domino-playing circles. Clothes and music were also important. The Caribbean people, says one "digger" descendant, "were the unquestioned leaders of glamour and glitter." "Let me tell you," says West Indian Benjamin Jordan. "To see people at night. Saturday night they have dances in different places. People put up huts and have dance parties and the rest of it. On Saturday night, it was a joyful time in Culebra. Liquor was common at that time. You give a dollar or a dollar and a half for a quart. That did a lot. To see those people dancing and making merry . . . Boy!" Another West Indian remembered "the elegant quadrille dances, men and women graciously moving though the many fancy figures" to the music of "Calypsos, mambos and meringues."

For policeman Harry Franck, Saturday nights, when the men had just been paid, was "the vortex of trouble on the Isthmus." On one occasion he went into "the rough and tumble" of New Gatún, where he encountered "a singing, howling, swarming multitude." With a colleague, he went into one of the bars, or, more exactly, the white side of it. "Beyond the lattice-work that is the 'color line' in Zone dispensaries," he wrote. "West Indians were dancing wild, crowded 'hoedowns' and 'shuffles' amid much howling and more liquidation; on our side a few Spanish laborers quietly sipped their liquor."

Indeed, the "Silver and Gold" distinction made no exception for Saturday nights or any other time or place in the Zone. Away from the works, there was next to no mixing between the races. In fact, the system was ever tightened. In February 1908, Taft, to please the unions as he prepared his bid for the presidency, declared that only U.S. citizens (and, after a protest, Panamanians) could be on the Gold Roll. The last of the West Indians were demoted, but the order also further complicated the tortuous euphemism of the Gold/Silver distinction. For one thing, there were a number of black U.S. citizens working for the ICC. Some five hundred had been recruited during the early years, almost all on the Silver Roll. It had been hoped that they would be good at "managing" the West Indians. But the authorities soon realized they had made a mistake—the American blacks were far less malleable and passive than the imported "third-country" workforce. As a West Indian writes, "The majority of them were employed as team drivers, and when delivering goods would refuse to unload same, claiming they were no labourers, they were team drivers. They also were tutoring the other employees to act accordingly. In the view of the fact, they were sent back home." "We had colored Americans working, good men, skilful men," remembered another West Indian. "But they can't pull with the White Americans always a fight and trouble." Furthermore, the small number on Gold Roll contracts vigorously protested when, as blacks, they were refused service at Gold Commissaries, or ordered to take off their hats "although no such requirement is made of white employees." Consequently, to preserve the color criterion that underpinned the Gold/Silver distinction, no more U.S. blacks were given Gold Roll contracts, and by February 1909 only one such employee remained, a Henry Williams.

So by 1908 there were hardly any nonwhite Gold employees left, but when Taft made his nationality order as far as Gold and Silver was concerned, it opened a can of worms for the authorities. Soon after, Goethals received a petition from ten Silver Roll American blacks complaining that as U.S. citizens they were entitled to the lavish Gold Roll privileges. After much discussion among the top brass, a compromise was decided on whereby the men were given home and sick leave entitlements, were paid in gold, but were still officially Silver Roll and thus excluded from clubhouses and commissaries.

Another protestor, Henry W. Scott, proved more of a handful. In early January 1910, he complained that he had been denied a foreman position in the Pacific Division because, he was told, "he was colored and not eligible for employment on the Gold Roll." Utterly fed up, he now wanted a job in Panama City, where the "prejudice feeling" did not exist "as on the Canal Zone." "My father having performed distinguished service in the Civil War. And on behalf of the twelve million American colored people and taxpayers, I most respectfully make application for one of the above places," he ended. But he had also been in touch with his senator back in the States, Wesley L. Jones, who, it turned out, had fought with his father in the Civil War. Jones wrote to Goethals, "Mr. Scott is part colored but I understand he is a young man of splendid ability."

Goethals had to tread carefully. Not only was the racial segregation of the Zone legally dubious, but also the Republican Party had sold itself as the defender of the blacks. He wrote back to the senator on January 24, 1910: "The fact of his being an American citizen does not entitle him to employment on the gold roll, as employment on the gold and silver rolls, respectively, depends entirely upon the class of work our employees do and not upon their nationality or color."

Cases like this highlight the confusions, contradictions, and hypocrisy of the Gold/Silver distinction. Happily for the authorities, the number of these awkward American blacks continued to dwindle. In July 1912 there were only sixty-nine at work for the ICC. The following year, only fifteen remained and this threat to the "logic" of the system was almost gone.

◄◄◄◄— —►►►►

*L*ater generations of Panamanian Antilleans, when looking at the actions of the American blacks or the Spaniards, would accuse their West Indian "silvermen" fathers and grandfathers of passivity during the construction period in the face of poor working conditions and the discriminatory policies of the canal authorities. Certainly, there would be no organized West Indian labor resistance until well after the canal was finished and the workforce much depleted. But many factors weighed against concerted labor action during the construction period. For one thing, there was still a surplus of labor on the islands. At the end of 1907 over two thousand men were actually laid off at the completion of the building work, and by the end of 1909 Karner could pack up his recruiting operation in Barbados as labor needs were more than being met by independent emigration. The result was a pool of some five thousand unemployed and usually desperate West Indians living in Colón or elsewhere from which the ICC could draw as and when it liked. As the *Star and Herald* noted, every man had "the knowledge that there are ten hungry applicants for each vacancy who will like the conditions well enough." Furthermore, there was little tradition of organized labor in the islands, and the West Indian community was, for now, divided by loyalty to individual islands.

The West Indians were also kept in line by the vigorous and often

violent efforts of the Zone police to punish even the mildest infringement. If this was not enough to curtail organized action, there
was the daily struggle to make ends meet when often three-quarters
of a wage would have to be spent on rent. There was also the exhausting fight against malaria, pneumonia, other diseases, and the effects of accidents. The West Indian accounts nearly all tell of at least
one stay in the hospital, often many more. By 1914, Gorgas's sanitation squads had drained more than a hundred square miles of swamp
through the building of nearly two thousand miles of ditches and
drains. But although infection and mortality rates kept on falling,
malaria and its recurring symptoms of agonizing fever and shaking,
followed by mind-numbing lethargy, would continue to affect many
of the inhabitants of the Zone. In 1914, nearly half the workforce,
over 24,000 people, were admitted to the hospital at some time during the year for a variety of illnesses or accidents.

The two simplest explanations for the lack of West Indian protest
or action against the ICC's regime were provided by a resident of
Colón, Mr. Foster Burns, who in 2004 was 104 years old. First, he said
plainly, the men wanted and needed the money. However it looks
now, work on the canal was the best get-rich (or at least stop-being-
hungry) scheme on offer. Second, the men were so busy working that
they had no time or energy left for anything else. This certainly rings
true. Although most American employees—with the exception of a
few foremen and doctors—were limited to an eight-hour day by a law
of Congress, Stevens had secured a special clause exempting "alien"
labor on the canal from this stipulation, so the West Indians worked
ten hours a day for six days a week. And this was before overtime (often compulsory and unpaid) and the journey to and from work.

The actual labor was usually backbreaking, and frequently carried
out, of course, in very difficult conditions. There were few cushy jobs
available to the black workers. Albert Peters tells of how being assigned to a dredge involved having to continually dive into the
muddy, slimy water to free the suction pump. In the burning heat or
ankle-deep mud of "Hell's Gorge," thousands carried heavy and dan-

gerous dynamite boxes, manned the largest and most violent drills ever seen, and stoked suffocating, red-hot steam furnaces on shovels or locomotives. And from 1909 onward, an increasing proportion of the laborers were working on the giant locks—the "concrete cathedrals"—being built at either end of the central "bridge of water." Here the work was, if anything, even more dangerous and unpleasant than in the Cut.

"LORD HOW PIERCING!"

It had been the "monstrous experiment" of the plan for the Gatún Dam that had attracted most criticism in the United States. In fact, there was nothing unprecedented about the dam apart from its scale. More justified were worries about its siting—over two deep geological gorges filled with dubious alluvial material. The plan was to block the Chagres valley at Gatún with an enormous, essentially earth structure one and a half miles long. The height was adjusted in the course of the building, but ended up being 115 feet above sea level, 30 feet above the planned level of the lake at 85 feet above sea level. At its top it was to be 100 feet wide, then 500 feet at the lake's surface and almost half a mile wide at the bottom. Between the two gorges across the dam site was a hill of solid rock, which would serve to anchor the structure and to provide the site for the spillway, through which the waters of the Chagres would be funneled and thence flow to the sea at San Lorenzo. Consisting of a convex wall 800 feet long and nearly 100 feet high, the spillway was to be the new jailer of the formidable Chagres River. For the planned locks to work properly, it was important that the level of the new river should not deviate from its 85-foot level by more than 2 feet. Within the wall of the spillway were a series of openings with massive steel gates. When all the gates were lifted, the spillway could cope with a discharge of 182,000 feet per second, judged to be the worst that the Chagres could throw at it. Next to the spillway a hydroelectric station was planned, to generate enough electrical current from the falling water to supply all the canal's energy needs. The triple-tiered double locks would be built at the dam's eastern end.

The dam itself was well suited to the height and length requirements of the chosen site, but more important it was to be constructed largely of the materials excavated from elsewhere along the canal line. A dam in concrete would have been equally feasible, but a great deal more expensive. Earth dams are not complex structures and are sometimes also referred to as gravity dams, because that is exactly how they perform; the resultant lake is held back purely by the huge mass of the dam and thus the friction at the base between the dam structure and the existing ground on which it is founded. The principle of earth dams is based on the fact that most clays are impervious. To construct such a dam, one builds in layers. First, outer walls of hard rock are laid down on both the upstream and down-stream faces. This is to hold the earth and clay filler in the construction phase, but also to protect against scour in the permanent case (from the lake on the upstream face and storm water on the down-stream). The next layer inside both faces is then normally constructed of soil and smaller rocks/stones, and then the central core is composed exclusively of appropriate clay. The clay can either be placed "dry" and compacted using rollers, or liquefied and pumped in. As the slurry drains and dries it will harden and become impervious.

At first all went well. To prevent organic matter forming a potentially porous layer under the dam, the six-hundred-acre site had to be meticulously cleared of its rich cover of tropical jungle. This task was completed by the end of 1907, and the dam site was barren. It reminded one visitor of the scene of a battle in some unimaginable war to come: "an ugly denuded waste of land . . . stubble was everywhere, and standing out like pockmarks were hundreds of black ash heaps where the greenery had been burned. Across this soggy wasteland . . . a dredge in the Chagres sucked mud from one place and vomited it into another; and dynamite crews sent up enormous geysers of rock and water. Men in gangs of forty to a hundred swarmed about the valley, all in the blue shirts and khaki trousers of the Zone Commissary, while the air was filled with the babel of more than twenty languages." As well as the dam site, it was necessary to clear all the large trees from the future route of the shipping lane through Lake Gatún. Barbadian Edgar Simmons described this process: up to fifteen holes were cut in the trunks of the trees, which were then stuffed with explosives: "Three sticks of dynamite, with a cap and coil, about 18 inches long, and covered with mud. So all are set for evening," he wrote. "After the 5:15 passenger train pass for Panama, we start lighting. Some of us has up to 65 or 72 holes to light . . . Nine of us start out, each one with two sticks of fire in our hand, running and lighting, at the same time trying to clear ourselves before the first set begin bursting on us. Then it's like Hell . . . it was something to watch seeing the pieces of trees flying in the air."

In 1907 the Chagres flowed through four routes to the sea: its old riverbed, the French canal, and the two diversion channels the French had built either side of their waterway. All four flowed through the site of the new dam. The Western Diversion was the lowest and this was widened and deepened, while the other three channels were dammed without any complications. The plan was to start work on the eastern end of the dam and the spillway, and then close the West Diversion when it was time for the river to be diverted through the spillway.

Shovels started cutting a channel through Spillway Hill while suction dredges thoroughly cleaned out the old river and canal beds. Then two parallel lines of trestles were erected at 30 feet above sea level along the upriver and downriver faces of the dam some 4,000 feet apart. On these were laid rail tracks to carry cars of rocks to create the two stone "toes" that would hold the innards of the dam in place. Locomotives from Culebra or the Mindi Hills started arriving regularly and slowly the rock walls began to crawl across the wide valley. Meanwhile a suction dredge began pumping in between the walls a mixture of clay and water sucked up from the bed of the old French canal behind the dam site. Toward the end of 1908 a solid wall of rock, 60 feet high, had been laid out along the extremities of the dam.

Back in the States, the doubters were still vociferous, and now Bunau-Varilla had added his comments: water would seep through, emptying the lake, he said; the dam should have been located at Bohío (as per the French lock plan), where there was better bedrock; Gatún Dam would develop fissures and would be damaged by even a light earthquake. Then, at end of November came the news that everybody had been dreading. "Collapse of the Gatún Dam" read one headline in the United States. "Chagres River plunges through Gap in Isthmian Wall." It turned out that an American journalist in Panama had noticed that a large section of the southern "toe," some

200 feet, had slipped by 20 feet where it crossed the line of the old French canal. Goethals denied any serious problem and was backed up by John Stevens, who wrote an article denouncing "the outbreak of yellow fever journalism in regard to the Gatún Dam."

But with their predictions of doom seemingly confirmed, the press kept the story running. The *New York Times*, a longtime enemy of Roosevelt and his Panama route, declared that the canal had to be begun anew at Nicaragua. Taft was quickly dispatched to Panama with some experts in tow to find out the truth about the dam. He confirmed Goethals's line that the slip was not serious, and rounded on critics of the great project, accusing them of creating a "fire in the rear . . . calculated to break down the nervous system of those persons on the Isthmus working day and night, tooth and toenail to build the greatest enterprise of two centuries."

The damage to the "toe" was repaired, and early in 1909 the first concrete was poured at the spillway site. Throughout the year, the massive dam structure began to take shape, rising to block the valley. By the end of 1910 four dredges and more than ten locomotives were at work, adding between them over a million cubic yards a month to the mass of the dam. As the new chasm was being created in the Cut, much of the spoil removed ended up as the new mountain at Gatún. The peak year of building was 1911, when there were two thousand men at work and over a hundred trainloads of rock and earth were being dumped every day. There were further alarms: in October 1911, 1,000 feet of the dam's eastern end settled a few feet, and in August the following year about 800 feet of the crest of the dam dropped 20 feet. On other occasions, as with the walls of the Cut, the dam writhed and twisted as it sought a new equilibrium, wrecking track and threatening the lives of the locomotive drivers. But these were largely movements within the fill, rather than a slip of the entire structure, and as the clay center of the dam dried out and hardened, so the period of greatest danger passed.

With the Panama Railroad relocated on higher ground, it was time to start filling the new lake. At the end of April, preparations were complete for the closing off of the West Diversion. The engineers knew that the final taming of the Chagres River would not be easy. For one thing, delays meant that the river level was 7 feet above its lowest dry-season level, and more rains were on the way. Furthermore, the West Diversion ran directly over a deep gorge, with mud to great depths. It was also about 20 feet lower than the bottom of the spillway, through which the river was now to be directed. This meant that the river would need to rise by this height before it would begin to find the new outlet.

Huge trestles were driven into the mud of the channel, and hundreds of flatcars, loaded with rock from Culebra, were readied nearby. The plan was simply to unload the rock into the current faster than it could be washed away.

Starting at either side, rocks were dumped from the trestles around the clock for four days. Initially, all was fine, but as the channel contracted, the flow picked up power and pace. When it had shrunk to 80 feet wide and 6 feet deep, as fast as the spoil was dumped it was washed away. Even rocks weighing a ton were lifted up and carried off by the powerful Chagres current. A great mass of old twisted French rails was brought up to the site and thrown off the trestle into the open section. As predicted, the rails snarled on the trestle piles, forming a web that started to catch and hold the bigger rocks. But this also transferred huge pressure onto the trestle itself, which groaned and trembled, then broke, with parts starting to move downstream. The water rushed through again, and parts of the surviving dam slid and collapsed.

But the battle was not lost. Men clambered out onto the trestles to repair them, more cars were brought up frantically to dump rock, and a dredge started pumping clay upstream of the dam breach to reduce the force on the trestles. Finally the dam held, and as the water at last found the outlet of the heavily regulated spillway, the destructive force of the Chagres, the bane of the French effort, was gone forever.

With the West Diversion closed, the water was allowed to back up and the lake began to rise at 2 inches a day. Eventually the water would cover 164 square miles of jungle, as well as several villages and much of the digging of the French. Some villagers refused to move out and had to be forcibly evicted. For many of them the drowning of the Chagres valley was like a biblical flood. A way of life based on the river, which long predated Columbus's first voyage, was coming to an end. "It is not hard to realize why the bush native does not love the American," wrote Harry Franck, who took a trip out on the growing lake in a police launch in mid-1912. "Suppose a throng of unsympathetic foreigners suddenly appeared resolved to turn all the world you knew into a lake, just because that absurd outside world wanted to float steamers you never knew the use of, from somewhere you never heard of, to somewhere you did not know."

⟨⟨⟨⟨⟨─⟩⟩⟩⟩⟩

The first task in constructing the locks had been to excavate to bedrock the basins in which they were to be built. For Gatún, this meant digging a hole a mile and a quarter long, 200 yards wide, and 50 feet deep—the removal of nearly 7 million cubic yards of rock and silt. Most difficult was the lowest of the three basins, whose bottom was 66 feet below sea level, and whose sides constantly slipped. As the engineer in charge wrote, "No one expected on returning to work in the morning to find things as they were left the evening before." Even though there were temporary dams at both ends of the lock basins, there was a constant danger of seepage and floods. American Harry Cole worked on the locks on the Pacific side—one pair at Pedro Miguel, two at Miraflores. In the lowest basin on the Miraflores locks—"an extremely dangerous place to work"—he experienced the same problems. "Sometimes, in the rainy season," he wrote, "even the small rivers became large rivers and often overflowed and inundated much of the construction work, putting even our drainage pumps out of action. Canal banks would break loose, cover up lock wall foundations, fill up culverts, submerge railroad service tracks and cause weeks of delay to clean up and put the work in order again. Those were our heart-breaking times."

As excavation continued on the lower basins, in late 1909 actual construction started on the completed upper basin of the Gatún Locks. The lock component of the 1906 plan had attracted almost as much criticism as the dam. Certainly, the locks were a gamble. Nothing of the sort even remotely as large had been built before, and the choice of concrete as the primary building material, mainly to save time, was even more daring. Today, concrete technology is an industry in its own right, as it can be a more difficult material to work with than it first seems. In the early 1900s little was known about the properties of concrete and the basic materials (sand, gravel, cement, and water) were simply thrown together in a fairly fixed proportion, mixed, and poured. That the locks at the Panama Canal are still working nearly a hundred years later without any major problem in the concrete is testament to the standard of design and construction employed.

The structural design of the locks was unremarkable. They were to be constructed of "mass concrete," that is, there was to be little use of steel reinforcement bars. This type of structure, like the Gatún Dam, relies mainly on the enormous mass of material present to withstand the loads imposed upon it. In fact, the sidewalls of the locks are structurally similar to miniature dams. The massive width of the bottom of the wall, some 50 feet, creates an equally large frictional resistance to the force of the water pushing against it when the lock is full. The wall becomes thinner and thinner as the height increases and the applied hydraulic force reduces.

The key to building a major concrete structure was the same as that for the excavation works at the Cut: creating an organized and balanced production line. In this, Goethals was equally as successful at the locks as Stevens had been in the Culebra Cut. To build any concrete structure, the wet concrete must be poured into giant "molds," referred to as shutters. Traditionally, these are made of wood. In massive structures such as the Panama locks, using wood becomes extremely wasteful, time-consuming, and thus expensive, as the molds can only be used two or three times before being scrapped. Goethals therefore opted to use shutters made of steel, which has a very high initial cost, but a relatively low total lifetime cost. Such a shutter weighed many hundreds of tons and constituted a major feat of precise manufacture in itself. These main shutters were then mounted on rails, running parallel to the walls, so that they could be easily moved.

An enormous amount of concrete was required. For the Gatún Locks alone, 2 million cubic yards would be poured. The cement came from the States, about five million bags or barrels of it. Obviously it made sense to source the stone and sand from nearer to the site. The Commission sent a party to try to secure sand from San Blas, which although ninety miles from Colón, had the best quality for cement. But this area was inhabited by Cuna Indians, who had long memories: "They did not look with favour on visits from the white men, whom they suspected were searching not for sand but for gold," reported one of the engineers. The Americans were led before a seventy-year-old local chief, "seated on a block of timber, and he

A Traveling trolleys
B Machinery houses containing electrical operating apparatus
C Operators' cabs
D 2-cubic-yard bucket for placing concrete

E Double-track trestle from which the concrete buckets are served
F Side walls of locks, showing side wall and floor culverts
G Center wall and center wall culvert
H Operating tunnel

Chamber cranes at Miraflores

motioned his visitors to a seat on the sand at his feet. An air of great solemnity surrounded the proceedings." The visitors outlined their plans to connect the two oceans by a canal, and how this would bring a better price for the Indians' coconuts and ivory. "The Chief listened," the account continues, "but when the story was finished he said that God had given the Indians their country, the land and the water, and that which God had given to the Indians they would neither sell or give to the white man." That was his final word, and permission to anchor for the night was only granted on the condition that the Americans left the next morning and did not return. So the rock for the gravel, including old stones from the fortress of San Felipe de Todo Fierro, ended up coming from Portobelo, where a crushing plant was built, and the beach at Nombre de Dios was stripped of its sand, all to feed the voracious appetite of the Gatún Locks. On the Pacific side suitable rock and sand were found much closer to the lock sites, but to supply Gatún required barges negotiating the dangers of a sea journey of between twenty and forty miles. Any stoppages from bad weather would upset the brilliant mechanized system Goethals had now established to deliver the mixed concrete to where it was needed. Once the barges from up the coast arrived at Colón, they made their way up the newly redredged old French canal to Gatún, where unloading facilities and a mixing plant had been established. The concrete was assembled by the use of an ingenious system of small electric cars carrying buckets passing under hoppers containing sand, crushed stone, or cement. These would end up above one of the eight giant mixers, underneath which other similar cars waited for the finished concrete.

Spanning the site were four giant, 800-foot-long cableways, supported on either side of the great basin by towers 85 feet high. As each pair of buckets was filled with 6 tons of liquid concrete, the car moved off and was then picked up by a hook on the cableway and taken off to the site. At the same time, an empty skip returning from the site was set down on the railcar.

The system worked brilliantly. In one year a million cubic yards of concrete were delivered to be molded and set. The walls were built in 36-foot sections all the way to the top, which took about a week. Then the scaffolding, shutters, and cableway towers, all rail-mounted, were simply shifted along to the next section.

On the Pacific side concrete was batched on-site and lifted to the required position using a tower crane. Here even more concrete was used for the single lock at Pedro Miguel and the double tier at Miraflores. A small dam was also required at Miraflores in conjunction with the locks, forming the tiny Miraflores Lake, but this structure presented no serious difficulties.

The lock basins are the construction marvel of the canal. They are massive, a hundred thousand tons of concrete each, 1,000 feet long and more than 100 feet wide. Seen full of water they are impressive enough, but those who stood on the empty floor and gazed upward at the sheer, featureless walls, more than 80 feet high, taller than a six-story building, were awestruck. "These locks are more than just tons of concrete," commented one such visitor, "they are the gate to that pathway of which Columbus dreamed and for which Hudson died. They are the answer of courage and faith to doubt and unbelief. In them are the blood and sinew of a great and hopeful nation, the fulfillment of ancient ideals and the promise of a larger growth to come . . . I left with the feeling that follows a service in a great cathedral."

⟪⟪⟪-⟫⟫⟫

The mechanical marvel of the canal was the machinery of the locks. For one thing, the entire system was powered by electricity (supplied from the hydroplant next to the spillway), a great innovation at a time when steam- and horse-powered systems were the norm, and the electrification of factories was in its infancy. The power that did the hard work of lifting or lowering ships was, of course, gravity, the filling of a lock with water from the lake or a higher lock or the release of water to farther down the system. Water was drained or admitted through tunnels 18 feet in diameter, built lengthwise within the center and wide walls of the locks. Running perpendicular to these were smaller tunnels or culverts under the floors of the locks, fourteen per chamber. Each had five evenly spaced openings in to the floor, so that when water was admitted the turbulence would be minimized. The main culverts had large steel gates as valves. The principle was ancient: to fill a lock, the valve at the lower end would be closed and the upper one opened, and vice versa to drain it. Each lock had a lift of an unprecedented 28 feet, and the system aimed to raise or lower a ship this distance in just fifteen minutes.

Worries voiced in the U.S. press prompted the adoption of a series of stringent safety measures to avert the worst-case scenario of a ship smashing through the upper lock, causing the lake to pour through the breach. No ship would pass through the locks under its own steam. Instead the movement of the ships would be controlled by a group of powerful electrical cars, mounted on rails at the lock's edge, each in control through a windlass, a steel cable, attached to the ship. Each lock had a double gate, and a chain ran in front of the mouth of the top lock to catch and slow any vessel approaching in a dangerous way. Failing that, an emergency dam could be lowered across the channel within minutes.

All of the mechanisms for the lock operation were controlled from one position, where a working replica of the locks had been made, with the controls for each machine adjacent to its model. In addition, a system of safeguards meant that it was impossible, for instance, to open a culvert valve if the relevant lock gates were not firmly shut.

The manufacture of the lock gates was the only substantial part of the canal work that was subcontracted. A Pittsburgh firm, McClintic-Marshall, started assembly and installation in May 1911 at Gatún, August at Pedro Miguel, and at Miraflores in September 1912. The lock gates were designed to close into a flattened V. When open they slotted into a recess in the lock wall. Each individual gate was 65 feet wide and 7 feet thick and varied in height from 47 to 82 feet depending on its position. The highest were the bottom gates at Miraflores, which had to cope with the Pacific tides. The gates were opened and closed by giant wheels within the lock gates. These needed to be hugely powerful machines, but the gates weighed less than they looked. They were hollow, consisting of steel plates riveted on to a steel frame, and watertight so relatively buoyant. At their base were rollers, which ran on enormous steel plates embedded into the floor of the lock.

Few ships at that time needed anything like the space the giant locks provided, so intermediate gates were installed so that vessels less than 600 feet long could pass through more quickly and with less expenditure of water. So in all there were forty-six pairs constructed and installed. The great steel gates were one of the most spectacular sights on the Isthmus, particularly while the lock chambers were still empty and their huge size could be appreciated.

However, the work on the gates also figures, along with the explosion at Bas Obispo, as the worst memory of the construction period for the West Indian workers. The money was good—McClintic-Marshall paid US$0.25 an hour, more than double the basic labor wage—but the work was among the most dangerous anywhere. As a West Indian work song from the time had it:

Yuh gets more money for that job than working in the cut
But it all depends muh honey on if yuh don't get hut
For if you ever get a drop yuh surely have to die
For dem gates lawd gad gal is seventy five feet high.

In mid-1912, when work on the gates was well advanced, Harry Franck went to the Gatún Locks looking for a man accused of theft. "I found myself racing across the narrow plank bridges above the yawning gulf of the locks, with far below tiny men and toy trains, now in and out among the cathedral-like flying buttresses, under the giant arches past staring signs of "DANGER" on every hand . . . I descended to the very floor of the locks, far below the earth, and tramped the long half-miles of the three flights between soaring concrete walls ... On them resounded the roar of the compressed air riveters and all the way up the sheer faces, growing smaller and smaller as they neared the sky, were McClintic-Marshall men driving into place red-hot rivets, thrown at them viciously by negroes at the forges."

This was the worst job of all. The riveters, using heavy pneumatic hammers, worked on scaffolding that normally consisted of chains running down the face of the gate to which hooked planks were attached one above the other. There were four men per plank, and any sudden movement could unbalance and unhook the platform; if one came down from above, it usually took a few lower ones with it.

Eustace Tabois remembered a particularly gruesome accident at Gatún. "We were working there one Sunday," he said. "I was inside the gate, right at one of the portholes, and I just happened to look out. I saw a shadow come down like that. And when I look out I saw this man down below. The scaffold break away with him and he went right down and the plank down there with him a spike went right though his head. Kill him dead, kill him dead. Man used to die every day." "Scuffles would break away," said James Ashby, "hurting many and sometimes killing men instantly. Lord how piercing!" As another West Indian commented, "The family of those men working on those locks were always fearful as to who may be next to fall."

It was the same on the Pacific side. Jamaican Nehemiah Douglas was working on the giant gates at Miraflores when the cable holding his plank broke, "kill[ing] some men, on the spot. The amount of blood that flowed gave the appearance of a little gully," he later wrote, "and when I saw what appeared to be an island of blood, I got nervous, I think, because how I got down, I do not know; but I got down and ran like never run before, straight home in Paraiso." Many stayed away after witnessing incidents like this, even if they had pay to collect, but Douglas returned and was soon after hit by a crane and received a fractured skull.

Nevertheless, with the money that could be earned, men still "poured like sand" to go and work on the locks. However many were injured or killed, "there were always others to take their places without hesitation." This became more urgent as the project progressed. It was obvious that the well-paid work was not going to be around for that much longer. The canal project was now nearing its triumphant conclusion.

THE LAND DIVIDED, THE WORLD UNITED

During the four last years of construction, nearly 100,000 American and European visitors arrived in Panama to view work on the canal. Interest was so great that steamship lines diverted vessels from other routes to the Caribbean. At Ancón the Isthmian Canal Commission created a tourist station with a lecture room, relief maps, and models of the locks. Tourists could also visit the work site by taking a special train whose open sightseeing cars had been converted from Panama Railroad flatcars.

Back in the States, Tin Pan Alley was busy churning out hits such as "Where the Oceans Meet in Panama (That's Where I'll Meet You)" and "The Pamela," and the press eagerly reported, alongside sombre news of rising tensions in Europe, each and every landmark and breakthrough.

Work on the west breakwater from Toro Point in Limón Bay started in 1910. As the local rock was too soft to withstand the power of the "northers," 12- to 18-ton rocks were blasted from the quarry in Portobelo and shipped by sea to be dumped by barges along the outside of the breakwater line. Then a series of creosoted piles were driven in to form a trestle on the inland side. Next, local stone was loaded into flatcars, pushed out along the trestle, and unloaded by the plow method on the inside of the line of hard rock. Work progressed steadily and Colón became a safe harbor for the first time. The east breakwater caused more problems, mainly because the French had dredged deep channels across its line, but it was completed in 1915. The digging inland did not all go smoothly. At Mindi huge amounts of explosives were required to break up the rock, and there were constant problems from flooding. However, by the summer of 1912 only a small belt of land 1,000 feet wide separated the open Atlantic channel from the site of the Gatún Locks. By August 1913 it was the same at the other end of the canal, with just a dike holding the waters of the Pacific back from the Miraflores Locks.

Construction had also got under way for the running of the canal after completion. A new Administration Building was built at Balboa, as La Boca had been renamed, while on Toro Point and Margarita Island in Limón Bay and on the islands of Perico, Flamenco, and Naos in the Bay of Panama 16-inch guns were installed, the largest then in the possession of the United States military. Elsewhere, smaller-bore artillery was sited, along with mortar batteries, to repel a land-based attack. In all, some $15 million was spent on fortifying the canal from attack by sea or by land.

At 4:30 p.m. on May 20, 1913, shovels No. 222 and No. 230 met "nose to nose" at the center of the Cut. At 40 feet above sea level, the Cut had reached its full planned depth. The mighty shovels whirred and clanked to a stop and the men cheered and threw their hats in the air. Whistles were sounded all along the gorge and photographers recorded the event. Now all the shovels could concentrate on removing the massive slides from the eastern end of the Cut.

Further red-letter days followed thick and fast. On June 27, 1913, the last of the Gatún Dam spillway gates was closed, allowing the lake to now rise to its full height. On August 31, a Sunday, so that, Goethals suggested, "everyone could join the fun," a huge charge was exploded in the dike between the Miraflores Lock and the Pacific channel. The hundreds of spectators then settled back to wait for high tide at noon. The Pacific tide at Panama comes in fast. Soon it was pouring over the breach in the dike, and then rushing in, clearing the dam debris as it went. Then the waters of the Pacific were lapping at the closed gates of the Miraflores Lock. Two days later the same operation was completed for the barrier below the Gatún Locks. Steadily, waters from the two oceans were moving inland to meet each other.

The locks were all completed by the end of the following month, and the Gatún Lock had been successfully tested. But in the Cut the battle against the slides was not going well. The slopes at Cucaracha and Culebra had been cut back to as gentle as one in five, but the movement of earth and rocks into the canal prism continued. In October it was decided to flood the Cut and complete the excavation "in the wet" with dredges. In September, the last steam shovel was moved out, the rails lifted and carried away, and old ties piled up and burned.

The huge earthen dike at Gamboa, which separated the Cut from the rising lake, had six large pipes in its base. These were now opened, and water started to pour into the gorge. Everyone who had worked on the canal had imagined and pictured in his mind's eye the appearance of the Cut when full of water. Now it was happening. Then, on October 10, 1913, in a stunt dreamed up by a newspaperman, President Woodrow Wilson pressed a button in Washington and relayed by telegraph from Washington to New York to Galveston to Panama the signal that blew the center of the dike to complete the flooding of the Cut, and, it was hoped, blast a passage through the slides at the eastern end. Just before the signal was sent, Rose van Hardeveld remembers, "There was a reverent silence" among the hundreds gathered to witness the spectacle. "No one spoke at all." Then, "there was a low rumble, a dull muffled B-O-O-M! A triple column shot high in the center, turned, and fell gracefully to both sides like a fountain. From the multitude came a spontaneous long, loud roar of such joy and relief that I felt sure I would remember the sound all my life. As the water poured out of the lake into the Cut, hats came off." Rose and the children could see their father Jan shaking hands with his boss. Both men were crying.

As the fountain of earth cleared, the spectators could see a great wave sweep down the channel. At its crest rode two small launches and a native dugout, in fierce competition to see who would be the first to get to the Pedro Miguel Locks at the other end of the Cut. But they were in for a disappointment. At the mighty Cucaracha slide the water was stopped. The frustration was immense. Massive amounts of dynamite were used and dredges were brought up from the Atlantic through the Gatún Locks and across the lake to work away at the blockage from that side. But nothing seemed to work. The explosions threw rocks and earth in the air only for them to seemingly land back in the same place. But then the river came to the rescue. After heavy rain the Chagres began to flood. In three days the level of the lake had risen by 3 feet. A small trench was dug out by hand over the Cucaracha blockage, and a trickle of water began to flow across it. As the water bit into the mud, the stream increased to a torrent, further clearing rocks and mud from its path. Soon the dry section behind the blockage was full, and dredges from the Pacific side could start work on the slide from the other direction. Floodlights allowed round-the-clock digging. An old French ladder dredge made the "pioneer cut" through the slide on December 10, 1913, to open the channel for the first time. Although there were still millions of cubic yards of slide material to be removed before an oceangoing vessel could make the transit, the waters of the two oceans were now unmistakably united.

By April 1914, the channel was wide enough for tugs and boats to pass through it, and when an American Hawaiian Steamship Line vessel showed up in the Bay of Panama wanting to move a cargo of tinned pineapples and sugar from Hawaii across the Isthmus, Goethals was able to have it taken through by lighter. Others followed, and by June the canal had taken over $7,000 in tolls.

Practice continued, however, on dealing with larger ships in the locks. In June, an old Panama Railroad steamer locked up and down the Gatún tier very slowly and carefully but without mishap. Meanwhile plans were finalized for a grand celebration to mark the official opening of the Panama Canal, set for August 15, 1914. The boat given the honor of passing through the canal was the *Ancon*, another Panama Railroad steamer. This was to be followed by a fleet of international warships—symbolizing global concord—sailing through from the Atlantic to the Pacific, arriving in San Francisco in time for the opening of the Panama-Pacific International Exposition. Leading the fleet would be the *Oregon*, whose famous race round the Horn during the Spanish War had done so much in the United States to build a case for a publicly funded canal. On board this vessel would be the U.S. president himself.

There was a final practice run on August 3, using the *Ancon*'s sister ship, the *Cristobal*. Not everything went according to plan. The "mules" in the locks had great difficulty holding the ship, as one burnt out a motor and another had its cable snapped. Nevertheless, it was not these incidents that overshadowed the first interoceanic transit by a seagoing vessel. Toward the end of the trip news came through from Europe: Germany had declared war on France. Philippe Bunau-Varilla had returned to Panama for the canal's opening, and was on board the *Cristobal* with his daughter Giselle. As soon as he heard the news, he declared to the other passengers, "Gentlemen, the two consuming ambitions of my life are fulfilled on the same day. The first, to see an ocean liner sail through the Panama Canal: the second, to see France and Germany at war."

So just as the great civilizing quest of the Panama Canal was coming to an end and the United States was taking her place as a global power, "Old Europe" was embarking on a ruinous and bloody war. The ending of the Victorian world of de Lesseps, foreshadowed by the Panama story, was now complete. Although the Panama-Pacific Exposition went on as planned, the festivities at the canal were canceled. The *Ancon* still made the official first trip, but it was a muted affair. There were no international dignitaries in attendance. Observing the transit from shore, Goethals followed its progress by railroad. Claude Mallet was on board, however; he was surely the only man present at both the de Lesseps inauguration of the project on a boat in the Bay of Panama in early 1880, and also at the official opening thirty-four years later. He wrote in his memoirs, "The canal has been a life's work to me. As it progressed, I became more and more absorbingly interested in every detail of the enterprise."

"Everything went like clockwork," reported Winifred James, English wife of one of the *Ancon*'s guests. "On board were all the foremost Panamanian citizens and politicians, headed by the President of the Republic and his pretty wife. The ministers and consuls of the different Powers stood in groups together talking of the war and to the ladies alternately . . . We slid slowly up to the first lock and through it; and everybody looked at his watch and wondered when it would be breakfast time."

There was no razzmatazz, no music, only a few flags among the largely silent crowd lining the tops of the lock walls. On board, the guests were served "mugs of cold tea and dishes of broken meats." Occasionally someone would get a burst of energy and go around slapping people's backs, saying what a great day it was, but on the whole most remained solemn. According to Winifred James, "Not very late in the morning the Panamanians began to inquire" if there was anything to drink on the ship. There wasn't.

Because of the war, the news of the official opening, so long anticipated, was consigned to the inside pages. "The Panama Canal is open to the commerce of the world. Henceforth ships may pass to and fro through that great waterway," announced the *New York Times* on page fourteen. The *Philadelphia Record*, however, commented that the "Unostentatious dedicatory act [was] a more appropriate celebration of the triumph of the arts of peace than if it had been associated with martial pomp and an array of destroyers and battleships." The peaceful American "Army of Panama" had fought for its country well. "The practical completion of this great achievement wins little attention from a world intent upon war and the news from Belgium and Alsace," wrote another paper. "Americans should find solemn pride in the thought that they have added much to a world from which other nations are taking so much away." How much, of course, could not have been imagined.

The day after the opening, Winifred James came across a squad of Martinican ex-canal workers in uniform marching down to the station to entrain to Colón and thence to fight for France in the war with "the tricolor waving above them and the *Marseillaise* playing them on. Beside them walked their women," she wrote, "the older ones wearing the gaudy bandana of the Martinique woman, which is the gayest of all the turbans. They were, men and women alike, smiling a little in a hypnotized way, caught up in the trance of the music and the flying colors. Probably none would come back. But that was nothing: the band was playing and they were going to fight for their country."

POSTSCRIPT
Whose Canal Is It, Anyway?

Whatever the news agenda at the beginning of August 1914, the opening of the Panama Canal was an achievement, an epic battle won, which still thrills nearly a hundred years later. Regardless of the motivation or the means, the end result of cutting in two the eight-thousand-mile-long maritime barrier of the American continent fulfilled the dream of four hundred years. In 1914 scores of books and articles were published in the United States celebrating the great achievement of the American construction leadership. And rightly so. The completion of the canal was at the time history's greatest engineering marvel and a victory of man over nature that would not be matched until the moon landings.

When one considers that this world record–breaking construction was carried out in tropical conditions, in a previously disease-ridden area with endemic political unrest, with no local workforce and two thousand miles from home base, the achievement becomes even more impressive.

That six pairs of locks were constructed, from start to finish, in approximately four years is remarkable, and would be considered a perfectly reasonable time frame even today. The Gatún Dam, also, unlike the hastily and cheaply built Johnstown dam, was a solid, professional, and lasting piece of work. And by making the Chagres River an ally rather than an enemy of the canal, the Americans mastered a problem that had ruined the French effort.

So the United States engineers managed to complete in ten years a goal that had defeated the French for over twenty-two. Between 1881 and 1903, the two French companies removed 73 million cubic yards of spoil. Although the Americans took out only 14 million cubic yards during the difficult early years, from 1907 onward Goethals's "Army of Panama" moved an astonishing 219 million cubic yards. Much credit for this excavation must go to Stevens's Railroad-era workers. Stevens built the digging machine, having learned from the mistakes of Wallace; Goethals merely had to turn the handle and, now and then, tighten the screws.

Furthermore, the end product was vastly superior to anything conceived by the French. The fact that the canal is still, a hundred years later, a key artery of world commerce, is testimony to how the Americans "thought big."

The French failed, of course, because of disease and because they ran out of money. They were also unlucky, suffering floods, fires, and revolution on the Isthmus, as well as the financial mugging by Trenor Park of the Panama Railroad Company. But they massively underestimated the size of the task they had taken on. De Lesseps's first calculation of the amount of excavation needed for the sea-level plan was only a quarter of that removed by the Americans for their lock-canal project. Furthermore, the sea-level plan, the culmination of centuries of wishful thinking about the Isthmus, was simply impossible—the slides in the Cut would have been even worse if the digging went down another 60 or 70 feet. As Goethals commented, there was simply not enough money in the world to pay for such a plan. For a private company looking for a return on its investment, it was hopeless.

The Americans, as has been seen, repeated many of the mistakes of the French, but they also had key advantages in addition to their much more reliable financial backing. Crucial to the morale of the white American workforce was the defeat of yellow fever and taming of malaria, made possible by discoveries that largely postdated the de Lesseps effort. The presence of the U.S. military and their firm grip on Panamanian politics meant that the Americans suffered none of the political instability, revolution, and violence that the French had to work around, in spite of the long-established local antipathy toward the "Yankees." Advances in precision manufacturing, assembly-line production, and steel technology, driven in part by the naval armaments and motor industries, meant that the U.S. machinery was far superior to that of the French. The Bucyrus shovels were capable of excavating at a rate three or four times greater than that of the best French machines. The Americans also had better drills and explosives and superior expertise in railroad transportation. And in Stevens and Goethals they found determined and accomplished leadership.

For all Theodore Roosevelt's bellicosity, the war against the Panama jungle and mountains would be the only battle he would fight as president. On several occasions—the choice of the Panama route, the creation of the Republic of Panama, the backing of Gorgas, and the choice of the lock and lake plan—his intervention was decisive. Certainly, Roosevelt was in no doubt where the credit should go. In 1908, as he was preparing to leave office, he wrote of the canal project to a newspaper editor in London: "This I can say absolutely was my own work, and could not have been accomplished save by me or by some man of my temperament." Out of office, he was even more boastful, saying to an audience at the University of California at Berkeley in 1911, "I am interested in the Panama Canal because I started it. If I had followed traditional, conservative methods I would have submitted a dignified State paper of probably 200 pages to Congress and the debates on it would have been going on yet; but I took the Isthmus, started the canal and then left Congress not to debate the canal, but to debate me and in portions of the public press the debate still goes on as to whether or not I acted properly in getting the canal but while the debate goes on the canal does too." What was key, Roosevelt pronounced in his autobiography, was that "somebody [namely, himself] was prepared to act with decision."

The speech in California, quoted and misquoted in newspapers across the United States, caused a sensation, and reignited the controversy of America's role in the "Panama Revolution." The whole affair, argued a contributor to the *North American Review* in 1912, had been a "Chapter of National Dishonor." A prominent U.S. historian described it as "an affront to international decency." Alfred Mahan himself replied to these attacks, writing, "The summary ejectment of Colombia from property which she could not improve herself, and against the improvement of which by another she raised frivolous obstacles, is precisely in line with transactions going on all over the world . . . India, Egypt, Persia, Tripoli, Tunis, Algiers, Morocco, all stand on the same general basis as Panama." Their occupation, he went on, was part of the "advance of the world."

Many Americans agreed that the ends justified the means, but most were uneasy about this sort of high-flown imperialism, especially after difficulties from "insurgents" persisted in the Philippines and Cuba. In fact, Democratic Party policy was now that Colombia had a legitimate grievance for the loss of Panama, and after the 1910 midterm elections they had a majority in the House of Representatives. So when Roosevelt made his "I took the Isthmus" speech, a resolution was introduced and approved calling for a fresh congressional investigation into the whole affair. There were also renewed protests and demands for international arbitration from Colombia, and this time, with Roosevelt off the scene, they were heard sympathetically. In 1911 the Taft administration sent James du Bois to Bogotá to secure an agreement.

The envoy was shocked at the strength of feeling in Colombia. "Confidence and trust in the justice and fairness of the United States, so long manifested, has vanished completely," he reported back to

Washington the following year. He also found the country's leadership to be nothing like Roosevelt's famous description: "instead of 'blackmailers' and 'bandits' the public men of Colombia compare well with the public men of other countries in intelligence and respectability," he wrote. "I deplore Colonel Roosevelt's bitter and misleading attack."

In 1914 the Wilson government offered Colombia a "sincere apology" and an indemnity of $25 million, but such was the vehemence of Roosevelt's attack on this measure that Congress backed off ratifying the new treaty. Then, in January 1919, Roosevelt died, and a major impediment to the deal was removed. There was also a new and powerful incentive to repair relations with Bogotá—what was thought at the time to be the world's largest reserve of oil had been found under the soil of Colombia, and the Anglo-Dutch company Shell looked set to control the supply. So with Colombia's permission to remove the clause stating "sincere regret," the treaty was ratified in early 1921 under Harding's Republican administration, and the $25 million, dubbed "canalimony" by one wit, was paid over.

Doubtless the agreement had as much to do with oil reserves and other business opportunities in Latin America as it did with righting a past wrong. U.S. investment in Colombia increased tenfold in the eight years after the deal. But for the *New York World* the paying of the indemnity was a vindication of the newspaper's investigation into "a most sordid and shameless conspiracy into which Theodore Roosevelt had dragged the United States Government in order to satisfy his personal ambition." "The most flagrant act of Prussianism in the history of the United States," the paper concluded, "is now definitely repudiated by the political party that ardently defended it for nearly eighteen years."

<<<<-->>>>

On August 24, 1914, the *Pleiades* steamed into New York to be met by a cacophony of whistles from all the ships in the harbor. The vessel and its cargo, 5,000 tons of lumber and general merchandise, was unremarkable enough. What had caused the outbreak of celebrations was that the *Pleiades* was the first ship to trade between San Francisco and New York via the new canal. In her fourteen years plying the trade routes of the world, it was her most profitable trip yet. The canal had shaved nearly eight thousand miles off the journey between the two cities, almost halving the time at sea. Now two voyages could be made in the time of one. The benefits of the canal for U.S. trade and shipping were there for all to see.

The first years of the canal, however, saw continuing challenges. Two months after the transit of the *Pleiades*, a huge slide at east Culebra completely blocked the channel in half an hour. As before, Goethals, still in charge, ordered his dredges and shovels to dig it all out once more, but the following year saw more slides and the waterway blocked again for all but the smallest vessels, this time for seven months, and President Wilson was forced to return to a two-ocean navy, exactly what the canal had been built to avoid.

In fact, the problem of slides was never solved. All the canal maintenance teams could do was to remove the spoil and keep their fingers crossed. As recently as 1974, 250,000 cubic yards slid into the Cut, reducing it to one-way traffic and costing more than $2 million to remove.

The canal was also sporadically closed when, during the dry season, the level of Lake Gatún fell below that needed to operate the locks. So early 1935 saw the completion of a new structure at Alhajuela, the Madden Dam, which held a higher, secondary reserve of water to hold back extreme floods and to feed the larger, lower lake when necessary.

When it was found that the new aircraft carriers were too wide for the locks, the United States army engineers started work on two giant new lock basins at either end of the canal. But with America's entry into World War II, the project was shelved. By the end of the war, the United States fleet was so vast that the canal's original purpose—avoiding having to support a two-ocean navy—had been outgrown,

although much use was made of the canal for ferrying men and materials for the Korean and Vietnam wars. Just as useful strategically
were the army and air force bases in the Zone, from which U.S. power
could be (and was) projected throughout Central America and northern South America.

The canal is now Panama's after two generations of struggle
against the United States to regain control of their country. The bases
are gone, and the canal has returned to the peaceful purpose always
intended by idealists like Humboldt and de Lesseps. The checkpoints
that prevented Panamanians from driving into the Zone are still there
but abandoned and dilapidated, and the neat rows of identical houses
for the U.S. administrators and military are now home to Panamanians, who, with their "dislike of uniformity," have been busy person-
alizing them, adding scruffy lean-tos or extending verandas in a
higgledy-piggledy fashion.

Opponents of the 1999 handover argued that the Panamanians
would be unable to run the canal efficiently, but they have been
proved wrong. Canal improvements have continued steadily and
threats to the water supply, so vital for the huge locks, have been addressed. Now the ACP, the Autoridad del Canal de Panamá, has proposed an ambitious plan to build two giant new lock systems at either
end of the canal to cope with the increasing number of post-
Panamax container ships and the currently vast traffic from manufacturing centers in East Asia to the United States' East Coast. Work
began in 2007.

While wishing the project well, it is impossible to avoid hearing
echoes of the canal's long history. There is a Technical Commission
of international worthies (who even considered a sea-level scheme);
the work will be done, it is planned, by machines rather than men; by
2025 the enlarged capacity will be contributing eight times the canal's
current $500 million annual payment to the Panama treasury, or, as
William Paterson said three hundred years ago, "trade will increase
trade, and money will beget money."

⪻⪻⪻⫸⫸⫸

ℬetween 1904 and 1914 the U.S. government paid out about $400 million for its canal. It was not until the 1950s, however, that the venture started showing a profit, far longer than private capital would have required. There were, of course, other costs as well. According to the official figures, just over six thousand employees died in ICC hospitals during the American construction period, of whom about three hundred were from the United States. As we have seen, this overall figure is likely to be an underestimate. Those who suffered most were the humble "silvermen."

At the end of the construction period, some of the canal workers had made good, some had not. A number did return home, however, with a large enough nest egg to buy some land, or set up a small business, or just to impress their friends. "The returned Panama Canal labourer is an uncommonly vain fellow," commented one observer in Barbados. "He struts along in all the glory of a gay tweed suit, a cylindrical collar and a flaring necktie." Like "Colón Man" in Jamaica a generation before, returnees to Barbados brought with them a less subservient attitude and a new cosmopolitanism. They would be at the forefront of the social upheavals of the 1920s and 1930s that eventually led to political decolonization. Also, support for Marcus Garvey's Universal Negro Improvement Association would be strongest among those who had worked in Central America. Garvey had worked as a newspaper editor in Colón during the last years of the construction period, and his approach was characterized by internationalism, accentuating the identity of interests among blacks all over the world in place of narrow national loyalties. He was also a materialist—"Wealth is strength, wealth is power," he wrote—and saw the Panama money earned by the blacks as a liberating force.

But not everyone returned home with their pockets rattling with coins. Jamaican Z. McKenzie remembered that "the completion of the waterway Brought great Desolation on the W.I. [West Indian] employees . . . The wage during the Canal Construction was so small that we could not put by any Savings in the Bank. Hence the majority of us left empty handed, to live or die." In fact many were like Albert Bannister, who wrote, "I would be glad to go home but I can't go home empty handed." Some 45,000 Barbadians went to Panama, and of these only about half returned home at the end of the construction period. Barbados had a population of only 200,000, so the effect on the island was dramatic. For one thing, the planters no longer had the pool of cheap labor that had sustained their inefficient practices. And even more than in Jamaica a generation before, the demographics of the country were radically altered. As late as 1921 there were less than 400 males per 1,000 females on the island.

Of those who did not return, some enlisted in the British or French armies and were shipped to Europe. Others took jobs on the United Fruit or the sugar plantations in Guatemala, Cuba, and South America. A large number also stayed in Panama, of whom about 7,000 were kept on in the employ of the canal, often at lower wages than they had been paid during the construction period. Their treatment by the canal authorities was pretty much consistent with what had gone before, with the Gold/Silver Roll system as firm as ever and strikers or activists ruthlessly deported. If anything, some of them comment, it was worse, as the esprit de corps of the construction period did not last. They were also targeted by nationalist Panamanians, who from the 1930s and 1940s onward tried to purge their country of non-Hispanic elements.

Saddest of all, perhaps, was the treatment of the old-timers who had worked during the construction and then stayed with the canal for the rest of their working lives. Initially, there was no pension at all, then in the 1930s the canal authorities offered the men "disability relief" of one dollar a month per year worked, up to a maximum of $25. Inspectors would come to their houses and if they had possessions of any value, or if another family member worked, this sum was reduced.

One man who had worked for thirty-eight years for the canal, without a single week's holiday and having suffered numerous injuries in the course of his work, was told that he was to be retired and was given fifteen days' notice to quit his Canal Zone quarters. He eventually found a small apartment in Colón for $25 a month, which was the sum total of his pension. His son described in 1946 how his father was "receiving not enough to live a comfortable life for his remaining days. Broken in body and spirit, he calmly smokes his faithful old pipe waiting for the call of his Maker."

"Who dug the canal?" asks Jules LeCurrieux. "Who suffered most even until now? Who died most? Who but the West Indian negroes." LeCurrieux worked from 1906 to 1938, in the course of which he was blinded in one eye while building the relocated railroad. When he was "retired," he received $17.50 a month, "which was too small to live on."

Many of the letters to the "Competition for the Best True Stories . . ." held in 1963, contain pathetic pleas for help with subsistence. A doctor who treated a lot of the old-timers in their last days told how the majority had chronic health problems not caused by the difficult conditions in which they had worked, but, shockingly, from malnutrition.

Most of the West Indians signed off their accounts for the competition with mixed feelings. Unlike the thousands who worked and died on the French canal, at least there was something to show for their efforts. As one digger put it, "I am glad to see that all my sweat, tears, and all those deaths were not in vain." Having been part of the great achievement of the canal was a source of great pride. "It is a job well done," wrote one Jamaican, "and a help to mankind." "I got to be a man," said another.

Harrigan Austin, who had arrived in 1905 hungry enough to attack bags of sugar on the wharf, wrote about the "untold benefits to the world at large" that the canal brought. " 'Tis reasonable in any big war or any such projects as this, something will happen," he went on. "Some must suffer for the good and welfare of the others for where there is no Cross there may be no Crown . . . Thank God, the canal has been finished and has become a blessing to the world at large. A great accomplishment, the work of a Great Nation—May God Bless America."

George Martin, who looked back fondly on the days when he could afford ham and ice-cream, concluded: "The work of the construction days was a hard and rough struggle, but it was done cheerfully, and faithfully; thus giving the American people their hearts' desire."

Other old-timers were less gracious about their treatment. Benjamin Jordan, who back in 1905 had lied about his age to get selected for a Karner contract, testified in 1984 that although he had not let the "discrimination take hold" of him, there were now, at the end of his life, feelings that he could no longer "put in a corner." "For my years with the Panama Canal," he said, "there is a feeling that I have not been treated as I should. I still enjoy life, like some of the others who survived. The fact still remains: much blood was spilt, and no one cared about it. But I'm still alive, under God's care and will always remember: the good that you do lives with you."

NOTES

Abbreviations
FO Public Record Office, Kew, London, Foreign Office Records.
RG Record Group, National Archives, Suitland, Maryland.
MCCZ Manuscript Collection of the Canal Zone Library-Museum, Library of Congress, Washington, DC.

Preface: The Battle to Build the Canal
xxi   **Bahamas-born Albert Peters** Isthmian Historical Society, "Competition for the Best True Stories of Life and Work on the Isthmus of Panama During the Construction of the Panama Canal," Balboa, 1963, Box 25 MCCZ.
xxi   **Alfred Dottin,** in "Competition for the Best True Stories."
xxi   **Constantine Parkinson** Ibid.
xxii   **"Some of the costs of the canal are here"** Franck, *Zone Policeman 88*, p. 85.
xxii   **"some sort of semi-slavery"** Harrigan Austin, in "Competition for the Best True Stories."
xxii   **"Many times I met death at the door"** J. T. Hughes, in "Competition for the Best True Stories."
xxii   **"We worked in rain, sun, fire"** Prince Green, in "Competition for the Best True Stories."

xxiii   **"greatest liberty ever taken with nature"** James Bryce, quoted in LaFeber, *The Panama Canal: The Crisis in Historical Perspective*, p. 4.

Chapter One: "The Keys to the Universe"

1   **"Do but open these doors"** National Library of Scotland, Adv MS83.7.3,f 44v.

5   **"shewing them the great maine sea"** Peter Martyr, *De orbe novo*. In Hakluyt, *Collection of the Early Voyages, Travels, and Discoveries*, vol. 5, p. 253.

6   **"If there are mountains there are also hands"** Enrique de Vedia, ed., *Historiadores primitivos de Indias*, vol. 1, p. 222.

7   **"would open the door to the Portuguese"** Quoted in Anguizola, *Philippe Bunau-Varilla*, pp. 3–4.

8   **"no mountain range at all"** Lionel Wafer, quoted in Duval, *From Cadiz to Cathay*, p. 10.

8   **"talks too much and raises people's expectations"** National Archives of Scotland, GD26/13/43/27.

9   **"Being starved and abandoned by the world"** Letter from Robert Drummond, August 11, 1699, National Library of Scotland: Adv Ms 83.7.3, f.22.

Chapter Two: Rivalry and Stalemate

12   **"I am assured . . . a canal appeared very practicable"** Jefferson, *Writings*, vol. 1, p. 518.

13   **"The American continents"** Quoted in Siegfreid, *Suez and Panama*, p. 224.

13   **"would immortalise a government occupied with the interests of humanity"** Humboldt, *Political Essay on the Kingdom of New Spain*, p. 77.

13   **Goethe, who** Quoted in Collin, *Theodore Roosevelt's Caribbean*, p. 129.

15   **"veritable capital of the world"** Quoted in Siegfreid, *Suez and Panama*, p. 223.

16   **"present a human barrier of such formidable power"** John A. Lloyd, "On the Facilities for a Ship Canal Communication . . . through the Isthmus of Panama," Institute of Civil Engineers, *Minutes of Proceedings*, vol. 9, 1850, p. 242.

16   **"superstitious . . . Billiards, cockpits, gambling and smoking"** Ibid., p. 59.

16   **A visitor from Bogotá in the 1830s** Castillero, *Historia de Panama*, p. 87.

17   **"an absurdity"** Quoted in Mack, *The Land Divided*, p. 128.

Chapter Three: Gold Rush

22   **"low, miserable town, of thirty thatched huts"** Hotchkiss, *On the Ebb*, p. 84.

22   **"The houses are only hovels"** "Across the Isthmus in 1850: The Journey of Daniel A. Horn," quoted in Perez-Penero, *Before the Five Frontiers*, p. 82.

22   **"Half are full-blooded negroes"** Quoted in Ibid., p. 84.

22   **"one of the filthiest places we ever saw"** Richards, ed., *California Gold Rush Merchant*, p. 7.

22   **"the birthplace of a malignant fever"** Marryat, *Mountains and Molehills*, pp. 1–3.

22 **"as disconcerting as hell"** John Easter Minter, *The Chagres: River of Westward Passage*, p. 238, quoted in Perez-Penero, *Before the Five Frontiers*, p. 85.

23 **"The eye does not become wearied"** Marryat, *Mountains and Molehills*, pp. 1–3.

23 **Some of the men carried as much as three hundred pounds** J. D. Borthwick, *Three Years in California*, p. 34, quoted in Brands, *The Age of Gold*, p. 81.

23 **"so like a nightmare"** Frémont, *A Year of American Travel*, p. 34.

23 **"the main street is composed almost entirely of hotels"** Marryat, *Mountains and Molehills*, p. 5.

24 **"I knew nothing of the great risk in traveling alone"** Julius H. Pratt, "To California by Panama in '49," *Century Illustrated Monthly Magazine* 41, no. 6, April 1891, pp. 915–17.

24 **"weak sway of the New Granada Republic"** Seacole, *Wonderful Adventures*, p. xx.

25 **"Terribly bullied"** Ibid., p. xx.

26 **"No imposing ceremony inaugurated"** Otis, *History of the Panama Railroad.*

26 **"It was a virgin swamp"** Ibid., p. 26.

27 **"carried his noonday luncheon in his hat"** Otis, *History of the Panama Railroad*, p. 12.

27 **"wore the pale hue of ghosts."** Seacole, *Wonderful Adventures*, p. 64.

Chapter Four: "A Natural Culminating Point"

28 **"intended to be, to a certain extent prohibitory"** Otis, *History of the Panama Railroad*, p. 24.

29 **"British consul's precarious corrugated iron dwelling"** Ibid., p. 58.

29 **"I thought I had never seen a more luckless, dreary spot"** Seacole, *Wonderful Adventures*, p. 64.

30 **"as filthy and odorous as any slavers"** Schott, *Rails across Panama*, p. 177.

30 **"We could name many persons"** Quoted in Senior, "The Panama Railway," *Jamaica Journal*, June 1980, p. 68.

31 **all but two of the fifty American technicians . . .** McCullough, *The Path between the Seas*, p. 38.

31 **One railroad historian . . .** Schott, *Rails across Panama*, pp. 192–93.

31 **"workers who toppled over in the jungle"** Ibid., p. 139.

32 **"a bare-footed, coatless, harum-scarum looking set"** Tomes, *Panama in 1855*, p. 123.

32 **in the process publicly flogging the Panamanian official . . .** Conniff, *Panama and the United States*, p. 28.

33 **A forty-foot-deep cut was dug near Paraíso . . .** Nelson, *Five Years at Panama*, p. 148.

33 **"no one work . . . has accomplished so much"** Otis, *History of the Panama Railroad*, p. 15.

34 **estimates are as high as $7 to 9 million, or $170,000 per mile . . .** *New York Tribune*, March 13, 1855.

36 **"better class of shop-keepers are Mulattoes"** *Panama Star and Herald*, December 27, 1856.

Chapter Five: The Competing Routes

41 **"It is proved beyond all doubt that Dr. Cullen never was in the interior"** Mack, *The Land Divided*, p. 255.

41 **"mystical and imaginative"** Ripley, *The Capitalists and Colombia*, p. 45.

42 **"The Department has entrusted to you a duty"** McCullough, *The Path between the Seas*, p. 20.

43 **"it [would] one day be covered with sails from every clime"** *H. Misc. Doc. 113*, 42d Cong., 3rd Sess., p. 41, quoted in Mack, *The Land Divided*, p. 243.

44 **"the deep cut would probably be subject to land-slides"** *Sen. Ex. Doc. 15*, 46th Cong., 1st Sess., p. 5.

Chapter Six: "Le Grand Français"

47 **"We are, gentlemen, soldiers under fire"** Bunau-Varilla, *Panama*, p. 52.

49 **"astonish[ing] the world by the great deeds"** Quoted in Siegfried, *Suez and Panama*, p. 236.

51 **"man eminent for originality"** *The Times*, July 2, 1870.

51 **"You exercise a charm"** Lesseps, *Recollections of Forty Years*, vol. 2, p. 294.

52 **"will help to wed the whole universe"** Quoted in Siegfried, *Suez and Panama*, p. 60.

52 **"Is it not a glorious thing"** Lesseps, *Recollections of Forty Years*, p. 172.

54 **"Our hope is to fill these waters with all the ships"** Ibid., p. 184.

55 **"You should start preparations immediately"** Wyse to Reclus, February 2, 1878, quoted in Fauconnier, *Panama: Armand Reclus*, p. 105.

56 **Four were in Darién . . .** Wyse, Reclus, et Sosa, *Rapport sur les Etudes de la Commission Internationale d'exploration de L'Isthme Americain*, p. 48.

Chapter Seven: The Fatal Decision

60 **"Tragic scenes"** *New York Tribune,* May 5, 1879.

60 **"Business has been paralysed"** Hugh Mallet to Foreign Office, June 17, 1879, FO55/269.

63 **"involved so much uncertainty"** Menocal, "Intrigues at the Paris Canal Conference," *North American Review*, September 1879, p. 16.

63 **"provide for the whole drainage"** *Instructions to Rear Admiral Daniel Ammen . . .* , p. 11.

63 **"threw off the mantle of indifference"** Quoted in McCullough, *The Path between the Seas*, p. 78.

64 **De Lépinay himself, although favoring Panama** Congrès International D'Études du Canal Interocéanique, *Compte Rendu Des Séances*, pp. 293–99, 355.

65   he claimed that he had investigated its potential Wyse, *Le Canal de Panama*, p. 191.

65   He also argued that the new lake *Instructions to Rear Admiral Daniel Ammen . . .*, p. 19.

67   "May that illustrious man" *Le Matin*, May 30, 1879, quoted in Anguizola, *Philippe Bunau-Varilla*, p. 38.

68   "A careful examination of the names of the French delegates" Menocal, "Intrigues at the Paris Canal Conference."

68   "relative consideration of natural advantages" *Instructions to Rear Admiral Daniel Ammen . . .*, p. 10.

68   "a comedy of the most deplorable kind" Johnston, "Interoceanic Ship Canal Discussion," *Journal of the American Geographical Society* 11 (1879): 172–80.

68   Menocal, for his part, was sure *Instructions to Rear Admiral Daniel Ammen . . .*, p. 21.

69   "prefigures for us an era of complications and difficulties" *New York World*, January 1, 1880.

70   "The financial organs were hostile" Quoted in McCullough, *The Path between the Seas*, p. 102.

Chapter Eight: The Riches of France

73   "Mr. Lesseps' enterprise" *Star and Herald*, January 1, 1880.

74   "wearing the diplomatic smile" Robinson, *Fifty Years at Panama*, p. 139.

74   "The Canal will be made" Ibid., p. 140.

75   "every one of the [city's] 14,000 inhabitants" *New York World*, January 22, 1880.

75   "Such an air of neatness" *New York Tribune*, January 22, 1880.

75   "gave éclat to the occasion" Robinson, *Fifty Years at Panama*, p. 143.

76   "unanimous in their expressions of gratification" *Star and Herald*, January 8, 1880.

76   "His mind is unalterably made up" *New York Tribune*, January 22, 1880.

76   "Mr. Lesseps is an accomplished horseman" *Star and Herald*, January 5, 1880.

77   "as dark as Arabs" Robinson, *Fifty Years at Panama*, p. 144.

77   "bright with myriad lights" *Star and Herald*, February 7, 1880.

77   dance "all night like a boy" Robinson, *Fifty Years at Panama*, p. 146.

77   "The engineering difficulties" *Star and Herald*, January 16, 1880.

79   "vastly to the regret of the people" *Star and Herald*, February 14, 1880.

80   "Blanchet does nothing" Wyse to Reclus, January 24, 1880, quoted in Fauconnier, *Panama: Armand Reclus et le Canal des Deux Océans*, p. 170.

80   "proper predominance over the seas" *New York World*, January 2, 1880.

80   The *New York Times* thought that the sea-level canal *New York Times*, January 25, 1880.

80   "All this looks like business" *New York Tribune*, January 23, 1880.

81   "Now is the time for the Government to make up its mind" *New York Tribune*, February 10, 1880.

81   **"where one is used to working for the civilization of the world"** Fauconnier, *Panama*, p. 167.

82   **"the enterprise of M. Lesseps"** *Star and Herald,* February 17, 1880.

82   **"I have offered America 300,000 of the shares"** *Star and Herald*, April 21, 1880.

83   **"The policy of this country is a canal under American control"** *Sen. Exec. Doc. No. 112,* 46th Cong., 2d Sess., pp. 1–2.

83   **"When M. de Lesseps gets ready to leave Washington to-morrow"** *New York Tribune*, March 9, 1880.

83   **"President's message assured the political stability of the canal"** *Bulletin du Canal Interocéanique*, March 15, 1880.

84   **"In these provincial tours"** Johnston, "Interoceanic Ship Canal Discussion," *Journal of the American Geographical Society* 11 (1879): 172–80.

84   **"few miles of oozy quagmire and jungle"** *The Times*, May 3, 1880.

85   **"It is a region"** *London Standard*, December 8, 1880.

85   **500-franc shares in Suez were now worth** McCullough, *The Path between the Seas,* p. 125.

86   **"Capital and science have never had such an opportunity"** Quoted in *Bulletin du Canal Interocéanique*, December 1, 1880.

86   **"At that time they realized the poetry of capitalism"** Quoted in Siegfried, *Suez and Panama*, p. 240.

88   **"The company now has a legal existence and a name"** *Star and Herald*, March 12, 1881.

88   **"The worry is that it will weaken the United States"** *New York Tribune*, December 16, 1880.

88   **"insist on acquiring from Colombia the territory"** Ibid., January 6, 1881.

Chapter Nine: "Travail Commencé"

89   **"Travail Commencé"** Quoted in *Bulletin du Canal Interocéanique*, February 15, 1881.

90   **"Mais, bah!"** Cermoise, *Deux Ans à Panama*, pp. 1–107.

96   **The first criticism that Reclus made was leveled at the choice of men** Reclus to Charles de Lesseps, April 30, 1881, quoted in Fauconnier, *Panama*, pp. 186–88.

98   **Ernst Dichman, did everything in his power** Bennett to Foreign Office, May 11, 1880, FO55/274; also *Star and Herald*, May 8, 1880.

98   **"all alliances with the United States"** Arthur O'Leary in Bogotá to Granville, April 5, 1881, FO420/36.

98   **considered denouncing the 1846 Treaty** Letter from Carlos Holguin, July 9, 1881, FO420/36.

99   **"an alliance against the United States"** Secretary of State Blaine to James P. Lowell, June 24, 1881, "Correspondence respecting the Projected Panama Canal Presented to both houses of Parliament 1882." British Library microfilm, Mic. A. 19266, FO420/36.

99 **"would be glad to see England and France take joint measures"** Letter from Mr. Langley in Madrid to Granville, September 23, 1881, FO420/37.

100 **"enable the United States to keep military possession of the canal"** Sackville-West to Granville, January 12, 1882, FO420/37.

100 **"manifestly unjust"** Blaine to Mr. Lowell, November 19, 1881, FO420/37.

100 **"Mr. Blaine had overshot the mark"** *New York Herald*, January 20, 1882.

101 **"Everyone had his own room!"** Cermoise, *Deux Ans à Panama*, p. 109.

101 **"We said goodbye with a certain sadness"** Ibid., p. 128.

103 **Only one in ten newly arrived laborers** McCullough, *The Path between the Seas*, p. 133.

103 **"Mr. de Lesseps contemplates making up what is short"** *Star and Herald*, March 12, 1881.

104 **"learn a foreign language"** or **"seek adventure"** Quoted in Newton, *The Silver Men*, p. 7.

105 **"A trip to Colón?"** *Barbados Herald*, August 6, 1885.

105 **"pretentious, and always complaining"** Quoted in Siegfried, *Suez and Panama*, p. 252.

106 **"They were excellent workers"** Cermoise, *Deux Ans à Panama*, p. 247.

106 **"are left when ill to die in the streets of Colón"** "Governor's Report on the blue book 1881–2," p. 32, quoted in Petras, *Jamaican Labor Migration*, p. 112.

Chapter Ten: Fever

108 **"evidently in a state of delirium"** *Bulletin du Canal Interocéanique,* September 1, 1881.

111 **"There was a dismal period for the administration"** Cermoise, *Deux Ans à Panama*, p. 129.

111 **"At the moment, the state of health conditions"** Verbrugghe to Reclus, October 5, 1881, quoted in Fauconnier, *Panama*, pp. 208–9.

111 **"No epidemic of maladie had manifested itself"** *Star and Herald*, October 1, 1881.

112 **"Mr. Blanchet's death is an irreparable loss"** Bennett to Granville, November 10, 1881, FO420/36.

112 **The best estimate is that about fifty men died** *Star and Herald*, February 22, 1882; and Newton, *The Silver Men*, p. 126.

112 **"the hospital rooms are so vast"** Jos, *Guadeloupéens et Martiniquais au Canal de Panama*, p. 46.

113 **"She is one of those rare women"** *New York Herald*, August 22, 1881.

113 **"There's only one certain way to diagnose fever"** Cermoise, *Deux Ans à Panama*, p. 148.

115 **"*la section de la grande tranchée*"** Chamberlaine report, May 18, 1882, FO420/37.

115 **"invaded by a persistent tiredness"** Cermoise, *Deux Ans à Panama*, p. 230.

117 **"all but produced an earthquake"** Nelson, *Five Years at Panama*, p. 178.

118   **"I have spent two of the best years of my youth"** Cermoise, *Deux Ans à Panama*, p. 301.

118   **"After two years' work . . . we are much farther advanced"** *Bulletin du Canal Interocéanique*, December 8, 1882.

118   **"applications for shares showering him from all quarters of France"** *New York Tribune*, September 28, 1882.

119   **"The truth is that during the trial period"** Chambre des Députés, *5e Législature, Session de 1893, Rapport Général*... vol. 1, p. 451.

119   **"aged a good deal"** *New York Tribune*, quoted in the *Star and Herald*, June 23, 1883.

Chapter Eleven: Jules Dingler

121   **"busy . . . and bright with hope"** Nelson, *Five Years at Panama*, p. 230.

121   **"The work moves steadily on"** *Star and Herald*, November 21, 1884.

122   **"I intend to show the world that only the drunk and the dissipated"** Haskin, *The Panama Canal*, p. 194.

122   **"This result has surprised all"** *Star and Herald*, November 9, 1883.

123   **"determined to have a finger in the canal pie"** Robinson, *Fifty Years at Panama*, p. 151.

124   **an American naval officer** Rodgers, *Progress of Work on Panama Ship-Canal*, January 27, 1884 (Sen. Doc. 123, 48th Cong., 1st Sess.)

124   **"So the visitor to Gatún"** *Star and Herald*, October 14, 1884.

125   **"From morning till night"** Rodgers, *Progress of Work on Panama Ship-Canal*, January 27, 1884.

126   **"A stampede took place which is hardly possible to describe"** Quoted in *Star and Herald*, January 26, 1884.

126   **"Now and again you see a great swell"** Senior, "The Colon People," *Jamaica Journal*, March 1978, p. 70.

127   **"The infatuation to go seems to have taken hold"** *Daily Gleaner*, May 7, 1883, quoted in Senior, "The Colon People," p. 64.

127   **"a flag of liberation"** Senior, "West Indian Participation in the Construction of the Panama Canal," p. 40.

127   **"We are not of those who think it a calamity"** Quoted in *Star and Herald*, February 14, 1884.

127   **"the great outflow from the Colony of labourers"** *Star and Herald*, May 18, 1883.

128   **Kill my partner / Kill my partner** "West Indian Work Songs," MCCZ, Box 33.

128   **"They have a way of shifting for themselves"** *Star and Herald*, January 29, 1884, p. 79.

129   **"I perceive that these men are partial in their protection"** Letter of March 29, 1883, FO55/297.

129   **"a ruinously expensive method"** *New York World*, February 8, 1885.

130   **"Damage amounting to thousands of dollars"** *Montreal Gazette*, August 24, 1884.

130   **"of a character and complexity to defy description"** Sibert and Stevens, *The Construction of the Panama Canal*, p. 79.

130   **the Company lost some 10 percent of the work it paid for** J. Bigelow private diary, March 2, 1886.

130   **"There was no system or organisation"** Jeremiah Waisome, "Competition for the Best True Stories."

131   **"The rainy season, at last set in"** *Star and Herald*, May 25, 1883.

131   **"The heavy downpours of late"** *Star and Herald*, May 26, 1884.

132   **"the water will have to be hung up on the sides of the mountains"** Paper read before the Franklin Institute, October 22, 1884, by Charles Colné.

132   **"Fresh engineering difficulties present themselves"** Admiral Lyon to Foreign Office, November 29, 1883, FO420/50.

133   **"A day of reckoning is coming"** *Montreal Gazette*, August 24, 1884.

133   **"It is probable the present company will go into bankruptcy"** *New York Herald*, November 1, 1884.

134   **"It is generally believed here that the present Company"** Mallet to Foreign Office, July 5, 1884, FO55/304.

134   **"It would be a pity that a work such as this should be left partially completed"** *Star and Herald*, July 5, 1884.

134   **"Under such circumstances, there is something amounting to heroism"** *New York Herald*, December 2, 1883.

135   **"Death becomes a grim joke, burial a travesty"** *New York Tribune*, August 8, 1886.

135   **"Probably if the French had been trying to propagate Yellow Fever"** Gorgas, *Sanitation*, p. 232.

136   **"thousand dying with yellow fever"** Charles Wilson, unpublished memoir, p. 74, Box 11, MCCZ.

136   **"As for the men"** *Montreal Gazette*, August 24, 1884.

136   **"burials averaged from thirty to forty per day"** Nelson, *Five Years at Panama*, p. 7.

137   **"My poor husband is in a despair that is painful to see"** Edgar-Bonnet, *Ferdinand de Lesseps*, p. 184.

137   **"Mr. Dingler was but 20 years of age"** *Star and Herald*, February 25, 1884.

138   **"exalted the energy of those who were filled with a sincere love"** Bunau-Varilla, *Panama*, p. 44.

139   **"abominable neglect of all sanitary measures"** *Star and Herald*, January 28, 1884.

139   **"host of idle loafers, who infect the town"** *Star and Herald*, October 25, 1884.

139   **"thanks to abstemious habits."** Nelson, *Five Years at Panama*, p. 17.

139   **"Woe to the feeble person who doesn't know how to quench his thirst!"** Reclus, *Panama & Darien*, p. 130.

139   **"designed for nothing but hasty drinking,"** Cermoise, *Deux Ans à Panama*, pp. 52–53.

140   **"a veritable sink of iniquity,"** Bishop, *The Panama Gateway*, p. 88.

140   "the hardest drinking and the most immoral place I have ever known" Mallet, *Pioneer Diplomat.*

140   "spirit of venality and corruption" Robinson, *Fifty Years at Panama*, p. 61.

140   "There is a general belief held by many intelligent people" Nelson, *Five Years at Panama*, p. 18.

141   "assembly rooms, provided with books, periodicals, and various indoor games" *Bulletin du Canal Interocéanique,* July 18, 1883.

141   "A great enormous hall with a stone floor was the bar-room" Cermoise, *Deux Ans à Panama*, pp. 52–53.

141   "passions run high owing to the constant proximity of death" Dansette, *Les Affaires de Panama*, pp. 24–25.

141   "the Sword of Damocles hangs over everyone" Mimande, *Souvenirs d'un Echappe de Panama*, pp. 60–61.

141   "death and la fête are perpetually hand in hand" Cermoise, *Deux Ans à Panama*, p. 145.

142   "foreign men of dubious reputation" Perez-Penero, *Before the Five Frontiers*, p. 113.

142   "which as usual was occasioned by the vile rum" *Star and Herald*, May 22, 1883.

142   "an agglomeration of all nations" *Star and Herald*, September 18, 1883.

143   billed as a hole of 33 meters Zévaès, *Le Scandale du Panama*, p. 24.

Chapter Twelve: Annus Horribilis

144   "not unlikely" *New York Times*, quoted in *Panama Star and Herald*, February 3, 1882.

145   "the British recently took possession of Egypt and the Suez canal" *New York Sun*, November 6, 1884.

145   "be so fortified as to become a second Gibraltar" Lord Lyons in Paris to Granville, December 22, 1884, FO420/50.

146   muttering darkly to the British ambassador Sackville-West to Granville, December 26, 1884, FO420/50.

147   Britain should also have one, built at Tehuantepec. Sackville-West to Granville, December 28, 1884. FO420/50

148   "described every Canal functionary" F.R. St. John, British Minister in Bogotá to Granville, March 2, 1885, FO420/51.

149   the Colombian minister shared his grave concerns with the British ambassador Sackville-West to Granville, January 27, 1885, FO420/51.

150   "At 2 a.m. on the 16th" *Star and Herald,* March 19, 1885.

151   "rebel bullets and cannon balls" Leay note to Mallet, April 3, 1885, FO55/313.

152   "The firing was hot and reckless in the extreme" Mallet to Foreign Office, April 4, 1885, FO55/313.

153   "The entry of the American marines into the city" Mallet to Foreign Officer, April 27, 1885, FO55/313.

153   "the presence [of the U.S. force] is only temporary" U.S. Navy Department,

Report of Commander Bowman H. McCalla upon the Naval Expedition to the Isthmus of Panama, April 1885.

155 **"The State will never be free from such revolutionary nonsense"** *Star and Herald*, March 20, 1885.

156 **"were ignorant of Isthmian affairs"** Mallet to Foreign Office, August 10, 1885, FO55/313.

156 **Arthur Webb, a Jamaican** Eyewitness reports submitted to vice-consul Leay, sent to London by Mallet, August 10, 1885, FO55/313.

157 **"I have never before witnessed anything so horribly sickening"** Statement to Leay by C. H. Burns, May 10, 1885.

158 **"In all these fights between Jamaicans and Colombians"** *Star and Herald*, May 9, 1885.

158 **"It must also be borne in mind,"** Mallet to governor of Jamaica, July 6, 1885, FO55/313.

159 **"that the enterprise will be ready for the world's commerce"** Mallet to Foreign Office, March 4, 1885, FO55/313.

159 **"The Panama canal is in such a state that its ultimate completion is beyond question"** *New York Tribune*, May 8, 1885.

160 **"Mr. Varilla's tremendous mental capacity"** Letter from Wulsin, May 28, 1906, in Bigelow Papers, New York Public Library, Box 24.

160 **"His versatility was fantastic"** Quoted in Anguizola, *Philippe Bunau-Varilla*, p. 68.

161 **Menocal visited in August** *New York Times*, August 18, 1885.

161 **"Is Monsieur de Lesseps a Canal Digger, or a Grave Digger?"** *Harper's Weekly*, September 3, 1881.

163 **"like a human bunch of grapes"** Bunau-Varilla, *Panama*, p. 54.

163 **"Rain poured in torrents"** *Star and Herald*, December 4, 1885.

163 **"I saw they were covered with the most enormous and deadly spiders"** Bunau-Varilla, *Panama*, p. 55.

163 **Lieutenant William Kimball, who toured the works soon after** Kimball, *Special Intelligence Report on the Progress of the Work during the Year 1885.*

166 **"The contagion of my confidence in our success"** Bunau-Varilla, *Panama*, p. 53.

166 **"It is an impressive fact that there is money value in the prestige of M. de Lesseps"** *New York Tribune*, August 16, 1885.

166 **"As for human life, that is always cheap."** Kimball, *Special Intelligence Report on the Progress of the Work during the Year 1885*, p. 32.

167 **"under no circumstances would negroes be admitted"** J. B. Poylo to Mallet, August 8, 1885.

167 **"Many a man of them had been happy to enlist"** Bunau-Varilla, *Panama*, p. 44.

168 **"I had reached a state of semi-coma"** Mallet, *Pioneer Diplomat.*

168 **"should the works cease"** Consul Sadler to Marquis of Salisbury, January 27, 1886, FO 55/325.

Chapter Thirteen: Collapse and Scandal

170   **"that it was probably a scheme to use my name as an ex-Minister to France"** Bigelow private diary, January 31, 1886.

170   **"The success of the Panama business"** Molinari, *A Panama*, p. 25.

171   **"I was pleased to find that Grace and the old Baron got on admirably together"** Bigelow diary, February 18, 1886.

171   **"When we left they gave us repeated cheers"** Bigelow diary, February 19, 1886.

172   **"take a share in its management"** Bigelow diary, February 22, 1886.

172   **"His stay is one continued fête"** Sadler to Foreign Office, February 26, 1886, FO55/325.

173   **"Even if the piercing of the Isthmus presents enormous difficulties"** Molinari, *A Panama* p. 68.

173   **"often conflicting and rarely more than approximative"** Bigelow, *The Panama Canal. Report of the Hon. John Bigelow*, p. 4.

173   **"insalubrity"** Ibid., p. 12.

173   **"people of small means"** Ibid., p. 22,

174   **"secure to the United States"** Ibid., p. 24.

176   **"a violent vibration of my bed"** Bunau-Varilla, *Panama*, p. 61.

176   **"They are trying to shelve me"** *The Times*, July 13, 1886.

177   **Of thirty Italians who had arrived together twelve months earlier** *New York Tribune*, August 22, 1886.

177   **"Every month or two I would lose a man, perhaps two men"** *Hearings 3110,* Sen. Doc. 253, 57th Cong., 1st Sess., p. 100.

177   **"insane recklessness"** *New York Tribune*, August 29, 1886.

178   **"a dismal failure"** Bunau-Varilla, *Panama*, p. 68.

179   **"creditable"** Rogers, *Intelligence Report of the Panama Canal*, p. 34.

181   **"During my stay in Colón"** Sweetman, *Paul Gaugin*, p. 169.

182   **"the perfect, the final, project"** Bunau-Varilla, *Panama*, p. 80.

185   **"All France is joined in the completion of the Panama Canal"** Chambre des Députés, *5e Législature, Session de 1893, Rapport Général . . .* , pp. 101–2.

186   **"I appeal to all Frenchmen"** *Bulletin du Canal Interocéanique*, December 2, 1888.

186   **journalist Emily Crawford** *New York Tribune*, December 13 and 14, 1888.

188   **"like a stroke of paralysis"** Robinson, *Fifty Years at Panama*, p. 147.

188   **"There are hundreds [of destitute Jamaicans] absolutely starving"** *Star and Herald*, April 6, 1889.

189   **But stern warnings from the new U.S. president Benjamin Harrison** President Harrison's inauguration speech, March 4, 1889.

189   **"What have you done with the money?"** Drumont, *La Dernière Bataille*, p. 362.

189   **"He had apparently recovered all his strength"** Smith, *The Life and Enterprises of Ferdinand De Lesseps*, p. 310.

189   **"dissipating"** funds **"in a manner . . . more consistent with the personal views and interests of the administrators"** Chambres des Députés, *5e Législature, Session de 1893, No. 2921*, vol. 3, pp. 217–18.

191   "excessive optimism" Cour d'Appel de Paris, Première Chambre: *Plaidoirie de Me.*
        Henri Barboux pour MM. Ferdinand et Charles de Lesseps, p. 185.

192   "face was drawn and his skin yellowed" Courau, *Ferdinand de Lesseps*, p. 237.

194   "one of the enterprises which made some of the most scandalously exces-
        sive profits" Quoted in Skinner, *France and Panama*, p. 75.

195   "It would never have come to anything" Bunau-Varilla, *Panama*, p. 156.

Chapter Fourteen: Heroes and Villains—the "Battle of the Routes"

200   "The construction of a such a maritime highway" Annual Message, Decem-
        ber 5, 1898.

201   "The Nicaragua canal is a purely national affair" *New York Herald*, January 30,
        1902.

202   "He is one of the readiest talkers in town" *New York World*, October 4, 1908.

202   "involved almost every branch of professional activity" Quoted in Harding,
        The Untold Story of Panama, p. 3.

203   "There was a hole in Panama into which a lot of French money had been
        sunk" United States Congress House of Representatives, *The Story of Panama*,
        p. 6.

204   "the lawyer Cromwell" Bunau-Varilla, *Panama*, p. 10.

204   "Once you have touched Panama, you never lose the infection" Harding, *The
        Untold Story of Panama*, p. 88.

204   "the revolutionist who promoted and made possible the revolution" United
        States Congress House of Representatives, *The Story of Panama*, p. 61.

205   "masterful mind, whetted on the grindstone of corporation cunning"
        Quoted in Ibid., p. 94.

205   "no one in the United States doubted that the Panama Canal in itself was an
        impossibility" Harding, *The Untold Story of Panama*, p. 5.

205   "We must make our plans with Napoleonic strategy" Ibid., p. 5.

205   "ubiquitous and ever present" McCullough, *The Path between the Seas*, p. 273.

206   "mysterious influences" Harding, *The Untold Story of Panama*, p. 2.

206   "under the control, management and ownership of the United States"
        Quoted in Skinner, *France and Panama*, p. 138.

206   "for hours on the most profound study of the technical sides of the ques-
        tion" United States Congress House of Representatives, *The Story of Panama*,
        p. 224.

207   "the scales had fallen from their eyes" Bunau-Varilla, *Panama*, p. 166.

208   "all the difficulties of obtaining the necessary rights . . . on the Panama
        route" Sen. Doc. 5, 56th Cong., 2d Sess., pp. 43–44, quoted in Mack, *The Land Di-
        vided*, p. 425.

209   "Towards midnight as I was about to go out for a breath of fresh air" Bunau-
        Varilla, *Panama*, p. 184ff.

212   "No single great material work which remains to be undertaken" Quoted in
        McCullough, *The Path between the Seas*, p. 249.

212 **"If that canal is open to the warships of an enemy"** Thayer, *Theodore Roosevelt: An Intimate Biography*, vol. 2, p. 339.

213 **"strengthen our position enormously"** Beale, *Theodore Roosevelt and the Rise of American Power*, pp. 147–48.

213 **"ruptured the dikes placed against so-called American imperialism"** Miner, *The Fight for the Panama Route*, p. 232.

215 **"legitimate means"** United States Congress House of Representatives, *The Story of Panama*, p. 169.

215 **"The Colombians . . . have negro blood enough to make them lazy"** *Harper's Weekly*, August 23, 1902.

216 **"Talk about buying a lawsuit"** *New York World*, quoted in *Star and Herald*, February 22, 1902.

217 **"poison the minds of people"** Senate debate, 57th Cong., 1st Sess.

217 **"It is the certainty of moral defilement"** Anguizola, *Philippe Bunau-Varilla*, p. 215.

217 **"If the vote were to be taken under this impression"** Bunau-Varilla, *Panama*, p. 247.

Chapter Fifteen: "I Took the Isthmus"

220 **"a crowd of French jail-birds"** Collin, *Theodore Roosevelt's Caribbean*, p. 218.

220 **"Few of the members who will assemble in Bogotá"** *Star and Herald*, March 14, 1903.

221 **"a great deal of illness"** Mallet private letter, June 1, 1903.

221 **"give rise to unpatriotic feelings"** Miner, *The Fight for the Panama Route*, p. 292.

222 **"Not an atom of our sovereignty nor a stone of our territory"** *El Correo Naçional*, February 3, 1903.

222 **"our nation has insisted"** John Bigelow Papers, New York Public Library, Box 24.

223 **"It is the conviction of his irresistible superiority and vigor that makes the Yankee"** Quoted in Miner, *The Fight for the Panama Route*, p. 265.

223 **"from approbation to suspicion and from suspicion to decided opposition"** Skinner, *France and Panama*, p. 208.

223 **"History will say of me"** Miner, *The Fight for the Panama Route*, p. 233.

224 **"We pointed out"** United States Congress House of Representatives, *The Story of Panama*, pp. 278–79.

224 **"greedy little anthropoids"** Anguizola, *Philippe Bunau-Varilla*, p. 226.

224 **"If Colombia should now reject the treaty"** Miner, *The Fight for the Panama Route*, p. 285.

225 **"The only party"** Anguizola, *Philippe Bunau-Varilla*, p. 223.

225 **"President Roosevelt is determined"** *New York World*, June 13, 1903.

226 **"Any amendment whatever or unnecessary delay"** Miner, *The Fight for the Panama Route*, p. 308.

226 **"Make it as strong as you can"** Pringle, *Theodore Roosevelt: A Biography*, p. 311.

227   **"the foolish and homicidal corruptionists in Bogota"** Bishop, *Theodore Roosevelt*, vol. 1, p. 278.

227   **"I know, for having heard him say so, how intensely he wants it"** Jusserand, *What Me Befell*, p. 252.

228   **"We might make another treaty, not with Colombia, but with Panama"** *New York Herald*, August 15, 1903.

228   **"It is altogether likely there will be an insurrection on the Isthmus"** Bemis, ed., *The American Secretaries of State and their Diplomacy*, vol. 9, pp. 163–64.

229   **"a thousand offers in the direction of assisting the revolution"** United States Congress House of Representatives, *The Story of Panama*, p. 362.

229   **"The United States would build the Panama Canal"** Ibid., pp. 359–60.

230   **"Revolutionary agents of Panama [are] here"** Collin, *Theodore Roosevelt's Caribbean*, p. 249.

230   **"All is lost"** Bunau-Varilla, *Panama*, p. 291.

231   **"I have no doubt that he was able to make a very accurate guess"** Miner, *The Fight for the Panama Route*, p. 359.

231   **"I held all the threads of a revolution on the Isthmus"** Bunau-Varilla, *Panama*, p. 297.

233   **"If I succeeded in this task the Canal was saved"** Ibid., pp. 329–30.

235   **"If you will aid us"** United States Congress House of Representatives, *The Story of Panama*, p. 390.

235   **"There was nothing that did not show the greatest cordiality"** Espino, *How Wall Street Created a Nation*, p. 106.

237   **"resumed their independence"** Mack, *The Land Divided*, p. 463.

237   **"*Viva La Republica de Panama!*"** *Star and Herald*, November 11, 1903.

238   **"a second Boer War"** *New York Tribune*, November 24, 1903.

238   **"it is preferable to see the Colombian race exterminated"** Anguizola, *Philippe Bunau-Varilla*, p. 276.

239   **"revolution of the canal, by the canal, for the canal"** *Birmingham Age-Herald*, November 7, 1903.

239   **"It is another step in the imperial policy"** *Pittsburgh Post*, November 7, 1903.

239   **"hot-headed and immature"** *Little Rock (Arkansas) Gazette*, November 7, 1903, quoted in Graham, *The "Interests of Civilization"?*, p. 49.

239   **"It begins to look as if nobody can touch that Panama ditch"** *Salt Lake Herald*, quoted in *Literary Digest*, November 27, 1903.

239   **"stolen property"** *New York Times*, December 29, 1903.

239   **"The thing is done, there is no way of undoing it"** *Houston Post*, November 12, 1903.

239   **"The world must move on"** *San Francisco Chronicle*, November 18, 1903.

240   **"The country ought to be ringing with the protests"** Graham, *The "Interests of Civilization"?*, pp. 127–28.

240   **"Mr. President, I am glad you did not start the rabbit to running"** Quoted in *New York Commercial Advertiser*, November 12, 1903.

240   **"I did not lift a finger to incite the revolutionists"** Collin, *Theodore Roosevelt's Caribbean*, p. 267.

241   "It is reported that we have made the revolution" Jusserand, *What Me Befell*, p. 253.

242   "Mr. Secretary of State, the situation harbors the same fatal germs" Bunau-Varilla, *Panama*, p. 358.

244   "What do you think, Mr. Minister" Ibid., p. 366.

244   "Remember that ten days ago the Panamanians were still Colombians" Weisberger, "The Strange Affair of the Taking of the Panama Canal Zone," *American Heritage* 27, p. 75.

245   "As for your poor old dad" McCullough, *The Path between the Seas*, p. 392.

246   "inflammatory, unnecessary and offensive" Collin, *Theodore Roosevelt's Caribbean*, p. 281.

246   "very satisfactory, vastly advantageous to the United States" McCullough, *The Path between the Seas*, p. 392.

246   the new treaty was many times worse for Panama, as Hay later admitted Cullom, *Fifty Years of Public Service*, p. 383.

246   "We separated not without emotion" Bunau-Varilla, *Panama*, p. 377.

246   "I greeted the travelers with the happy news!" Ibid., pp. 377–78.

247   "What do you think of the canal treaty?" Mallet private letter, November 25, 1903.

248   "it sounds very much like we wrote it ourselves" Bunau-Varilla, *Panama*, p. 427.

248   "stolen in the most bare-faced manner from Colombia" 58th Cong., 2d Sess., p. 871, January 19, 1904.

248   "rising as one man," "but the one man was in the White House" 58th Cong., 2d Sess., p. 706, January 13, 1904.

248   "but the beginning of systematic policy of aggression" Ibid., p. 709.

249   "I fear that we have got too large to be just" Ibid., p. 401, December 19, 1903.

249   "You might whip the dog, but would you throw away the rabbit?" *New York Times*, January 8, 1904.

249   "to our future political, commercial, and naval expansion" Quoted in Graham, *The "Interests of Civilization"?*, p. 126.

249   "From the point of view of world politics" Charles Henry Huberich, *The Trans-Isthmian Canal: A Study in American Diplomatic History* (Austin, Texas, 1904), p. 31, quoted in Graham, *The "Interests of Civilization"?*, p. 126.

250   "the great Frenchman, whose genius has consecrated the Isthmus" Quoted in Anguizola, *Philippe Bunau-Varilla*, p. 289.

250   "somebody unexpectedly seized my hands" Bunau-Varilla, *Panama*, p. 428.

250   "great uneasiness caused among my friends by my action" Roosevelt to Spooner, January 20, 1904, quoted in Collin, *Theodore Roosevelt's Caribbean*, p. 306.

250   "The one thing for which I deserved most credit in my entire administration" Major, *Prize Possession*, p. 63.

251   "more to an empire than a Republic" Graham, *The "Interests of Civilization"?*, p. 144.

251   "Tell our speakers to dwell more on the Panama Canal" Collin, *Theodore Roosevelt's Caribbean*, p. 306.

251   **"We stand today, apparently in the shadow of a great defeat"** Graham, *The "Interests of Civilization"?*, p. 150.

Chapter Sixteen: *"Make the Dirt Fly"*

253   **"In America, anything is possible,"** Hardeveld, *Make the Dirt Fly*, p. 5.

253   **George Martin** "Competition for the Best True Stories."

254   **"is nothing in the nature of the work"** *New York Tribune*, January 23, 1904.

254   **"solid inevitability"** Skinner, *France and Panama*, p. 2.

254   **"the results be achieved"** McCullough, *The Path between the Seas*, p. 408.

254   **"Old Man of the Sea"** Gorgas and Hendrick, *William Crawford Gorgas*, p. 170.

255   **"I feel that the sanitary and hygiene problems"** Roosevelt to Morison, February 24, 1904, quoted in McCullough, *The Path between the Seas*, p. 406.

256   **some 70 percent had the enlarged spleen of the malaria carrier** Gorgas, *Engineering Record*, May 1904.

256   **"he was sure every member of the Commission hoped that a sea-level canal would be built"** Mallet to Lord Landsdowne, April 27, 1904, FO881/8429.

257   **"They have taken all the meat and left the bone"** Mallet private letter, June 16, 1904.

257   **"The Isthmus is swarming with Yankees already"** Mallet private letter, June 10, 1904.

257   **"Panama without mosquitoes?"** Mallet private letter, June 2, 1904.

257   **"such a God forsaken place where the French have so finally failed!"** Hibbard account, MCCZ, Box 22.

258   **"The rainy season had just commenced"** Karner, *More Recollections*, p. 11.

259   **"There was, I realized, a stupendous piece of work before us"** Quoted in Dock, ed., *A History of Nursing*, p. 300.

259   **"A more prolific source would be hard to imagine."** Le Prince and Orenstein, *Mosquito Control in Panama*, p. 20ff.

259   **"only jungle and chaos from one end of the Isthmus to the other"** McCullough, *The Path between the Seas*, p. 439.

260   **Joseph Le Prince found several trees** Le Prince and Orenstein, *Mosquito Control in Panama*, p. 17.

260   **"excellently recorded [which] proved to be of great use"** Sibert and Stevens, *The Construction of the Panama Canal*, p. 11.

260   **"a fairly good condition, and were systematically stored"** Wallace, "Preliminary Work on the Panama Canal," *Engineering Magazine*, October 1905.

260   **"Splendid workmanship was shown on these machines"** Sibert and Stevens, *The Construction of the Panama Canal*, p. 13.

260   **"considerable work had been done on the channel from La Boca to Miraflores"** Ibid., p. 11.

261   **"vastly more than the popular impression"** McCullough, *The Path between the Seas*, p. 441.

261   **The idea of a plan that would render much of the French digging** James

Thomas Ford, "The Present Condition and Prospects of the Panama Canal Work," Institute of Civil Engineers, *Minutes of Proceedings*, February 5, 1901.

262   **"afford convenient passage for vessels of the largest tonnage"** Quoted in Miner, *The Fight for the Panama Route*, pp. 408–9.

263   **"Lizards and gaudy snakes crawled and scuttled"** Waldo, "The Panama Canal Work, and the Workers," *Engineering Magazine*, p. 327.

263   **"indescribably filthy"** Maltby, "In at the Start at Panama," *Civil Engineering*, August 1945, p. 324.

263   **"As the use of cheap steel had not become the practice"** Sibert and Stevens, *The Construction of the Panama Canal*, pp. 86–87.

264   **Soon after his arrival, Maltby tried to organize** Maltby, "In at the Start at Panama," *Civil Engineering*, June 1945, p. 262.

264   **"I intend that those fellows on the hill"** Quoted in Gorgas and Hendrick, *William Crawford Gorgas*, p. 161.

265   **240,000 perfectly made hinges** Bates, *Retrieval at Panama*, p. 30.

265   **"Suitable quarters and accommodations could not be provided"** Wallace, "Preliminary Work on the Panama Canal," *Engineering Magazine*, October 1905.

266   **"before there was any way to care for them properly"** Maltby, "In at the Start at Panama," *Civil Engineering*, June 1945, p. 262.

266   **"A heavy suitcase in each hand, no light anywhere"** Hardeveld, *Make the Dirt Fly*, pp. 8–9.

267   **"apprehension," "homesickness"** Jessie Murdoch account, *Chagres Yearbook*, 1913, p. 43ff.

267   **"the wreck of the French companies"** James Williams unpublished account, MCCZ, Box 35.

267   **"We were supposed to have furniture issued to us"** "The Early Days" by John J. Meehan, *Chagres Yearbook*, 1913, p. 137ff.

268   **"I am thoroughly sick of this country and everything to do with the canal"** Quoted in Pepperman, *Who Built the Panama Canal?*, p. 61.

268   **"There have been many errors and much wastage and pilfering of money"** Boni, *Panamá, Italia y los Italianos*, p. 129.

268   **"supplies taking for ever to arrive"** Wallace, "Preliminary Work on the Panama Canal," *Engineering Magazine*, October 1905.

269   **A request was posted for twenty-five track foremen** Lewis, *The West Indian in Panama*, p. 97.

269   **"were not examined at all"** Karner, *More Recollections*, p. 25.

269   **"I have two sons who wish to go to Panama to work on the Canal"** Letter of February 17, 1905, Charles M. Swinehart file, RG 185.

269   **"railroad men who were blacklisted on the American railroads"** McCullough, *The Path between the Seas*, p. 444.

269   **"Americans will put their coats on for meals"** Sands, *Our Jungle Diplomacy*, p. 14.

270   **"the people of Panama look upon Americans as noisy, grabbing bullies"** Fraser, *Panama and What It Means*, p. 185.

270   **"The average American has the utmost contempt for a Panaman"** Bishop, *The Panama Gateway*, p. 121.

270   **"Panama must conduct itself as a civilized nation"** Mallet private letter, January 10, 1904.

271   **"revolutionary firebrand" and "notorious hater of foreigners"** U.S. consul Barrett to Hay, August 9, 1904, Hay Papers, Library of Congress.

271   **"any Latin American nation who fused her destiny with that of the United States"** Mellander, *The United States in Panamanian Politics*, p. 71.

272   **"I look upon the Republic of Panama as doomed"** Mallet private letter, June 29, 1904.

272   **"Opinion here amongst the natives is spreading"** Mallet private letter, July 25, 1904.

272   **"very loud spoken," "vulgar" and "full of self-assurance"** Mallet private letters, July 25, 1904 and March 9, 1905.

272   **Soon after, an anonymous flyer was distributed** Mallet private letter, August 28, 1904.

273   **"festering with intrigue"** Sands, *Our Jungle Diplomacy*, p. 14.

274   **"whither Theodore Roosevelt and his 'Yankee imperialism' might be tending"** Ibid., p. 44.

274   **"Don Santiago was aware"** Ibid., p. 62.

274   **started appearing in New York newspapers** For example, *New York Herald*, October 4, 1904.

275   **"a kind of Opera Bouffe republic and nation"** LaFeber, *The Panama Canal: The Crisis in Historical Perspective*, p. 40.

275   **"Though the heaviest man, in weight, in the room"** Karner, *More Recollections*, p. 78.

276   **One shipment of laborers was met by agents of the Municipal Engineering Division** Lindsay-Poland, *Emperors in the Jungle*, p. 135.

276   **"there was no surplus throughout Central or South America"** Wood in Goethals, ed. *The Panama Canal: An Engineering Treatise*, vol. 1, p. 191.

276   **estimated that some eight to ten thousand workers** Hains, "The Labor Problem on the Panama Canal," *North American Review*, July 1906.

277   **"useless to discuss the question of utilizing the white race"** 1906 *Hearings* quoted in Major, *Prize Possession*, p. 81.

277   **"The native population is wholly unavailable"** Hains, "The Labor Problem on the Panama Canal."

277   **"fairly industrious; not addicted to drink"** Ibid., p. 50.

278   **"He does loaf about a good deal"** Major, *Prize Possession*, p. 82.

278   **"natural markets for unskilled labor"** Wood in Goethals, ed., *The Panama Canal: An Engineering Treatise*, vol. 1, p. 194.

279   **"The island has always been and still is run for the whites"** Edwards, *Panama, the Canal, the Country, the People*, p. 21.

280   **"I shipped only sixteen laborers"** Karner, *More Recollections*, pp. 106–7.

282   **"which nearly buried the shovel from sight"** Ibid., p. 40.

282   **"there is little probability of finding a satisfactory location"** Report of the

Chief Engineer Isthmian Canal Commission, June 1, 1904–February 1, 1905, Washington, DC, 1905.

283   **"remove the principal elements of uncertainty now existing in regard to the project as a whole"** Ibid.

283   **"I want you to build up an organization so complete and efficient"** Maltby, "In at the Start at Panama," *Civil Engineering,* June 1945, p. 260.

Chapter Seventeen: Yellow Jack

284   **"for in a year or so there will be no mosquitoes there!"** Le Prince and Orenstein, *Mosquito Control in Panama,* p. iv.

287   **"yellow fever's first encounter with one who became its implacable foe"** Gorgas and Hendrick, *William Crawford Gorgas,* p. 4.

287   **"we were rather inclined to make light of his ideas"** Gorgas, *Sanitation in Panama,* pp. 14–16.

287   **"chlorinated lime"** Gorgas and Hendrick, *William Crawford Gorgas,* p. 86.

289   **"Of all the silly and nonsensical rigmarole about yellow fever"** *Washington Post,* November 2, 1900.

291   **"When I think of the absence of yellow fever from Havana"** Gorgas and Hendrick, *William Crawford Gorgas,* p. 133.

291   **"I fear an epidemic is inevitable"** Ibid., p. 170.

292   **"our work in Cuba and Panama will be looked upon as the earliest demonstration"** *Journal of the American Medical Association,* June 19, 1909.

292   **"the veriest balderdash"** Gorgas and Hendrick, *William Crawford Gorgas,* p. 162.

292   **"I'm your friend, Gorgas, and I'm trying to set you right"** Ibid., p. 164.

292   **"The world requires at least ten years to understand a new idea"** McCullough, *The Path between the Seas,* p. 405.

293   **"clean, healthy, moral Americans"** Ibid., p. 451.

293   **"Consequently," Joseph Le Prince complains** Le Prince, *Mosquito Control in Panama,* p. 299.

293   **"without having to wipe the mosquitoes off every second"** Mallet private letter, August 3, 1904.

293   **"a convert to the mosquito theory"** Mallet private letter, January 19, 1905.

293   **"existed at practically every house in town"** Le Prince, *Mosquito Control in Panama,* p. 272.

294   **"To attempt it is a dream, an illusion"** Quoted in Rink, *The Land Divided, the World United,* p. 102.

294   **"Le Prince," Johnson said, "you're off on the upper story!"** Gorgas and Hendrick, *William Crawford Gorgas,* p. 172.

295   **"Some yellow fever cases exist in the San Tomas hospital"** Mallet private letter, January 14, 1905.

295   **"If you should be unwell here or if anything should happen to you"** Barrett Papers, Library of Congress.

295   **"revealed a dishpan of water standing outside the cook's headquarters"** Gorgas and Hendrick, *William Crawford Gorgas,* pp. 178–79.

295   **"the saddest incident in the history of the American colony"** Davis to Wallace, January 17, 1905, General Correspondence, RG 185.

296   **"one of the saddest graveyards in the world"** Sullivan, *Our Times*, vol. 1, p. 455.

296   **"darkened the whole Isthmus"** Gorgas and Hendrick, *William Crawford Gorgas*, p. 174.

296   **"The rush to get away"** Ibid., p. 173.

296   **"the place where the 'ghost walks' "** *Galveston Daily Gleaner*, quoted in *Star and Herald*, January 13, 1905.

296   **"Unless something is done and done quickly"** *Star and Herald*, February 20, 1905.

298   It was . . . like **"the ending of many a bright young man I have seen on the battlefield"** Davis to Wallace, May 2, 1905, quoted in Duval, *And the Mountains Will Move*, p. 176.

298   **"Everybody here seems to be sitting on a tack"** Pepperman, *Who Built the Panama Canal?*, p. 59.

298   a young stenographer **"rose from his chair and shrieked"** Carr, "The Panama Canal," *The Outlook*, May 5, 1906.

298   **"yellow fever . . . completely filled the atmosphere"** Gorgas and Hendrick, *William Crawford Gorgas*, p. 168.

298   **One returning nurse** *New York Tribune*, July 6, 1905.

298   **about three-quarters of the white workforce** Pepperman, *Who Built the Panama Canal?* p. 58.

299   **"The military regime in Panama"** Waldo, "The Panama Canal Work, and the Workers," *Engineering Magazine*, January 5, 1907, p. 323.

300   **"gruff, domineering"** Gorgas and Hendrick, *William Crawford Gorgas*, p. 194.

301   **"Smells and filth, Mr. President"** Ibid., pp. 198–202.

301   **"huge in all three dimensions"** Sands, *Our Jungle Diplomacy*, p. 62.

301   **"It would perhaps be difficult to find any spot on earth"** *Star and Herald*, May 8, 1905.

301   **"ill-paid, over-worked, ill-housed, ill-fed"** Magoon to Shonts, June 3, 1905, quoted in Duval, *Mountains*, p. 178.

303   **"For mere lucre you change your position overnight"** Pepperman, *Who Built the Panama Canal?*, p. 121.

303   **"We felt like an army deserted by its general"** Maltby, "In at the Start at Panama," *Civil Engineering*, July 1945, p. 322.

303   **"the effect [of Wallace's resignation] upon the workers at the Isthmus"** Gorgas and Hendrick, *William Crawford Gorgas*, p. 174.

Chapter Eighteen: Restart

304   **"Then I was asked to meet . . . Cromwell"** Stevens, "An Engineer's Recollections," *Engineering News-Record*, September 5, 1935, p. 332.

305   **shocked at discovering that there were more canal employees** Pepperman, *Who Built the Panama Canal?*, p. 130.

305   **"The condition of affairs on the Isthmus"** Stevens, "A Momentous Hour at Panama," *Journal of the Franklin Institute,* July 1930.

305   **"scared out of their boots"** Stevens' statement, January 16, 1906, *Hearings No. 18,* 59th Cong., 2d Sess., vol. 1, p. 38.

305   **"no organization worthy of the name"** Stevens, "An Engineer's Recollections," *Engineering News-Record,* September 5, 1935, p. 256.

305   **"the idiotic howl"** Stevens, "The Truth of History," in Bennett, *History of the Panama Canal,* p. 218.

305   **"I believe I faced about as discouraging a proposition"** Stevens, "The Truth of History," in Bennett, *History of the Panama Canal,* p. 210.

306   **"keep his eye on the ball"** Pepperman, *Who Built the Panama Canal?,* p. 135.

306   **"There are three diseases in Panama"** Bishop, *Goethals: Genius of the Panama Canal,* p. 133.

306   **"I have had as much or more actual personal experience in manual labor"** Maltby, "In at the Start at Panama," *Civil Engineering,* July 1945, p. 324.

307   **"Come to Panama on the first train, Stevens."** Ibid., p. 322

307   **"I cannot conceive how they did the work they did"** Stevens's statement, January 16, 1906, *Hearings No. 18,* 59th Cong., 2d Sess., vol. 1.

307   **"I determined from the start"** Stevens, "The Truth of History," in Bennett, *History of the Panama Canal,* p. 212.

308   **"a machine in every way superior to any in existence"** Sibert and Stevens, *The Construction of the Panama Canal,* p. 88.

308   **"The problem was simply one of transportation."** Ibid., p. 76.

308   **"two streaks of rust and a right of way"** Maltby, "In at the Start at Panama, *Civil Engineering,* July 1945, p. 324.

308   **"thirty years behind the times"** Mallet to Foreign Office, August 30, 1905, FO881/8765.

308   **no sidings** Sibert and Stevens, *The Construction of the Panama Canal,* p. 41.

308   **"A collision has its good points as well as its bad ones"** Stevens, "The Truth of History," in Bennett, *History of the Panama Canal,* p. 121.

309   **"crank" for Chinese labour** Karner, *More Recollections,* p. 131.

309   **"two colored men stepped from a rowboat to the landing"** Ibid., p. 114.

309   **Arthur Bullard** Edwards, *Panama, the Canal, the Country, the People,* p. 29ff.

309   **Benjamin Jordan** *Diggers,* documentary produced and directed by Roman Foster.

310   **"one of the greatest engineering feats the world has ever undertaken"** John Bowen in *Diggers* documentary.

310   **"Why you don't hit de manager in de head"** Richardson, *Panama Money in Barbados,* p. 106.

311   **"Everything looked so strange, so different to home"** Egbert Leslie, in *Diggers* documentary.

312   **Harrigan Austin** "Competition for the Best True Stories."

313   **John Butcher** Ibid.

314   **"One could scarcely breathe God's free air"** *Colón Independent,* April 20, 1906.

315   **the "serious disturbance"** Mallet to Foreign Office, May 6, 1905, FO881/8765.

315   **"In Jamaica a constable is a peacemaker"** Slosson and Richardson, "An Isthmian Carpenter's Story: A Jamaican Negro," *The Independent*, April 19, 1906.

315   **"Instead of the canal bringing with it those good old times"** *Colón Independent*, December 6, 1904.

316   **On a wage of seldom more than a dollar a day** Major, *Prize Possession*, p. 101.

316   **Coffee and bread brought to the works by West Indian women** Amos Clarke in "Competition for the Best True Stories."

316   **"Things were very different in those days"** Slosson and Richardson, "An Isthmian Carpenter's Story: A Jamaican Negro," *The Independent*, April 19, 1906.

316   **"In their anxiety to save money"** Karner, *More Recollections*, p. 142.

317   **"I have looked into hundreds of their pots"** John Foster Carr, "The Silver Men," *The Outlook*, May 19, 1906.

317   **in October 1905, there were twenty-six, all West Indians** United States Isthmian Canal Commission, *Population and Deaths from Various Diseases*, 1907.

317   **In November 1905, journalist Poultney Bigelow** Bigelow, "Our Mismanagement at Panama," *The Independent*, January 4, 1906.

318   **"Notwithstanding nearly six thousand new laborers were brought in"** Stevens to Shonts, December 14, 1905, RG 185 2-B-1.

319   **frail "disposition to labor"** United States Isthmian Canal Commission, *Annual Report*, 1906.

319   **"The West Indian's every movement is slow and bungling"** Carr, "The Silver Men," *The Outlook*, May 19, 1906.

319   **"They were not getting proper food in sufficient and regular amounts"** Sibert and Stevens, *The Construction of the Panama Canal*, p. 133.

320   **By February 1906, there were over fifty in operation** Stevens to Shonts, February 16, 1906, RG 185 2-E-1.

320   **"the leavings from the hotels"** Chatfield, *Light on Dark Places*, p. 148.

320   **LeCurrieux's family** "Competition for the Best True Stories."

321   **Henry de Lisser visited one of the barracks** Lisser, *Jamaicans in Colon and the Canal Zone*, quoted in Newton, *The Silver Men*, p. 149.

321   **"The discipline maintained in the labour camps is severe"** Mallet letter to Governor of Jamaica, November 30, 1906, FO 371/300.

322   **"This rule worked well"** Sibert and Stevens, *The Construction of the Panama Canal*, p. 97.

322   **"At midnight when everyone is asleep"** *Colón Independent*, September 12, 1906.

323   **"deep foreboding"** Hardeveld, *Make the Dirt Fly*, p. 18ff.

327   **"Special inducements were added"** Sibert and Stevens, *The Construction of the Panama Canal*, p. 119.

Chapter Nineteen: The Railroad Era

328   **"the great waste of money"** Stevens, "A Momentous Hour at Panama," *Journal of the Franklin Institute*, July 1930.

329   **"that there was a big, thick white cloud of smoke"** Alfonso Suazo in "Competition for the Best True Stories."

330   **"We became so clean, orderly, and 'dried out'"** Maltby, "In at the Start at Panama," *Civil Engineering*, August 1945, p. 360.

331   **"the strong smell of decomposed fish has gone"** Mallet private letter, September 5, 1906.

332   **"the day of the good-for-nothing tropical tramp"** Carr, "The Panama Canal," *The Outlook*, May 5, 1906.

332   **"weeding out the faint-hearted and incompetent"** Pepperman, *Who Built the Panama Canal?* pp. 11–12.

332   **"The men themselves, have distinctive virtues"** Carr, "The Panama Canal," *The Outlook*, May 5, 1906.

333   **"Normal family life is becoming established"** Slosson and Richardson, "Life on the Canal Zone," *The Independent*, March 22, 1906.

333   **"Most of the young men on the Isthmus have absolutely no places of amusement"** John Barrett in *Star and Herald*, February 27, 1905.

334   **"positive forces for evil"** Quoted in Mack, *The Land Divided*, p. 549.

334   **"use money appropriated for the construction of the Canal"** Karner, *More Recollections*, p. 22.

335   **"Stevens lives on the line"** Mallet private letter, September 5, 1905.

335   **"Stevens' sturdy, competent presence"** Sands, *Our Jungle Diplomacy*, p. 40.

336   **"I am not running things"** Chatfield, *Light on Dark Places*, p. 64.

336   **"So many men sent down here drink to excess"** Ibid., p. 51.

336   **"Like many other people here in positions of authority"** Ibid., p. 67.

337   **clerk starting work on a salary of $2500** Carr, "The Panama Canal," *The Outlook*, May 5, 1906.

337   **could now report more regular wages** Mallet to Sir Edward Grey, January 31, 1906. FO881/8892

337   **"have returned [from Panama] with money"** *Barbados Agricultural Reporter*, March 3, 1906, quoted in Richardson, *Panama Money in Barbados*, p. 116.

337   **"innate respect for authority"** Sibert and Stevens, *The Construction of the Panama Canal*, p. 125.

337   **described conditions as "unsatisfactory"** Mallet to Foreign Office, August 14, 1905, FO881/8765

338   **"a capacity to develop into subforemen"** Stevens to Shonts, December 14, 1905, RG185 2-B-1.

338   **"No one will ever know, no one can realize"** Stevens, "The Truth of History," in Bennett, *History of the Panama Canal*, p. 211.

339   **"Stock Gambler's Plan to Make Millions!"** *New York World*, January 17, 1904.

339   **"a group of canal promoters and speculators and lobbyists"** *New York Times*, December 29, 1903.

340   **"I do not think there is a place on the face of the globe"** Pepperman, *Who Built the Panama Canal?*, p. 279.

340   **"I have heard all those things and many more"** Chatfield, *Light on Dark Places*, p. 189.

341   **"Many of the prominent American newspapers"** Townley Report, May 3, 1906, FO881/8892.

342   **"I had been told to build a house"** McCullough, *The Path between the Seas*, p. 481.

Chapter Twenty: The Digging Machine

343   **"Such a canal would undoubtedly be the best in the end if feasible"** *Engineering Record*, February 24, 1906.

344   **"One genius proposed to wash the entire cut"** Sibert and Stevens, *The Construction of the Panama Canal*, p. 76.

344   **"discovered an unknown way through this mysterious labyrinth"** Bigelow, *The Panama Canal and the Daughters of Danaus*, p. 40.

344   **"Mr. Randolph . . . advises M. P. Buneau Varilla"** Note of November 7, 1905, Bigelow Papers, New York Public Library, Box 24.

345   **"the most important document in the engineering history"** *Engineering Record*, January 10, 1906, p. 211.

346   **"narrow gorge" would be "tortuous"** Shonts quoted in Pepperman, *Who Built the Panama Canal?*, p. 208.

346   **"Such a waterway is far from meeting the conception"** Abbot, "The Panama Canal: Projects of The Board of Consulting Engineers," *Engineering Magazine*, July 1906, p. 483.

348   **"personal study of the conditions"** Stevens, "An Engineer's Recollections," *Engineering News-Record*, September 5, 1935, p. 40.

348   **"the difficulties and dangers of navigation"** *Washington Post*, February 20, 1906.

350   **"simply preposterous piece of work"** Quoted in Bigelow, *The Panama Canal and the Daughters of Danaus*, p. 35.

350   **"the greatest engineering conflict of the canal"** Bates, *Crisis at Panama*, pp. 32–34.

351   **"Hard rains had set in by this time"** Hardeveld, *Make the Dirt Fly*, p. 47.

351   **"came bounding up the steps three at a time"** Hardeveld, *Make the Dirt Fly*, p. 44.

352   **"The rule marked the first definite break"** "The Early Days," by John J. Meehan, *Chagres Yearbook*, 1913, p. 142.

353   **"Distinctive social lines were drawn on the Isthmus"** Sibert and Stevens, *The Construction of the Panama Canal*, p. 98.

353   **"sounded as though some one was throwing boulders"** Chatfield, *Light on Dark Places*, p. 118.

353   **"The meat served is almost always beef, and such beef!"** Ibid., p. 127.

353   **"was worse than usual, which was only just possible"** Ibid., p. 155.

354   **"severely manhandled"** Taft to Magoon, June 4, 1906, quoted in Major, *Prize Possession*, p. 121.

355   **"guarantee public order and constitutional succession"** Mellander, *Charles Edward Magoon*, p. 78.

355   **"in that territory [in] which [disorder] can be prevented"** Ibid., p. 80.

356   **"party feeling is very bitter"** Magoon annual report, 1905, RG185.

356   **the *Diario de Panama*, described the choice for the voters** *El Diario de Panama*, April 21, 1906.

356   **"a senior Conservative declared"** De La Guardia quoted in Mellander, *The United States in Panamanian Politics*, p. 88.

356   **"suppress any insurrection in any part of the Republic"** Taft to Magoon, April 26, 1906, General Correspondence (ICC) 1905–14, RG185.

356   **"customary" for government candidates to win elections** Mallet to Foreign Office, May 21, 1906, FO371/101.

356   **"explicit directions have been given to the police"** *Star and Herald*, May 18, 1906.

357   **Mallet put this down** Mallet to Foreign Office, May 30, 1906, FO371/101.

357   **"Negro influence"** Quoted in Major, *Prize Possession*, p. 118.

357   **"The police [who owed their jobs to the ruling government] voted the first time in uniform"** Sands, *Our Jungle Diplomacy*, p. 65.

358   **"prevailing clannishness"** Sibert and Stevens, *The Construction of the Panama Canal*, p. 115.

358   **"There is no sense in putting so many different races together"** Slosson and Richardson, "An Isthmian Carpenter's Story: A Jamaican Negro," *The Independent*, April 19, 1906.

358   **"some sort of hazy idea had gotten into their heads"** Sibert and Stevens, *The Construction of the Panama Canal*, p. 115.

358   **"three separate nationalities of laborers"** Stevens to Shonts, May 4, 1906, Panama Canal Commission File (PCC) 2-E-1.

359   **"The American is too proud to work with his hands!"** Lewis, *The West Indian in Panama*, p. 35.

359   **"Everybody in his area was so scared of disease"** Interview with Mr. William Donadío, Panama City, August 17, 2004.

360   **"The Spaniard is certainly the more intelligent and better worker"** Thompson, "The Labour Problems of the Panama Canal," *Engineering* (London) May 3, 1907.

360   **"It did exactly what was expected in changing the self-confidence of the negroes"** Sibert and Stevens, *The Construction of the Panama Canal*, p. 118.

361   **"practically all with malaria"** Carr, "The Work of the Sanitary Force," *The Outlook*, May 12, 1906.

361   **During the headline-grabbing yellow fever epidemic of May to August** Bishop, *The Panama Gateway*, p. 243.

361   **seventy-five people a day with the disease** Chatfield, *Light on Dark Places*, p. 142.

361   **"This rainy season has been a heavy trial on the canal builders"** *New York Herald*, August 1, 1906,

362   **the cases that came to the attention of the medical system** Newton, *The Silver Men*, pp. 152–54.

362   **an astonishing 80 percent of the overall workforce** Le Prince and Orenstein, *Mosquito Control in Panama*, p. 228.

362   **West Indian Rufus Forde** "Competition for the Best True Stories."

362   **Jamaican James Williams** Ibid.

363   **St. Lucian Charles Thomas** Ibid.

363   **Barbadian Clifford Hunt** Ibid.

364   **"The question of controlling malaria"** Le Prince and Orenstein, *Mosquito Control in Panama*, p. 24.

365   **"like fighting all the beasts of the jungle"** Gorgas and Hendrick, *William Crawford Gorgas*, p. 226.

365   **"Very patient negroes were necessary"** Le Prince and Orenstein, *Mosquito Control in Panama*, p. 113.

366   **"larvae of dragon flies and water beetles"** Ibid., p. 185.

367   **"the cause of many break downs in the constitution"** Mallet private letter, June 10, 1906.

367   **John Prescod** "Competition for the Best True Stories."

367   **"The prevailing illness is malaria"** Chatfield, *Light on Dark Places*, p. 103.

367   **"I went to the Cristóbal dispensary this morning"** Ibid., p. 150.

367   **Albert Peters** "Competition for the Best True Stories."

367   **Barbadian Amos Parks** Ibid.

368   **"the horrible and unfamiliar noise at night"** Hardeveld, *Make the Dirt Fly*, p. 49ff.

369   **Therefore the excavation was planned to proceed** Sibert and Stevens, *The Construction of the Panama Canal*, p. 77.

370   **The U.S. locomotives could haul four or five times the volume** Pepperman, *Who Built the Panama Canal?*, p. 38.

370   **a single rock weighing some thirty-four tons** Sibert and Stevens, *The Construction of the Panama Canal*, p. 89.

373   **"ran over a colored man"** Chatfield, *Light on Dark Places*, p. 198.

Chapter Twenty-one: Segregation

376   **"There is much talk about the anticipated visit of the president"** Chatfield, *Light on Dark Places*, p. 150.

376   **"seemed obsessed with the idea that someone was trying to hide something from him"** Maltby, "In at the Start at Panama," *Civil Engineering*, September 1945, p. 422.

376   **"when the president was at Cristóbal"** Chatfield, *Light on Dark Places*, p. 210.

376   **"A Strenuous Exhibition on the Isthmus"** McCullough, *The Path between the Seas*, p. 496.

377   **"He was intensely energetic"** Maltby, "In at the Start at Panama," p. 421.

378   **"Every man seems animated with the idea that he is doing a necessary part of the canal"** Thompson, "The Labour Problems of the Panama Canal," *Engineering* (London), May 3, 1907.

378   **At Gatún over a hundred new borings had been made on the dam site** Mallet to Grey, January 31, 1907, FO881/8897.

378 **"something which will redound immeasurably to the credit of America"** Pepperman, *Who Built the Panama Canal?*, pp. 13–14.

379 **"the heartiest contempt and indignation"** Ibid., p. 292.

379 **"Those cooking sheds with their muddy floors"** McCullough, *The Path between the Seas*, p. 502–3.

379 **"The higher death rate is, in our opinion, due to circumstances"** *Colón Independent*, August 24, 1906.

380 **"Wretched little houses rest on stilts"** Chatfield, *Light on Dark Places*, p. 137.

381 **"a striking lack of appreciation"** Lindsay-Poland, *Emperors in the Jungle*, p. 35.

381 **"racial and ethnic discrimination by the U.S. Government"** Conniff in Publication of the Proceedings of Symposium held at the University of the West Indies, p. 43.

381 **"Panama is below the Mason and Dixon Line"** Franck, *Zone Policeman 88*, p. 65.

381 **"If the stronger and cleverer race is free to impose its will"** Woodward, *The Strange Career of Jim Crow*, p. 72.

382 **In 1896 Louisiana had contained 130,000 black voters** Ibid., p. 85.

383 **These included foremen, office clerks, and teachers.** Petras, *Jamaican Labor Migration*, p. 150.

383 **"solution to troubles growing out of the intermingling of the races"** Haskin, *The Panama Canal*, p. 160.

383 **"It would, I think, be very impolitic to separate"** Commissary manager to Stevens, February 15, 1907, RG185 2-C-55.

385 **"Any northerner can say 'nigger' as glibly as a Carolinian"** Franck, *Zone Policeman 88*, p. 225.

385 **"was made to feel the prejudice against her color"** *New York Age*, quoted by the *Colón Independent*, December 29, 1905.

385 **"My father read of Panama and thought it a wonderful place"** Mrs. Taylor, interviewed by Eunice Mason.

386 **Jeremiah Waisome** "Competition for the Best True Stories."

386 **"often seen the threat of the slave-driver in the foreman's eye"** Carr, "The Silver Men," *The Outlook*, May 19, 1906, p. 118.

386 **"Among the white employees on the 'gold roll' some times an employee would use his hands"** Letter of Ralph B. Irwin, MCCZ, Box 35.

387 **"the he-man type"** Hardeveld, *Make the Dirt Fly*, p. 114ff.

387 **"it cost twenty-five dollars to lick a Jamaican negro"** Grier, *On the Canal Zone*, p. 71.

387 **"straighten himself up and say to the foreman"** Karner, *More Recollections*, p. 40.

388 **"developed an excessive regard for the English"** Publication of the Proceedings of Symposium held at the University of the West Indies, p. 64.

388 **" 'Pay me,' I says, 'or I'll stick de British bulldog on all yo' Omericans!' "** Walrond, *Tropic Death*, p. 42.

388 **"You couldn't talk back"** Constantine Parkinson, in *Diggers* documentary.

389 **"little better than the West Indian negro"** Gaillard to Goethals, July 12, 1907, RG 185.

389 **"the efficiency of the Spaniards did not hold up"** Sibert and Stevens, *The Construction of the Panama Canal*, p. 118.

389 **nearly half of those recruited during 1906 were gone by the beginning of the following year** Mallet to Grey, January 31, 1907, FO881/8897.

390 **But clashes between Spaniards and police continued** Navas, *El movimiento obrero en Panamá*, pp. 143–44.

390 **"People are falling ill the whole time"** *El Socialista*, December 21, 1906, quoted in Marco, *Los Obreros espanoles*, p. 18.

390 **"The labourers' lives are not highly valued"** *El Socialista*, May 14, 1909, quoted in Marco, *Los Obreros espanoles*, p. 32

390 **A Naples paper claimed that most of the workers had died** Boni, *Panamá, Italia y los Italianos*, p. 144.

390 **"My own private opinion"** Stevens to Shonts, January 18, 1907, RG 185 2-E-1.

391 **the deployment of no less than sixty-three Bucyrus shovels** Waldo, "The Present Status of the Panama Canal, *Engineering*, March 15, 1907.

392 **"Stevens must get out at once"** Roosevelt to Taft, February 12, 1907, Taft Papers, Taft-Roosevelt, Box 3, quoted in Duval, *And the Mountains Will Move*, p. 259.

392 **"blow up the Republican Party"** McCullough, *The Path between the Seas*, p. 506.

392 **"an immoderate amount of adulation"** Mallet to Foreign Office, April 9, 1907, FO 881/9201.

392 **"well-planned and well-built machine"** Stevens, "An Engineer's Recollections," *Engineering News-Record*, September 5, 1935, p. 52.

393 **"I know you pretty well now"** Maltby, "In at the Start at Panama," *Civil Engineering*, September 1945, p. 423.

393 **"Don't talk, dig"** *Star and Herald*, March 1, 1907.

394 **"in the charge of men who will stay on the job"** Mack, *The Land Divided*, p. 501.

Chapter Twenty-two: "The Army of Panama"

396 **"Colonel Goethals here is to be chairman"** Sullivan, *Our Times*, vol. 1, p. 466.

396 **"most absolute despot in the world"** Bishop, *Goethals: Genius of the Panama Canal*, p. 239.

396 **"It was asserted that the Department of Government"** Goethals, ed., *The Panama Canal: An Engineering Treatise*, vol. 1, p. 46.

396 **"a case of just plain straight duty"** Bishop, *Goethals: Genius of the Panama Canal*, p. 149.

397 **"I expect to be chief of the division of engineers"** *Star and Herald*, March 19, 1907.

397 **"The magnitude of the work grows and grows on me"** Goethals to his son, March 17, 1907, Goethals Papers, Library of Congress.

398 **"Yellow Peril"** Hardeveld, *Make the Dirt Fly*, p. 99.

399   **"the President, in his talks"** Sibert and Stevens, *The Construction of the Panama Canal*, p. 268.

400   **"was not necessary to the work of building the canal"** Petras, *Jamaican Labor Migration*, p. 180.

400   **"I have no complaint of any kind"** Panama Police Department Report, May 14, 1907, RG185 2-E-1.

401   **"Supposed ill treatment"** U.S. Senate, *Report of Special Commission Appointed to Investigate Conditions of Labor and Housing of Government Employees of the Isthmus of Panama*, December 8, 1908, p. 51.

401   **"professional agitators"** *Canal Record*, March 25, 1908.

401   **"At the present time all of our superintendents and foremen are unanimously of the opinion"** Goethals to Spanish chargé d'affairs at the legation in Panama, April 17, 1909, RG85.

403   **"The biggest boss is King Yardage"** Blythe, "Life in Spigotty Land," *Philadelphia Saturday Evening Post*, March 21, 1908.

404   **"the last vestige of fear and uncertainty seemed to have left"** Hardeveld, *Make the Dirt Fly*, p. 131.

405   **"we were surrounded"** Jessie Murdoch account, *Chagres Yearbook*, 1913, p. 58.

405   **By May 1908 there were well over a thousand families in the Zone** *Report of Special Commission Appointed to Investigate Conditions of Labor and Housing of Government Employees of the Isthmus of Panama*, December 8, 1908, p. 7.

405   **"It is doubtful, to be sure, whether one-fourth of the 'Zoners' "** Franck, *Zone Policeman 88*, p. 220.

405   **"one of the brand new cottages over the hill"** Hardeveld, *Make the Dirt Fly*, p. 110ff.

406   **"not until the business depression"** *Report of Special Commission Appointed to Investigate Conditions of Labor and Housing of Government Employees of the Isthmus of Panama*, December 8, 1908, pp. 11–12.

406   **the turnover of skilled workers was nearly 60 percent** Haskin, *The Panama Canal*, p. 529.

406   **"Anyone who stays here through a year of it becomes depressed"** Ghent, "Work and Welfare on the Canal," *Independent*, April 29, 1909, p. 910.

407   **"They fill a necessary place in the somewhat artificial life on the canal zone"** *Report of Special Commission Appointed to Investigate Conditions of Labor and Housing of Government Employees of the Isthmus of Panama*, December 8, 1908, p. 19.

408   **"to be furnished by Sidney Landon, character delineator"** *Canal Record*, September 11, 1907.

408   **"a really active American community"** Hardeveld, *Make the Dirt Fly*, p. 130.

409   **"He says it is not home, but on the order of a boarding school,"** Letter of Courtney Lindsay, May 8, 1907, MCCZ, Boxes 9 and 10.

409   **"Every day I am better pleased that I came"** Letter of Courtney Lindsay, June 12, 1907.

409   **"things are not always very clean"** Letter of Courtney Lindsay, July 6, 1907.

409   **"I have adapted myself pretty well"** Letter of Courtney Lindsay, July 27, 1907.

409   **"The Tivoli is giving a reception and dance tonight"** Letter of Courtney Lindsay, July 6, 1907.

409   **Pineapples are only 15 cents** Letter of Courtney Lindsay, July 17, 1907.

410   **"things have already begun to slack up"** Letter of Courtney Lindsay, June 27, 1907.

410   **"Now what can they tell about it?"** Letter of Courtney Lindsay, November 12, 1907.

410   **"the novelty has worn off"** Letter of Courtney Lindsay, December 1, 1907.

410   **"Empire Lady Minstrels"** Letter of Courtney Lindsay, March 22, 1908.

411   **"Nothing ever happens here"** Letter of Courtney Lindsay, November 6, 1908.

411   **"Am beginning to like Culebra better"** Letter of Courtney Lindsay, December 7, 1908.

411   **"broke into Culebra society"** Letter of Courtney Lindsay, January, 10, 1909.

411   **"that a dry season night down here, with a moon"** Letter of Courtney Lindsay, October 28, 1910.

411   **"She's just about the nicest thing in the girl line there is"** Letter of Courtney Lindsay, November 17, 1911.

412   **"The commissary is an assured success"** Ghent, "Work and Welfare on the Canal," *Independent*, April 29, 1909, p. 914.

412   **"First of all, there ain't any democracy down here"** Edwards, *Panama*, p. 572.

412   **"the establishment of an autocratic form of government"** Thompson, "The Labour Problems of the Panama Canal," *Engineering* (London), May 3, 1907.

412   **"enlightened despotism"** Franck, *Zone Policeman 88*, p. 205.

412   **"omnipresent"** Hardeveld, *Make the Dirt Fly*, pp. 99–100.

412   **"Goethals dominates over everybody and everything"** Mallet's Annual Report 1910, FO881/9841.

413   **"You can't realize what the Chief Engineer is"** Letter of Courtney Lindsay, April 3, 1908.

413   **"The system is one that would be very repugnant to Englishmen"** Thompson, "The Labour Problems of the Panama Canal," *Engineering* (London), May 3, 1907.

413   **"judicial terrorism"** Ghent, "Work and Welfare on the Canal," *Independent*, April 29, 1909, p. 913.

413   **"there has grown up in Panama circles somewhat of a tendency to monopolize patriotism"** Waldo, "The Panama Canal Work, and the Workers," *Engineering Magazine*, January 1907, p. 15.

414   **"Caste lines are as sharply drawn as in India"** Franck, *Zone Policeman 88*, p. 219.

414   a **"drearily efficient state"** Sands, *Our Jungle Diplomacy*, p. 25.

414   **"a chestless youth"** Franck, *Zone Policeman 88*, p. 10ff.

416   **"We have such control in Panama"** Major, *Prize Possession*, p. 126.

416   **"extremely tactful and friendly towards everybody"** Mallet's Annual Report 1910, FO881/9841.

416   **"a racial inability to refrain long from abuse of power"** George Weitzel quoted in Major, *Prize Possession*, p. 125.

416 **"It is really farcical to talk of Panama as an independent state"** Mallet to Grey, August 22, 1910, FO371/944.

417 **"docile to American wishes"** Mallet to Foreign Office, May 8, 1913, FO881/10293.

417 **a story that accused Taft's influential brother Charles** *New York World,* October 3 and 6, 1908.

418 **"I have never known in my lengthy experience in company matters"** Harding, *The Untold Story of Panama,* p. 35.

418 **"There are many peculiar circumstances about the Panama canal business"** Niemeier, *The Story of Panama,* p. 124.

Chapter Twenty-three: "Hell's Gorge"

420 **"a tropical glacier—of mud instead of ice"** Smithsonian online exhibition, http://www.sil.si.edu/Exhibitions/Make-the-Dirt-Fly.

420 **"it required night and day work to save our equipment"** Mallet to Foreign Office, January 31, 1908, FO 881/9201.

421 **"most formidable of the canal enterprise"** Goethals, ed., *The Panama Canal: An Engineering Treatise,* vol. 1, p. 337.

421 **"like snow off a roof"** McCullough, *The Path between the Seas,* p. 551.

421 **Spaniard Antonio Sanchez** Interview with Mr. William Donadío, Panama City, August 17, 2004.

422 **"the old hill politely slid back again"** Smithsonian online exhibition, http://www.sil.si.edu/Exhibitions/Make-the-Dirt-Fly.

422 **"Today you dig and tomorrow it slides"** Albert Bannister in "Competition for the Best True Stories."

422 **"was a land of the fantastic and the unexpected"** Bishop, *The Panama Gateway,* pp. 193–94.

422 **"The difficulties we are liable to encounter are unknown"** Mallet to Foreign Office, January 31, 1908, FO 881/9201.

422 **"this material has or will ultimately make its own design"** Sibert and Stevens, *The Construction of the Panama Canal,* p. 166.

422 **"found themselves handling hard rock one hour"** Goethals, ed., *The Panama Canal,* vol. 1, p. 346.

423 **seventy-six miles of construction track** Ibid., p. 346.

424 **"The Cut is a tremendous demonstration"** Archer, *Through Afro-America,* p. 287.

424 **"heroic human endeavour"** James, *A Woman in the Wilderness,* p. 96.

424 **"They are generally comfortable men and women of 50 or more"** William Baxter account, *Chagres Yearbook,* 1913, p. 59ff.

425 **Arnold Small** *Diggers* documentary.

425 **"John Prescod"** "Competition for the Best True Stories."

425 **"I had never saw so much rain in all my life"** Rufus Forde, in "Competition for the Best True Stories."

425   "The different levels varied from ten to twenty feet" Franck, *Zone Policeman 88*, p. 115.

427   **Jamaican Z. McKenzie** "Competition for the Best True Stories."

427   **Amos Clarke** Ibid.

428   "Two days later, all of us who had become such close friends" Hardeveld, *Make the Dirt Fly*, pp. 136–37.

429   "at the end of long years of patient, exacting work" Sibert and Stevens, *The Construction of the Panama Canal*, p. 10.

429   **George Martin** "Competition for the Best True Stories."

430   **netted 1,800 specimens in a week** Le Prince and Orenstein, *Mosquito Control in Panama*, p. 210.

431   "fine body of disciplined and skilled workmen" Mallet to Foreign Office, May 8, 1913, FO881/10293.

432   **the West Indian laborer had lived down his bad reputation** Haskin, *The Panama Canal*, pp. 154, 162.

432   "the negroes from the British West Indies" Franck, *Zone Policeman 88*, p. 123.

432   "What was the black culture" Victor Smythe in Russell, *The Last Buffalo*, p. 15.

433   "They lived chiefly in windowless, six-by-eight rooms" Franck, *Zone Policeman 88*, p. 40.

433   "On Sunday morning every religious community is busy" Carr, "The Panama Canal," *The Outlook*, May 5, 1906.

433   "a forum for expression on many issues" Westerman, *Los immigrantes antillanos en Panamá*, p. 23.

433   "tame them and provide a relief valve" Luis Navas, *El movimiento obrero en Panamá*, p. 250.

434   "were the unquestioned leaders of glamour and glitter" Russell, *The Last Buffalo*, p. 34.

434   "To see people at night" Benjamin Jordan in *Diggers* documentary.

434   "the elegant quadrille dances" Russell, *The Last Buffalo*, p. 37.

435   "the vortex of trouble on the Isthmus" Frank, *Zone Policeman 88*, p. 79.

435   "The majority of them were employed as team drivers" Enrique Plummer, in "Competition for the Best True Stories."

436   "although no such requirement is made of white employees" Goethals to Henry A. Hart, John Thomas, March 18, 1910, 2-C-55, pt. 1, General Correspondence, 1904–14, RG 185.

436   **no more U.S. blacks were given Gold Roll contracts** Gaillard (acting chairman and chief engineer) to Jackson Smith, February 11, 1908.

436   **by February 1909 only one such employee remained, a Henry Williams** Letters of February 8 and May 22, 1909.

436   "he was colored and not eligible for employment on the Gold Roll" Letter to Goethals, January 10, 1910.

437   **In July 1912 there were only sixty-nine** Letter to Goethals, July 9, 1912.

437   **The following year, only fifteen remained** Letter to Goethals, March 5, 1913.

437   **"the knowledge that there are ten hungry applicants"** *Star and Herald*, September 7, 1907.

438   **a resident of Colón, Mr. Foster Burns** Interview with Mr. Foster Burns, Colón, August 19, 2004.

Chapter Twenty-four: "Lord How Piercing!"

442   **"an ugly denuded waste of land"** Lee, *The Strength to Move Mountains*, p. 172.

442   **Barbadian Edgar Simmons** "Competition for the Best True Stories."

443   **"Chagres River plunges"** Lee, *The Strength to Move Mountains*, p. 183.

444   **"the outbreak of yellow fever journalism"** Ibid., p. 185.

444   **"fire in the rear"** Ibid., p. 189.

446   **"It is not hard to realize"** Franck, *Zone Policeman 88*, p. 307.

446   **"No one expected on returning to work in the morning"** Sibert and Stevens, *The Construction of the Panama Canal*, p. 205.

446   **American Harry Cole** "Some Episodes in Connection with the Construction of the Pacific Division of the Panama Canal," 1908–1914 by Harry O. Cole, unpublished memoir 1947, Box 1, MCCZ.

448   **"They did not look with favour"** Cameron, *The Impossible Dream*, p. 189.

450   **"These locks are more than just tons of concrete"** Lee, *The Strength to Move Mountains*, p. 263.

452   **"Yuh gets more money for that job than working in the cut"** "West Indian Work Songs," Box 33, MCCZ.

452   **"I found myself racing across the narrow plank bridges"** Franck, *Zone Policeman 88*, p. 181.

453   **Eustace Tabois** *Diggers* documentary.

453   **"hurting many and sometimes killing men instantly"** James Ashby, in "Competition for the Best True Stories."

453   **"The family of those men working on those locks"** T. H. Riley in "Competition for the Best True Stories."

453   **Jamaican Nehemiah Douglas** "Competition for the Best True Stories."

454   **"poured like sand"** Rufus Forde in "Competition for the Best True Stories."

Chapter Twenty-five: The Land Divided, The World United

457   **"There was a reverent silence"** Hardeveld, *Make the Dirt Fly*, p. 142.

459   **"Gentlemen, the two consuming ambitions of my life"** Cameron, *The Impossible Dream*, p. 254.

460   **"On board were all the foremost Panamanian citizens and politicians"** James, *A Woman in the Wilderness*, p. 94ff.

460   **"Unostentatious dedicatory act [was] a more appropriate celebration"** Lee, *The Strength to Move Mountains*, p. 283.

Postscript: Whose Canal Is It, Anyway?

464   **"This I can say absolutely was my own work"** Roosevelt, *The Letters of Theodore Roosevelt*, vol. 6, p. 1444.

464   **"I am interested in the Panama Canal because I started it"** *New York Times*, March 24, 1911.

465   **"somebody [namely, himself] was prepared to act with decision"** Roosevelt, *An Autobiography*, p. 553.

465   **argued a contributor to the *North American Review*** Leander T. Chamberlain, "A Chapter of National Dishonor," *North American Review*, February 1912.

465   **"an affront to international decency"** Elmer Ellis quoted in Graham, *The "Interests of Civilization"?*, p. 178.

465   **"The summary ejectment of Colombia"** Mahan, "Was Panama 'A Chapter of National Dishonor'?," *North American Review* 196, 1912.

466   **dubbed "canalimony"** Graham, *The "Interests of Civilization"?* p. 158.

466   **"a most sordid and shameless conspiracy"** *New York World*, April 24, 1921.

469   **"The returned Panama Canal labourer"** Richardson, *Panama Money in Barbados*, p. 149.

469   **Jamaican Z. Mackenzie** "Competition for the Best True Stories."

471   **One man who had worked for thirty-eight years for the canal** Petras, *Jamaican Labor Migration*, pp. 227–28.

471   **A doctor who treated a lot of the old-timers** Interview with Dr. Hedley C. Lennon, Panama City, August 18, 2004.

471   **"I am glad to see that all my sweat"** Alfred E. Dottin in "Competition for the Best True Stories."

471   **"It is a job well done"** S. Smith in "Competition for the Best True Stories."

471   **"I got to be a man"** *Diggers* documentary.

SELECT BIBLIOGRAPHY

Abbot, Willis, J. *Panama and the Canal in Pictures and Prose.* New York & London, 1913.

Acosta, José de. *Historia natural y moral de las Indias occidentales ó América,* vol. 2. Madrid, 1787.

Anguizola, Gustave. *Philippe Bunau-Varilla: The Man Behind the Panama Canal.* Chicago, 1980.

Archer, William. *Through Afro-America: An English Reading of the Race Problem.* London, 1910.

Arias, Harmodio. *The Panama Canal: A Study in International Law and Diplomacy.* London, 1911.

Bailey, Thomas. *A Diplomatic History of the American People.* New York, 1947.

Barrett, J. *The Panama Canal: What It Is, What It Means.* Washington, 1913.

Bates, Lindon Wallace. *The Crisis at Panama.* New York, 1906.

———. *Retrieval at Panama.* New York, 1907.

Beach, Rex. *The Ne'er do Well.* New York, 1911.

Beale, Howard. *Theodore Roosevelt and the Rise of American Power.* Baltimore, 1956.

Beisanz, John and Mavis. *The People of Panama.* New York, 1955.

Bemis, Samuel Flagg, ed. *The American Secretaries of State and Their Diplomacy.* New York, 1958.

Bennett, Ira E. *History of the Panama Canal.* Washington, D.C., 1915.

Bethell, Leslie, ed. *Cambridge History of Latin America.* Vol. VII. Cambridge and New York, 1990.

Bidwell, Charles. *The Isthmus of Panama.* London, 1865.

Bigelow, John. *The Panama Canal. Report of the Hon. John Bigelow, Delegated by the Chamber of Commerce of New York to Assist at the Inspection of the Panama Canal in February 1886.* New York, 1886.

———. *The Panama Canal and the Daughters of Danaus.* New York, 1908.

Bigelow, Poultney. "Our Mismanagement at Panama." *The Independent,* January 4, 1906.

Birmingham, Stephen. *Our Crowd: The Great Jewish Families of New York.* New York, 1967.

Bishop, Joseph Bucklin. *The Panama Gateway.* New York, 1913.

———. *Theodore Roosevelt and His Time Shown in His Own Letters.* New York, 1920.

———. *Goethals: Genius of the Panama Canal: A Biography.* New York, 1930.

Boni, Diego dal. *Panamá, Italia y los Italianos en la época de la construcción del Canal (1880–1915).* Panama, 2000.

Borthwick, J. D. *Three Years in California.* Edinburgh and London, 1857.

Brands, H. W. *The Age of Gold.* London, 2005.

Bunau-Varilla, Philippe. *Panama: The Creation, Destruction, and Resurrection.* New York, 1914.

Burnett, Robert. *The Life of Paul Gauguin.* New York, 1937.

Burton, John, ed. *The Darien Papers.* Edinburgh, 1849.

Cameron, Ian. *The Impossible Dream: The Building of the Panama Canal.* London, 1971.

Carr, John Foster. Various articles from *The Outlook,* April 28, May 5, 12, 19, 1906.

Castillero Pimentel, Ernesto. *Panamá y los Estados Unidos.* Panama City, 1973.

Castillero Reyes, Ernesto J. *Historia de la Comunicacion Interoceanica,* 1939, quotes from 1999 ed. Panama.

———. *Historia de Panama.* Panama, 1962.

Cermoise, Henri. *Deux Ans à Panama: Notes et Recits d'un Ingenieur au Canal.* Paris, 1886.

Chamberlain, Leander T. "A Chapter of National Dishonor." *North American Review,* February 1912.

Chambre des Députés, *5e Législature, Session de 1893, Rapport Général. . . .* Paris, 1893.

Chatfield, Mary. *Light on Dark Places.* New York, 1908.

Clapp, Margaret. *Forgotten First Citizen: John Bigelow.* Boston, 1947.

Collin, Richard. *Theodore Roosevelt's Caribbean: The Panama Canal, the Monroe Doctrine and the Latin American Context.* Baton Rouge, 1990.

Congrès des Science Géographique, Cosmographique et Commerciales. *Compte Rendu.* Antwerp, 1872.

Congrès International D'Études du Canal Interocéanique. *Compte Rendu Des Séances.* Paris, 1879.

Conniff, Michael L. *Black Labor on a White Canal—Panama 1904–1981.* Pittsburgh, 1985.

———. *Panama and the United States: The Forced Alliance.* Athens, Ga., 1992.

Conrad, Joseph. *Nostromo: A Tale of the Seaboard.* London and New York, 1904.

Cornish, Vaughan. *The Panama Canal and Its Makers.* London, 1909.

Courau, Robert. *Ferdinand de Lesseps.* Paris, 1932.

Cullom, Shelby Moore. *Fifty Years of Public Service.* Chicago, 1911.

Dansette, Adrien. *Les Affaires de Panama.* Paris, 1934.

Davis, Raymond A. "West Indian Workers on the Panama Canal: A Split Labor Market Interpretation." PhD diss., Stanford, 1981.

Dean, Arthur H. *William Nelson Cromwell.* New York, 1957.

Dock, Lavinia. L., ed. *A History of Nursing.* 4 vols. New York, 1912.

Donadío, William Daniel. *The Thorns of the Rose.* Colón, 1999.

Drumont, Edouard. *La Dernière Bataille.* Paris, 1890.

Duval, Miles. *From Cadiz to Cathay.* Stanford, 1940.

———. *And the Mountains Will Move.* Stanford, 1947.

Edgar-Bonnet, G. *Ferdinand de Lesseps*. Paris, 1951.

Edwards, Albert (pseudonym of Bullard, Arthur). *Panama, the Canal, the Country, the People*. New York, 1911.

Espino, Oviedo Diaz. *How Wall Street Created a Nation*. New York, 2001.

Fauconnier, Gérard. *Panama: Armand Reclus et le Canal des Deux Océans*. Paris, 2004.

Franck, Harry A. *Zone Policeman 88*. New York, 1913.

Fraser, John Foster. *Panama and What It Means*. London, 1913.

Frederick, Rhonda D. *Colón Man a Come: Mythographies of Panamá Canal Migration*. Lanham, 2005.

Frémont, Jesse Benton. *A Year of American Travel: Narrative of Personal Experience*. California, 1878.

Ghent, W. J. "Labor and the Commissary at Panama" and "Work and Welfare on the Canal." *The Independent* 66: (April–June 1909).

Goethals, George W. *Government of the Canal Zone*. Princeton, 1915.

——, ed. *The Panama Canal: An Engineering Treatise*, 2 vols. New York, 1916.

Gorgas, Marie D., and Burton J. Hendrick. *William Crawford Gorgas: His Life and Work*. New York, 1915.

Gorgas, William Crawford. *Sanitation in Panama*. New York, 1915.

Graham, Terence. *The "Interests of Civilization"?: Reaction in the United States Against the "Seizure" of the Panama Canal Zone, 1903–1904*. Sweden, 1983.

Great Britain, Foreign Office. *Correspondence Respecting the Projected Panama Canal . . . 1882*. London, 1883.

Grier, Thomas Graham. *On the Canal Zone*. Chicago, 1908.

Guerrero, Luis C. and Jose G. Lorente. *Los Obreros Espanoles en Panama*. Havana, 1908.

Hains, Brig. Gen. Peter. "The Labor Problem on the Panama Canal." *North American Review*, July 1906.

Hardeveld, Rose van. *Make the Dirt Fly*. Hollywood, Calif., 1956.

Harding, Earl. *The Untold Story of Panama*. New York, 1959.

Haskin, Frederic. J. *The Panama Canal*. New York, 1913.

Healy, David, *U.S. Expansionism: The Imperialist Urge in the 1890s*. Madison, Wis., 1970.

Healy, Phyllis Foster. "Mary Eugenie Hibbard: Nurse, Gentlewoman and Patriot." Unpublished thesis, University of Texas at Austin, 1990.

Helms, Mary W. *Ancient Panama: Chiefs in Search of Power*. Austin, Tex., 1976.

Hill, Robert A., ed. *Marcus Garvey and the Universal Negro Association Papers*. Berkeley, Calif., 1983.

Hotchkiss, Charles F. *On the Ebb*. New Haven, 1878.

Howarth, David. *The Golden Isthmus*. London, 1966.

Humboldt, Alexander von. *Political Essay on the Kingdom of New Spain*. London, 1811.

Instructions to Rear Admiral Daniel Ammen and Civil Engineer A.G. Menocal, U.S. Navy, Delegates on the Part of the United States to the Interoceanic Canal Congress, Held at Paris May, 1879, and Reports of the Proceedings of the Congress. Washington, 1879.

Isthmian Historical Society. "Competition for the Best True Stories of Life and Work on the Isthmus of Panama During the Construction of the Panama Canal." Balboa, 1963, Box 25 MCCZ.

Jaén Suárez, Omar. *La población del Istmo de Panamá*. Madrid, 1998.

James, Winifred. *A Woman in the Wilderness.* London, 1915.

Jefferson, Thomas. *Writings.* New York, 1859.

Jessup, Philip C. *Elihu Root.* New York, 1938.

Johnson, W. F. *Four Centuries of the Panama Canal.* New York, 1906.

Johnson, Willis Fletcher, ed. *Addresses and Papers of Theodore Roosevelt.* New York, 1909.

Johnston, Dr. William E. "Interoceanic Ship Canal Discussion." *Journal of the American Geographical Society* 11, 1879.

Jusserand, J. J. *What Me Befell.* Boston, 1933.

Karner, William J. *More Recollections.* New York, 1921.

Kemble, John Haskell. *The Panama Route, 1848–1869.* Berkeley, Calif., 1943.

Kimball, William Wirt. *Special Intelligence Report on the Progress of the Work during the Year 1885.* 49th Cong., 1st Sess., House of Representatives, Misc. Doc. No. 395, Washington, 1886.

LaFeber, W. *The Panama Canal: The Crisis in Historical Perspective.* New York, 1978 (quotes from updated edition, New York, 1989).

Lamming, George. *In the Castle of My Skin.* London, 1953.

LaRosa, Michael, and German R. Mejia, ed. *The United States Discovers Panama: The Writings of Soldiers, Scholars, Scientists and Scoundrels, 1850–1905.* Lanham, Md., 2004.

Lee, W. S. *The Strength to Move Mountains.* New York, 1958.

Lemaitre, Eduardo. *Panamá y su separción de Colombia.* Bogotá, 1971.

Le Prince, Joseph A., and A. J. Orenstein. *Mosquito Control in Panama.* New York and London, 1916.

Lesseps, Ferdinand de. *Recollections of Forty Years.* London, 1887.

Lewis, Lancelot S. *The West Indian in Panama: Black Labor in Panama 1850–1914.* Washington, D.C., 1980.

Lindsay-Poland, John. *Emperors in the Jungle: The Hidden History of the U.S. in Panama.* Durham, N.C., and London, 2003.

Lisser, Henry de. *Jamaicans in Colon and the Canal Zone.* Kingston, Jamaica, 1906.

Lloyd, John A. "On the Facilities for a Ship Canal Communication . . . through the Isthmus of Panama." Institute of Civil Engineers, *Minutes of Proceedings,* vol. 9, 1850.

Lull, Edward. *Reports of Explorations and Surveys for the Location of Interoceanic Ship Canal through the Isthmus of Panama.* Washington, D.C., 1879.

Mack, Gerstle. *The Land Divided.* New York, 1944.

Mahan, Captain A. T. *The Influence of Sea Power on History.* Boston, 1890.

———. *The Interest of America in Sea Power Present and Future.* Boston, 1898.

———. "Was Panama 'A Chapter of National Dishonor'?" *North American Review,* October 1912.

Major, John. *Prize Possession: The United States and the Panama Canal, 1903–1979.* Cambridge, 1993.

Mallet, Sir Claude Coventry. "Pioneer Diplomat," unpublished memoir.

Maltby, Frank. "In at the Start at Panama." *Civil Engineering,* June–September 1945.

Marco Serra, Yolanda. *Los Obreros espanoles en la construccion del Canal de Panama.* Panama, 1997.

Maréchal, Henri. *Voyage d'un Actionnaire à Panamá.* Paris, 1885.

Marryat, Frank. *Mountains and Molehills; or, Recollections of a Burnt Journal.* 1855; reprint, Philadelphia, 1962.

Marshall, Peter. *Demanding the Impossible: A History of Anarchism.* London, 1992.

McCain, William. *United States and the Republic of Panama*. Durham, N.C., 1937.

McKay, Claude. *Banana Bottom*. San Diego, 1933.

McCullough, David. *The Path between the Seas*. New York, 1977.

Mellander, Gustavo A. *Charles Edward Magoon, the Panama Years*. Panama, 1999.

———. *The United States in Panamanian Politics: The Intriguing Formative Years*. Danville, Ill., 1971.

Menocal, A. G. "Intrigues at the Paris Canal Conference." *North American Review*, September 1879.

Mimande, Paul. *Souvenirs d'un Echappe de Panama*. Paris, 1893.

Miner, Dwight Carol. *The Fight for the Panama Route: The Story of the Spooner Act and the Hay-Herran Treaty*. New York, 1940 (quotes from 1966 ed., Octagon Books Inc., New York).

Molinari, M. G. de. *A Panama: L'Isthme de Panama, La Martinque, Haiti*. Paris, 1887.

Mollier, Jean-Yves. *Le Scandale de Panama*. Paris, 1991.

Navas, Luis. *El movimiento obrero en Panamá 1880–1914*. Panama, 1974.

Nelson, Wolfred. *Five Years at Panama*. New York, 1889.

Newton, Velma. *The Silver Men: West Indian Labour Migration to Panama, 1850–1914*. Kingston, Jamaica, 1984.

Niemeier, Jean Gilbreath. *The Story of Panama*. Portland, 1968.

Otis, Fessenden N. *History of the Panama Railroad*. New York, 1867.

Parks, E. Taylor. *Colombia and the United States, 1765–1934*. Durham, N.C., 1935.

Patterson, John. "Latin American Reactions to the Panamanian Revolution of 1903." *Hispanic American Historical Review* 24 (1944).

Pearcy, Thomas L. *We Answer Only to God: Politics and the Military in Panama, 1903–1947*. Albuquerque, 1998.

Pepperman, Leon W. *Who Built the Panama Canal?* New York, 1915.

Perez-Penero, Alex. *Before the Five Frontiers*. New York, 1978.

Petras, Elizabeth McClean. *Jamaican Labor Migration: White Capital and Black Labor, 1850–1930*. Boulder and London, 1988.

Pringle, Henry F. *Theodore Roosevelt: A Biography*. New York, 1931.

Puri, Shalini, ed. *Marginal Migrations: The Circulation of Cultures within the Caribbean*. Oxford, 2003.

Reclus Armand. *Panama & Darien*. Paris, 1884.

Reyes, Rafael. *The Two Americas*. London, 1914.

Richards, Benjamin. B., ed. *California Gold Rush Merchant: The Journal of Stephen Chapin Davis*. San Marino, 1956.

Richardson, Bonham C. *Panama Money in Barbados 1900–1920*. Knoxville, Tenn., 1985.

Rink, Paul. *The Land Divided, the World United*. New York, 1963.

Ripley, J. Fred. *The Capitalists and Colombia*. New York, 1931.

Robinson, Tracy. *Fifty Years at Panama*. New York, 1911.

Rodgers, Lt. Raymond P. *Progress of Work on Panama Ship-Canal* (Senate Doc. 123, 48th Cong., 1st Sess.). Washington, 1884.

Rodrigues, José Carlos. *The Panama Canal*. New York, 1885.

Rogers, Lieutenant Charles C. *Intelligence Report of the Panama Canal* (House Misc. Doc. 599, 50th Cong., 1st Sess.). Washington, 1889.

Roosevelt, Theodore. *The Letters of Theodore Roosevelt* (ed. Elting E. Morison et al.) Harvard, 1951–54, 8 vols.

———. *An Autobiography*. New York, 1913.

Russell, Carlos E. *An Old Woman Remembers*. New York, 1995.

———. *The Last Buffalo*. Charlotte, N.C., 2003.

Sands, William Franklin. *Our Jungle Diplomacy*. Chapel Hill, N.C., 1944.

Schott, Joseph L. *Rails across Panama*. New York, 1867.

Scott, William Rufus. *The Americans in Panama*. New York, 1912.

Seacole, Mary. *Wonderful Adventures of Mrs. Mary Seacole in Many Lands*. OUP 1988 edition.

Senior, Olive. "The Colon People." *Jamaica Journal*, March and September 1978; "The Panama Railway." *Jamaica Journal*, June 1980.

Sibert, W. L., and J. F. Stevens. *The Construction of the Panama Canal*. New York, 1915.

Siegfreid, André. *Suez and Panama*. New York, 1940.

Simon, Maron J. *The Panama Affair*. New York, 1971.

Sisnett, Cano, and Manuel Octavio, ed. *Pedro Prestan: cien años después*. Panama, 1985.

Skinner, James M. *France and Panama: The Unknown Years, 1894–1908*. New York, 1988.

Slosson, Edwin, and Gardner Richardson. "Life on the Canal Zone." *The Independent*, March 22, 1906.

———. "An Isthmian Carpenter's Story: A Jamaican Negro." *The Independent*, April 19, 1906.

Smith, G. Barnett. *The Life and Enterprises of Ferdinand De Lesseps*. London, 1895.

Stevens, John F. "An Engineer's Recollections." *Engineering News-Record*, vol. 115 (September 5, 1935).

———. "A Momentous Hour at Panama." *Journal of the Franklin Institute*, July 1930.

Stiner, William F. Klaus de Albuquerque, and Roy S. Bryce-Laporte, eds. *Return Migration and Remittances: Developing a Caribbean Perspective*. Washington, 1982.

Sullivan, Lieutenant John T. *Report of Historical and Technical Information . . .* Washington, 1883 (House Exec. Doc. 107, 47th Cong., 2d Sess.).

Sullivan, Mark. *Our Times*. New York, 1928.

Sweetman, David. *Paul Gauguin*. London, 1995.

Thayer, William R. *Theodore Roosevelt: An Intimate Biography*. New York, 1919.

Thompson, A. Beeby. "The Labour Problems of the Panama Canal." *Engineering* (London), May 3, 1907.

Tomes, Robert. *Panama in 1885*. New York, 1855.

Trautwine, John C. "Rough Notes of an Exploration for an Inter-oceanic Canal Route by Way of the Rivers Atranto and San Juan." *Franklin Institute Journal* 57, no. 5, May 1854.

Tuchman, Barbara. *The Proud Tower*. New York, 1966.

United States Congress House of Representatives. *The Story of Panama: Hearings on the Rainey Resolution*. 62d Cong., 2d Sess., Washington, 1913.

United States Congress. *Report of the Isthmian Canal Commission 1899–1901*. Washington, D.C., 1904.

United States Isthmian Canal Commission. *Annual Reports*. Washington, 1906.

———. *Annual Reports of the Department of Sanitation*. Washington, 1908.

———. *Population and Deaths from Various Diseases . . .* Washington, 1907.

———. *Report of the Isthmian Canal Commission, 1899–1901*. Washington, D.C., 1904.

United States of America Navy Department. *Report of Commander Bowman H. McCalla upon the Naval Expedition to the Isthmus of Panama, April 1885.*

———. *Reports of Explorations and Surveys.* Washington, D.C., 1879.

———. *Papers on Naval Operations during the Year Ending July 1885.* Washington, D.C., 1885.

United States Senate. *Report of Special Commission Appointed to Investigate Conditions of Labor and Housing of Government Employees of the Isthmus of Panama,* 60th Cong., 2d Sess., Document No. 539, Washington, 1908.

Vedia, Enrique de, ed. *Historiadores primitivos de Indias.* Madrid, 1852.

Vivian, James. "The 'Taking' of the Canal Zone: Myth and Reality." *Diplomatic History* 4, 1980.

Waldo, Fullerton L. "An Engineer's Life in the Field on the Isthmus." *Engineering,* December 1905.

———. "The Panama Canal Work, and the Workers." *Engineering Magazine,* January 5, 1907.

———. "The Present Status of the Panama Canal." *Engineering,* March 15, 1907.

Wallace, John F. "Preliminary Work on the Panama Canal." *Engineering Magazine,* October 1905.

Walrond, Eric. *Tropic Death.* New York, 1926 (quotes from Collier Books ed., 1972).

Ward, Christopher. *Imperial Panama: Commerce and Conflict in Isthmian America 1550–1800.* Albuquerque, 1993.

Watts, David. *The West Indies.* London, 1987.

Weir, Hugh C. *The Conquest of the Isthmus.* New York, 1909.

Weisberger, Bernard. "The Strange Affair of the Taking of the Panama Canal Zone." *American Heritage* 27, October 1976.

Westerman, George W. *Los immigrantes antillanos en Panamá.* Panama, 1980.

———. "Historical Notes on West Indians on the Isthmus of Panama." *Phylon* 22:4 (Winter 1961).

———. "Gold and Silver Men." *Crisis* 54:12 (December 1947).

"West Indian Participation in the Construction of the Panama Canal." Publication of the Proceedings of Symposium held at the University of the West Indies, Mona, Jamaica, June 15–17, 2000.

Woodward, C. Vann. *The Strange Career of Jim Crow.* New York, 1955 (quotes from 2002 paperback ed.).

Wyse, Lucien N–B. *Rapport sur les Etudes de la Commission Internationale d'exploration de L'Isthme du Darien.* Paris, 1877.

———, and Reclus, Armand et Sosa P. *Rapport sur les Etudes de la Commission Internationale d'exploration de L'Isthme Americain.* Paris, 1879.

———. *Le Canal de Panama.* Paris, 1886.

Zévaès, Alexander. *Le Scandale du Panama.* Paris, 1931.

Zimmerman, Warren. *First Great Triumph.* New York, 2002.

INDEX